DATE DUE

DEMCO 38-296

HISPANIC
MARKET
HANDBOOK

HISPANIC MARKET HANDBOOK

The definitive source for reaching this lucrative segment of American consumers

M. ISABEL VALDÉS
&
MARTA H. SEOANE

Forewords by
Michael J. Naples and
Ennio Quevedo-García

Gale Research Inc.

An International Thomson Publishing Company

I(T)P

NEW YORK • LONDON • BONN • BOSTON • DETROIT • MADRID
MELBOURNE • MEXICO CITY • PARIS • SINGAPORE • TOKYO
TORONTO • WASHINGTON • ALBANY NY • BELMONT CA • CINCINNATI OH

Gale Research Inc. Staff

Rebecca Nelson, *Developmental Editor;* Marie Ellavich, *Associate Editor;* Kelle S. Sisung, *Contributing Editor;* Camille Killens, Jolen M. Gedridge, *Contributing Associate Editors;* Lawrence W. Baker, *Senior Developmental Editor;* Greg Michael, *Acquiring Editor*

Mark C. Howell, *Page Designer;* Tracey Rowens, *Art Director;* Cynthia Baldwin, *Product Design Manager*

C. J. Jonik, *Desktop Publisher;* Willie F. Mathis, *Camera Operator;* Barbara J. Yarrow, *Graphic Services Supervisor*

Mary Kelley, *Production Associate;* Evi Seoud, *Assistant Production Manager;* Mary Beth Trimper, *Production Director*

LySandra Davis, *Data Entry Associate;* Gwendolyn S. Tucker, *Data Entry Coordinator;* Benita L. Spight, *Data Entry Manager*

Typesetting by Marco Di Vita, The Graphix Group

 ™ This book is printed on acid-free paper that meets the minimum requirements of American National Standard for Information Sciences—Permanence Paper for Printed Library Materials. ANSI Z39.48-1984.

Valdés, M. Isabel.
    Hispanic market handbook / M. Isabel Valdés and Marta H. Seoane.
        p.   cm.
    Includes bibliographical references and index.
    ISBN 0-8103-8500-7
    1. Hispanic Americans as consumers—Handbooks, manuals, etc. 2. Marketing research—United States—Handbooks, manuals, etc. 3. Marketing—United States—Handbooks, manuals, etc. I. Seoane, Marta H. II. Title
HC110.C6V347   1995
658.8'348—dc20   95-3268
                                                                                                    CIP

Printed in the United States of America

To my two children, second-generation Hispanics,
Gabriel and Clara;
And to my husband
Julio

—M. I. V.

To my staunchest supporters,
my husband
Kingsley
and our son
Alexander

—M. H. S.

Contents

Foreword xiii
Preface xvii

Chapter 1: Identifying the Hispanic Consumer 1
 • Hispanic Population Trends in the United States • His-
panic Heritage and Social Networks • Who Is Hispanic?
 • Reasons for Hispanic Migration to the United States
 • Hispanic Ethnicity and the Marketplace • Understanding
the Hispanic Consumer Market

   Figures 19
   Tables 26

Chapter 2: Hispanic Demographics and Trends 37
 • A Hispanic Renaissance • How Hispanic Growth Affects
the Marketplace • A Hispanic Market without Immigration • Key Hispanic Market Trends • Hispanic Households • A Regional View of the Market • City Dwellers
 • Hispanic Subgroups

   At a Glance 66
   Figures 77
   Tables 84

Chapter 3: Hispanics as Consumers 113
• Where Hispanic Income Is Concentrated • Hispanic
Affluence •Hispanic Income Sources • Hispanic Spending
• Market Opportunities

    At a Glance 128
    Figures 129
    Tables 145

Chapter 4: Culture and the Hispanic Consumer 159
• "It's Not Only a Matter of Language" • What is Culture?
•Communicating in a Bicultural Context • "To Sell Me Is
to Know Me" • Understanding and Thinking in a Different
Culture • Managing Acculturation and Diversity • Cul-
tural Diversity among U.S. Hispanics

    Figures 206
    Tables 207

Chapter 5: Language and the Hispanic Consumer 213
• Information Overload • The Role of Language • Spanish
in the United States • The Isolated or Spanish-Dominant
Hispanic Consumer • Spanish and Hispanics • Bilinguals
• Communicating with Acculturated Hispanics • Manag-
ing Language Diversity

    Figures 235
    Tables 241

Chapter 6: Hispanic Media in the U.S. 251
• Dynamics of Hispanic Media Use • An Overview of the
U.S. Hispanic Media • Multi-Media Strategies and the
Hispanic Consumer • Language Segmentation and Media
Preference: California

    At a Glance 282
    Figures 286
    Tables 295

Contents

Chapter 7: Reaching Hispanics 313
  • Marketing to Hispanics • Targeting Hispanic Market
  Segments •Marketing to Hispanic Women • Marketing to
  Hispanic Youth •Couponing and the Hispanic Consumer
  • Advertising to Hispanics •Community Marketing
                Figures 351
                Tables 361

Chapter 8: Market Research 369
  • Marketing Research and Hispanics • Conceptualization,
  Sampling, and Survey Issues • Segmenting the Hispanic
  Market • Door-to-Door *vs.* Telephone Studies
                Tables 398

Chapter 9: Principles in Action: Case Studies 411
  • Tianguis Stores: The Right Idea at the Right Time • Bank
  of America's Introduction of System-Wide Bilingual ATMs
  • Western Union • CIBA Vision's Illusions • Inter-American Book Services: Selling Spanish-Language Books
  through Direct Marketing Vehicles • California Avocado
  Commission: Hispanic Advertising Campaign • Education
  Now And Babies Later (ENABL) • Immigration and Naturalization Service Amnesty

Sourcebook: Who to Call for What 455
  Consultants • Directories • Electronic Resources • Jour-
  nals and Magazines • National Hispanic Organizations
  • Newsletters •Newspapers • Representatives of Hispanic
  Media • Research Centers • Top 25 Hispanic-owned
  Businesses

Index 475

Forewords:

Perspectives from the Field

The *Hispanic Market Handbook* is a ground-breaking work, one that will be influential as the defining summary of this important segment of the U.S. population in the closing years of the twentieth century.

For the first time, everything the marketer needs to know about the U.S. Hispanic market growth phenomenon in order to zero in on its marketing potential has been assembled in one place. The *Hispanic Market Handbook* successfully brings clarity, and therefore visibility, to the Hispanic market—as it is and what it is becoming, providing insights that marketers will find compelling.

The *Handbook* covers all areas relevant to anyone who is seeking to understand the Hispanic market—from definitions to demographics, language, cultural orientation, and the market's many segments. Chapter headings tell the story:

 ✧ Identifying the Hispanic Consumer
 ✧ Demographics and Trends
 ✧ Hispanics as Consumers
 ✧ Culture and the Hispanic Consumer

An Emerging U.S. Market Segment

By Michael J. Naples, President, Advertising Research Foundation

❖ Language and the Hispanic Consumer

❖ Hispanic Media in the U.S.

❖ Reaching Hispanics

❖ Market Research

❖ Case Studies

In recent years the Advertising Research Foundation (ARF) has begun to pay greater attention to the growing importance of Hispanic and other ethnic groups with the 1990 establishment of the ARF Ethnic Research Steering Committee. The mission of this group is to strengthen the validity and the credibility of ethnic market research, which demonstrates the effectiveness of ethnic media and the potential of ethnic markets. Clearly, without sound and valid research on ethnic markets, the quality of decisions, and therefore the effectiveness of ethnic marketing strategies, is at risk.

A particularly important part of the Handbook (Chapter 8) deals with research, setting forth an overall framework about how to approach valid research of the Hispanic market. It represents an important statement on the value of sound research and will help the reader understand how Hispanic market research differs from that of the general market.

We are all indebted to Isabel Valdés and Marta Seoane for providing us with such a comprehensive and up-to-date evaluation of an emerging U.S. market segment, which by the beginning of the next century will exceed 30 million people.

Two Cultural Worlds

By Ennio L. Quevedo-García, Bank of America

In the year 2030, 48.2 percent of this country's total consumer growth will be in the Hispanic population. In that same year, only 9.1 percent of our nation's consumer growth will be attributable to the non-Hispanic white consumer. Hispanic household growth will out-pace the general market in the 1990s by growing 48 percent compared to a 13 percent growth in the general market. Hispanics also continue to make impressive gains economically. Between now and the year 2000, Hispanic disposable income will increase by 93 percent compared to a projected increase of only 34 percent in the general market.

The presence of the Hispanic consumer in the United States of America is by no means a recent phenomenon. By the time the English "pilgrims" and the Native inhabitants of what is now New England encountered each other, the Spanish colonial settlement of Santa Fe (New Mexico) had been a thriving economic hub for more than 150 years. The present-day states of California, Arizona, New Mexico, Texas, Nevada, and Colorado belonged to Mexico long before they were annexed to the United States as a result of the war with Mexico, which culminated in the 1848 Treaty of Guadalupe Hidalgo. Since then, people from every Latin American nation have continued to immigrate and contribute to the economic and cultural development of this country.

When modern-day Hispanic immigrants come to the United States, they enter a nation that has already undergone centuries of Hispanization. Thus, the U.S. Hispanic, different from members of any other cultural group, has been able to take part in mainstream America without having to forfeit his or her Latino culture. The Spanish language and Hispanic culture and value system are destined to survive in the United States. And so, the uniquely U.S. Hispanic consumer psychographic trend is not one of acculturation from Spanish to English, or Latino culture to Anglo culture, but rather from monolingual/monocultural Latino to bilingualism and biculturalism. The Hispanic consumer has the special advantage of being able to leverage the best of the two cultural worlds in which he/she lives. In a recent national survey, over 95 percent of the U.S. Hispanic citizens who responded strongly identified themselves as "Hispanic" as well as a U.S. citizen.

If we apply the old marketing adage, "demographics is destiny" to the incredible past, present, and projected future of the U.S. Latino market, even the modestly prudent business person can quickly deduce that success in the U.S. consumer environment greatly depends on business' ability to effectively market its products and services to all segments of the U.S. Latino market.

Although the Hispanic market, along with its very distinct subsegments, has the potential to be very profitable, it is also very complex, under-researched, and still very much an enigma to the vast majority of marketing professionals. Due to its complexities, the successful Hispanic marketer must be willing to let go of standard general market approaches and become a pioneer. True success in the U.S. Latino market takes dedication, perseverance, and highly developed skills.

The U.S. Latino market, as with any valid consumer group, is constantly changing and is made of many distinct but reachable sub-segments. In this book, Isabel Valdés and Marta Seoane have done an outstanding job of describing the complexities of the U.S. Latino consumer market. The authors are indeed true visionaries and pioneers, who very early rejected the "let's just translate everything we have into Spanish" approach to the market. The Hispanic consumer has a very unique psychology that directly affects buying decisions. The keys to success in the market are understanding that unique psychology and developing strategies that are compatible with the Latino view of the world.

The good news is that there is a substantial track record of major corporations that have been successful in their outreach to this market. Some of these companies/organizations have shared their success stories in Chapter 9, where eight case studies have been reprinted. There are three basic elements that set apart the companies/organizations that are successfully reaching the Hispanic market. First, they enjoy a sincere commitment from their senior management to become the dominant player in the Hispanic market. (This commitment is demonstrated by allocating the appropriate monetary resources to ensure success.) Second, they have had the insight to hire qualified and dedicated Hispanic marketers who have the skills and the cultural sensitivity necessary to be effective in the Latino arena. And third, they have enough trust in their Hispanic marketing talent to allow them to implement their strategies, even though they might seem unorthodox when compared to a general market approach.

As a member of the U.S. Latino community, I take pride in the publication of this *Handbook* as a symbol of the economic progress that my people continue to make in the United States, which, for many is their country of birth and for many others is their country of choice.

Preface

Writing a book about U.S. Hispanic consumers had been on my mind for some time. When Greg Michael at Gale Research suggested putting the idea down on paper, it was evident that the time had come for me to collect the information and experiences gained through many years researching and studying the Hispanic community, as a marketing consultant and as the president and founder of the marketing research firm Hispanic Market Connections. Dr. Marta H. Seoane joined the venture in its early stages. As a demographer and sociologist, she has conducted research on Latin American populations and has completed other demographic studies. Beyond our common professional interests, we are both Hispanics, we both earned our graduate degrees at American universities, and we have both lived in the United States for many years.

Behind each book there is a vision. For the *Hispanic Market Handbook* it was to convey the fundamental differences that distinguish U.S. Hispanic consumers from mainstream American consumers, and to do it in a way that makes the facts and the principles accessible and understandable. Growing competition among American businesses to reach the Hispanic market and secure the Hispanic consumer's "share of mind" make this book necessary.

The U.S. Hispanic population has been growing exponentially for years, but only recently have the intricacy and the potential of this market been realized. Marketing research has shown that Hispanics interact with society, perceive life, and behave differently from non-Hispanics. The behavioral gap between Hispanic and non-Hispanic consumers has steadily widened—*not* narrowed as had been expected. Here we suggest an explanation for this phenomenon: The underlying cultural differences between Hispanics and non-Hispanics play an important role in consumer behavior. Both Anglo and Hispanic cultures organize their values, and hence, their priorities, around different axes, which affect the decisions they make day to day. Advertising and marketing campaigns and media programs have been more successful reaching a Hispanic audience when they have been specifically created and developed for the Hispanic consumer.

The *Handbook* provides a multitude of facts and figures documenting the Hispanic population in the United States. We also discuss the interpretation of those statistics, as well as the analytical tools, strategic thinking, and planning that are essential to a successful marketing or advertising campaign.

We have relied both on qualitative and quantitative data to form our argument, and we have made every effort to ensure the accuracy of our information. The principal instruments we have used are surveys, the U.S. population censuses, and Hispanic Market Connection's national studies and database. We also tapped secondary sources, such as journal articles, books, and other professional publications. Through the cooperation of the companies and agencies that launched the advertising/marketing campaigns, we have included eight case studies illustrating the points presented in the text.

This has been a collaborative effort. Marta contributed to the conceptualization of the book, performed most of the demographic analysis, and provided insight into the subjects of several chapters. The original idea benefitted greatly from her input.

Many of my organizing thoughts were inspired by the works of Celia Falicov, Ph.D., and Carlos Sluzki, M.D., who, at a spring 1982 seminar, provided new direction in my thinking and lit an everlasting light. Further, as Marta and I wrote and re-wrote, we appreciated the input of our clients and colleagues.

Our offices in Los Altos, California, became the headquarters for our research and writing. Airports, airplanes, convention centers, and our homes also provided space for revising, updating, and editing.

We hope that this book will help businesses and other organizations better understand and reach the U.S. Hispanic consumer market, which is not only growing in numbers, but in economic force.

—M.I.V.

Without the foresight and vision of Greg Michael, a director of new publications at Gale Research, this book would have only been a concept not realized—a need to be fulfilled. Greg, and later, Developmental Editor Becky Nelson, provided encouragement, direction, and support throughout the sometimes overwhelming process of researching and writing this book. It is in challenging moments that we learn how much we depend on each other to make things happen. We are highly indebted to both Greg and Becky for their whole-hearted commitment to see the book through its many stages. We also owe special thanks to copy editors Gina Misiroglu and Bob Griffin for their roles in improving the clarity and flow of the writing of two English-second-language speakers. Ala Ramonita Q. Wilson was instrumental in typing the manuscript and many times salvaged hastily scribbled notes, which otherwise might have been lost. Many, many thanks for her dedication and professionalism. We also thank Associate Editor Marie Ellavich and data entry whizzes Angela Darling (in New York) and LySandra Davis (at Gale Research in Detroit), who all managed to decipher the many directions in the manuscript. Thanks also to Lynn Noble who helped us conduct bibliographic research.

We also want to acknowledge the inspiration and encouragement of our friends and colleagues, including Héctor and Norma Orcí, David Hausmann, Peggy Goff, Dolores Kunda, Ennio Quevedo-García, Armando Chapelli, Jesus Chavarria, Sara Sunshine, Roberto Torres, Carlos Santiago, Judi Jones, Augustin Huneeus,

Dr. Celia Correas de Zapata, Edward T. Lewis, and Christy Hauberger. We would also like to acknowledge Donnelly Marketing Information Services for their cooperation and assistance in compiling data.

We owe special thanks to Dr. Kingsley Davis, a legend to all who are involved in demographics, for his ongoing contribution, and to Dr. Davis Heer for the direction he provided our demographic analysis.

We want to especially thank our case study contributors who took time from their busy schedules to provide the studies and accompanying materials — Bonnie Morrow (AT&T, formerly of Western Union), Dolores Valdés Zacky (Valdés Zacky and Associates), Pat Perea and Palmira Arellano (Sosa, Bromley, Aguilar and Associates), Michael Heinley and Robert Morrison (formerly of Dorland Sweeney Jones), Héctor Orcí (La Agencia de Orcí y Asociados), Alvaro de Regil (Mercatec Direct), Ennio Quevedo-García (Bank of America), and Gayle Geary (Gardner, Geary, Coll & Young).

We wish to acknowledge the ongoing support of clients who made possible the implementation of Hispanic Market Connection's regional studies, which provided primary and original data: Pacific Bell, Mervyn's, Pepsi, *La Opinión*, Telemundo, WSNS-Channel 44 (Chicago), Merck Laboratories, NYNEX, First Chicago Bank, Coors, Bell Atlantic, and Nielsen Household Services.

Finally, we want to thank the staff at Hispanic Market Connections, especially Jannet Torres and Diana Loayza, who have been instrumental in the implementation of the National Hispanic Database studies.

Our most sincere and loving thanks to our husbands, Julio Aranovich and Kingsley Davis, and to our children, Gabriel and Clara Aranovich-Valdés and Alexander Seoane-Davis, for sharing many hours of family time to help us make this dream come true.

M. Isabel Valdés
Marta H. Seoane
Los Altos, California
January 1995

CHAPTER 1

■ Hispanic Population Trends in the United States

■ Hispanic Heritage and Social Networks

■ Who Is Hispanic?

■ Reasons for Hispanic Migration to the United States

■ Hispanic Ethnicity and the Marketplace

■ Understanding the Hispanic Consumer Market

Identifying the

Hispanic Consumer

Why has the Hispanic consumer market become such a prominent subject in financial and marketing circles? The answer is simple and straightforward—opportunity—business opportunity. From a marketing perspective, the dramatic Hispanic population growth witnessed during the past few decades, and expected to continue for the foreseeable future, translates into sheer marketing and business opportunity.

For more than four decades a significant number of emigrants from every country in Latin America have become active members of the U.S. consumer market. It took only 30 years for the Hispanic market to triple in size, a trend that is sure to continue for a long time. Between 1960 and 1990 the number of Hispanic consumers increased from 6.9 million to more than 22 million, an absolute increase of 15 million people (Figure 1.1).

The marketing challenge for companies wishing to sell to the Hispanic market is not only to identify Hispanics but also to determine how they are different from non-Hispanics as well as how homogeneous they are as a group. Are Mexicans, Puerto Ricans, and Cubans alike? Is there a "Hispanic" culture that binds Hispanics together? What are Hispanics' likes and dislikes? How should businesses communicate with them? How should businesses factor into their marketing strategies the ongoing but slow assimilation process of Hispanics? What sort of informational sources are available to target Hispanics?

These and other considerations are explored in subsequent chapters. The present chapter provides an overview of the U.S. Hispanic market.

■ Hispanic Population Trends in the United States

The statistics are impressive. Depending upon the sources consulted, by the beginning of the twenty-first century, the number of Hispanics in the United States could exceed 30 million (Figure 1.2), approximately the current size of the population of Canada (27.4 million) or Argentina (33 million) and about one and a half times the population of Australia (18 million). Between 1960 and 1990 the proportion of Hispanics in the United States more than doubled, from 3.9 percent to 9 percent (Figure 1.3), and at the time of the 1990 census there were more than 9 million Hispanics who were foreign born (Edmonston and Passel, 1992, 42–43), giving the United States one of the largest Spanish-speaking populations in the world (Table 1.1).

By the year 2000, the number of Hispanic households is predicted to have more than doubled from the 1983 level, increasing from 4.1 million to over 9 million, a 59 percent increase and more than twice the expected increase for Afro-American households. In absolute numbers, the U.S. Hispanic market will add 3 million new households between 1990 and 2000, almost equaling the white, non-Hispanic market, which is projected to add 3.4 million new households during the same period (Table 1.2).

Hispanics in the continental United States are wealthier than most Hispanics living in Latin America. During the last decade, U.S. Hispanic aggregate income after taxes increased from $85 billion to $144 billion—an average annual increase of 6 percent

(Figure 1.4). In 1990 this group had an income per capita of $8,424 (Table 1.3). If current demographic and economic trends persist, the size of the U.S. Hispanic market and the amount of Hispanic disposable income will continue to accelerate well into the twenty-first century.

From a business perspective, such unprecedented population increase and economic growth are reflected daily in the marketplace, with the burgeoning number of Hispanic men, women, and children patronizing supermarkets, dealerships, general and specialty stores, and restaurants and conducting business in banks, credit unions, real estate and travel agencies, and so forth.

These trends in population, market size, and collective earnings are just a few significant facts about the Hispanic consumer market. To be effective, companies trying to sell to this market should learn more about the peculiarities of this rapidly growing population segment. For example, what are Hispanics like collectively? How diverse is this population? How are Hispanic consumers different from general market consumers? What are their buying preferences? How can businesses effectively appeal to Hispanic consumers?

■ Hispanic Heritage and Social Networks

Unlike the period preceding World War II, the last four decades have witnessed an influx of Hispanic immigrants into the United States from Puerto Rico, Cuba, Mexico, the Dominican Republic, and Central and South America. Net migration gains, combined with many more births than deaths, and political, economic, and social factors have greatly enhanced the visibility of Hispanics throughout the United States.

Today Hispanics are well established in American society, having developed a social infrastructure through which the ideas and values of their culture are preserved and transmitted to future generations. Hispanics' rapid population growth, purchasing power, business entrepreneurship, expanding communities, political participation, and communication networks, along with the growth of organizations dedicated to the study and preservation of Hispanic history and culture, have created for Hispanics a select and permanent niche in the American marketplace.

COMMUNITIES   Most Hispanic barrios, or neighborhoods, have evolved into well-organized communities with their own city council representatives, community activists, school boards, medical clinics, legal offices, and nonprofit associations. One of the most important social functions these communities provide is a sense of belonging, of cultural heritage.

Spanish is the prevalent language among adults in Hispanic neighborhoods. Children grow up bilingual. Most vendors talk to their customers in Spanish. Catholic churches, representing the dominant religion for Hispanics, reach their congregations through services conducted in Spanish. And a variety of shops and supermarkets satisfy consumers' longing for traditional Hispanic foods, clothing, and amenities along with their newly acquired tastes for American products.

Hispanic communities are expected to continue to grow in number and in population. Hispanics may soon be the majority population in states such as New Mexico, California, and Texas. In 1990 Hispanics comprised 38, 26, and 25 percent, respectively, of the total population of those states (Figure 1.5). Currently Hispanics in the Los Angeles basin account for more than 33 percent of the total population of the area (Center for the Continuing Study of the California Population, 1991, LA-11).

BUSINESSES   Not only are Hispanics significant consumers of mass market U.S. goods, they also contribute greatly to the marketplace as entrepreneurs and producers of goods and services. In 1987 there were 422,373 Hispanic-owned businesses in the United States, with total revenues of $25 billion (Table 1.4). In 1980, Miami, San Antonio, and Los Angeles-Long Beach registered Hispanic business ownership rates as high as 43 percent, 21 percent, and 14 percent, respectively (Table 1.5). In 1990 the top 500 Hispanic companies reported sales in excess of $9.8 billion (*U.S. Bureau of the Census*, 1991b).

POLITICS

Hispanics have become active in the political process and are influential at the federal, state, county, city, and local levels. As of 1993 there were over 5,170 elected Hispanic officials — 1,387 more than in 1989 (Table 1.6).

ASSOCIATIONS

In the United States there are more than 300 national organizations and more than 800 state, regional, and national chapters concerned with Hispanic Americans; about 200 libraries with special Hispanic collections; 300 museums, galleries, and other organizations featuring Hispanic culture; 200 university research centers studying Hispanic history and culture; and approximately 450 colleges and universities offering Hispanic courses or studies (*Hispanic Americans Information Directory 1994–95*, xi–xiv). (See Table 1.7 for approximate numbers of other Hispanic organizations and programs.)

MEDIA

In 1994 there were approximately 500 Hispanic serial publications including newspapers, periodicals, newsletters, and directories; 210 publishers of books and other literature by and about Hispanics; and about 325 radio and television stations and networks with programming aimed at the Hispanic community (*Hispanic Americans Information Directory 1994–95*, xi–xiv). (See Chapter 6 for an in-depth look at the Hispanic media scene.)

FESTIVALS

In 1990 alone there were fourteen Hispanic communities that organized festivities to celebrate patriotic or cultural events such as Mexican Independence Day. Some of these events attract huge crowds; in New York, the Feria Mundial Hispaña (Hispanic World Fair) attracts more than 400,000 people annually, and in Miami, the Hispanic Heritage Festival attracts more than half a million people annually (Table 1.8).

■ Who Is Hispanic?

Webster's Tenth New Collegiate Dictionary traces the origin of the word Hispanic to Hispania Iberian peninsula (Spain) and defines as Hispanic any person "of Latin American descent living in the United States, especially one of Cuban, Mexican, or Puerto

Rican origin." The Bureau of the Census used a more comprehensive definition at the time of the 1990 census. The bureau included as Hispanic persons in the categories Spanish, Spaniard, Mexican-American, Chicano, Puerto Rican, Cuban, and "other" (to identify respondents from other parts of Latin America). "Hispanic" is also the preferred term used today within the U.S. business community to identify this particular segment of the market.

Often the terms Latino and Hispanic are used interchangeably, although the term Latino seems to carry with it some soft political overtones. When a particular Hispanic group is referred to, however, the name of the country of origin is usually used. In current usage the term Latino refers more specifically to the peoples born in the Latin American region, regardless of race.

There is currently no consensus within the Hispanic community as to how its members should be collectively referred to. The term Hispanic is neither offensive nor preferable. Latino Voices, a major survey conducted among Mexicans, Puerto Ricans, and Cubans, found that foreign-born respondents overwhelmingly identified themselves with the name of their country of origin. The pattern of identification was similar among the U.S. native born, particularly among Mexicans but to a lesser degree among Puerto Ricans and Cubans, who seemed to have a stronger preference for Pan-ethnic labels, such as Latino, Hispanic, or Spanish-American (Figure 1.6).

Among the various subgroups, Mexican Americans tend to prefer the word Latino; Cubans appear to have no objection to the word Hispanic. (In others words both Hispanic and Latino are terms accepted by the Hispanic community.) Hispanics may be of any race. Most are Catholic and most trace their ancestry to a Spanish-speaking country.

HISPANIC SUBGROUPS   Mexicans, Puerto Ricans, and Cubans are the three largest Hispanic groups, according to the 1990 U.S. census (Figure 1.7). Peoples who trace their heritage to the countries of Central and South America form the other major Hispanic group. By virtue of being U.S. citizens, Puerto Ricans are in a special category. Those who were born on the mainland and consider themselves Puerto

Ricans are officially considered U.S. Hispanics. Those born on the U.S. commonwealth island of Puerto Rico are counted separately and are currently excluded from the Hispanic category. (Because it would be erroneous to exclude the 3.5 million population of Puerto Rico from the figures for the U.S. Hispanic market, Chapter 2 includes a special section on Puerto Rico.)

From a marketing perspective it makes a big difference whether consumers are born in the United States or elsewhere in Latin America because foreign and native-born Hispanics differ considerably in terms of language usage, media consumption, and cultural traits—all of which affect consumer research, marketing, and selling strategies. The significance of the number of foreign-born Hispanics is very hard to ignore. If residents of Puerto Rico are added to the number of U.S. Hispanics whose country of birth is other than the United States, then the total size of the Hispanic foreign-born population at the time of the last census was 9 million—about 2 million more consumers than there are in the country of Switzerland.

In addition, the number of foreign-born persons is actually much higher than that given in the official count. As often publicized, a large number of legal and undocumented immigrants were not counted at the time the census was taken. According to the United States Department of Justice, in 1990 the size of the undocumented Hispanic population ranged from 1.8 million to 3.1 million. The discrepancy clearly underestimates the true size of the foreign-born and of the Hispanic market in general.

One only need look at the numbers in Table 1.9 to realize how vital it is for marketers to take nativity into account when targeting Hispanics, particularly Mexican and Central and South American consumers. For these groups, which comprise a major share of the immigrant population, the proportion of foreign-born persons has increased steadily in the last three decades and is projected to continue to do so for some time. Foreign-born Cubans outnumber the native-born population despite a decline in immigration over the last decade. Chapter 7 addresses the issues that arise in marketing to the U.S.-born and foreign-born Hispanic segments.

■ Reasons for Hispanic Migration to the United States

Hispanic presence in what is now the United States dates back to 1513. The number of immigrants swelled after World War II. Recent surveys identify various motives for relocating to the United States. Of these, economic considerations rate highest among Mexicans, and political strife dominates with Cuban immigrants (de la Garza et al. 1992, 154). Family reunification, educational opportunities, new sources of financial investment, and the desire to start a new business in the United States are also important contributors to Hispanic immigration (Figure 1.8). Table 1.10 lists important sociopolitical landmarks in the history of the United States, Puerto Rico, Mexico, Cuba, and Central and South America that are at the core of the massive migration of Hispanics to the United States.

GEOGRAPHIC DISTRIBUTION   The geographical location of the different Latin American countries relative to the United States determines to a large extent the settlement patterns of the immigrants. Puerto Ricans tend to relocate in the Northeast (New York and Boston); Cubans, in the Southeast (Miami area); and Mexicans, in the Southwest (New Mexico, Texas, Arizona, and California). Figure 1.9 shows the distribution of the Hispanic population in the states.

Country of origin and relocation patterns of the immigrants have lent distinct characteristics to the rapidly growing Hispanic market.

■ Hispanic Ethnicity and the Marketplace

In the field of marketing, "Hispanic ethnicity" is a convenient term used to address a large, heterogeneous group rich in diversity and cultural subtleties. Every group considered Hispanic originates from Spain and from one of the Latin American countries. Each one of these countries has a unique national history, cultural background, demographic profile, and level of development, all of which contribute to their distinctiveness. Recognizing what these differences are is crucial to an effective marketing program, and is as essential as detecting the similarities that exist between the various nationalities. For marketing purposes, people from Portugal and Brazil, which are also of Latin origin, are not included in broad definition of Hispanic market because of the language difference, Portuguese.

■ Understanding the Hispanic Consumer Market

Uninterrupted migration has kept the Hispanic consumer market in a state of flux. Long before World War II, streams of foreign-born Hispanics flowed into the United States to satisfy the labor demands of the country's growing economy. Many were in the United States long before Texas and California were incorporated into the Union, and since then, their descendants have been active members of American society. Others have arrived during the past few minutes. Their backgrounds differ. Men, women, and children come from urban and rural areas all over North, Central, and South America. Some have more formal schooling than others. Large numbers come alone, others with their families. Most do not speak English. Despite their diversity, their cultural similarities, such as the Spanish language, far outweigh their differences.

Upon arrival in the United States, Hispanics come into contact with a different culture. Almost immediately they begin to realize that the life-styles, customs, aspirations, and values found in the new society are different from their own. What they considered "a given" in their own country is now questioned, reassessed, and sometimes replaced with a different viewpoint or way of doing things. As they become familiar with the traditions and the way of doing things in the United States, Hispanics develop new approaches to interacting, living, and understanding the world around them. Slowly but steadily the acculturation process carries on.

Acculturation

Gradually Hispanic consumers begin to shift from their native culture to that of the United States. Not everyone acculturates at the same pace. Many factors may accelerate or slow the process, such as where immigrants relocate or the degree of formal education upon arrival. The process of acculturation takes place at all levels of social interaction. Understanding its dynamics is critical to learning how to interact, communicate, and work with the Hispanic consumer market successfully.

Because new immigrants arrive daily, the acculturation process never ceases. This constant renewal makes the Hispanic consumer market a moving target. Advertisers and others who continually communicate with Hispanic customers and consumers need to do so at *all* levels of the cultural assimilation process. Ad campaigns and other marketing efforts targeting Hispanics must successfully communicate with a market that is conspicuously new as well as one that is well informed, brand aware, and loyal. Acculturation as it relates to the Hispanic consumer market is examined in depth in Chapter 3, and the dynamics of marketing to the diverse segments of the Hispanic market are discussed in Chapter 7.

Communication is a critical aspect during the transition between cultures. When two or more cultures coexist in the same society, as is the case with Anglo and Hispanic cultures, there is a greater risk that the receiver belonging to a culture different from the sender's will misinterpret the intended meaning in the message being delivered, even when the translated words are correct. The result is miscommunication and wasted promotional and marketing dollars. To be effective, campaigns to target Hispanic consumers must be in consonance with Hispanic culture at all message levels: symbolic, explicit, visual, and subliminal. How to achieve cultural consonance when communicating with the Hispanic market is discussed in detail in Chapters 4, 5, and 6.

Hispanics and the "Melting Pot"

Research conducted by Hispanic Market Connection's (a marketing research company), as well as investigations by many others studying Hispanics in various settings, indicates that important and identifiable cultural traits can be found in U.S. Hispanic families even when they have resided in the United States for several generations. In other words, the "melting pot" phenomenon is slow to occur, and much slower than some have suspected. Of all social traits, language is perhaps the most distinguishable characteristic of any culture, and probably the last one any immigrant group will give up. As has been documented extensively, given the choice, most first-generation U.S. Hispanic adults speak in Spanish rather than English, even if they are bilingual. Spanish-language usage is sure to continue well into the future if current immigration projections hold. According to Edmonston and Passel (1992, 43), by the year 2010 foreign-born Hispanic consumers may still account for about 40 percent (13.6 million) of the total Hispanic market, and second and later generations for about 60 percent (20.4 million). The role of language in Hispanic culture is discussed in detail in Chapter 5.

Multicultural Households

Hispanic consumers seldom acquire all their values from mainstream American culture. Rather, their aspirations, tastes, preferences, purchasing behavior, life-styles, and the activities surrounding buying decisions tend to be different from those of the overall market. In the Hispanic marketplace, first-generation consumers have preferences and tastes that were acquired and molded in their countries of origin. By contrast, Hispanic children born or raised in the United States acquire some of their values and preferences from their exposure to American culture through schools, friends, and media as well as from the beliefs and customs of their parents. The daily contact of Hispanic children with both Anglo and Hispanic traditions gives rise to households with dual value systems and dual preferences for toys, clothing, foods, and other consumer goods. For these reasons, Hispanic families frequently exhibit two distinct sets of aspirations, food preferences, cooking styles, consumption habits, and so on. Chapters 4, 5, and 7 include further discussions of multicultural households.

Culture

Latin American countries trace their cultural origins to Spain and Portugal. These two countries were once part of the Roman Empire, of which Latin was the official language and Catholicism the prevalent religion. During the Age of Discovery (circa 1400), Spain, and to a lesser extent Portugal, conquered large regions of the Western Hemisphere, including most of Central America, South America, the Caribbean, Mexico, and parts of what is today the United States, specifically, Texas, Arizona, and California; Hence the common cultural features shared by most Latin

American countries are the Spanish language and the Catholic faith.

Other factors connect Latin American countries with Spain and Portugal as well, for example, slower economic, technological, and scientific development. (Spain and Portugal were two of the last countries to join the Industrial Revolution.) Partly because of this slow development, many Latin American countries still have large rural or semirural populations with little formal education. Most of these countries are not well developed, and they all share in the struggle to compete with more technologically and economically advanced nations.

Most Latin American countries were also greatly influenced by indigenous cultures, having had their own pre-Columbian civilizations, for example, the Mayan and Aztecan in Mexico and the Incan in Peru. Others, such as Argentina, Uruguay, Chile, Peru, Paraguay, Cuba, and the Dominican Republic, were also influenced by large immigration flows from northern and eastern Europe, Africa, and Asia. The influence of these various cultures is noticeable in the music Hispanics sing and dance to, the different foods they eat, the religious and healing practices they follow, and their material items, such as their musical instruments and artifacts.

Cultural and regional differences become very relevant when the target audience is a particular Hispanic subgroup. The importance of these differences in marketing to Hispanics is discussed in more detail in Chapter 2 (see page 51).

Language "Pardon Me, Do You Speak English?" (Crispell, 1992, 4) is the title of a recent article reporting data on a new phenomenon—"linguistically isolated households," as the U.S. Census refers to those households in which no one is able to speak English well enough to communicate with English-speaking people. These households are culturally isolated as well. Their members are excluded from mainstream American culture and, to a large extent, are *unreachable* via traditional English-language advertising strategies and ads.

One recent investigation indicates that adult consumers' preference for the Spanish language is perhaps the strongest indicator of Hispanic culture in the United States (Hispanic Market Connections, 1992, pp. 26–31). After conducting thousands of interviews among Hispanic adults, Hispanic Market Connections (HMC) developed the Hispanic Language Segmentation©, a rating scale based on a battery of questions concerning usage and proficiency in Spanish and English. On the basis of respondents' language preference in media, HMC identified five groups in the Hispanic market today: Spanish dominant, Spanish preferred, true bilinguals, English preferred, and English dominant.

Media Usage

Most Hispanics utilize English and Spanish media. The frequency with which they choose one or the other varies drastically depending on language proficiency, length of residence in the United States, and formal educational level. As would be expected, the fewer the number of years they have lived in the United States, the lower their English proficiency and the greater the use of Spanish-language media. However, this rule does not apply across the board. Many long-term U.S. residents, and even second-generation Hispanics, choose more Spanish-language media than English-language.

The opposite tends to be true for those who are English dominant and English preferred. According to HMC statistics, people in these two groups partake of significantly more English than Spanish media, but they are a small percentage of the U.S. Hispanic market. Since a very large proportion of Hispanics arrived in the United States during the 1980s and 1990s, the Spanish-dominant and Spanish-preferred segments of the market are overwhelmingly large.

It stands to reason, then, that Spanish should be the language selected to advertise mass consumption-type products, such as personal care products, food, jeans, restaurants, over-the-counter medicines, and health-care services. English-language media, on the other hand, provide Hispanic bilinguals and English-preferred consumers with an informational forum of American social, entertainment, and political information, and therefore complement general market communications.

Values

Unlike American mainstream culture, which emerged from the Anglo-Saxon tradition, Hispanic culture was heavily influenced by Spain. Hence, Hispanic and Anglo values tend to be different, and, consequently, each culture reflects a uniquely different lifestyle. These differences and how they are involved in the acculturation process are discussed in detail in Chapter 4 (see page 180).

Customs Overall, Hispanics tend to be lighthearted and enjoy group activities involving relatives and friends. Special birthdays, such as the *Quinceañera* (a rite of passage for fifteen-year-old girls in some Latin American countries), and anniversaries, engagements, weddings, and religious ceremonies, such as baptisms and communions, tend to be elaborate and well attended. Close family ties are a tradition deeply rooted in Hispanic culture. As with other cultures, Hispanics are frequently seen shopping and sightseeing with family and friends. Individualism, while fostered in Anglo-Saxon tradition, is not as greatly valued in Hispanic culture.

Sentiments Regardless of how long they have lived in the United States, foreign-born Hispanics all had to leave their homes, their families, their friends, and the way they used to live. Some fled economic strife, others escaped political persecution, and still others had to face deportation. Whatever the reasons, some were forced and others chose to leave their native land. Some arrived in boats and by plane, others by foot and in cars or trucks.

Many Hispanics think of their native countries with longing, with nostalgia. Many dream of going back home someday, and others know they will never return. So, a need to create a home away from home has resulted in the development of small Latin corners. For example, Miami is known as Little Havana, and Southern California is "a piece of Latin America." Regardless of country of origin, the immigration experience contributes to the character and strength of U.S. Hispanics. They are nostalgic, courageous, hardworking, and committed.

Social Attributes In their home countries, most first-generation immigrant Hispanics encountered, the hardship of having to earn a living in a society where social and political conditions are so oppressive that it is impossible to achieve acceptable or minimal social status or material gains. One of the greatest attributes Hispanics see in the United States is its political freedom and the opportunities available for upward mobility brought about by an open society. The simple fact that such a large group of people attempt to move between countries in order to improve their living conditions reveals their eagerness to climb the social scale, and their determination to work hard and succeed for the sake of their children's future.

Regardless of the reasons for leaving their home country, Hispanics arrive in the United States searching for a better life and higher standards of living. Although as a group Hispanics may be at a disadvantage with regard to formal education, income, and working experience relative to other immigrants, they have certainly advanced their status. Their social, economic, and political gains during the past few decades exemplify their potential to be active contributors to American society and the marketplace. It is expected that Hispanics will continue to make gains and contributions at all levels in society.

■ *Reference*

American Marketing Association. "The New Majority: Marketing to Hispanic, African & Asian Americans." New York: AMA, 1993. Photocopy.

Bean, Frank D., and Marta Tienda. *The Hispanic Population of the United States.* New York: Russel Sage Foundation, 1990.

Center for the Continuing Study of the California Population. (CCSCP) *California Population Characteristics.* Palo Alto, Calif.: CCSC, 1991.

"Comparing the Hispanic and Non-Hispanic Markets: How Different Are They?" *The Journal of Services Marketing* 6, no. 2 (Spring 1992).

Crispell, Diane, ed. "Pardon Me, Do You Speak English?" *American Demographics.* Vol. 12, No. 8. 1992.

de la Garza, Rodolfo O., Louis DeSipio, F. Chris Garcia, John Garcia, and Angelo Falcon. *Latino Voices: Mexican, Puerto Rican, & Cuban Perspectives on American Politics.* Boulder, Colo.: Westview Press, 1992.

Edmonston, Barry, and Jeffrey S. Passel. *The Future Immigrant Population of the United States.* Washington, D.C.: The Urban Institute, 1992.

"The 500. Market Down, Hispanic Companies Up." In *Hispanic Business.* (June 1991): 30.

Guernica, Antonio, and Irene Kasperuk. *Reaching the Hispanic Market Effectively: The Media, the Market, the Methods.* New York: McGraw-Hill, 1982.

Hispanic Americans Information Directory 1994–95. Detroit, Mich.: Gale Research, 1994.

Hispanic Market Connections. *The National Hispanic Database: Northern California, 1992.* Los Altos, Calif.: HMC, 1992.

———. *The National Hispanic Database: Southern California, 1992.* Los Altos, Calif.: HMC, 1992.

Kanellos, Nicolás. *The Hispanic-American Alamanac.* Detroit, Mich.: Gale Research, 1993.

"MDI Hispanic Teen Poll," reviewed in "Research Alert" (newsletter) March 1992, 4. Brooklyn, N.Y.: EPM Communications.

Mulhern, Francis J., and Jerome D. Williams. "Hispanic Shopping Behavior: A Look at Actual Purchases and Income." Department of Marketing, Pennsylvania State University, 1993. Photocopy.

National Association of Latino Elected and Appointed Officials (NALEO) Educational Fund. *National Roster of Hispanic Elected Officials.* In Frank L. Schick and Renee Schick, eds., *Statistical Handbook on U.S. Hispanics.* Phoenix, Ariz.: Oryx Press, 1991.

"Number News." *American Demographics* (August 1992): 4–9.

Population Reference Bureau. *1992 World Population Data Sheet.* Washington, D.C.: PBR, 1992.

Schick, Frank L., and Renee Schick, eds. *Statistical Handbook on U.S. Hispanics.* Phoenix, Ariz.: Oryx Press, 1991.

Tienda, Marta, and Vilma Ortiz. "Hispanicity and the 1980 Census." Working paper no. 84–23. Center for Demography and Ecology, University of Wisconsin, 1984. Ithaca, N.Y.: TGE Demographics, 1992.

United Nations. *Demographic Yearbook.* New York: U.N., 1989.

U.S. Bureau of the Census. *1977 Economic Census. Survey of Minority Owned Business Enterprises. Minority Owned Business. Spanish Origin.* Washington, D.C.: Government Printing Office, 1980.

———. *The Hispanic Population in the United States: March 1991.* Population Characteristics, series P-20, no. 455. Washington, D.C.: Government Printing Office, 1991(a).

———. *1987 Economic Census. Survey of Minority-Owned Business Enterprises. Hispanic.* Washington, D.C.: Government Printing Office, August 1990–June 1991(a).

———. *1987 Economic Census. Survey of Minority-Owned Business Enterprises. Summary.* Washington, D.C.: Government Printing Office, 1991.

———. *Race and Hispanic Origin.* 1990 Census Profile, no. 2, 1991(b).

———. *Current Population Reports: Population Projections of the United States, by Age, Sex, Race, and Hispanic Origin: 1992–2050.* Washington, D.C.: Government Printing Office, 1992.

———. *Statistical Abstract of the United States: 1992.* 112th ed. Washington, D.C.: Government Printing Office, 1992.

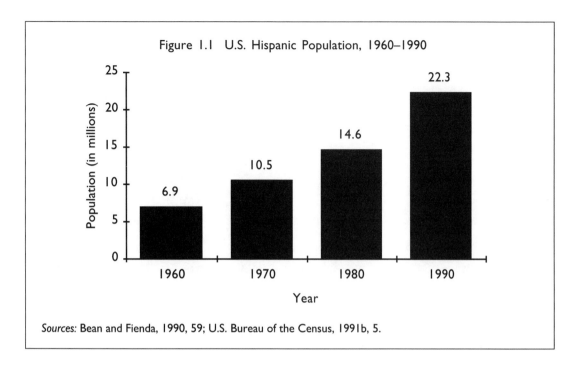

Figure 1.1 U.S. Hispanic Population, 1960–1990

Sources: Bean and Fienda, 1990, 59; U.S. Bureau of the Census, 1991b, 5.

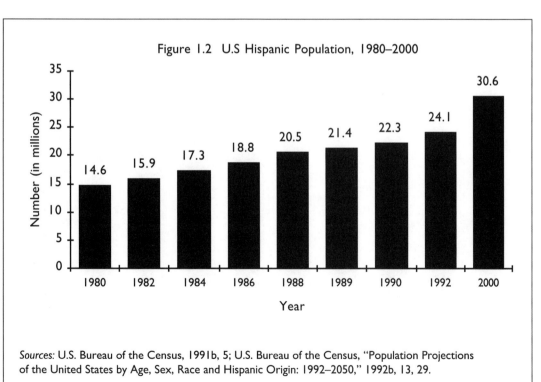

Figure 1.2 U.S Hispanic Population, 1980–2000

Sources: U.S. Bureau of the Census, 1991b, 5; U.S. Bureau of the Census, "Population Projections of the United States by Age, Sex, Race and Hispanic Origin: 1992–2050," 1992b, 13, 29.

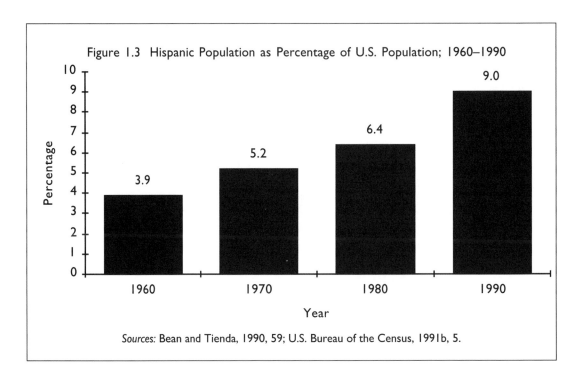

Figure 1.3 Hispanic Population as Percentage of U.S. Population; 1960–1990

Sources: Bean and Tienda, 1990, 59; U.S. Bureau of the Census, 1991b, 5.

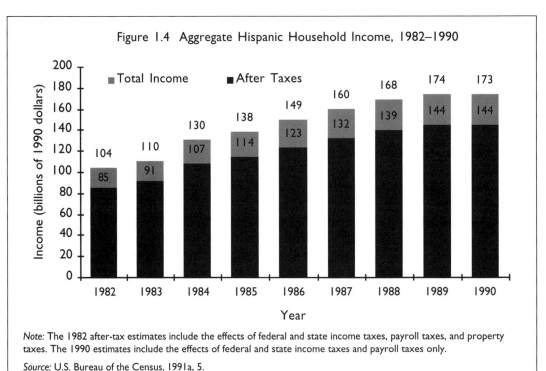

Figure 1.4 Aggregate Hispanic Household Income, 1982–1990

Note: The 1982 after-tax estimates include the effects of federal and state income taxes, payroll taxes, and property taxes. The 1990 estimates include the effects of federal and state income taxes and payroll taxes only.

Source: U.S. Bureau of the Census, 1991a, 5.

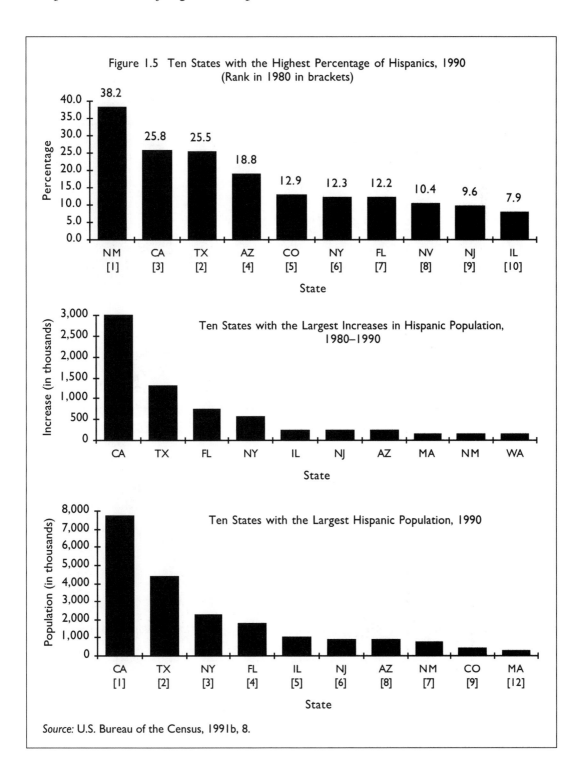

Figure 1.5 Ten States with the Highest Percentage of Hispanics, 1990
(Rank in 1980 in brackets)

Ten States with the Largest Increases in Hispanic Population, 1980–1990

Ten States with the Largest Hispanic Population, 1990

Source: U.S. Bureau of the Census, 1991b, 8.

Figure 1.6 Hispanic Self-Identification

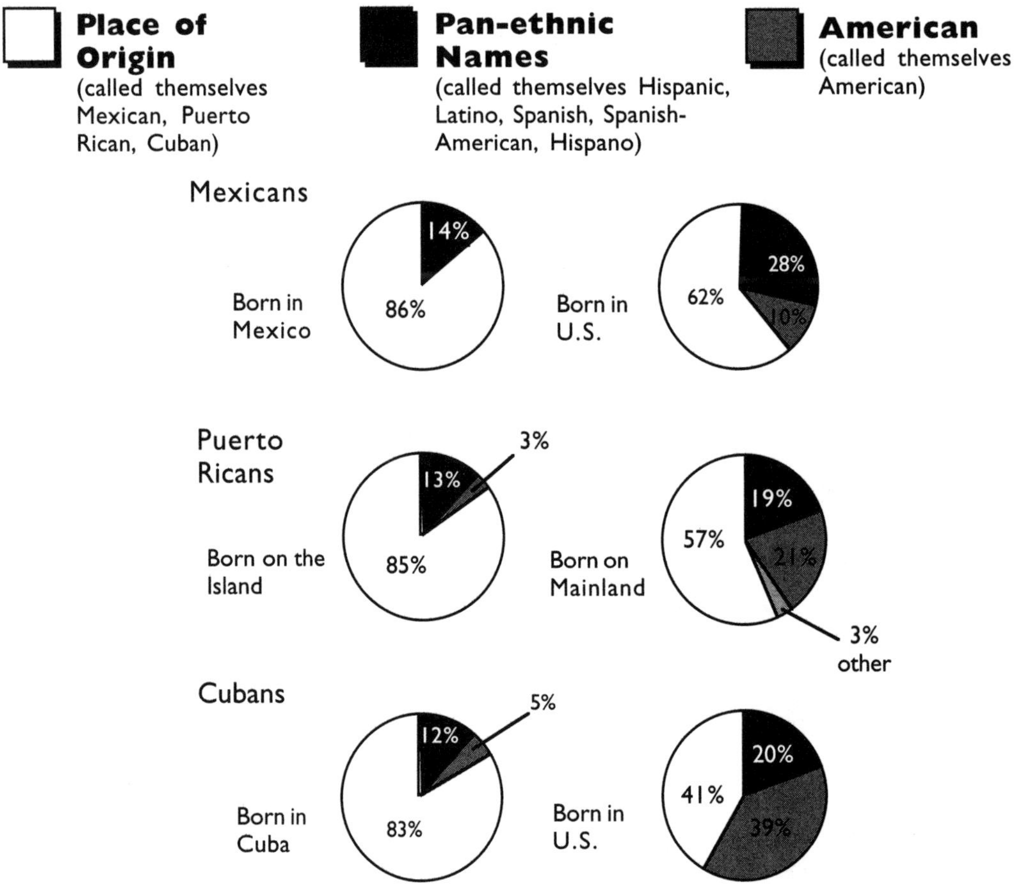

☐ **Place of Origin**
(called themselves Mexican, Puerto Rican, Cuban)

■ **Pan-ethnic Names**
(called themselves Hispanic, Latino, Spanish, Spanish-American, Hispano)

▨ **American**
(called themselves American)

Mexicans

Born in Mexico — 14% / 86%

Born in U.S. — 28% / 10% / 62%

Puerto Ricans

Born on the Island — 3% / 13% / 85%

Born on Mainland — 19% / 21% / 57% / 3% other

Cubans

Born in Cuba — 5% / 12% / 83%

Born in U.S. — 20% / 39% / 41%

Note: People living in the United States were asked how they identified themselves. Numbers may not add to 100 percent because of rounding.

Source: Reprinted from de la Garza et al., *Latino Voices: Mexican, Puerto Rican, and Cuban Perspectives on American Politics.* Boulder, Colo.: Westview Press, 1992.

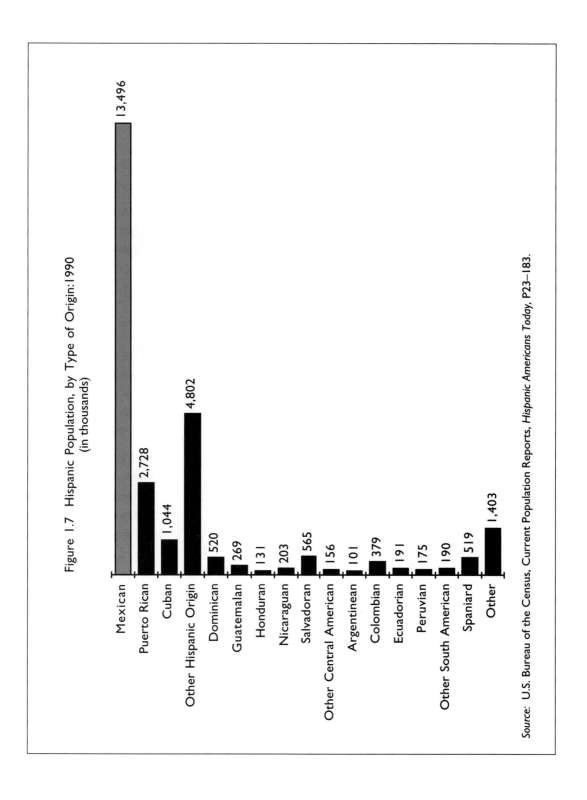

Figure 1.7 Hispanic Population, by Type of Origin: 1990 (in thousands)

Source: U.S. Bureau of the Census, Current Population Reports, *Hispanic Americans Today*, P23–183.

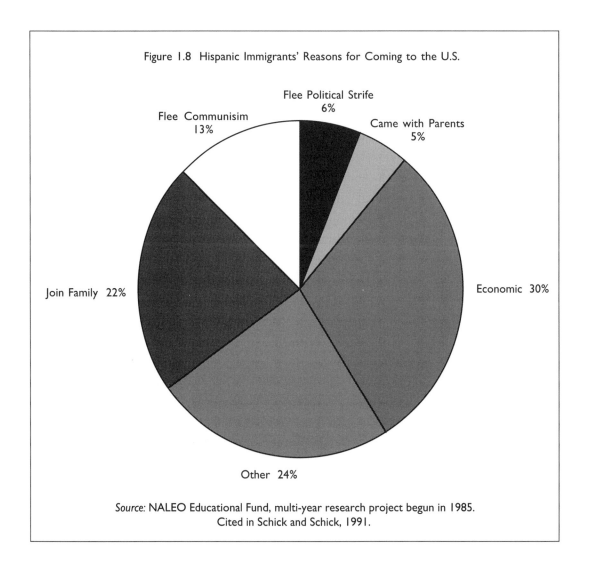

Figure 1.8 Hispanic Immigrants' Reasons for Coming to the U.S.

Flee Political Strife 6%

Came with Parents 5%

Flee Communisim 13%

Economic 30%

Join Family 22%

Other 24%

Source: NALEO Educational Fund, multi-year research project begun in 1985.
Cited in Schick and Schick, 1991.

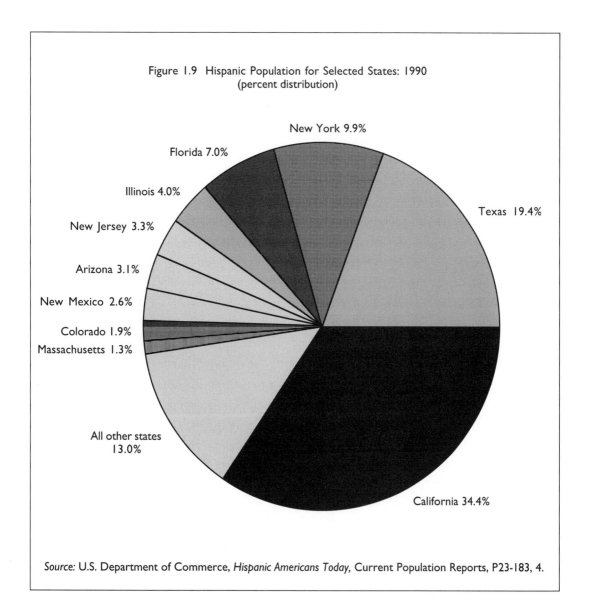

Figure 1.9   Hispanic Population for Selected States: 1990
(percent distribution)

New York 9.9%

Florida 7.0%

Illinois 4.0%

New Jersey 3.3%

Arizona 3.1%

New Mexico 2.6%

Colorado 1.9%

Massachusetts 1.3%

All other states
13.0%

Texas 19.4%

California 34.4%

Source: U.S. Department of Commerce, *Hispanic Americans Today,* Current Population Reports, P23-183, 4.

Table 1.1 Six Countries with Large Spanish-Speaking Populations, 1990

Country Population (Estimated)

Mexico	84,275,000
Spain	38,811,000
Argentina	31,929,000
Colombia	31,193,000
United States	22,354,000
Peru	21,792,000

Source: United Nations, *Demographic Yearbook,* 1989, 144.

Table 1.2 Household Projections, 1990–2000
(In thousands)

	1990	2000	Absolute Change 1990-2000	Percentage Change 1990-2000
Total households	91,950	103,810	11,860	12.9
Total households (white)	76,028	79,411	3,383	4.4
Total households (Afro-American)	10,307	12,441	2,134	20.7
Total households (Hispanic*)	6,365	9,422	3,057	48.0

*Hispanics of any race.
Source: TGE Demographics, 1992, 22, 33, 38.

Table 1.3 Hispanic Income per Capita, 1990

	Income per Capita (1990 dollars)
U.S.Hispanics	$8,424
Puerto Rico	6,470
Venezuela	2,560
Uruguay	2,560
Mexico	2,490
Argentina	2,370
Chile	1,940
Costa Rica	1,910
El Salvador	1,100
Guatemala	900
Honduras	590

Sources: U.S. Bureau of the Census, 1992b, 454; Population Reference Bureau, 1992.

Table 1.4 Growth of Hispanic-Owned Firms, Revenues, and Employees

Survey Year	Number of Businesses	Percentage Annual Growth	Revenue (billion $)	Percentage Annual Growth	Number of Employees	Percentage Annual Growth
1969	100,212	–	3.6	–	126,296	–
1972	120,108	6	5.3	14	149,656	6
1977	219,355	13	10.4	14	206,054	7
1982	233,975	1	11.8	2	154,791	6
1987	422,373	13	24.7	16	264,846	11

Notes: Growth percentages are expressed as compound annual rates. Data for surveys before 1982 reflect some differences from current methodology, however, the apparent slow growth between 1977 and 1982, including the decrease in employment, is real and reflects general economic conditions.

Sources: U.S. Bureau of the Census, August 1990–June 1991a, 2, 8, 9; 1980, 14–15.

Table 1.5　Hispanic Businesses Ranked by City

Rank[a]	Metropolitan Area	Number of Hispanic Businesses	Hispanic Population	Percentage Hispanic	Hispanic Business Rate[b]
1	Miami, FL	24,898	580,994	35.7%	42.9
2	Tampa-St. Petersburg, FL	2,686	79,431	5.1	33.8
3	Washington, DC-MD-VA	2,357	93,380	3.1	25.2
4	McAllen-Pharr-Edinburg, TX	5,766	230,212	81.3	25.0
5	Santa Barbara Santa Maria-Lompoc, CA	1,339	55,356	18.5	24.2
6	Laredo, TX	2,049	90,842	91.5	22.6
7	Houston, TX	9,276	424,903	14.6	21.8
8	San Francisco-Oakland, CA	7,649	351,698	10.8	21.7
9	Corpus Christi, TX	3,428	158,119	48.5	21.7
10	San Antonio, TX	10,341	481,511	44.9	21.5
11	Las Cruces, NM	1,071	50,204	52.1	21.3
12	Brownsville-Harlingen-San Benito, TX	3,377	161,654	77.1	20.9
13	Austin, TX	1,932	94,367	17.6	20.5
14	El Paso, TX	5,994	297,001	61.9	20.2
15	San Jose, CA	4,243	226,611	17.5	18.7
16	Anaheim-Santa Ana-Garden Grove, CA	5,317	286,339	14.8	18.6
17	Oxnard-Simi Valley-Ventura, CA	2,092	113,192	21.4	18.5
18	Albuquerque, NM	3,005	164,200	36.1	18.3
19	Sacramento, CA	1,852	101,694	10.0	18.2
20	Tucson, AZ	2,026	111,418	21.0	18.2
21	Dallas-Fort Worth, TX	4,493	249,614	8.4	18.0
22	Riverside-San Bernardino-Ontario, CA	5,218	290,280	18.6	18.0

Table 1.5 Hispanic Businesses Ranked by City (*continued*)

Rank[a]	Metropolitan Area	Number of Hispanic Businesses	Hispanic Population	Percentage Hispanic	Hispanic Business Rate[b]
24	San Diego, CA	4,903	275,177	14.8	17.8
25	Nassau-Suffolk, NY	1,659	101,975	3.9	16.4
26	Jersey City, NJ	2,367	145,163	26.1	16.3
27	Stockton, CA	1,002	66,565	19.2	15.1
28	Fresno, CA	2,266	150,790	29.3	15.0
29	Los Angeles-Long Beach, CA	29,982	2,066,103	27.7	14.5
30	Salinas-Seaside-Monterey, CA	1,074	75,129	25.9	14.3
31	Bakersfield, CA	1,170	87,026	21.6	13.4
32	Visalia-Tulare-Portersville, CA	979	73,298	29.8	13.4
33	Phoenix, AZ	2,631	199,003	13.2	13.2
34	Detroit, MI	852	71,606	1.6	11.9
35	Boston-Lowell-Brockton-Lawrence-Haverhill, MA	782	66,417	2.4	11.8
36	Newark, NY	1,541	132,372	6.7	11.6
37	Philadelphia, PA-NJ	1,133	116,280	2.5	9.7
38	Honolulu, HI	484	54,561	7.2	8.9
39	Paterson-Clifton-Passaic, NJ	543	62,123	13.9	8.7
40	New York, NY-NJ	12,292	1,493,148	16.4	8.2
41	Chicago, IL	4,562	580,609	8.2	7.9

[a]Metropolitan areas with at least 50,000 Hispanics in 1980, ranked by Hispanic business rate.
[b]Number of Hispanic-owned businesses per 1,000 Hispanics in population.

Source: U.S. Bureau of the Census, *Survey of Minority-Owned Business Enterprises,* 1980 and 1982.

Table 1.6 Hispanic Elected U.S. Officials by Level of Government, 1993

	Number	Percentage of Total Hispanic Elected Officials
FEDERAL		
U.S. senators	0	–
U.S. representatives	17	0.33
STATE		
State officials[a]	7	0.13
State legislators	156	3.01
County officials	406	7.85
Municipal officials	1,474	28.51
Judicial/law enforcement	633	12.24
Educational/school boards	2,332	45.10
Special districts	145	2.80
Total 1993	**5,170**	**(100)**

[a]Total of state officials includes governors and other elected officials within the executive branch.

Source: NALEO Education Fund. National Association of Latino Elected Officials *1993 National Roster of Hispanic Elected Officials.* Table 8, ix, 1993.

Table 1.7 Indicators of Hispanic Culture and Business

Hispanic organizations/activities	Approximate number[a] in U.S.
National organizations	300
Regional, state and local organizations	800
Library collections	200
Museum and other cultural organizations	300
Research centers	200
Awards, honors, prizes	110
Hispanic studies programs	450
Bilingual and migrant education programs	100
Scholarships, fellowships, and loans	125
Federal government agencies	215
Federal domestic assistance programs	70
State and local government agencies	320
Businesses[b]	500
Publications	500
Publishers	210
Broadcast media	325
Videos	600

[a]Numbers are approximate.

[b]Lists the top 500 U.S. Hispanic businesses only.

Source: Hispanic Americans Information Directory 1994–95, xi-xiv.

Table 1.8 Hispanic Festivals, 1990[a]

Date	Festival	Location	Estimated Attendance
April	Tucson Festival	Tucson, AZ	–
May	Olvera Street Cinco de Mayo	Los Angeles, CA	100,000+
May	Cinco de Mayo	Santa Ana, CA	100,000+
May	Cinco de Mayo, Semana Latina	Henderson, CO	20,000+
May	Cinco de Mayo Festival	Grand Prairie, TX	–
May	Fiesta Mexicana/Chili Cook-Off	Shreveport, LA	15,000+
May	Tejano Conjunto Festival	San Antonio, TX	35,000+
May	New Jersey Hispanic Heritage Festival and Concert	Ocean City, NJ	30,000+
July	4th of July Fajita Cook-Off	Mesquite, TX	15,000+
July	Viva Mexico	Chicago, IL	100,000+
July	Feria Mundial Hispana	New York, NY	400,000+
July	Hispanic-American Cultural Fest	Washington, D.C.	250,000+
August	New York Latino Festival	New York, NY	50,000+
August	Chicago's Pan-American Festival	Chicago, IL	100,000+
August	Feria Artesana	Albuquerque, NM	20,000+
August	Old Spanish Days Fiesta	Santa Barbara, CA	–
August	Fiesta Mexicana	Milwaukee, WI	–
September	Fiesta de Santa Fe	Santa Fe, NM	–
September	16th of September Fiesta	Calexico, CA	–
September	International Mariachi Festival	Los Angeles, CA	30,000+
October	The Whole Enchilada Fiesta	Las Cruces, NM	–
October	Hispanic Heritage Festival	Miami, FL	500,000+
November	Festival de las Super Estrellas	Houston, TX	30,000+

[a]List is not all-inclusive.

Sources: SRDS; Festivals U.S.A. by Kathleen Thompson Hill. New York, N.Y.: John Wiley & Sons, 1988.

Table 1.9 Distribution of Hispanic Population by National Origin

		1960	1970	1980	1990
Mexican					
	Foreign born	17%	18%	26%	33%
	Native born	83%	82%	74%	67%
Puerto Rican					
	Island Born	68%	54%	51%	45%
	Mainland Born	32%	46%	49%	55%
Cuban					
	Foreign Born	65%	73%	77%	72%
	Native-born	36%	27%	23%	28%
Central/South American					
	Foreign Born	62%	69%	80%	77%
	Native-born	38%	31%	20%	23%
Other Hispanic					
	Foreign Born	18%	12%	17%	15%
	Native-born	82%	88%	83%	85%

Sources: Data for 1960–1980 is from the 1980 Public Use Microdata Sample A, cited in Bean and Tienda, 1990, 110–11. Data for 1990 is from the U.S. Bureau of the Census, 1990, 3, 4, 10, 15, 23. Figures for persons of Puerto Rican origin were derived from Bureau of the Census tape STF3, matrices P11 and P42, 1990.

Table 1.10 Chronology of Hispanic Presence in the United States

Spanish

1690	First permanent Spanish settlement in Texas.
1691	Expansion to Arizona and Texas.
1766	San Francisco presidio becomes the northernmost frontier Spanish outpost.
1769	First Spanish mission in Alta, California (San Diego).

Mexican

1781	Independence from New Spain. The Republic of Mexico is born.
1821	Mexico acquires its independence from Spain. Permanent colonies exist in coastal California, southern Arizona, southern Texas, southern Colorado, and most of Texas.
1823	Anglo colonization of Mexican Texas begins at the request of Mexican representative.
1836	Anglo settlers declare the Republic of Texas independent of Mexico. Mexicans are forced off their properties and many move to Mexico.
1845	Texas is officially annexed to the United States.
1846	The United States invades Mexico. The treaty of Guadalupe ends the war. Half of land area of Mexico, including Texas, California, most of Arizona and New Mexico, parts of Colorado, Utah and Nevada is ceded to the United States. About 75,000 people choose to become U.S. citizens.
1880	Mexican immigration to the United States is stimulated by the advent of the railroad.
1910	Mexican revolution begins. Hundreds of people flee from Mexico and settle in the southwestern United States.
1917	During World War I, "temporary" Mexican farm workers, railroad laborers, and miners are permitted to enter the United States to work.
1917	Immigration Act, imposing literacy requirement on all immigrants, is designed to curtail immigration from Asia and Eastern Europe. Mexico and Puerto Rico become major sources of workers.

Cuban

1563	Earliest settlement in North America in Saint Augustine, Florida.
1770–90	50,000 African slaves are reportedly taken to Cuba to work in sugar production.
1776	Spanish presence expands in Florida, which is ceded by the French.
1783	The United States purchases Florida from Spain.
1840–70	125,000 Chinese arrive in Cuba to work as cane-cutters, build railroads, and serve as domestics in the cities. Retail trade expands with the influx of Spaniard merchants, who open the first general stores, called *bodegas*.

(continued next page)

Table 1.10 Chronology of Hispanic Presence in the United States (*continued*)

1868	Cubans leave for Europe and the United States in sizable numbers during Cuba's first major attempt at independence.
1880	Slavery is abolished. Population becomes more heterogenous.
1897	Spain grants autonomy to Cuba and Puerto Rico.
1898	Treaty of Paris between Spain and the United States grants Cuba and Puerto Rico to the United States.
1902	Cuba declares its independence from the United States.
1959	Castro takes power. Large-scale immigration to the United States.
1965	Second wave of Cuban refugees includes many relatives of former exiles.
1966–73	Cuban airlift. About 10 percent of the island population emigrates during this time. Most are of European origin, middle-class, well educated, landowners, professionals, and business people.
1980	Third wave of Cuban refugees, Marielitos, who are less educated, are of lower economic status, and are mostly non-European, begins to immigrate to the United States.
1994	*Balceros,* or rafters, flee harsh economic conditions in Cuba. Thousands arrive in the United States; many are picked up at sea by U.S. coast guard and are taken back to the U.S. base at Guantanamo, Cuba, where temporary camps are set up.

Puerto Rican

1898	In the Treaty of Paris, Spain transfers Puerto Rico and Cuba to the United States.
1900	The Foraker Act establishes a civilian government in Puerto Rico under U.S. dominance. Islanders elect their own House of Representatives but are not allowed to vote in Washington.
1930	United States controls 44 percent of cultivated land in Puerto Rico. Private capital controls 60 percent of banks, public services and all maritime lines.
1930–34	About 20 percent of Puerto Ricans on the mainland return to the island.
1944	Operation Bootstrap is initiated by the Puerto Rican government to meet U.S. labor demands of Worl War II. Encourages industrialization in the island and stimulates migration to the mainland.
1950	Puerto Rico becomes a U.S. commonwealth.
1950–1960	Early employment pattern: menial jobs in service sector, light factory work.
1959	Unlike Mexicans or Cubans, Puerto Ricans encounter minimum red tape to enter or re-enter the United States.
1978	The United Nations recognizes Puerto Rico as a colony of the United States.

Source: Kanellos, 1993, xxi–xxix.

CHAPTER 2

■ A Hispanic Renaissance

■ How Hispanic Growth Affects the Marketplace

■ A Hispanic Market without Immigration

■ Key Hispanic Market Trends

■ Hispanic Households

■ A Regional View of the Market

■ City Dwellers

■ Hispanic Subgroups

Hispanic Demographics
and Trends

■ **A Hispanic Renaissance**

The U.S. Hispanic consumer market is undergoing a renaissance, the result of a very rapid population increase that has dramatically transformed the U.S. demographic landscape and business environment in a relatively short period of time. A significant number of North, Central, and South American and Caribbean Hispanics have joined the ranks of U.S. consumers, creating new market niches and rekindling old ones. In addition, hundreds of Hispanic infants are born across the United States every day, enlarging the market for baby products and services; they are also the juvenile and adult consumers of the future. The demographic significance of U.S. Hispanics is such that the Bureau of the Census has a special branch (the Ethnic and Hispanic Branch) for collecting, analyzing, and disseminating information about Hispanics.

Businesses, advertisers, and marketers in particular make use of Hispanic demographics and trends daily. They routinely seek information that will answer questions about Hispanic market size and growth: which groups live where, what income averages are, who purchases what, and many, many other such questions. These questions are the subject of this chapter. First we discuss Hispanic growth as it affects primarily three main consumer groups: the young, older Hispanics, and women. We also explore how changing household demographics reflect changing Hispanic life-styles.

Then we focus on the geographic distribution of the Hispanic market—the main regions, states, and metropolitan areas where Hispanics live. Information on the fastest- and slowest-growing metropolitan areas in the ten leading Hispanic states is also provided.

Finally, we look at the subgroups that make up the Hispanic market. The purpose of this is twofold: (1) to assess the contribution of each subgroup to the changing demographic trends discussed in the first section, and (2) to provide a sociodemographic profile of each of the main groups—Mexicans, Puerto Ricans, Cubans, and Central and South Americans.

Scope of the Hispanic Renaissance

The U.S. Hispanic market is booming and there are no signs that the expansion will subside in the near future. According to the Census Bureau, as of 1990 there were 22.3 million Hispanics in the United States (Table 2.1)—7.4 million more than in 1980, and 15.5 million more than in 1960. In the long run marketers can expect to see the number of Hispanic consumers increase 17 million from the 1990 level by 2010 and 48 million by 2040—a cumulative increase of 48 million people in only fifty years. As the country advances to the second half of the twenty-first century, the number of Hispanics is expected to reach 81 million (Figure 2.1), roughly equal to the current population of Mexico.

The U.S. Bureau of the Census (1992b, xx), projects that every year after 1995 Hispanics could add more consumers to the United States than any other group, including non-Hispanic whites. By 2010 the number of U.S. Hispanics (39 million) will exceed that of Afro-Americans (38 million) and Asian-Americans (16 million). In fewer than forty years the Hispanic share of the U.S. population will increase from 9 percent to more than 20 per-

cent (Figure 2.2). The Census Bureau also projects that at current rates, by 2015 the Hispanic population will double its size to
reach 44 million (1992b, 43).

■ How Hispanic Growth Affects the Marketplace

Simply put, the historical increase in Hispanic population is the
result of a cumulative excess of births over deaths coupled with
gains through immigration. Each one of these components of
growth is significant in its own right, and each brings a different
set of dynamics to the marketplace.

Hispanic births will increasingly add more babies, teenagers and **BIRTHS**
younger parents to the consumer pool, as the Hispanic share of
all U.S. births is projected to increase from 14 to 29 percent
between 1992 and 2050. Contributing to the increase is the tendency for Hispanic women to have more children (2.5) than non-
Hispanic white women (1.8). Higher fertility will remain a
distinct feature of the Hispanic market (U.S. Bureau of the Census, 1992b, xxii).

For business a high-fertility population means younger consumers overall. For example, by the beginning of the next century more than one-third of U.S. Hispanics (11.4 million people)
will be under twenty years of age; only one-fourth of non-Hispanic whites will be in that category (Tables 2.2 and 2.3). Current
rates of Hispanic childbearing open up enormous possibilities for
companies with products and services appealing to families,
young parents, unmarried couples, mothers, singles, teenagers,
school-age children, preschoolers, toddlers, and babies.

Net immigration, the number of immigrants in the United States **IMMIGRATION**
minus the number who leave, is as responsible for the growth of
the Hispanic market as natural increase (more births than
deaths). The immediate effect of continuous immigration on the
marketplace is to raise the number of Hispanic adults ages 20 to
34 relative to the non-Hispanic white population (Figure 2.3).
Official estimates are that during the 1980s more than 3 million

additional Hispanic immigrants settled in the United States; that is, on average, in each year of the decade more than 300,000 foreign-born Hispanics made their permanent residence in this country.

Drawing from the immigration figures for the 1980s, the Bureau of the Census projects that between 1990 and 2050 an additional 24,000 Hispanic immigrants will be added every year, bringing the annual number to 324,000. This figure includes legal and illegal immigration and represents 37 percent of all annual net immigration into the United states (Figure 2.4). Other sources, however, have arrived at much higher figures. For example, demographers at the Urban Institute, a research organization on economics and social issues, located in Washington, D.C., project annual immigration figures of 380,000 during the 1990s and 401,000 by the year 2005 (Edmonston and Passell, 1992, 18, 38). Estimates aside, both sources agree that Hispanic immigration will continue to be significant. Understanding the role of immigration in market dynamics is essential to marketers, advertisers, and the media because immigration determines the number of foreign-born consumers there will be in the United States.

Foreign-Born Consumers The sheer number of foreign-born Hispanics adds to the complexity of targeting the Hispanic market. Urban Institute demographers B. Edmonston and J. Passel project that the number of foreign-born Hispanics could climb from 9.1 million in 1990 to 15 million in 2010 (Table 2.4). If this occurs, then the foreign-born will continue to have a substantial share of the market, representing 39 percent of the total U.S. Hispanic population.

These numbers redefine the rules of the marketplace, particularly with regard to language, culture, life-styles, communication, consumption patterns, and demand for certain goods and services. For example, foreign-born Hispanics are much more likely to use Spanish as their primary language. As a group, they are older than native Hispanics. They tend to rent a home rather than own one; they are far more likely to send remittances home than are U.S.-born Hispanics; and they tend to live in large households.

Banks and financial institutions, in particular, can benefit tremendously from the patronage of foreign-born Hispanics. Money transfers between the United States and Latin America are a multibillion dollar business. The dollar amount of money transferred from Mexicans in the United States to their families in Mexico, for instance, is such that it accounts for the third-largest source of income for the Mexican government. These international money transfers open up enormous opportunities in the areas of domestic and international banking and financial services. Other industries that can and are benefitting from the foreign-born Hispanic market segment are the telephone companies, the travel and entertainment industries, and restaurants serving Latin American cuisine.

■ A Hispanic Market without Immigration

For those concerned with the market implications of more restrictive immigration policies, the answer is that even without immigration, the Hispanic market will continue to grow. Despite its obvious contribution to the Hispanic population, immigration plays a lesser role than that of natural increase, births minus deaths. In the unlikely event of zero immigration, the Bureau of the Census still projects 51 million Hispanics by the year 2050, about 30 million fewer than with the expected number of immigrants but still twice the size of the Hispanic population in 1990.

■ Key Hispanic Market Trends

Because the Hispanic population is increasing across almost every age level (see Tables 2.2 and 2.3), marketers need to know for planning purposes which consumer age groups will likely increase and how fast. In lieu of a crystal ball to predict the future, demographers make various assumptions about how populations change over time. The estimates or projections are based on assumptions about future trends in fertility, life expectancy, and net immigration. The results (called series) are usually labeled low, middle, or high to indicate how each component is expected to vary. For example, Hispanic fertility rates are assumed to decrease 10 percent after the year 2000 in the "middle series," to decrease by 20 percent in the "low series," and to increase by 10 percent in the "high series" (Bureau of the Census 1992b, xi). The closer the assumptions are to fact, the greater the accuracy of the estimates. The trends described in the discussion that follows are based on the "middle series."

THE YOUTH MARKET If one accepts the Census Bureau's middle series estimates as likely, then marketers whose products or services are consumed by Hispanic infants, children, and teenagers will definitely have the upper hand. The Hispanic population is, and will likely remain, younger than the U.S. total population for a long time to come. The age pyramids in Figure 2.3 provide planners with an insight into which Hispanic age groups they may wish to target. For Hispanics, the pyramid has a wide base reflecting a youthful population, the result of high birth rates. The thickening or bulging of the pyramid around ages 20 to 34 reflects the short-term effect of continuous immigration. By contrast, in the pyramid for whites the narrow base and thickening around ages 25 to 34 is the result of fewer births and the aging of the baby boom generation. For Hispanics, the top of the pyramid, indicating the older population, is also much thinner than the pyramid for whites. In other words, from a demographic perspective these are two quite different markets.

THE MATURE MARKET Those doing long-range planning can benefit by keeping their eyes on the mature market, as the differences in age distribution between Hispanics and whites are projected to narrow with time. The trends point to fewer births, longer life spans, and steady streams of immigrants, all of which tend to shift the weight of the population from the younger to the older groups. As a result of the interplay of these factors, the median age moves upward. For example, between 1980 and 1990, the median age for Hispanics increased from 23.2 to 26.2; by 2010 the median age is expected to be 29 (Table 2.2).

MARKET EXPECTATIONS If the Bureau of the Census middle series projections are used as a starting point for planning, Tables 2.2 and 2.3 show what the age composition of the Hispanic market may look like by the year 2010.

Between 1990 and 2010, each single age group will increase in size. During the same period, the under 45-age group will lose (and the over-45 group will gain) 8.9 percentage points, a sign of a gradually aging market. What gains are expected in each group?

Children and teenagers, a major consumption group, will continue to be the largest segment of the market, as they are also expected to sustain the largest gains of all age groups listed in Table 2.2. So, between 1990 and 2010, the last year in the table, marketers could be looking at an additional 5.4 million people under age 20 as their numbers will increase from 8.6 million to 14 million, a 63 percent increase in 20 years.

With regard to the mature market, Hispanic consumers entering their middle years will comprise another group that business should watch. The category composed of ages 30 to 44 will sustain the second largest increase and is expected to add more than 3 million people between 1990 and 2010, a 62 percent gain. This is an important group because consumers in their thirties and forties are most likely to buy or rent homes, which has a positive affect on the financial and construction industries. Those in their late forties and early fifties, the 45 to 54 group, will almost triple between 1990 and 2010. It is expected that they will expand by 3.1 million people over twenty years, a 182 percent increase during the period. Hispanics who are 55 and over will add 3.4 million, a 147 percent increase during the same period. Of all age groups listed in Table 2.2, those in their twenties will sustain the smallest gains, 1.7 million, or 36 percent between 1990 and 2010.

■ Hispanic Households

Household and family statistics are of major interest to marketers and advertisers because households and families reflect major consumption units. In addition, in times of economic upswing, an increase in the number of households translates into more housing units, more construction, and more business opportunities for the housing industry and the real estate market.

The number of Hispanic households has increased dramatically in the last twenty years. (The Bureau of the Census considers a household Hispanic if the householder, that is, the person who rents or owns a housing unit, claims to be of Hispanic origin, regardless of how many other people live there, or how many claim Hispanic origin.) Between 1970 and 1990 their number almost tripled, from 2.3 million to 6 million. By 1992 Hispanics occupied 4 million more households than in 1970, and 2.7 million more than in 1980 (Table 2.5). By the year 2000, marketers, advertisers, and the media may be looking at more than 9.4 million Hispanic households—a 48 percent increase in ten years (Table 2.6). During the 1990s the number of Hispanic households could grow faster than the Hispanic population, partly because of the large increase expected in the growth of nonfamily households (for example, young adults leaving home to live on their own). To illustrate the magnitude of the changes ahead, suffice it to say that although Hispanic households represent only 7 percent of all U.S. households, one new household in four is expected to be headed by a Hispanic during the 1990s (Table 2.7) (TGE Demographics, 1992, 10).

Demographically, Hispanic households are quite different from non-Hispanic ones. In general, Hispanic households are bigger, for at least two reasons. First, as has been noted, Hispanics tend to have more children. Second, it is quite common to find friends and family living together in a single household or in multiple-family households, with more than one nuclear family residing in the same dwelling. In 1992, 25 percent of all Hispanic households had five or more people living in them, compared with 8 percent for non-Hispanic white households.

Hispanic households are also different because of language. According to the 1990 census, there are more than 7.7 million Hispanics with limited knowledge of English and a household population of 4.5 million with almost no knowledge of it (U.S. Bureau of the Census, 1993, 79).

Hispanic householders are younger than the national average. In 1990 the median age of Hispanic householders was 40, versus 46 for the total population (U.S. Bureau of the Census, 1993a, 54, 268). The trend, however, is changing, shifting toward older householders. By the year 2000, there will be fewer Hispanic householders in their twenties. As the population ages, the renters and mortgage holders will increasingly be older Hispanics, particularly those in the 45–54 age group, whose numbers are expected to increase by 79 percent during the decade (Table 2.7). According to the *American Housing Survey*, in 1991 the median age for Hispanic homeowners was 48 compared with 35 for renters (Bureau of the Census 1993a, 54, 268).

Knowing household size is important when marketing to Hispanics. Depending on the size of a household, more or less money is earned and spent, and spent differently. In this regard Hispanic households are very different from non-Hispanic white households. Larger Hispanic households generally have higher average incomes, particularly if the number of persons is seven or more. For whites, average income peaks when the household reaches a size of four and then declines (U.S. Bureau of the Census, 1992c, 447). Also, because Hispanic households are bigger, more of the budget is allocated for food and clothing than in other groups (see "Hispanics as Consumers," Chapter 3).

HOUSEHOLD SIZE

From a marketing perspective, Hispanic households differ from those of other groups in that it takes fewer of them to reach the same number of people. In 1992 the average size of a Hispanic household was 3.45 persons, compared with 2.49 persons for non-Hispanic whites. This means that even if marketers reached fewer Hispanic households, they would still reach many more consumers. For example, if the same television commercial reached 100,000 Hispanic and 100,000 non-Hispanic white households, an estimated 96,000 more Hispanic consumers would view it—345,000 versus 249,000.

The surge in the number of Hispanic households new diversity in the marketplace. Fewer Hispanics now live as married couples; more live as single parents; more are living with friends or other unrelated individuals; and more men and women are living alone. Family households (according to the Census Bureau, a Hispanic family household is one in which the householder, in addition to being of Hispanic origin, is also related by birth, marriage, or adoption to at least one other person in the house), however, still prevail over all other forms—a demographic expression of the high value Hispanics attach to the family. For the last twenty years, the number of households with families has been increas-

HOUSEHOLDS IN TRANSITION: Family Households

ing steadily, with more than 3 million added since 1970. In 1992, the number of Hispanic family households was 5.2 million, or 81 percent of all Hispanic households (Table 2.5). That number is projected to grow to 7.7 million by 2000 (Table 2.6).

Clearly, most Hispanics still live in more traditional family settings. In 1992 households with husband and wife present accounted for 68 percent of all Hispanic households, or 3.5 million (Table 2.8). The steady increase in the number of households with single parents, however, tells marketers that changes in Hispanic life-styles are occurring. Whereas the share of households with husband and wife present has declined since the 1970s, during the same time the share of family households headed by single men or women has increased from 19 percent to 31 percent (Table 2.8), or from 389,000 to 1.5 million.

Households without Families Households not meeting the Census Bureau criteria for a Hispanic family household are considered unrelated or nonfamily households. As with single-parent family households, the number of nonfamily households has also increased steadily. There were 1.19 million such households in 1992 (Table 2.8), and they are projected to increase by 533,000, or 45 percent, by the year 2000 (Table 2.7). Non-related households present a set of dynamics, needs, and consumption patterns uniquely different from those of family households.

Women and Households The changes in family relationships have given women a leading role they have not experienced in the past. For instance, more single-parent Hispanic households are headed by women than men, 24 percent versus 7 percent. When Hispanic women do participate in the traditional family environment, they play a key part in deciding how the family income is spent. Not only are Hispanic women more likely to make purchasing decisions, they are also the ones more likely to shop for household goods and necessities. Hispanic women are becoming increasingly more independent and self-reliant. In the process, they have become even more indispensable to household economics. In addition to contributing about 42 percent of the family income, they continue to be the principal keepers of the young. All of this makes them central figures in marketing dynamics.

The number of Hispanic women is significant and growing. In 1992 there were more than 11 million U.S. Hispanic women, and their number is expected to reach 19 million in 2010. In 1992 over 61 percent of all women ages 18 and over were married, and the rest were single (never married, 23 percent; widowed, 7 percent; and divorced, 9 percent) (U.S. Bureau of the Census 1993d, 53). The number of households (both family and non-family) headed by females in 1992 totaled 1.8 million — nearly a four-fold increase over the 1970 figure of 455,000. In 1992, 24 percent of all family households and 45 percent of all nonfamily households were headed by women (Table 2.8).

More and more Hispanic women are either working or looking for a job. According to the Bureau of the Census, 52 percent of Hispanic women ages 16 and over were in the labor force in 1992, (Figure 2.5). Between 1980 and 1990 they joined the labor force faster than Hispanic men and faster than non-Hispanic women. (Non-Hispanic whites includes Anglos, other Europeans and people from the Middle East.) During that decade the number of Hispanic women in the labor force increased by 54 percent; the rate of increase for both Hispanic men and Anglo women was 23 percent.

Hispanic women also have increased earning power. In just six years, from 1986 to 1992, the proportion of women earning less than $10,000 declined from 67 percent to 46 percent, while those earning $25,000 or more increased from 3.8 percent to 15 percent (U.S. Bureau of the Census, 1988, 26; 1994, 12). The relevance of this demographic group in marketing to Hispanics is discussed in Chapter 7, beginning on page 330.

■ A Regional View of the Market

The preponderance of the U.S. Hispanic market is located in the cities and large metropolitan areas of the West, the South, and the Northeast where 82 percent of Hispanics live. Ten states (California, Texas, New York, Florida, Illinois, New Jersey, Arizona, New Mexico, Colorado, and Massachusetts) have historically been main centers of attraction for Hispanics, and in 1990 accounted for 87 percent of the total Hispanic population (Table 2.9). California, Texas, New York, and Florida alone represent 71 percent of the total Hispanic population, or 16 million.

The same ten states accounted for about 89 percent of the total Hispanic population increase during the 1980s. During this time, however, the number of Hispanics increased very rapidly in every region of the United States. Even the South, which includes Texas and Florida, had a 51 percent gain despite the decrease in Hispanic population experienced by seven states in that region (Table 2.10). The large distribution of Hispanic consumers in a relatively few states makes them easily accessible to marketers, advertisers, and the media.

■ City Dwellers

Hispanic immigrants come from big cities, small towns, and rural areas in Latin America and the Caribbean, but when they enter the United States the vast majority tend to relocate in large metropolitan areas. In 1990 about 72 percent of all Hispanics lived in metropolitan areas (MAs). A metropolitan area consists of "a core area containing a large population nucleus together with adjacent communities having a high degree of social and economic integration with that core" (U.S. Bureau of the Census, 1993d, 916). During the 1980s all metropolitan areas containing 100,000 or more Hispanics (Table 2.11) had increases in the Hispanic population, ranging from 15 percent in Corpus Christi, Texas, to 136 percent in Riverside-San Bernardino, California (Table 2.12). Also, during the 1980s, eleven metropolitan areas (MAs) increased their Hispanic population to well over 100,000 (Table 2.12).

Some metropolitan areas are predominantly Hispanic. For example, the Laredo, Texas, metropolitan area is about 94 percent Hispanic, and the Brownsville-Harlingen and McAllen-Edinburgh-Mission metros are 81 percent and 85 percent Hispanic, respectively. Another important center with a large Hispanic concentration and consumer base is the Los Angeles-Long Beach metropolitan area, which continues to offer some of the best opportunities for mass marketing. This metro area, which is about 40 percent Hispanic and growing, is home to over 3.3 million Hispanics, primarily of Mexican origin. The Los Angeles-Long Beach area alone contains about 15 percent of all U.S. Hispanic consumers. During the 1980s this large consumer base grew as rapidly as 5 percent per year.

Other large population centers are currently growing even faster than the Los Angeles-Long Beach area, in large part owing to rapid expansion of the Hispanic population. In California, for example, the metropolitan areas of Riverside-San Bernardino and Anaheim-Santa Ana grew at annual average rates of 9 percent and 7 percent respectively during the 1980s (Table 2.13). In Texas, the metropolitan areas of Dallas and Houston also sustained comparable growth, as did Tucson, Arizona. Florida added two metropolitan areas with Hispanic populations exceeding 100,000, and together the Hispanic population of the three metropolitan areas (Miami-Hialeah, Tampa-St. Petersburg-Clearwater, and Ft. Lauderdale-Hollywood-Pompano Beach) grew at an annual rate of 7.5 percent (Table 2.13).

New York, with close to 2 million Hispanics, also had very rapid growth during the 1980s, although not as fast as the Nassau-Suffolk, New York, area, which grew at about 5 percent per year. The Hispanic population of many other metropolitan areas grew at comparable rates (Table 2.13).

■ Hispanic Subgroups

Bound by a common heritage, yet exhibiting distinctive traits and characteristics, Hispanic subgroups present unique business opportunities. Each group has definitely carved out its own niche and made its own contributions to the marketplace. The following discussion summarizes the key demographic variables of each subgroup: Mexicans, mainland and island Puerto Ricans, Cubans, and Central and South Americans. For a detailed look at the cultural characteristics of Hispanic subgroups see page 189.

MARKET GROWTH OF SUBGROUPS

All Hispanic subgroups sustained very rapid growth during the 1980s. Central and South Americans led the market in growth. Rates of growth for these groups are not readily available, but figures for 1980 immigration levels (see below) and other indicators place the annual rates beyond that of Mexicans (4.4 percent). The national Hispanic average growth was 4.2 percent. The growth rate of Puerto Ricans was 3.1 percent, and of Cubans 2.6 percent. If 1980s growth rates are used as estimates of future growth and 1990 taken as the base year, it would take each group the amount of time shown in the table below to double in size.

Mexicans	16 years	(2006)	27 million
Mainland Puerto Ricans	23 years	(2013)	5.4 million
Cubans	27 years	(2017)	2.1 million

With over 13 million consumers in 1990 and an expected 27 million in 2006, Mexicans make up the lion's share of the Hispanic market. Alone they account for 60 percent of all Hispanics in the United States.

A striking feature of each subgroup is the large number of foreign-born people. According to the 1990 census, the figures are as follows: Central Americans, 79 percent; South Americans, 75 percent; Cubans, 72 percent; and Mexicans, 33 percent. Puerto Ricans are U.S. citizens and fall in a category of their own, so the proportion of foreign born is very small, only 1.2 percent. However, if one considers island-born Puerto Ricans as foreign born, the figure for that group would be 4.5 percent (U.S. Bureau of the Census, 1993c, 5–8, 11–12, 21).

The presence in each group of millions of foreign-born consumers for whom Spanish is the primary language presents definite marketing challenges and opportunities. Although the ability to speak English varies with each group, in each the number of consumers who speak little or no English at all is very high. This is particularly true for Mexicans, 4.4 million of whom are foreign born, a figure that exceeds by more than 700,000 the entire population of U.S. Cubans and mainland Puerto Ricans combined. About 40 percent of Mexican consumers ages 5 and over claimed they could not speak English very well at the time of the 1990 census. For the other subgroups, the percentage who claimed not to speak English very well was as follows: Cubans, 49 percent; Puerto Ricans, 33 percent; Central Americans, 60 percent; and South Americans, 49 percent (U.S. Bureau of the Census, 1993, 4–5, 81–83, 87, 97). Chapters 4 and 5 examine in detail the marketing ramifications of having to deal with different cultural and linguistic backgrounds.

The business potential offered by each demographic group is phenomenal. For example, marketers with products and services appealing to the Hispanic youth market are well advised to look to the Southwest, as Mexicans will turn out to be the Hispanic baby boomers of tomorrow. Mexican infants, children, and teenagers account for 70 percent of all U.S. Hispanics under age 20. Mexican women have more children than women in any of the major Hispanic groups, which makes them the greatest contributors to the youth market. Out of 8.6 million Hispanics under age 20 in 1993, over 6 million were of Mexican origin.

At the opposite end of the scale and with a much smaller population, Cubans provide the opportunity to venture into the Hispanic mature market, as one-third of all Cubans were 55 years of age or older in 1992. This is not to say, however, that marketers should overlook seniors in other Hispanic subgroups. For example, there are large numbers of mature Mexican consumers. In 1993 there were 1.3 million Mexicans ages 55 and over, a market larger than the size of the entire U.S. Cuban population (U.S. Bureau of the Census, 1994, 11).

Earlier in this chapter Hispanic life-styles were discussed in terms of changing household demographics. The changes are noticeable across all groups but are visible among some more than others, particularly among women, who have emerged as very important economic agents in their own right. As noted, more of them are living alone, with or without children, and more are joining the labor force. For example, 43 percent of Puerto Rican and 28 percent of Cuban households are headed by women, which makes them the sole decision makers about what products or services to buy. In the other subgroups the figures are also high. For instance, for Central and South Americans and Mexicans the statistics are 28 percent and 23 percent, respectively (U.S. Bureau of the Census, 1994, 17).

Many factors, such as level of formal education, income, and occupation, contribute to changes in consumer life-styles. These factors, in turn, greatly influence a consumer's purchasing decisions. As for Hispanic subgroups, Cubans and South Americans tend to have more formal education than Mexicans, Puerto Ricans, or Central Americans. Among adults ages 25 and over, both groups have more high school and college graduates than Mexicans, Puerto Ricans, or Central Americans. Island and mainland Puerto Ricans have a higher proportion of high school and university graduates than Mexicans or Central Americans (Table 2.21).

Cubans and South Americans are also the wealthiest subgroups. Half of all U.S. Cuban and South American families have incomes above $32,000, while about 4 percent of them have incomes above $100,000. In addition, Cubans have the highest percentage of people in professional occupations (U.S. Bureau of the Census, 1993c, 159, 174).

Each of the groups discussed is important in some way, and all combined offer excellent opportunities for businesses to increase their sales. In addition, each group can act as a test market for products, services, and marketing techniques. Marketers and advertisers can look, for instance, at Mexicans as leading indicators in the Hispanic youth market, and Cubans in the Hispanic mature market.

SUBGROUP PROFILES

Mexicans

✧ Market Size. Mexican consumers are the largest segment of the U.S. Hispanic market, accounting for more than 60 percent of the total (Figure 2.6). In 1990 there were more than 13 million people of Mexican origin in the United States (Table 2.14). During the 1980s the market grew at unprecedented speed: approximately 475,000 potential consumers were added to the market each year, for a total of 4.7 million Hispanics for the decade. At current rates, it will take only until 2006 for the U.S. Mexican population to double its present size to 27 million (U.S. Bureau of the Census, 1991d, 3).

✧ Geographic Distribution. The heart of the Mexican market is in the southwestern United States. In 1990, 83.2 percent of the U.S. Mexican population was clustered in California, Texas,

Arizona, New Mexico, and Colorado. In addition, three other states (Illinois, Florida, and Michigan) and the District of Columbia had Mexican populations of 100,000 or more. These eight states plus D.C. accounted for 91 percent of the entire Mexican population (Table 2.14).

✧ Nativity, Time of Entry, and Language Spoken. Contrary to popular belief, the majority of U.S. Mexicans are natives (67 percent) rather than foreign born (33 percent). Of those who are foreign born, half entered the United States during the 1980s. (Certainly, this figure underestimates the number of foreign-born Mexicans who were not counted in the 1990 Census.) About 80 percent speak a language other than English, and about 40 percent "did not speak English very well" at the time of the 1990 census. Among Mexicans 5 years of age and over, about 24 percent live in linguistically isolated households, that is, in households where no person over the age of 14 can speak English (U.S. Bureau of the Census, 1993c, 81).

✧ Demographic Characteristics. There are more U.S. Mexican men than women—50 percent versus 49 percent (Table 2.15). U.S. Mexican consumers are the youngest among all Hispanics, with a median age of 24.4 in 1992. U.S. Mexicans account for about 70 percent of all U.S. Hispanics under age 20. For all practical purposes U.S. Mexicans are the heart of the Hispanic youth market. About 23 percent of the population are under 10 years of age, and over 41 percent are under age 20. Over 19 percent are in their twenties, and another 23 percent are in their thirties and mid-forties. About 84 percent of the U.S. Mexican population are under 45 years of age, and only about 16 percent are over 45 years of age. The result is 5.8 million infants, children, and teenagers, and 5.9 million adults in their twenties, thirties, and mid-forties. There were 1.3 million in their late forties and fifties, and 971,000, close to a million, over age 60 (Table 2.16). The youth segment of the Mexican market is largely U.S. born while the adult portion is heavily foreign-born. About 72 percent of all Mexicans under age 20 were born in the United States while 46 percent over that age are immigrants.

✧ Marital Status. Among U.S. Mexicans 15 years of age and older, more than half are married; about one-third have never been married; and about one in ten are either widowed or divorced (Table 2.17).

✧ Households. The mean number of persons per household is 3.73. U.S. Mexican households totaled 3.7 million in 1992, accounting for about 60 percent of all Hispanic households. Mexican households are large, and about one-third have five or more persons living in them. Family households are more common than nonfamily units. Households with married couples are much more prevalent than family households headed by single women or men, although one-fourth of all households were headed by single women (Table 2.18).

✧ Household and Family Income. About 45 percent of all U.S. Mexican households and families have incomes of $25,000 or more, while about 13 percent have incomes of $50,000 or more (Table 2.19).

✧ Education and Labor Force Participation. More than 66 percent of U.S. Mexicans are in the labor force. Labor force participation is higher for men than for women, 80 percent versus 52 percent (Figure 2.5; Table 2.20). More U.S. Mexican women tend to be in managerial and administrative positions than men, 53.5 percent versus 23.3 percent, and more tend to be in service occupations, 25 percent versus 17 percent. More men work in agricultural activities than women, 11 percent versus 3 percent. Almost 50 percent of all employed men work on precision production, craft and repair, or as operators, fabricators, or laborers. A large proportion of U.S. Mexicans ages 25 years or older are high school graduates, and about 6 percent have at least a bachelor's degree (Table 2.21).

✧ Other Statistics. In 1992, 44 percent of all householders either owned or were buying a home, 86 percent had some type of telephone service, and nearly 98 percent accepted telephone interviews (U.S. Bureau of the Census, 1993b, 19).

Mainland Puerto Ricans

✧ Market Size. In 1990, 2.7 million Puerto Ricans, or 12 percent of the total Hispanic population, lived on the mainland. Rapid growth during the 1980s added 714,000 consumers by the end of the decade. If the current annual rate of growth (3.1 percent) continues, by 2013 the number of Puerto Ricans on the mainland will double in size to 5.4 million (U.S. Bureau of the Census, 1991d, 3).

✧ Geographic Distribution. The eastern United States is to mainland Puerto Ricans what the southwestern United States is to the Mexican population. In 1990, more than 1.4 million Puerto Ricans (52 percent of the U.S total) were clustered in New York and New Jersey. And 35 percent resided in Florida (9.1 percent), Pennsylvania (5.5 percent), Massachusetts (5.5 percent), Connecticut (5.4 percent), Illinois (5.4 percent), and California (4.6 percent), with these eight states accounting for 87 percent of the total mainland population (Table 2.22).

✧ Demographic Profile. There are more Puerto Rican women than men, 51 percent versus 49 percent (Table 2.15). Mainland Puerto Ricans are the second-youngest Hispanic subgroup, after Mexicans, with a median age of 27. Thirty-eight percent of Puerto Ricans are under 20 years of age, and 29 percent are between ages 30 and 49. About 10 percent are 55 years old or older (Table 2.23).

✧ Marital Status. Half of all Puerto Ricans ages 15 years and older are single (never married, widowed, or divorced). At just over 49 percent, mainland Puerto Ricans have the lowest proportion of married persons among all Hispanic subgroups (Table 2.24).

✧ Households. The mean number of persons per household is 2.9. Mainland Puerto Rican households totaled 820,000 in 1992, accounting for about 13 percent of all U.S. Hispanic households. Puerto Rican households are generally smaller than those in other subgroups. Puerto Ricans have the largest proportion of nonfamily households of any other group—24.4 percent—and the largest percentage of households headed by single women or men, 41.3 and 18.2 percent (Table 2.25).

✧ Household and Family Income. About 38 percent of mainland Puerto Rican households, and over 43 percent of families, have incomes of $25,000 or more; about 16 percent of all households and 18 percent of all families have incomes of $50,000 or more (Table 2.26). Affluent families, those with incomes over

$50,000, are more prevalent among Puerto Ricans than among Mexicans or Central Americans.

✧ Education and Labor Force Participation. Since the 1950s native Puerto Ricans have traveled to the mainland in search of employment and better economic opportunities. Labor force participation among mainland Puerto Ricans was 57 percent in 1992. At that time there were 898,000 Puerto Ricans working or looking for a job. Of those, 88 percent were actually gainfully employed. In addition, Puerto Rican women have become a vital asset to the market; the labor force participation rate for female Puerto Ricans was 45 percent, while the rate for men was 70 percent (Table 2.27).

Puerto Ricans ages 25 and over have higher levels of education than Mexicans and Central Americans but lower levels than the other Hispanic groups. More than 53 percent have four years of high school or more, and 9.5 percent have four years of college or more (Table 2.21). The higher educational level of Puerto Ricans compared with the Mexican subgroup is reflected in the occupational structure of both groups. About 50 percent of employed Puerto Ricans work in managerial, professional, technical, and administrative support, as do 34 percent of Mexicans (U.S. Bureau of the Census, 1993d, 397).

✧ Other Statistics. In 1992 about 24 percent of householders either owned or were buying a home. Only about 82 percent of Puerto Rican households have telephone service (U.S. Bureau of the Census 1993b, 19).

Island Puerto Ricans   ✧ Market Size. In 1990 the population of Puerto Rico was 3.5 million. Between the 1980 and 1990 censuses, population growth was much slower than on the mainland (2.2 percent versus 3.9 percent annually), partly, it could be hypothesized, because of the large number of people (more than 270,000) leaving the island (U.S. Bureau of the Census 1993d, 822).

✧ Demographic Profile. Like their counterparts on the mainland, Puerto Ricans on the island are growing older. Between 1970 and 1990 the median age of the population increased from 21.6 to 28.5 — a gain of almost 7 years (U.S. bureau of the Census, 1993d, 822).

✧ Households. The mean number of persons per household is 3.3. The mean number of persons per family in Puerto Rico is 3.7, whereas on the mainland it is 2.9 (U.S. Bureau of the Census 1993d, 823–5).

✧ Marital Status. Island Puerto Ricans resemble the other Hispanic subgroups in their marital status. More island than mainland Puerto Ricans tend to be married. In 1990 over 58 percent of island Puerto Ricans age 15 and older were married versus 45 percent of mainland Puerto Ricans (U.S. Bureau of the Census 1993c, 6; 1993d, 823).

✧ Household and Family Income. Higher wages and employment opportunities draw island Puerto Ricans to the mainland. In 1991 Puerto Ricans had a median family income of $9,988 on the island and $20,654 on the mainland (Table 2.26). In 1990 labor force participation among island Puerto Ricans was lower than among mainland Puerto Ricans, 47 percent versus 60 percent. Seventy-nine percent of those in the labor force were actually working, versus 87 percent on the mainland. Unemployment is higher in Puerto Rico than on the mainland, 14 percent versus 10.3 percent (U.S. Bureau of the Census 1993c, 120, 158; 1993d, 823).

Cubans

✧ Market Size. U.S. Cuban consumers are the smallest segment of the Hispanic market, accounting for only 5 percent (Figure 2.6). In 1990 there were more than 1 million people of Cuban origin in the United States. During the 1990s the Cuban market grew at an annual rate of 2.6 percent, which is much slower than the other Hispanic subgroups. At the present rate this market will double by 2017. More than 24,000 U.S. Cubans were added to the population each year during the 1980s (U.S. Bureau of the Census, 1991d, 3).

✧ Geographic Distribution. The core of the Cuban market is in the Southeast. In 1990 more than 64 percent of the total U.S. Cuban population of 1,053,000 lived in Florida alone (Table 2.28). In addition, more than 8 percent lived in New Jersey, and 7 percent in California; the rest were scattered across the nation (U.S. Bureau of the Census, 1993d, 31).

✧ Nativity, Time of Entry, and Language Spoken. Cubans are primarily foreign born, with 72 percent born outside the United States. More than 74 percent of all foreign-born Cubans arrived in the United States prior to 1980. More than 89 percent spoke a language other than English, and about 49 percent "did not speak English very well" at the time of the 1990 census. Among Cubans age 5 or over, about 28 percent lived in households where no person over 14 years of age could speak English (U.S. Bureau of the Census, 1993c, 7–8, 83; 1993c, B-25).

✧ Demographic Profile. There are more U.S. Cuban women than men, 52 percent versus 48 percent (Table 2.15). The median age for U.S. Cubans is 40. This group is considerably older than any of the other Hispanic subgroups and older than the non-Hispanic white population. About 30 percent of Cubans are age 55 or older. Twenty-two percent of Cubans are age 20 or under, whereas 41 percent of U.S. Mexicans are. Of a population of 1 million, more than 300,000 are age 55 or over (Table 2.29).

✧ Marital Status. About 58 percent of the population ages 15 and older are married. About one-fourth have never been married, and approximately one out of six are either widowed or divorced (Table 2.30).

✧ Households. the mean number of persons per household is 2.7. U.S. Cuban households account for a small percentage of all U.S. Hispanic households, about 6 percent, but they represented approximately 22 percent of all Hispanic households in the Miami metro area in 1992. There were 395,000 households in 1992. U.S. Cubans have the smallest households among Hispanics—51 percent are composed of one or two persons. About 25 percent of all households were nonfamily units, and 31 percent were headed by single women with or without children (Table 2.31).

✧ Household and Family Income. The mean household income was $35,599 in 1991. About 53 percent of all U.S. Cuban households had incomes of $25,000 or more, and 24 percent had incomes of at least $50,000 (Table 2.32). Cubans, together with South Americans, are wealthier than any other Hispanic group.

✧ Education and Labor Force Participation. More than 61 percent of U.S. Cubans ages 16 and over are in the labor force.

Out of the 538,000 who are either working or looking for a job, 487,000 or 90 percent are employed. Labor force participation is higher for men than for women, 72 percent versus 52 percent (Figure 2.5). At 9.4 percent, the unemployment rate is the lowest of all Hispanic subgroups (Table 2.33). Almost as many men as women are in white-collar occupations, and almost twice as many women as men are in technical and administrative jobs, 48.5 percent versus 25 percent (U.S. Bureau of the Census, 1993b, 13–15). After South Americans, U.S. Cubans have more formal education than any other Hispanic subgroup—57 percent completed high school, and 19 percent have earned a bachelor's degree (Table 2.21).

✧ Other Statistics. In 1992 as many U.S. Cubans were likely to be renters as homeowners; however, they were more likely to be homeowners than any of the other Hispanic subgroups. More of them had telephones in their homes (95 percent) (U.S. Bureau of the Census, 1993b, 19).

✧ Market Size. There were more than 2.3 million Hispanics in 1992 whose country of origin was in Central or South America (Table 2.34). About 78 percent of Central Americans are Salvadorans, Guatemalans, and Nicaraguans, with Salvadorans being the largest group. About 72 percent of all South Americans are Colombians, Ecuadorians, and Peruvians, with Colombians alone representing about 36 percent of all South Americans in the United States.

Central and South Americans

✧ Geographic Distribution. The heart of the Central American market is in California, where about 50 percent of all U.S. Central Americans reside. Two other states with significant concentrations are Florida and New York. South Americans, on the other hand, are more spread out. The largest segment of this market is in New York, with a concentration of 27 percent. Three other states with large concentrations of South Americans are California, Florida, and New Jersey (Table 2.35).

✧ Nativity, Time of Entry, and Language Spoken. This group is primarily foreign born; 79 percent of all Central Americans and 75 percent of all South Americans were born outside the United States. Fifty-five percent of all Central Americans and 38

percent of all South Americans arrived in the United States during the 1980s. About 92 percent of Central Americans and 90 percent of South Americans spoke a language other than English at
the time of the 1990 census. Fewer Central Americans "speak
English very well" than South Americans, 60 percent versus 49
percent. Among Central Americans 5 years of age and over, 40
percent live in households where English is hardly spoken, versus
28 percent of South Americans (U.S. Bureau of the Census
1993c, 11, 21, 87, 97).

✧ Demographic Profile. There are as many men as there are
women in these subgroups. Central Americans are younger than
South Americans; the median age for Central Americans is 27, and
for South Americans, 31. About 30 percent (712,000) of Central
and South Americans are under age 20. About 34 percent
(838,000) are between ages 20 and 34. About 70 percent of Central
Americans are under age 35. Of a combined Central and South
American population of 2.3 million, 198,000 are age 55 or older
(Table 2.36). Most (90 percent) of Central and South Americans
are foreign born (U.S. Bureau of the Census, 1993c, 11–12, 21).

✧ Marital Status. More South Americans are married (55
percent), widowed (0.7 percent) and divorced (9 percent) than
Central Americans (47 percent, 0.6 percent, and 7 percent)
(Table 2.37).

✧ Households. The mean number of persons per household
is 3.9 for Central Americans and 3.2 for South Americans. South
American households tend to be smaller than those of Central
Americans. Thirty-seven percent of South American households
have at least two persons, and 21 percent have five or more people living in them, compared with 25 percent and 36 percent for
Central Americans (Table 2.38). There were 900,000 Central and
South American households in the United States in 1992. As with
other Hispanic subgroups, there are more family than nonfamily
households — 81 percent among Central and South Americans.
Households with married couples are the predominant kind, and
households headed by single women with or without children (16
percent) are less prevalent.

✧ Household and Family Income. According to the 1990

census, South Americans are considerably more affluent than Central Americans, surpassing Central Americans in per capita income, $12,119 versus $8,005; in median family income, $32,087 versus $23,619; and in median household income, $30,716 versus $24,695. About 24 percent of all South American households and 15 percent of all Central American households have earnings in the $50,000–$100,000 range (U.S. Bureau of the Census 1993c, 163 and 173).

✧ Education and Labor Force Participation. Of a population of 2.3 million Central and South Americans, 1.8 million, or 73 percent, are in the labor force. And of the 1.8 million, 1.3 million, or 72 percent, are employed. As with other ethnic segments, labor force participation is higher for men than for women (Figure 2.5). Many more South and Central Americans (48 percent and 30 percent, respectively) work in white-collar occupations (U.S. Bureau of the Census, 1993c, 125, 135). South Americans have higher educational attainment than Central Americans; 71 percent of South Americans and 46 percent of Central Americans are at least high school graduates. Similarly, 8.2 percent and 3.2 percent respectively, have professional degrees (Table 2.21). Most Central and South Americans tend to be renters, 78 and 64 percent respectively; fewer Central Americans own a house, 22 percent, as compared to South Americans, 36 percent (U.S. Bureau of the Census, 1993c, 201, 211).

✧ Other Statistics. Eighty-nine percent have telephones (U.S. Bureau of the Census, 1993b, 19).

■ *References*

Bean, Frank D., and Marta Tienda. *The Hispanic Population of the United States*. New York: Russel Sage Foundation, 1990.

Donnelley Marketing Information Services, 1990.

Edmonston, Barry, and Jeffrey S. Passel. *The Future Immigrant Population of the United States*. Washington, D.C.: Urban Institute, 1992.

National Association of Latino Elected and Appointed Officials (NALEO) Educational Fund. *The National Latino Immigrant Survey*. Washington, D.C.: NALEO, 1989.

TGE Demographics. *Consumer Household Projections by Age, Type of Household, Race, and Hispanic Origin 1990–2000*. Ithaca, New York: TGE Demographics, 1992.

U.S. Bureau of the Census. *Statistical Abstract of the United States: 1984.* 104th ed. Washington, D.C.: Government Printing Office, 1983.

———. *Statistical Abstract of the United States: 1988.* 108th ed. Washington, D.C.: Government Printing Office, 1987.

———. *The Hispanic Population of the United States: March 1986 and 1987. Current Population Reports,* ser. P-20, no. 434. Washington, D.C.: Government Printing Office, 1988.

———. *Historical Statistics of the United States: Colonial Times to 1957.* Washington, D.C.: Government Printing Office, 1990.

———. *Persons of Hispanic Origin by Type for the United States and States: 1990.* Special Tables 1, 2, 3. Washington, D.C.: Government Printing Office, 1990a.

———. *Persons of Hispanic Origin for the United States: 1990.* CPH-L-91. 1990 Census Special Tabulations, Ethnic and Hispanic Branch. Washington, D.C.: Government Printing Office, 1990b.

———. "United States Population Estimates by Age, Sex, Race and Hispanic Origin: 1980 to 1988," by Frederick W. Hollman. *Current Population Reports,* ser. P-25, no. 1045. Washington, D.C.: Government Printing Office, 1990c.

———. *The Hispanic Population in the United States: March 1991. Current Population Reports,* ser. P-20, no. 455. Washington, D.C: Government Printing Office, 1991a.

———. *Race and Hispanic Origin.* 1990 Census Profile no. 2. Washington, D.C.: Government Printing Office, 1991b.

———. *Statistical Abstract of the United States: 1991.* 111th ed. Washington, D.C.: Government Printing Office, 1991c.

———. *Race and Hispanic Origin for the United States.* Table 1, Summary Tape File 1A. Press Release CB91–215, 1991d.

———. *The Foreign Born Population in the United States: 1990,* by Susan J. Lapham. CPH-L-98. Ethnic and Hispanic Branch. Washington, D.C.: Government Printing Office, 1992a.

———. *Population Projections of the United States, by Age, Sex, Race, and Hispanic Origin: 1992 to 2050,* by Jennifer Cheeseman Day. *Current Population Reports,* ser. P-25, no. 1092. Washington, D.C.: Government Printing Office, 1992b.

———. *Statistical Abstract of the United States: 1992.* 112th ed. Washington, D.C.: Government Printing Office, 1992c.

———. *American Housing Survey for the United States in 1991. Current Housing Reports.* H150/91. Washington, D.C.: Government Printing Office, 1993a.

———. *The Hispanic Population in the United States: March 1992,* by Jesus Garcia. *Current Population Reports,* ser. P-20, no. 465RV. Washington, D.C.: Government Printing Office, 1993b.

———. *Persons of Hispanic Origin in the United States.* 1990 Census of Population. CP–3. Washington, D.C.: Government Printing Office, 1993c.

———. *Hispanic Americans Today. Current Population Reports,* ser. P-23, no. 183. Washington, D.C.: Government Printing Office, 1993e.

———. *The Hispanic Population in the United States: March 1993,* by Patricia A. Montgomery. *Current Population Reports,* ser. P-20, no. 475. Washington, D.C.: Government Printing Office, 1994.

———. *1990 Profiles of the Hispanic Population: Selected Characteristics by Hispanic Origin.* Publication CPH-L-150. N.d.

United States Bureau of Labor Statistics. *Employment in Perspective: Minority Workers.* Report 829. Washington, D.C.: Government Printing Office, second quarter, 1992.

At a Glance . . .
Hispanic Population Growth

The Hispanic population reached 22.3 million in 1990.

In 1990 there were 7.7 million more Hispanic consumers than in 1980 and 15 million more than in 1960.

17 million more Hispanics will be added from 1990 to 2010, and 40 million by 2040.

Every year after 1995 Hispanics may account for more U.S. consumers than any other group.

By 2010 the Hispanic population will surpass that of African-Americans and Asians.

More than 3 million Hispanic immigrants settled in the United States during the 1980s.

As many as 380,000 Hispanic immigrants each year will be added to the population during the 1990s.

Even without immigration, the number of Hispanics could reach 51 million by 2050.

By 2010 there will be 15 million foreign-born Hispanics living in the United States.

At a Glance . . .
Miscellaneous Facts about Hispanics

They are younger than white non-Hispanics.

Hispanic homeowners are younger than non-Hispanic homeowners and renters.

Hispanic households are larger than white non-Hispanic households.

It takes fewer Hispanic households to reach more consumers.

Hispanics tend to live in metropolitan areas.

Riverside-San Bernardino, California, is the fastest-growing metropolitan area (MA).

Foreign-born Hispanics will comprise a greater portion of the Hispanic consumer market in the future.

At a Glance . . .
Mexican and Central American Demographics, 1990

	Mexicans	Salvadorans	Nicaraguans	Guatemalans
Population	13,393,208	565,081	202,658	268,779
Percentage of Central Americans	—	43	15	20
Market location, percentage in	California: 46	California: 60	California: 36	California: 59
	Texas: 30	Texas: 10	Florida: 39	New York: 8
	Other: 24	Other: 30	Other: 25	Texas: 33
Population under Age of 20	42%	33%	35%	31%
Median Age	24	29	27	27
Labor Force Participation	68%	76%	73%	75%
(persons 16 years and over)				
Education				
(persons 25 years and over)				
High School	44%	34%	61%	38%
Bachelor's Degree	6.3%	5%	15%	6%
Income (1989)				
Average family income	$29,564	$27,014	$31,277	$28,581
Average household income	$29,151	$28,832	$31,758	$30,152
Per capita income	$7,447	$7,201	$7,995	$7,761
Workers in Family				
Two or more	59%	64%	67%	64%
Household Size				
Households	3,302,208	137,946	49,197	66,397
1–2 persons	29%	19%	24%	21%
3–4 persons	37%	40%	37%	40%
5 or more persons	34%	41%	39%	39%

(continued next page)

Mexican and Central American Demographics, 1990 (*continued*)

	Mexicans	Salvadorans	Nicaraguans	Guatemalans
Ability to Speak English (persons 5 years and over)	11,567,198	508,393	185,312	243,625
Non-English Speaking Households	23.7%	47.1%	40%	44%

Sources: Hispanic Market Connections; Donnelly Marketing Information Services.

At a Glance . . .
Puerto Rican Demographics

	Mainland Born	**Island Born**
Population (1990)	2.6 million	3.5 million
Market location	66% in New York, New Jersey, Florida, and Puerto Rico	–
Percent women	51	51
Median age	26.9	28.4
Labor force participation, percentage	60 (1990)	47
Average family income	$27,908 (1991)	22,772 (1991)
Number of families	619,000	886,000
Average number of persons per family	3.49	3.7
Number of households	820,000	1,055,000
Average number of persons per household	2.99	3.3

Note: Figures for mainland Puerto Ricans are for 1992 and for Island Puerto Ricans for 1990.

Source: U.S. Bureau of the Census, 1993d, 823, 825; 1993, 13–19.

At a Glance . . .
California Metropolitan Areas (MAs) with Large Hispanic Concentration, 1980–1990

Metro Areas with 100,000 or More Hispanics   Hispanic Population

    14 MAs (1990) 7,024,963
    10 MAs (1980) 3,865,855

Gains (1980–1990)

Total increase:	3,159,108
Percent increase:	82
Annual percent increase:	6.3[a]

Fastest-growing: Riverside-San Bernardino	9 percent annually[a]
Largest: Los Angeles-Long Beach	3,351,242
Smallest: Stockton	112,673

Metro Areas Reaching 100,000 Hispanics since 1980:

Bakersfield	151,995
Visalia-Tulare-Porterville	120,893
Salinas-Seaside-Monterey	119,570
Stockton	112,673

[a]Compounded annually.

Sources: Hispanic Market Connections, Inc.; Donnelly Marketing Information Services.

At a Glance . . .

Texas Metropolitan Areas (MAs) with Large Hispanic Concentration, 1980–1990

Metro Areas with 100,000 or More Hispanics   **Hispanic Population**

   10 MAs (1990) 3,265,200
   7 MAs (1980) 1,906,786

Gains (1980–1990)

Total increase:	1,358,414
Percent increase:	71
Annual percent increase:	5.5[a]

Fastest-growing: Dallas	5.8 percent annually[a]
Largest: San Antonio	629,290
Smallest: Laredo	125,060

Metro Areas Reaching 100,000 Hispanics since 1980:

Austin	159,842
Fort Worth-Arlington	150,033
Laredo	125,060

[a]Compounded annually.

Sources: Hispanic Market Connections, Inc.; Donnelly Marketing Information Services.

At a Glance . . .
New York Metropolitan Areas (MAs) with Large Hispanic Concentration, 1980–1990

Metro Areas with 100,000 or More Hispanics   Hispanic Population

    2 MAs (1990) 2,054,900
    2 MAs (1980) 1,566,609

Gains (1980–1990)

    Total increase: 488,291
    Percent increase: 31
    Annual percent increase: 2.7[a]

Fastest-growing: Nassau-Suffolk   4.9 percent annually[a]
Largest: New York   1,889,662
Smallest: Nassau-Suffolk   165,238

Metro Areas Reaching 100,000 Hispanics since 1980:

[a]Compounded annually.

Sources: Hispanic Market Connections, Inc.; Donnelly Marketing Information Services.

At a Glance . . .
Florida Metropolitan Areas (MAs) with Large Hispanic Concentration, 1980–1990

Metro Areas with 100,000 or More Hispanics   **Hispanic Population**

   3 MAs (1990) 1,201,094
   1 MA (1980) 580,994

Gains (1980–1990)

   Total increase: 620,099
   Percent increase: 107
   Annual percent increase: 7.5[a]

Fastest-growing: Ft. Lauderdale-Hollywood-Pompano Beach   103 percent annually[a]
Largest: Miami-Hialeah   953,407
Smallest: Ft. Lauderdale-Hollywood-Pompano Beach   108,439

Metro Areas Reaching 100,000 Hispanics since 1980:

   Tampa-St. Petersburg-Clearwater   139,248
   Ft. Lauderdale-Hollywood-Pompano Beach   108,439

[a]Compounded annually.

Sources: Hispanic Market Connections, Inc.; Donnelly Marketing Information Services.

At a Glance . . .
Illinois Metropolitan Areas (MAs) with Large Hispanic Concentration, 1980–1990

Metro Areas with 100,000 or More Hispanics   **Hispanic Population**

   1 MA (1990) 734,827
   1 MA (1980) 519,649

Gains (1980–1990)

   Total increase: 215,178
   Percent increase: 41.4
   Annual percent increase: 3.5[a]

Largest: Chicago

[a]Compounded annually.

Sources: Hispanic Market Connections, Inc.; Donnelly Marketing Information Services.

At a Glance . . .
New Jersey Metropolitan Areas (MAs) with Large Hispanic Concentration, 1980–1990

Metro Areas with 100,000 or More Hispanics   **Hispanic Population**

   4 MAs (1990) 693,612
   3 MAs (1980) 391,499

Gains (1980–1990)

   Total increase: 302,113
   Percent increase: 77.2
   Annual percent increase: 5.9[a]

Fastest-growing: Philadelphia PA-NJ   4.1 percent annually[a]
Largest: Newark   188,299
Smallest: Bergen-Passaic   147,868

Metro Areas Reaching 100,000 Hispanics since 1980:

   Bergen-Passaic   147,868

[a]Compounded annually.

Sources: Hispanic Market Connections, Inc.; Donnelly Marketing Information Services.

At a Glance . . .
Colorado Metropolitan Areas (MAs) with Large Hispanic Concentration, 1980–1990

Metro Areas with 100,000 or More Hispanics   **Hispanic Population**

   1 MA (1990) 211,005
   1 MA (1980) 163,394

Gains (1980–1990)

   Total increase: 47,611
   Percent increase: 29.1
   Annual percent increase: 2.6[a]

Largest: Denver

Metro Areas Reaching 100,000 Hispanics since 1980:

   none

[a]Compounded annually.

Sources: Hispanic Market Connections, Inc.; Donnelly Marketing Information Services.

At a Glance . . .
Arizona Metropolitan Areas (MAs) with Large Hispanic Concentration, 1980–1990

Metro Areas with 100,000 or More Hispanics   **Hispanic Population**

2 MAs (1990) 508,760
2 MAs (1980) 310,421

Gains (1980–1990)

Total increase:	198,339
Percent increase:	64
Annual percent increase:	5.1[a]

Fastest-growing: Phoenix	5.7 percent annually[a]
Largest: Phoenix	345,498
Smallest: Tucson	163,262

Metro Areas Reaching 100,000 Hispanics since 1980:

[a]Compounded annually.

Sources: Hispanic Market Connections, Inc.; Donnelly Marketing Information Services.

At a Glance . . .
Washington, D.C., Maryland, Virginia Metropolitan Areas (MAs)
with Large Hispanic Concentration, 1990

Metro Areas with 100,00 or More Hispanics   **Hispanic Population**

1 MA (1990) . . . . .224,786[a]

[a]The Washington, D.C., Metropolitan Area includes counties in Maryland and Virginia.

Sources: Hispanic Market Connections, Inc.; Donnelly Marketing Information Services.

At a Glance . . .
U.S. Metropolitan Areas (MAs) with Large Hispanic Concentration—Summary

Total (Combined) Population of MAs with 100,000 or More Hispanics, 1990:   79,279,518
Percentage Hispanic: 20.5

Metro Areas with 100,000 or More Hispanics   **Hispanic Population**

   40 MAs (1990) 16,226,340
   28 MAs (1980) 9,459,827

Gains (1980–1990)

   Total increase: 6,766,513
   Percent increase: 71.6
   Annual percent increase: 5.5

Fastest-growing: Ft. Lauderdale-Hollywood-Pompano Beach, FL   103 percent annually
Slowest-growing: Corpus Christi, TX   1.4 percent annually

Largest (1990): Los Angeles-Long Beach, CA   3,351,242
Largest (1980): Los Angeles-Long Beach, CA   2,066,103

Smallest (1990): Fort Lauderdale-Hollywood-Pompano Beach, FL   108,439
Smallest (1980): Nassau-Suffolk, NY   101,975

Sources: Hispanic Market Connections, Inc.; Donnelly Marketing Information Services.

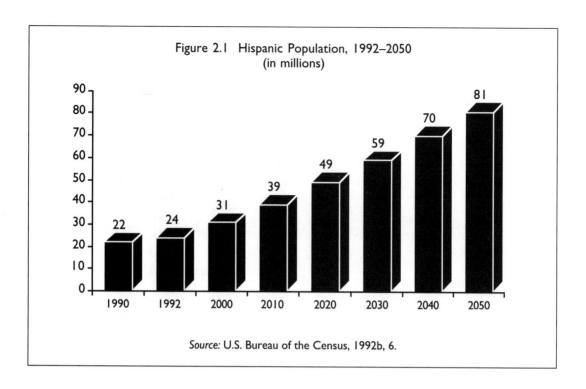

Figure 2.1   Hispanic Population, 1992–2050
(in millions)

Source: U.S. Bureau of the Census, 1992b, 6.

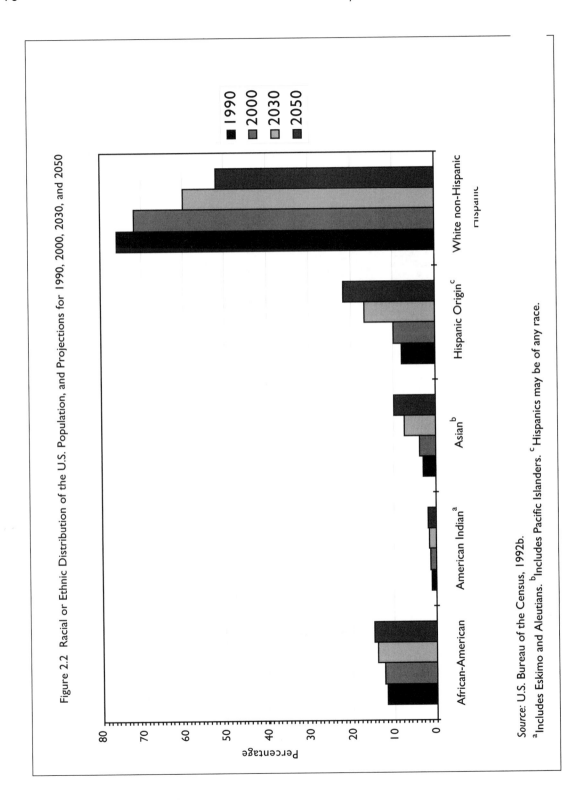

Figure 2.2 Racial or Ethnic Distribution of the U.S. Population, and Projections for 1990, 2000, 2030, and 2050

Source: U.S. Bureau of the Census, 1992b.

[a]Includes Eskimo and Aleutians. [b]Includes Pacific Islanders. [c]Hispanics may be of any race.

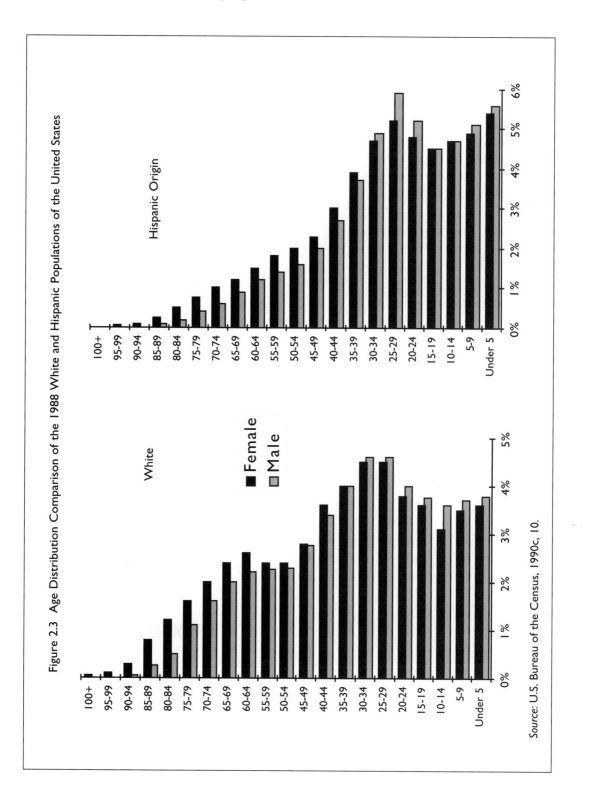

Figure 2.3 Age Distribution Comparison of the 1988 White and Hispanic Populations of the United States

Source: U.S. Bureau of the Census, 1990c, 10.

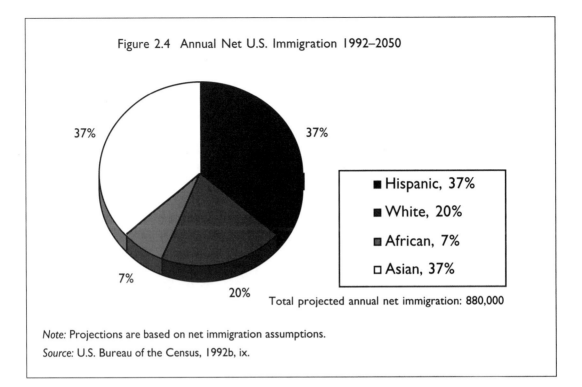

Figure 2.4 Annual Net U.S. Immigration 1992–2050

37%

37%

7%

20%

■ Hispanic, 37%

■ White, 20%

■ African, 7%

□ Asian, 37%

Total projected annual net immigration: 880,000

Note: Projections are based on net immigration assumptions.

Source: U.S. Bureau of the Census, 1992b, ix.

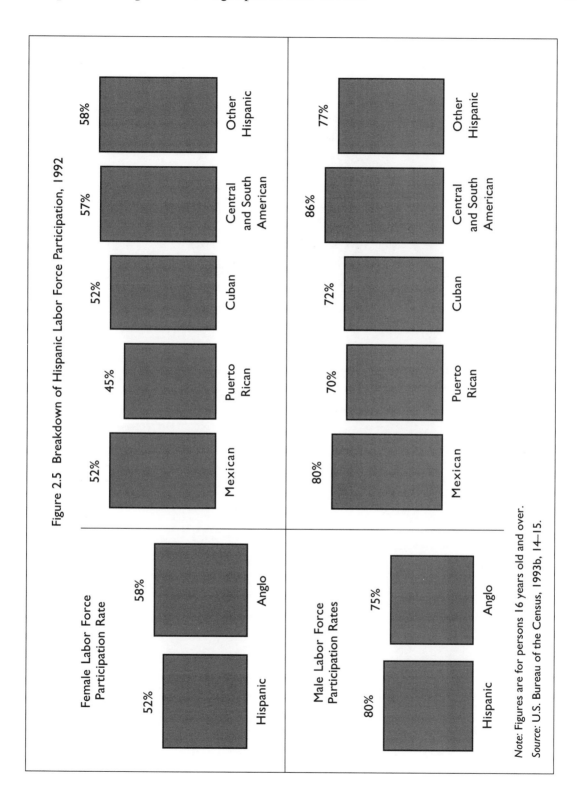

Figure 2.5 Breakdown of Hispanic Labor Force Participation, 1992

Note: Figures are for persons 16 years old and over.

Source: U.S. Bureau of the Census, 1993b, 14–15.

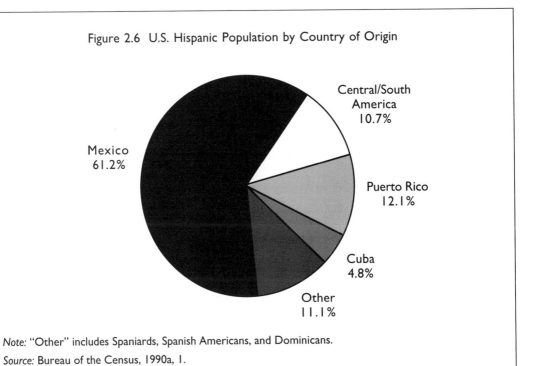

Figure 2.6 U.S. Hispanic Population by Country of Origin

Note: "Other" includes Spaniards, Spanish Americans, and Dominicans.

Source: Bureau of the Census, 1990a, 1.

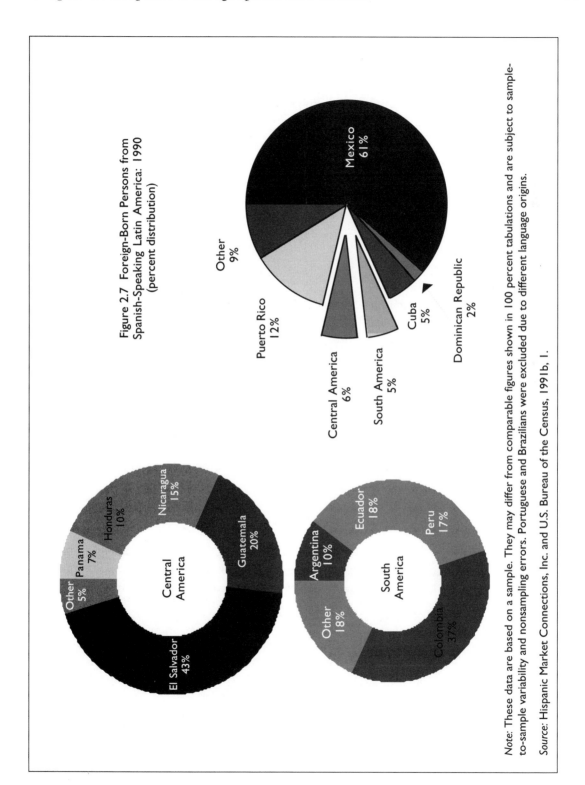

Figure 2.7 Foreign-Born Persons from Spanish-Speaking Latin America: 1990 (percent distribution)

Mexico 61%

Other 9%

Puerto Rico 12%

Central America 6%

South America 5%

Cuba 5%

Dominican Republic 2%

Central America

El Salvador 43%
Guatemala 20%
Nicaragua 15%
Honduras 10%
Panama 7%
Other 5%

South America

Colombia 37%
Ecuador 18%
Peru 17%
Argentina 10%
Other 18%

Note: These data are based on a sample. They may differ from comparable figures shown in 100 percent tabulations and are subject to sample-to-sample variability and nonsampling errors. Portuguese and Brazilians were excluded due to different language origins.

Source: Hispanic Market Connections, Inc. and U.S. Bureau of the Census, 1991b, I.

Table 2.1 Alternative Projections of the U.S. Population, by Race/Ethnicity, 1980-2040
(Populations in millions)

	Total	Total White	Total White, Non-Hispanic	Asian	Black	Hispanic[a]	Other
1980							
Census	226.5	194.7	180.9	3.6	26.1	14.6	1.3
PRB[b]	226.5	195.6	181.0	4.4	26.5	14.6	–
1990							
Census	248.7	208.7	188.3	7.0	29.3	22.3	1.8
UI[b]	248.8	209.5	187.1	7.3	30.0	22.4	2.0
2000							
Census	274.8	224.6	196.7	11.6	33.8	30.6	2.1
PRB	279.1	230.6	200.3	12.1	36.4	30.3	–
UI	276.9	228.7	198.4	12.0	34.1	30.3	2.1
2020							
Census	322.5	250.6	206.2	21.8	42.9	48.9	2.7
PRB	316.9	252.2	205.6	20.3	44.4	46.6	–
UI	320.6	255.5	208.4	22.7	40.2	47.1	2.2
2040							
Census	364.4	268.8	205.6	33.1	52.3	69.8	3.6
PRB	333.4	257.2	196.9	27.8	48.4	60.3	–
UI	355.5	274.7	210.5	34.5	44.1	64.2	2.2
	(1)	(2)	(3)	(4)	(5)	(6)	(7)

[a]Hispanics may be of any race

[b]PRB (Population Reference Bureau); UI (Urban Institute)

Notes:

– Column 1 = the sum of columns 3 through 7.

– Other includes American Indian, Eskimo, and Aleut.

– Census figures for Total White = the sum of the White Non-Hispanic (column 3) and the White Hispanic populations. The figures for the White Hispanic population are: 13,807 (1980); 20,404 (1990); 27,893 (2000); 44,425 (2020); and 63,191 (2040). Hispanics are excluded from the Asian, Black, and Other catagories.

– Population Reference Bureau (PRB) figures for Total White = the sum of the White Non-Hispanic (column 3) and the Hispanic (column 6) populations; the figures for Asians and Other are combined.

– Urban Institute (UI) figures for Total White = sum of the White Non-Hispanic (column 3) and the Hispanic (column 6) populations. Figures for Other includes some Hispanics.

Sources: Table adapted from Edmonston and Passel, 1992, 39, 44. Census data (2000, 2020, 2040): U.S. Bureau of the Census, 1992a, 28–29, 44–45, 53; 1992b, 18. U.S. Bureau of the Census, *Statistical Abstract of the United States,* 1994, 17–18. Figures in table are derived from the middle series projection.

Table 2.2 Age Composition of the Hispanic Population

Total population (million)	1980 14.9	1990 22.4	2000 30.6	2010 39.3
Under 20	6,281,000	8,638,000	11,434,000	13,966,000
Under 5	1,663,000	2,388,000	3,055,000	3,683,000
5 to 9	1,537,000	2,194,000	2,945,000	3,480,000
10 to 14	1,475,000	2,002,000	2,817,000	3,404,000
15 to 19	1,606,000	2,054,000	2,617,000	3,399,000
20 to 29	2,962,000	4,645,000	5,008,000	6,326,000
20 to 24	1,586,000	2,304,000	2,490,000	3,303,000
25 to 29	1,376,000	2,341,000	2,518,000	3,023,000
30 to 44	2,695,000	5,007,000	7,503,000	8,388,000
30 to 34	1,129,000	2,062,000	2,682,000	2,828,000
35 to 39	854,000	1,661,000	2,608,000	2,757,000
40 to 44	712,000	1,284,000	2,213,000	2,803,000
45 to 54	1,186,000	1,710,000	3,029,000	4,800,000
45 to 49	622,000	954,000	1,715,000	2,619,000
50 to 54	564,000	756,000	1,314,000	2,181,000
55 to 64	775,000	1,193,000	1,729,000	2,993,000
55 to 59	454,000	639,000	965,000	1,702,000
60 to 64	321,000	554,000	764,000	1,291,000
65 and over	709,000	1,161,000	1,135,000	2,838,000
Median age	23.2	26.2	27.8	29

Source: U.S. Bureau of the Census, 1992b, 28–29, 38, 41.

Table 2.3 Age Composition of the Hispanic Population: In Percentages

Total population (millions)	1980 14.9	1990 22.4	2000 30.6	2010 39.3
Under 20	42.9	38.6	37.4	35.5
Under 5	11.4	10.7	10.0	9.4
5 to 9	10.5	9.8	9.6	8.8
10 to 14	10.1	8.9	9.2	8.6
15 to 19	10.9	9.2	8.9	8.6
20 to 29	20.3	20.8	16.4	16.1
20 to 24	10.8	10.3	8.1	8.4
25 to 29	9.4	10.5	8.2	7.7
30 to 44	18.4	22.4	24.5	21.3
30 to 34	7.7	9.2	8.8	7.2
35 to 39	5.8	7.4	8.5	7.0
40 to 44	4.9	5.7	7.2	7.1
45 to 54	8.1	7.6	9.9	12.2
45 to 49	4.2	4.3	5.6	6.7
50 to 54	3.9	3.4	4.3	5.5
55 to 64	5.3	5.3	5.6	7.6
55 to 59	3.1	2.9	3.2	4.3
60 to 64	2.2	2.5	2.5	3.3
65 and over	4.8	5.2	3.7	7.2

Note: Data for 2000 and later not strictly comparable with previous year. Percentages may not add to total due to rounding.

Source: U.S. Bureau of the Census, 1992b, 28–29, 38, 41; 1992c, 18.

Table 2.4 U.S. Hispanic Population by Generation

Year	Total	Foreign Born (millions)	Total Native (millions)	Second Generation (millions)	Third Generation (millions)	Fourth+ Generation (millions)
1990	22.4	9.1 (40.9%)	13.2 (59.1%)	6.1 (27.2%)	3.1 (14.0%)	4.0 (17.9%)
2000	30.3	12.2 (40.4%)	18.1 (59.6%)	9.3 (30.7%)	3.8 (12.7%)	4.9 (16.3%)
2010	38.6	15.1 (39.1%)	23.5 (60.9%)	12.6 (32.6%)	4.9 (12.7%)	6.0 (15.6%)
2020	47.1	17.6 (37.3%)	29.5 (62.7%)	15.6 (33.1%)	6.6 (14.1%)	7.3 (15.6%)
2030	55.8	19.5 (35.0%)	36.2 (65.0%)	18.5 (33.2%)	9.0 (16.2%)	8.7 (15.6%)
2040	64.2	20.9 (32.6%)	43.3 (67.4%)	21.3 (33.1%)	11.6 (18.1%)	10.4 (16.2)

Source: Edmonston and Passel, 1992, 43.

Table 2.5 U.S. Hispanic Households, 1970–92

	1992	(%)	1990	(%)	1980	(%)	1970	(%)
All Hispanic Households	6,379,000	100.0	5,933,000	100.0	3,683,000	100.0	2,303,000	100.0
Family	5,180,000	81.2	4,840,000	81.6	3,029,000	82.2	2,004,000	87.0
Nonfamily	1,199,000	18.8	1,093,000	18.4	654,000	17.8	299,000	13.0

Source: U.S. Bureau of the Census 1992c, 47; 1992b, 18–19.

Table 2.6 Hispanic Household Projections, 1990–2000[a]

Age of householder	1990			1995			2000		
	All Households	Family Households	Nonfamily Households	All Households	Family Households	Nonfamily Households	All Households	Family Households	Nonfamily Households
Under 25	629	471	159	639	478	161	703	526	177
25 to 34	1,865	1,583	282	2,251	1,911	339	2,411	2,049	362
35 to 44	1,499	1,310	189	1,977	1,727	250	2,507	2,189	317
45 to 54	975	832	143	1,302	1,112	190	1,743	1,488	255
55 to 64	692	541	151	804	629	175	990	776	215
65 to 74	491	343	148	623	437	187	724	508	216
75+	213	112	101	264	139	125	344	181	163
Total	6,365	5,193	1,172	7,859	6,432	1,426	9,422	7,717	1,705

[a]Figures in thousands.

Note: Figures for 1990 not comparable with figures in Tables 2.5, 2.7, 2.8.

Source: TGE Demographics 1992, 38.

Table 2.7 Projected Gain in Number of Hispanic Households, 1990–2000

	All Households (thousands)	(%)	Family Households (thousands)	(%)	Nonfamily Households (thousands)	(%)
Age of Householder						
Under 25	73	11.8	55	11.7	18	11.3
25 to 34	546	29.3	466	29.4	80	28.4
35 to 44	1,007	67.2	879	67.1	128	67.7
45 to 54	768	78.8	656	78.8	112	78.3
55 to 64	298	43.1	235	43.4	64	42.4
65 to 74	233	47.5	165	48.1	68	45.9
75+	131	61.5	69	61.6	62	61.4
Total	3,056	48.1	2,525	48.6	532	45.4

Source: TGE Demographics, 1992, 38.

Overall Household Projections 1990–2000
(Households in Thousands)

	1990	2000	Absolute Change	Percent Change
Total Households[a]	91,950	103,832	11,882	13
White HHs	76,028	79,411	3,383	4
Black HHs	10,307	12,441	2,134	21
Hispanic[b] HHs	6,365	9,422	3,057	48

[a]Total Households = White HHs + Black HHs + (Asian and other races not included in the projections).

[b]Hispanics may be of any race.

Note: White, Black, and Hispanic households do not add up to total households because Hispanics may be of any race. Also, Asian and "other races" households are not included in this projection.

Source: TGE Demographics, 1992, 10.

Table 2.8 Households in Transition

	1992		1990		1980		1970	
	(thousands)	(%)	(thousands)	(%)	(thousands)	(%)	(thousands)	(%)
All family households	5,180	–	4,840	–	3,030	–	2,004	–
Married couples	3,534	68	3,395	70	2,282	75	1,615	81
Female-headed households	1,263	24	1,116	23	610	20	307	15
Male-headed households	383	7	329	7	138	5	82	4
Nonfamily households	1,199	–	1,093	–	654	–	299	–
Female-headed households	542	45	506	46	435	44	148	49
Male-headed households	657	55	587	54	365	56	150	50

Note: Percentages may not total 100 due to rounding.

Source: U.S. Bureau of the Census, 1992c, 47; 1993b, 18–19.

Table 2.9 Ten States with the Largest Hispanic Population, 1980, 1990

	1990 (thousands)	1980 (thousands)	Net Increase (thousands)	Percentage Increase
California	7,688	4,544	3,144	69.2
Texas	4,340	2,986	1,354	45.3
New York	2,214	1,659	555	33.4
Florida	1,574	858	716	83.4
Illinois	904	636	268	42.1
New Jersey	740	492	248	50.4
Arizona	688	441	247	56.0
New Mexico	579	477	102	21.4
Colorado	424	340	84	24.7
Massachusetts	288	141	147	104.2
Total, Ten States	19,439	12,574	6,865	54.6
Total, U.S. Hispanic	22,354	14,609	7,745	53.0
Percentage of Total U.S. Hispanic Population in Ten States	86.9	86.0	88.6	

Note: Rank in 1990.
Source: U.S. Bureau of the Census, 1991b, 4–5.

Table 2.10 Hispanic Population Loss in Seven Southern States

	1990 (thousands)	1980 (thousands)	Percent Change
W. Virginia	8	13	-38.5
S. Carolina	31	33	-6.1
Kentucky	22	27	-18.5
Tennessee	33	34	-2.9
Alabama	25	33	-24.2
Mississippi	16	25	-36.0
Louisiana	93	99	-6.1
Total Loss	228	264	-13.6

Source: U.S. Bureau of the Census, 1991b, 4–5.

Table 2.11 Metropolitan Areas (MAs) with 100,000 or More Hispanics, 1990

MA	Population	Total Hispanic	Percent Hispanic
Los Angeles-Long Beach, CA	8,863,164	3,351,242	37.8
New York, NY	8,546,846	1,889,662	22.1
Miami-Hialeah, FL	1,937,094	953,407	49.2
Chicago, IL	6,069,974	734,827	12.1
Houston, TX	3,301,937	707,356	21.4
Riverside-San Bernardino, CA	2,588,793	686,096	26.5
San Antonio, TX	1,302,099	620,290	47.6
Anaheim-Santa Ana, CA	2,410,556	564,828	23.4
San Diego, CA	2,498,016	510,781	20.4
El Paso, TX	591,610	411,619	69.6
Dallas, TX	2,553,362	368,884	14.4
Phoenix, AZ	2,122,101	345,498	16.3
McAllen-Edinburg-Mission, TX	383,545	326,972	85.2
San Jose, CA	1,497,577	314,564	21.0
Oakland, CA	2,082,914	273,087	13.1
Fresno, CA	667,490	236,634	35.5
San Francisco, CA	1,603,678	233,274	14.5
Washington, DC-MD-VA	3,923,574	224,786	5.7
Brownsville-Harlingen, TX	260,120	212,995	81.9
Denver, CO	1,622,980	211,005	13.0

(continued next page)

Table 2.11 Metropolitan Areas (MAs) with 100,000 or More Hispanics, 1990 (*continued*)

MA	Population	Total Hispanic	Percent Hispanic
Newark, NJ	1,824,321	188,299	10.3
Jersey City, NJ	553,099	183,465	33.2
Corpus Christi, TX	349,894	181,860	52.0
Albuquerque, NM	480,577	178,310	37.1
Oxnard-Ventura, CA	669,016	176,952	26.4
Philadelphia, PA-NJ	4,856,881	173,980	3.6
Sacramento, CA	1,481,102	172,374	11.6
Nassau-Suffolk, NY	2,609,212	165,238	6.3
Tucson, AZ	666,880	163,262	24.5
Austin, TX	781,572	159,942	20.5
Bakersfield, CA	543,477	151,995	28.0
Ft. Worth-Arlington, TX	1,332,053	150,033	11.3
Bergen-Passaic, NJ	1,278,440	147,868	11.6
Tampa-St. Petersburg-Clearwater, FL	2,067,959	139,248	6.7
Boston, MA	2,870,669	128,883	4.5
Laredo, TX	133,239	125,069	93.9
Visalia-Tulare-Porterville, CA	311,921	120,893	38.8
Salinas-Seaside-Monterey, CA	355,660	119,570	33.6
Stockton, CA	480,628	112,673	23.4
Fort Lauderdale-Hollywood Pompano Beach, FL	1,255,488	108,439	8.6
Total	79,279,578	16,226,340	20.5

Sources: Hispanic Market Connections, Inc.; Donnelly Marketing Information Services.

Table 2.12 Hispanic Gains in Metropolitan Areas (MAs) with 100,000 or More Hispanics, 1980–1990

| | | | Hispanic Population Gains | |
	1990	1980	Absolute	Percent
Los Angeles-Long Beach	3,351,242	2,066,103	1,285,139	62.2
New York, NY	1,889,662	1,464,634	425,028	29.0
Miami-Hialeah, FL	953,407	580,994	372,413	64.1
Chicago, IL	734,827	519,649	215,178	41.4
Houston, TX	707,536	402,224	305,312	75.9
Riverside-San Bernardino, CA	686,096	290,280	395,816	136.4
San Antonio, TX	620,290	481,511	138,779	28.8
Anaheim, Santa Ana, CA	564,828	286,339	278,489	97.3
San Diego, CA	510,781	275,177	235,604	85.6
El Paso, TX,	411,619	297,001	114,618	38.6
Dallas, TX	368,884	176,065	192,819	109.5
Phoenix, AZ	345,498	199,003	146,495	73.6
McAllen-Edinburg, TX	326,972	230,212	96,760	42.0
San Jose, CA	314,564	226,611	87,953	38.8
Oakland, CA	273,087	185,782	87,305	47.0
Fresno, CA	236,634	150,790	85,844	56.9
San Francisco, CA	233,274	165,916	67,358	40.6
Washington, DC-MD-VA	224,786	–	–	–
Brownsville-Harlingen, TX	212,995	161,654	51,341	31.7
Denver, CO	211,005	163,394	47,611	29.1
Newark, NJ	188,299	130,056	58,243	44.8
Jersey City, NJ	183,465	145,163	38,302	26.4
Corpus Christi, TX	181,860	158,119	23,741	15.0
Albuquerque, NM	178,310	154,620	23,690	15.3

(continued next page)

Table 2.12 Hispanic Gains in Metropolitan Areas (MAs) with 100,000 or More Hispanics, 1980–1990 (*continued*)

	1990	1980	Hispanic Population Gains Absolute	Percent
Oxnard-Ventura, CA	176,952	113,192	63,760	56.3
Philadelphia, PA-NJ	173,980	116,280	57,700	49.6
Sacramento, CA	172,374	105,665	66,709	63.1
Nassau-Suffolk, NY	165,238	101,975	63,975	62.0
Tucson, AZ	163,262	111,418	51,844	46.5

MAs (with more than 100,000 Hispanics) added in 1990

	1990	1980	Absolute	Percent
Austin, TX	159,942	94,512	65,430	69.2
Bakersfield, CA	151,995	87,048	64,947	74.6
Ft. Worth-Arlington, TX	150,033	72,002	78,031	108.4
Bergen, Passaic, NJ	147,868	90,510	57,358	63.4
Tampa, St. Petersburg, Clearwater, FL	139,248	80,700	58,548	72.5
Boston, MA	128,883	67,344	61.539	91.4
Laredo, TX	125,069	90,090	34,979	38.8
Visalia-Tulare-Porterville, CA	120,893	73,308	47,585	64.9
Salinas-Seaside-Monterey, CA	119,570	75,110	44,460	59.2
Stockton, CA	112,673	66,624	46,049	69.1
Ft. Lauderdale,-Hollywood-Pompano Beach, FL	108,439	40,720	67,719	166.3

Sources: Hispanic Market Connections, Inc.; Donnnelly Marketing Information Services; U.S. Bureau of the Census, 1983, 22; 1987, 28–30, 33.

Table 2.13 Metropolitan Areas (MAs) with 100,000 or More Hispanics, 1980 and 1990

	1990	1980	(Average) Annual Percent Rate of Growth[a]
ARIZONA			
Phoenix	345,498	199,003	5.7
Tucson	163,262	111,418	3.9
Total	508,760	310,421	5.1
CALIFORNIA			
Los Angeles-Long Beach	3,351,242	2,066,103	4.9
Riverside-San Bernardino	686,096	290,280	9.0
Anaheim-Santa Ana	564,828	286,339	7.0
San Diego	510,781	275,177	6.4
San Jose	314,564	226,611	3.3
Oakland	273,087	185,782	3.9
Fresno	236,634	150,790	4.6
San Francisco	233,274	165,916	3.5
Oxnard-Ventura	176,952	113,192	4.6
Sacramento	172,374	105,665	5.0
Bakersfield[b]	151,995	87,048	5.7
Visalia-Tahoe-Porterville[b]	120,893	73,308	5.1
Salinas-Seaside-Monterey[b]	119,570	75,110	4.7
Stockton[b]	112,673	66,624	5.4
Total	7,024,963	4,167,945	5.3
COLORADO			
Denver	211,005	163,394	2.6
FLORIDA			
Miami-Hialeah	953,407	580,994	5.1
Tampa-St. Petersburg-Clearwater	139,248	80,700	5.6
Ft. Lauderdale-Hollywoodb-Pompano Beach	108,439	40,720	103.0
Total	1,201,094	580,994	7.15
ILLINOIS			
Chicago	734,827	519,649	3.5

(continued next page)

Table 2.13 Metropolitan Areas (MAs) with 100,000 or More Hispanics, 1980 and 1990
(*continued*)

	1990	1980	(Average) Annual Percent Rate of Growth[a]
NEW JERSEY			
Jersey City	183,465	145,163	2.3
Newark	188,299	130,056	3.8
Philadelphia PA-NJ	173,980	116,280	4.1
Bergen-Passaic[b]	147,868	90,510	
Total	693,612	482.009	3.7
NEW YORK			
New York	1,889,662	1,464,634	2.6
Nassau-Suffolk	165,238	101,975	4.9
Total	2,054,900	1,566,609	2.7
TEXAS			
San Antonio	620,290	481,511	2.6
Houston	707,536	402,224	5.8
El Paso	411,619	297,001	3.3
McAllen-Edinburg-Mission	326,972	230,212	3.6
Dallas	368,884	176,065	7.8
Brownsville-Harlingen	212,995	161,654	2.8
Corpus Christi	181,860	158,119	1.4
Austin[b]	159,942	94,512	5.4
Fort Worth-Arlington[b]	150,033	72,002	7.6
Laredo[b]	125,060	90,090	3.3
Total	3,265,200	2,163,390	4.2

[a]Compounded annually.

[b]Fewer than 100,000 Hispanics in 1980.

Sources: Hispanic Market Connections, Inc.; Donnelly Marketing Information Services; U.S. Bureau of the Census.

Table 2.14 States with Mexican-Origin Population of 100,000 or More, 1990

	Total Population	Percentage of U.S. Total
California	6,118,996	45.3
Texas	3,890,820	28.8
Illinois	623,688	4.6
Arizona	616,195	4.6
New Mexico	328,836	2.4
Colorado	282,478	2.1
Florida	161,499	1.2
Washington, D.C.	155,864	1.2
Michigan	138,312	1.0
Total, Eight States and D.C.	12,316,189	91.2
Total, U.S.	13,495,938	100

Note: Mexican-origin population includes U.S.- and foreign-born Mexicans.

Source: U.S. Bureau of the Census, 1990b.

Table 2.15 Sex Composition of the U.S. Hispanic Population by Origin, March 1992

	Mexican	Mainland Puerto Rican	Island Puerto Rican[*]	Cuban	Central American[*]	South American[*]
Sex						
Male	50.3	48.6	48.4	47.5	49.5	49.1
Female	49.1	51.4	51.6	52.5	50.5	50.9
Total	14,062	2,352	3,522	1,045	1,323	1,036

[*]Data for Central America, South America, and Island of Puerto Rico is for 1990.

Note: Figures in thousands.

Source: U.S. Bureau of the Census, 1993b, 13; 1993c, 11, 21; 1993d, 822.

Table 2.16 Age Distribution of U.S. Mexican Population, March 1992

Age	Total (thousands)	Percentage
Under 5 years	1,687	12
5–9 years	1,519	10.8
10–14 years	1,336	9.5
15–19 years	1,279	9.1
20–24 years	1,378	9.8
25–29 years	1,350	9.6
30–34 years	1,336	9.5
35–39 years	1,026	7.3
40–44 years	858	6.1
45–49 years	548	3.9
50–54 years	422	3
55–59 years	351	2.5
60–64 years	323	2.3
65–69 years	267	1.9
70 or more years	381	2.7
Total	14,062	100

Median age: 24.4

Note: Includes U.S.- and foreign-born Mexicans.

Source: U.S. Bureau of the Census, 1993b, 13.

Table 2.17 Marital Status of U.S. Mexican Population, 1992

Marital Status	Total (in thousands)	Percentage
Never married	3,129	32.9
Married	5,450	57.3
Widowed	352	3.7
Divorced	580	6.1
Total	9,512	100

Note: Figures are for persons 15 years of age and older. Totals may not add up to 100 due to rounding. Includes U.S.-born and foreign-born Mexicans.

Source: U.S. Bureau of the Census, 1993b, 13.

Table 2.18 Makeup of U.S. Mexican Households, March 1992

Type of Household	Total (in thousands)	Percentage
Family Households	3,130	84.0
Married/couples	2,228	59.8
Male head; no wife present	235	6.3
Female head; no husband present	667	17.9
Nonfamily Households	596	16.0
Male householder	346	9.3
Female householder	250	6.7
Total	3,726	100

Number of Persons in Household	Percentage
1	11.0
2	19.1
3	18.4
4	20.9
5	14.9
6	7.9
7 or more	7.8
Total	100

Total households: 3,726,000
Mean number of persons: 3.73

Note: Includes U.S.-born and foreign-born Mexicans.

Source: U.S. Bureau of the Census, 1993b, 19.

Table 2.19 Income of U.S. Mexican Households and Families, 1991

All Families	3,132,000	All Households	3,726,000
Less than $10,000	18.0%	Less than $10,000	18.9%
$10,000–$24,999	36.7%	$10,000–$24,999	36.4%
$25,000–$49,999	31.8%	$25,000–$49,999	31.6%
$50,000 or more	13.5%	$50,000 or more	13.1%
Median Income	$23,018	Median Income	$22,477
Mean Income	$27,968	Mean Income	$27,617

Note: Includes U.S.-born and foreign-born Mexicans.

Source: U.S. Bureau of the Census, 1993b, 19, 21.

Table 2.20 Labor Force Participation among U.S. Mexicans, March 1992

	Total	Male	Female
Total Population (in thousands)	9,229	4,698	4,530
Civilian Labor Force (in thousands)	6,119	3,783	2,336
Employed	5,404	3,314	2,091
Unemployed	716	469	245
Percentage of Total Population in Civilian Labor Force	66.3	80.5	51.6
Employed	88.3	87.6	89.5
Unemployed	11.7	12.4	10.5

Note: Figures are for persons age 16 and older. Includes U.S.-born and foreign-born Mexicans.

Source: U.S. Bureau of the Census, 1993b, 15.

Table 2.21 Hispanic Educational Attainment

	Mexican	Mainland Puerto Rican	Island Puerto Rican	Cuban	Central American	South American
Persons 25 years and over (thousands)	6,362	1,353	1,952	768	736	657
High school graduate or higher (%)	44.2	53.4	49.7	56.6	45.7	70.8
Bachelors degree or higher (%)	6.3	9.5	14.3	16.5	9.1	19.5
Graduate Degree or Higher (%)	2.0	3.2	NA	7.2	3.2	8.2

Note: 1990 data.

NA = not available.

Source: Hispanic Market Connections, Inc. and U.S. Bureau of the Census, 1993c.

Table 2.22 States with Puerto Rican Population of 100,000 or More, 1990

	Population	Percentage of U.S. Total
New York	1,086,601	39.8
New Jersey	320,133	11.7
Florida	247,010	9.1
Pennsylvania	148,988	5.5
Massachusetts	151,193	5.5
Connecticut	146,842	5.4
Illinois	146,059	5.4
California	126,417	4.6
Total, Eight States	2,373,243	87.0
Total, U.S.	2,727,754	100.0

Source: U.S. Bureau of the Census, 1993d, 31.

Table 2.23 Age Distribution of Mainland Puerto Rican Population, March 1992

Age	Total (in thousands)	Percentage
Under 5	254.0	10.8
5–9	216.4	9.2
10–14	240.0	10.2
15–19	195.2	8.3
20–24	181.1	7.7
25–29	230.5	9.8
30–34	197.6	8.4
35–39	188.2	8.0
40–44	162.3	6.9
45–49	131.7	5.6
50–54	112.9	4.8
55–59	70.6	3.0
60–64	56.4	2.4
65–69	40.5	1.7
70 and over	72.9	3.0
Total	2,352	100

Median age: 26.9

Source: U.S. Bureau of the Census, 1993b, 13.

Table 2.24 Marital Status of Mainland Puerto Rican Population, March 1992

Marital Status	Total (in thousands)	Percentage
Never married	613	37.3
Married	810	49.3
Widowed	80	4.9
Divorced	138	8.4
Total	1,641	100

Note: Figures are for persons age 15 and older.

Source: U.S. Bureau of the Census, 1993b, 13.

Table 2.25 Makeup of U.S. Puerto Rican Households, March 1992

Type of Household	Total (in thousands)	Percentage
Family Households	620	75.6
Married/couples	332	40.5
Male head; no wife present	34	4.2
Female head; no husband present	253	30.9
Nonfamily Households	200	24.4
Male householder	115	14.0
Female householder	85	10.4
Total	820	100

Number of Persons in Household	Percentage
1	19.9
2	23.9
3	21.1
4	18.6
5	9.8
6	4.0
7 or more	2.8
Total	100

Total households: 820,000
Mean number of persons: 2.99

Source: U.S. Bureau of the Census, 1993b, 19.

Table 2.26 Income of Mainland Puerto Rican Households and Families, March 1991

All Families	619,000	All Households	820,000
Less than $10,000	29.2%	Less than $10,000	33.4%
$10,000–$24,999	27.3%	$10,000–$24,999	28.5%
$25,000–$49,999	25.2%	$25,000–$49,999	21.7%
$50,000 or more	18.3%	$50,000 or more	16.5%
Median Income (dollars)	$20,654	Median Income	$17,967
Mean Income	$27,908	Mean Income	$25,736

Source: U.S. Bureau of the Census, 1993b, 19, 21.

Table 2.27 Labor Force Participation among Mainland Puerto Ricans, March 1992

	Total	Male	Female
Total Population (in thousands)	1,585	898	845
Civilian Labor Force (in thousands)	898	740	378
Employed	788	520	341
Unemployed	110	220	37
Percentage of Total Population in Civilian Labor Force	56.7	70.3	44.7
Employed	87.7	85.9	90.2
Unemployed	12.3	14.1	9.8

Note: Figures are for persons age 16 and older.
Source: U.S. Bureau of the Census, 1993b, 15.

Table 2.28 States with Large Cuban Populations, 1990

	Population	Percentage of U.S. Total
Florida	674,052	64
New Jersey	85,378	8.1
New York	74,345	7.1
California	71,977	6.8
Illinois	18,204	1.7
Texas	18,195	1.7
Total, Six States	942,151	89.4
Total, U.S.	1,053,197	100

Source: Hispanic Market Connections and U.S. Bureau of the Census, 1990b, 2–3.

Table 2.29 Age Distribution of the U.S. Cuban Population, 1992

Age	Total (thousands)	Percentage
Under 5	51.0	4.9
5–9	58.3	5.6
10–14	39.5	3.8
15–19	61.4	5.9
20–24	72.9	7.0
25–29	82.2	7.9
30–34	73.0	7.1
35–39	74.9	7.2
40–44	86.4	8.3
45–49	50.0	4.8
50–54	73.9	7.1
55–59	57.2	5.5
60–64	79.1	7.6
65–69	53.1	5.1
70 and over	127	12
Total	1,041	
Median age: 40.4		

Note: Percentages do not total 100 due to rounding.

Source: U.S. Bureau of the Census, 1993b, 13.

Table 2.30 Marital Status of the U.S. Cuban Population, March 1992

Marital Status	Total (thousands)	Percentage
Never Married	223	25.0
Married	518	58.0
Widowed	73.2	8.2
Divorced	79	8.8
Total	893	100

Note: Figures are for persons age 15 and over.
Source: U.S. Bureau of the Census, 1993b, 13.

Table 2.31 Composition of U.S. Cuban Households, March 1992

Type of Household	Total (thousands)	Percentage
Family Households	237	75.2
Married couples	221	55.9
Male head; no wife present	11	2.9
Female head; no husband present	65	16.4
Nonfamily Households	98	24.9
Male householder	41	10.5
Female householder	57	14.4
Total	395	100

Number of Persons in Household	Percentage
1	20.1
2	31.7
3	22.5
4	15.0
5	7.4
6	2.7
7	0.7

Total households : 395,000
Mean number of persons: 2.7

Source: U.S. Bureau of the Census, 1993b, 19.

Table 2.32 Income of U.S. Cuban Households and Families, 1991

All Families	296,000	All Households	395,000
Less than $10,000	13.4%	Less than $10,000	20.4%
$10,000–$24,999	25.4%	$10,000–$24,999	26.7%
$25,000–$49,999	32.9%	$25,000–$49,999	29.3%
$50,000 or more	28.3%	$50,000 or more	23.6%
Median income	$30,095	Median income	$26,593
Mean income	$40,030	Mean Income	$35,599

Source: U.S. Bureau of the Census, 1993b, 19, 21.

Table 2.33 Labor Force Participation among U.S. Cubans, March 1992

	Total		Male		Female	
	(thousands)	(%)	(thousands)	(%)	(thousands)	(%)
Cuban Population	874		420		454	
Civilian Labor Force	538	61.5	303	72.2	235	51.7
Employed	487	90.5	276	91.1	211	89.8
Unemployed	51	9.4	27	9.1	24	9.9

Note: Figures are for persons ages 16 and older.

Source: U.S. Bureau of the Census, 1993b, 19, 21.

Table 2.34 Persons of Hispanic Origin in the United States, 1990

	Total (in thousands)	Percentage
Total U.S. Population	248,710	
Total Persons of Hispanic Origin	21,900	100
Mexican	13,393	61.2
Puerto Rican	2,652	12.1
Cuban	1,053	4.8
Dominican	520	2.4
Central American	1,324	6.0
Costa Rican	57	0.3
Guatemalan	269	1.2
Honduran	131	0.6
Nicaraguan	203	0.9
Panamanian	92	0.4
Salvadoran	565	2.6
Other Central American	7	0.0
South American	1,036	4.7
Argentinian	101	0.5
Bolivian	38	0.2
Chilean	69	0.3
Colombian	379	1.7
Ecuadorian	191	0.9
Paraguayan	7	0.0
Peruvian	175	0.8
Uruguayan	22	0.1
Venezuelan	48	0.2
Other South American	6	0.0
Spaniard[a]	1057	4.8
All Other Hispanic Origin[b]	865	3.9
Not of Hispanic Origin	226,810	

[a]Study includes Spaniard, Spanish, and Spanish-Americans.

[b]Numbers include U.S. Central and South Americans.

Note: These data are based on a sample. They may differ from comparable figures shown in 100 percent tabulations and are subject to sample-to-sample variability and nonsampling errors. Portuguese and Brazilians were excluded due to different language origins.

Source: Hispanic Market Connections, Inc. and U.S. Bureau of the Census, 1991b, 1.

Table 2.35 States with Central and South American Populations of 100,000 or more, 1990

	Central Americans		South Americans	
	Population	Percentage of U.S. Total	Population	Percentage of U.S. Total
California	637,656	48.2	182,384	17.6
Florida	149,741	11.3	170,531	16.5
New Jersey	–	–	126,286	12.2
New York	142,415	10.7	279,101	26.9
Total, Four States	929,812	70.2	758,302	73.2
Total, U.S.	1,324,000	100	1,036,000	100

Source: Hispanic Market Connections, Inc. and U.S. Bureau of the Census, 1990b, 6, 11, 32, 34.

Table 2.36 Age Distribution of the U.S. Central and South American Population, 1990

Age	Central American Total (thousands)	Percentage	South American Total (thousands)	Percentage
Under 5	110.0	8.3	73.5	7.1
5–9	99.6	7.5	67.2	6.5
10–14	101.1	7.6	68.7	6.6
15–19	115.5	8.7	76.6	7.4
20–24	161	12.2	92.8	9.0
25–34	343.2	25.9	240.1	23.2
35–44	209.1	15.8	181.5	17.5
45–54	97.3	7.3	123.2	11.9
55–64	48.8	3.7	69.0	6.7
65 and over	38.2	2.9	42.4	4.1
Total	1,323.8	100	1,034	100

Median age: Central American 27.1   South American 30.8

Source: U.S. Bureau of the Census, 1993c, 11, 21.

Table 2.37 Marital Status of the U.S. Central and South American Population, 1990

| Marital Status | Central American | | South American | |
	Total (thousands)	Percentage	Total (thousands)	Percentage
Never Married	226	45.5	140	34.8
Married	234	47.1	222	55.2
Widowed	3	0.6	3	0.7
Divorced/Separated	34	6.8	37	9.2
Total	497	100	402	100

Note: Total may not add up to 100 due to rounding. Figures are for persons age 15 and older.

Source: U.S. Bureau of the Census, 1993b, 11, 21.

Table 2.38 Composition of U.S. Central and South American Households

Central and South American

Type of Household (1992)	Total (thousands)	Percentage
Family Households	734	81.3
Married couples	484	53.6
Male head; no wife present	70	7.8
Female head; no husband present	180	19.9
Nonfamily Households	169	18.7
Male householder	89.4	9.9
Female householder	79.5	8.8
Total	903	100

Number of Persons in Household (1990)	Central American Percentage	South American Percentage
1	9.2	15.0
2	15.8	22.4
3	18.4	20.4
4	20.6	20.7
5	15.8	12.1
6	9.3	5.3
7	10.8	3.9
Total	100	100
Total households (in thousands):	336	320
Mean number of persons:	3.9	3.2

Source: U.S. Bureau of the Census, 1993b, 19; 1993c, 49, 59.

CHAPTER 3

- Where Hispanic Income Is Concentrated
- Hispanic Affluence
- Hispanic Income Sources
- Hispanic Spending
- Market Opportunities

Hispanics as Consumers

Cultural heritage, the Spanish language, and . . . disposable income are three things most U.S. Hispanics have in common. Every day, Hispanic consumers pour billions of dollars into the U.S. economy. Regardless of how much money they make individually or how much better off one group may be compared to another, the end result stays the same: *U.S. Hispanics earn and spend more money than most Hispanics in Latin America* (Table 3.1).

According to the Census Bureau's *Current Population Survey,* which measures Hispanics' monthly income, in 1991 U.S. Hispanic households had an aggregate income of $184 billion. This number underestimates Hispanics' real income, however, because it excludes noncash benefits amounting to millions of dollars each year. Noncash benefits, such as contributions to retirement programs, medical and educational expenses, health insurance, subsidized housing, free transportation, and food stamps, free up a substantial dollar amount that Hispanic consumers spend on additional goods and services (U.S. Bureau of the Census, 1993b, 8). If noncash benefits are added to the $184 billion estimate, then total aggregate income for the U.S. Hispanic market could be as high or higher than $200 billion.

Money and financial resources greatly influence consumers' lifestyles, spending habits, and the types of goods and services they buy. This chapter describes how much money Hispanics make, how affluent they are, where and how they spend their money, and how Hispanic culture influences their decisions. These factors are closely tied to the goods and services Hispanics purchase and consume, their unique demographic characteristics, personal preferences, and cultural differences.

■ Where Hispanic Income Is Concentrated

The region with the largest concentration of Hispanic income is the Southwest (California, Texas, Arizona, New Mexico), which is also where most Hispanics reside, making this region the prime target for marketing to Hispanics. According to the Bureau of the Census, in 1990 the Southwest alone contained three-fourths of all Hispanic people (17 million), households (4.4 million), and incomes ($134 billion). Although the Midwest and the Northeast are not as heavily populated by Hispanics, Hispanic households in both regions combined generate substantial amounts of money, approximately $42 billion (Figure 3.1).

On average, Hispanic households tend to be better off financially in those states with lower concentrations of Hispanics (Figure 3.2). For example, in 1990 Maryland, Virginia, New Hampshire, and Alaska had households with much higher median household incomes than California (Figure 3.3; Table 3.2). Hispanic households in Maryland had a median income of $37,300, and in California, $28,209. The median income for Hispanic households in the above-mentioned four states was also higher than the $31,435 median for white non-Hispanics. In twenty-two states Hispanics had household incomes higher than the national Hispanic median of $24,156 (Table 3.2). And on average, Hispanic household income is 15 percent higher than that of African Americans

(Table 3.3). These figures challenge the notion that "Hispanics are not worthy as a market" because "they are all poor."

■ Hispanic Affluence

The growth in Hispanic income has been steady over the past couple of decades. In fact, Hispanics prospered greatly during the 1980s. For example, in 1991 there were relatively fewer households at the lower end of the income scale than in 1980. But the greatest gains took place at the other end of the scale, among the more affluent, those with incomes over $50,000 (Figure 3.4); a 26 percent increase was observed in this group during the past decade (Figure 3.5). In fact, in 1991 over one-fourth of Hispanic homeowners had incomes of $50,000 or more according to the American Housing Survey (U.S. Bureau of the Census, 1993a, 276). In terms of purchase behavior, the increase in household income means more disposable income. For example, Hispanics in higher income brackets who already own a home may be inclined to buy a better home or to make improvements to their current home. Renters may become first-time home-buyers. More Hispanic parents may send their children to college. They are more likely to purchase new automobiles, electronic goods, video and computer equipment, and so on. They are also more likely to vacation and travel to places other than their country of ancestry and stay in hotels or resorts.

Affluent Hispanics may also be more receptive to making long-term investments and purchasing other financial products such as money market funds, securities, life insurance and stocks. Hispanic Market Connections' research on financial investments and Hispanics has shown that many affluent Hispanics today are already looking for financial growth opportunities and ways to diversify their assets, but many do not know how to go about it. One main barrier is the language problem. Investment literature, including magazines and brochures, often is not available in Spanish, and companies frequently have no staff who speak Spanish or understand Hispanics' lack of familiarity with financial products.

Ford advertises the new Thunderbird in Spanish.

State Farm targeted the Hispanic audience with this ad in Hispanic Business *magazine.*

There are about 1 million Hispanic households in the United States with incomes of $50,000 or more (Table 3.4). Almost two-thirds of those households are in three states: California, Texas, and New York. About one-quarter are spread across Florida, New Jersey, Illinois, Arizona, New Mexico, the Washington, D.C., area, and Colorado (Table 3.5).

Finally, when deciding which Hispanic markets to target, companies should consider the following factors. Contrary to popular belief, there are many more affluent households among Mexicans than any other Hispanic group (Figure 3.6). As a group, however, Cubans are more affluent than Mexicans, with a larger proportion having incomes of $50,000 or more (Figure 3.7). What does this mean in practical terms? When targeting upscale Hispanics, companies should consider targeting both Mexicans and Cubans in areas where they are highly concentrated: California and Florida.

CALIFORNIA

California has the largest number of affluent Hispanics. Roughly 40 percent of all U.S. Hispanic households with incomes of $50,000 or more are found in the state (Table 3.5). Most affluent Hispanics in California live in large urban areas and suburbs. There are more than a quarter of a million affluent Hispanic households spread over six metropolitan areas in the southern part of California, including Los Angeles-Long Beach, Anaheim-Santa Ana, Riverside-San Bernardino, San Diego, Oxnard-Ventura, and Santa Barbara-Santa Maria-Lompoc. Together, these six areas account for 75 percent of all affluent households in the state. Hispanic affluence also exists in northern California, where about 61 percent of Hispanic households with incomes over $50,000 cluster in the San Jose, Oakland, and San Francisco metropolitan areas. All told, Hispanic affluence in northern California is spread over fifteen urban conglomerates (Table 3.6).

NEW YORK AND NEW JERSEY

New York and New Jersey follow California in affluence. When added together the two states account for 16 percent of all upper-income Hispanics. The New York-Newark-New Jersey metropolitan area offers ample opportunity to target this consumer segment, as over 94 percent of Hispanic households with incomes of $50,000 or more are found there (Table 3.7). In New Jersey over half of all upper-income Hispanic households are found in

Jersey City. In the adjacent counties of Monmouth and Ocean about a third of all Hispanic households may be considered upscale (Table 3.8).

Hispanic affluence is distributed over a wide geographic area in Texas. For example, out of almost 87,000 upscale households, 61 percent are found in the state's southern metropolitan areas of Houston, San Antonio, and Dallas. South of Houston, the Brazoria metro area has the highest concentration of affluent Hispanics, with 16 percent of all Hispanic households (8,430) reporting incomes of $50,000 or more at the last census (Table 3.9).

TEXAS

Upper-income Hispanics in Florida are concentrated primarily on the Atlantic coast of the Miami-Hialeah, Fort Lauderdale-Hollywood, and Pompano Beach metro areas, where about 80 percent of all affluent Florida Hispanic households are located. Another 18 percent is split between the urban conglomerates of Tampa-Petersburg-Clearwater in West Florida and toward the northeast, in the Orlando metro area (Table 3.10).

FLORIDA

Over 80 percent of all upscale Hispanic households in the state are located in the Chicago metropolitan area. To the Southwest, the Joliet metro area is an enclave of Hispanic affluence, with about 30 percent of all Hispanic households being upwardly mobile (Table 3.11).

ILLINOIS

Arizona, Colorado and New Mexico account for slightly more than 5 percent (about 41,300 households) of all affluent Hispanic households in the United States. The metropolitan areas of Phoenix, Arizona; Albuquerque, New Mexico, and Denver, Colorado are the most affluent in their states, containing 66 percent, 61 percent, and 73 percent respectively of all upscale Hispanic households (Tables 3.12, 3.13, and 3.14).

ARIZONA, COLORADO, AND NEW MEXICO

■ Hispanic Income Sources

About 89 percent of all Hispanic men and women in the labor force are employed. In addition, many Hispanics also receive

income from self-employment, Social Security, retirement benefits, and public assistance.

Large Hispanic households tend to drive the mean income
upward. For example, in 1990 Hispanic households with more
than seven people had mean incomes of $36,618, while two-per-
son households had mean incomes of $26,310.

Young adult and middle-age Hispanics ages 25 to 44 contributed
55 percent of all aggregate household Hispanic income in 1990.
Young adult and middle-age whites and African-Americans contributed 46 percent and 52 percent, respectively, of household
income for their groups. Hispanic teenagers and young adults
ages 15 to 24 contributed 7 percent to the Hispanic household
aggregate income; whites and African Americans contributed 3
percent and 4 percent respectively (U.S. Bureau of the Census,
1992b, 447). Whites and African Americans tend to remain in
school longer than Hispanics. Hispanics tend to join the labor
force somewhat earlier, which may explain in part why Hispanic
youth contribute more to the Hispanic household income.

■ Hispanic Spending

Hispanics spend about the same or more than non-Hispanic
whites and African Americans in eight key areas (Figure 3.8):

- Food consumed at home
- Rental housing
- Apparel
- Telephone services
- TV/radio and other sound equipment
- Personal care products
- Public transportation
- Cleaning supplies

As documented by the Consumer Expenditure Survey for
1990–1991 (U.S. Bureau of Labor Statistics, 1992), the spending
habits of Hispanics are somewhat different from those of other

consumer groups (Tables 3.15–3.17). For example, Hispanics allocate about three-fourths of their income to housing, food, transportation, and clothing (Figure 3.10), which is more than white non-Hispanics (68 percent) or African Americans (64 percent) do. They also spend 13 percent of their household incomes on personal insurance, pensions, health, and personal care. Another 11 percent is spent on entertainment, alcoholic beverages and tobacco, and reading and educational materials.

One area in which Hispanic spending trails behind other groups is life and health insurance. For example, according to the 1992 Consumer Expenditure Survey, Hispanics spend about $148 annually in life and other personal insurance, whereas non-Hispanics and African Americans spend $372 and $304 dollars, respectively (Figure 3.11). This lower insurance coverage can again be largely understood within the context of Hispanic cultural heritage. Until very recently, life, personal, and other types of insurance were not broadly promoted in Latin America. Only the more wealthy or educated groups in those countries have traditionally purchased life insurance, and governments have historically provided some form of health care; hence, to the masses, insurance has not been a familiar product.

Crown Royal goes after the Hispanic dollar with the slogan "you deserve to be treated like a king."

But this is changing rapidly. Research shows that Hispanics in the U.S. are learning fast about the benefits of insurance coverage. When businesses position, support, and promote these services to Hispanics, Hispanics have responded very positively. Successful promotions always include Spanish-language materials with introductory information that is simple and to the point. In sum, there is great potential for those insurance businesses who target Hispanics with culturally sensitive strategies.

■ Market Opportunities

In-home food preparation tends to be higher among Hispanics. Hispanics spend as much as white non-Hispanics and much more than African Americans on food. They also tend to eat more at home than the other two groups (Table 3.16). One reason for this

FOOD

difference is that Hispanic homes and families are larger, hence there are more people to feed. Another equally important reason has to do with the cultural aspect of food. Hispanics place high value on food and meal preparation and getting together to enjoy a delicious, home-cooked meal. Large meals are at the center of Hispanic home entertainment, and most entertainment occurs within the Hispanic family compound. It is very common that friends and extended family, parents and their children, aunts, uncles, cousins, and grandparents visit on weekends, holidays, and other days of celebration and share a meal. It is also very common for Hispanic families and individuals to gather for picnics at the park or at the beach. Food is involved in most Hispanic celebrations.

The foods Hispanics use to prepare meals reflects another cultural difference between Hispanics and non-Hispanics. For example, Hispanics spend more on cereals, bakery products, dairy items, meats, and vegetables than either white non-Hispanics or African Americans. Rice and beans are universal staples and essential components in many Hispanic menus and diets. Most Hispanics prefer beef over pork, poultry, or fish and consume twice as many eggs as white non-Hispanics and considerably more than African Americans. Hispanics generally prefer fresh fruits and vegetables over processed ones, but also spend more on processed foods than either of the other groups (Table 3.16). Figure 3.12 shows Hispanic food preferences for food consumed at home.

HOUSING   The home ownership rate is lower among Hispanics than white non-Hispanics, and Hispanics spend more money on rent than on mortgages. As shown in Figure 3.13, Hispanics paid less on mortgages ($2,423), interest, and property taxes than on rental units ($2,566) in 1990–91 (U.S. Bureau of Labor Statistics, 1992). Home ownership is also lower among foreign-born than native-born Hispanics (Table 3.18).

Demographic and cultural factors are responsible for this reliance on renting to the detriment of home ownership. First, immigration has a profound and almost immediate effect on the local housing market. The arrival of thousands of immigrants greatly increases the demand for rental housing, consequently raising the price people pay for rent in those areas.

Second, foreign-born Hispanics generally have lower incomes, fewer own real estate property, and as immigrants many have not developed a credit history. Hence, it is very difficult for many to obtain mortgage approvals to purchase homes without first becoming financially established. Third, cultural aspects also determine the buying behavior of immigrants. For example, the household purchase dynamics of foreign-born Hispanics reflects that of their country of birth. Because mortgages in most Hispanic countries tend to be prohibitively expensive or unavailable to most, many people who own homes build their own. Other barriers that limit Hispanic home buying are lack of familiarity with the home-purchasing process in the U.S., lack of Spanish-language advertising and materials to attract and entice new house buyers, and the dearth of personnel at banks, real estate agencies, and other institutions who can both speak the Spanish language and understand the Hispanic culture. Finally, many foreign-born Hispanic families that have the necessary income to purchase houses postpone the decision, thinking that they will return to their homelands.

The future thus holds great business potential for those in the real estate, banking, and housing industries who target Hispanics with culturally attuned efforts. According to the American Housing Survey, in 1991 the median age for Hispanic homeowners was 48 and for renters, 35 (U.S. Bureau of the Census, 1993a, 268). The median age for foreign-born Hispanics was 32, which indicates that 10 to 15 years down the road, when they are between 42 and 47 years old, a large number of them will be considering purchasing their first home in the United States.

Arthur Andersen targets young, college-educated Hispanics in this recruitment ad, showing two up-and-coming Latinos.

The rate of home ownership varies widely among Hispanic subgroups. For the three major Hispanic subgroups, ownership is higher among Cuban and Mexican households, 47 percent and 43 percent, respectively, and lowest for Puerto Rican households, 23 percent. But ownership was reportedly highest (50 percent) for Hispanic households in the "Other Hispanics" category which includes people from Spain (Figure 3.14).

Again, cultural insight is important in selling homes to Hispanics. Strategies targeting the Hispanic real estate market should differ for the foreign- and native-born, particularly for those whose

The message, "Sprint makes it possible for you to communicate more with your loved ones," hits home.

length of stay in the United States has been short, say, 10 years or less. To a Hispanic immigrant, buying a home is not only an investment decision but also a decision to stay in the United States permanently rather than keeping open the option of returning to the immigrant's country of origin. For most people, buying a home is a major decision involving putting down roots, and many Hispanics residing in the United States have not yet consciously decided that it will be their long-term homeland. Home ownership connotes stability and permanency. It is up to marketers to introduce to Hispanics alternative ways of thinking regarding home ownership and long-term investments in general. Also, the longer foreign-born Hispanics have resided in the United States, the more easily they can be motivated to purchase a home. Finally, as the native Hispanic population grows older, that population will contain a greater number of prospective buyers.

TELEPHONE SERVICES

AT&T's bilingual direct-mail piece. The spokesperson, soccer champion Pelé is well-known to Hispanics. The message, "Your connection to the world just got better," appeals to customers making international calls.

Hispanics are great consumers of telephone services, and they allocate more money to this area of household spending than either non-Hispanic whites or African Americans. Given the large number of foreign-born Hispanics now living in the United States and their family-oriented culture (see Chapter 4, p. 167), it is easy to understand their love affair with long-distance calls—it is important to them to stay in close touch with their families and friends. In 1990 and 1991 Hispanics spent an annual average of $661 per household on telephone services, amounting to about 38 percent of all Hispanic utility bills (Table 3.15), more than both non-Hispanic whites and African Americans. In terms of local calls, Hispanics are also frequent phone users. Communicating frequently with the children at home and with friends is a feature of the Hispanic culture.

Phone companies targeting Hispanics should always keep in mind that emotionally driven bilingual or Spanish-language advertising, information, and support are essential to attract, entice, and retain Hispanic customers. In addition, new arrivals (that is, foreign-born Hispanics) require special marketing attention and support because a very large percentage did not have phones in their homes before immigrating to the United States, owing to the much lower availability and high cost of telephone services in Latin America (Figure 3.15).

Telephone companies and related businesses should expect continuous growth in the Hispanic market. On the one hand, foreign-born Hispanics are projected to continue to migrate to the United States in large numbers well into the next century. On the other hand, Hispanics tend to relocate quite often within the U.S., leaving friends and relatives behind with whom they keep in close touch by phone. Therefore, Hispanics will continue to be heavy users of telephone services.

Major housekeeping expenditures include laundry, cleaning supplies, furniture, appliances, and miscellaneous household equipment. Hispanics spend on these items about 22 percent of the dollar amount marked for shelter expenses. On average, Hispanics spend more money ($1,124) than African Americans ($925) but less than non-Hispanic whites, ($1,689). Also, Hispanics spend more on laundry and cleaning supplies ($140) than either non-Hispanic whites ($112) or African Americans ($119) (Figure 3.16 and Table 3.15).

HOUSEKEEPING SUPPLIES/EQUIPMENT

Apparel and apparel services is the fourth-largest category in the Hispanic budget. On average, each household spends $1,736 on clothing and shoes (Table 3.17). Expenditures for women exceed those for men by about 1.5 times; those for girls exceed those for boys 7 percent to 6 percent; and expenditures for adults exceed those for children, 47 percent to 22 percent (Figure 3.17).

CLOTHING

Overall Hispanic households spend about the same as non-Hispanic white households and a little more than African-American households on apparel (Table 3.17). But relative to non-Hispanic whites, Hispanic households spend more on children and less on adults and on footwear. Hispanic households spend more on babies, girls, men, and on footwear and less on boys and women than African Americans (Figure 3.18 and Table 3.17).

As illustrated by these figures, clothing and footwear are big items in the mind-set of Hispanic consumers. Again, this attitude can be tied to demographic and cultural factors that contribute to our understanding of why Hispanics spend more than the other two groups. For instance, as previously discussed, Hispanics have larger families than the other two groups (U.S. Bureau of the Census, 1992, 52). Hispanic women have on average more

One of Sears' Spanish-language ads.

children than non-Hispanic whites and African Americans, which alone would indicate that Hispanic households need to spend more in clothes to dress their children. According to the U.S. Bureau of the Census (1991d, 53), in 1991 the average number of children per Hispanic family with children under 18 was 3.82, compared with 3.51 for African American families and 3.12 for white families.

Hispanics also tend to dress more formally. They usually like to dress up when visiting friends or relatives, going to church, to the movies, or just going to the local mall or grocery store. This appears to be more so for women and children than for men. And Hispanic women do spend more money on clothing per household than men (Figure 3.17 and Table 3.17). This formality in dressing habits is changing as well, as Hispanics learn that casual clothing are more comfortable and acceptable in American society.

In sum, Hispanics are an appealing market segment for manufacturers and services in several categories. Many food, clothing, retail, and telecommunications companies are aggressively competing today for their patronage. Given the Hispanic market's demographic trends and its growth in disposable income, savvy businesses are ensuring their share in the Hispanic market into the 21st century.

Levi's creates brand awareness among youngsters with this coloring book for preschoolers, called "Let's Get Dressed."

■ *References*

Hispanic Market Connections. *The National Hispanic Database: Northern California, 1992.* Los Altos, Calif. HMC, 1992a.

————. *The National Hispanic Database: Southern California, 1992.* Los Altos, Calif.: HMC, 1992.

————. *Chicago ADI Database.* Los Altos, Calif.: HMC, 1993.

Population Reference Bureau. *World Population Data Sheet.* Washington, D.C., 1993.

U.S. Bureau of the Census. *Household Income in 1989 for Households with a Hispanic Origin Householder.* CPH-L-94. Washington, D.C.: Bureau of the Census 1989.

————. *Hispanic Origin Persons Below Poverty Level by Age: 1990.* CPH-L-95. Washington, D.C.: USBC, 1990b 1989.

————. "Consumer Expenditure Survey, 1985–1986." Unpublished tables. Washington, D.C.: Department of Labor, November 22, 1991a.

————. "Consumer Expenditure Survey, 1989–1990." Unpublished Tables. Washington, D.C.: Department of Labor, December 10, 1991b.

———. "Consumer Expenditure Survey, 1990–1991." Unpublished Tables. Washington, D.C.: Department of Labor, December 30, 1991c.

———. *The Hispanic Population in the United States: March 1991. Current Population Reports*, series P-20, no. 455. Washington, D.C.: Government Printing Office, 1991d.

———. *Statistical Abstract of the United States: 1992.* 112th ed. Washington, D.C.: Government Printing Office, 1992a.

———. *American Housing Survey for the United States in 1991.* Current Housing Reports. H150/91. Washington, D.C.: Government Printing Office, 1993a.

———. *The Hispanic Population in the United States: March 1992.* By Jesus Garcia. Current Population Reports, series P-20, no. 465RV. Washington, D.C.: Government Printing Office, 1993b.

———. *The Hispanic Population in the United States: March 1993.* By Patricia A. Montgomery. Currents Population Reports, series P-20, no. 475. Washington, D.C.: Government Printing Office, 1994.

Levi's challenges the Hispanic inclination to dress more formally by showing a couple who looks stylish in their blue jeans. The slogan: "They always fit [well]."

At a Glance . . .
The Hispanic Consumer

U.S. Hispanics earn and spend large amounts of money.

U.S. Hispanics earn more per capita than Hispanics in Latin America.

California has the largest number of affluent Hispanic households in the United States.

As a group Cubans are more affluent than any other group.

In absolute numbers there are far more affluent Mexican U.S. households than Cuban ones—
488,106 versus 93,220 in 1991.

Hispanics spend proportionally more money on food than non-Hispanics.

Hispanics spend more money on clothing and telephone services than non-Hispanics.

Sources: Hispanic Market Connections, 1992; U.S. Bureau of the Census, 1993b.

Figure 3.1 The U.S. Hispanic Market

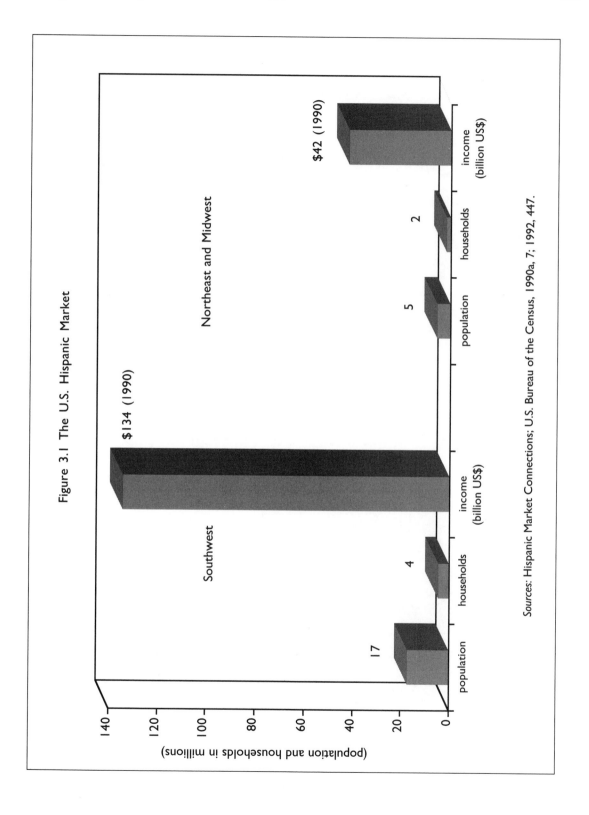

Sources: Hispanic Market Connections; U.S. Bureau of the Census, 1990a, 7; 1992, 447.

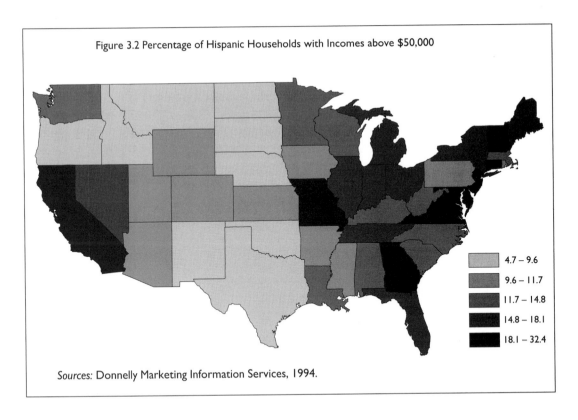

Figure 3.2 Percentage of Hispanic Households with Incomes above $50,000

	4.7 – 9.6
	9.6 – 11.7
	11.7 – 14.8
	14.8 – 18.1
	18.1 – 32.4

Sources: Donnelly Marketing Information Services, 1994.

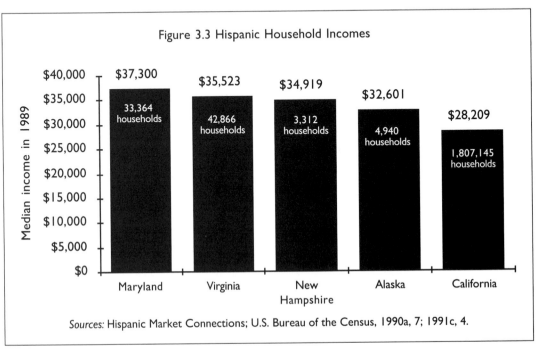

Figure 3.3 Hispanic Household Incomes

Median income in 1989

- Maryland: $37,300 — 33,364 households
- Virginia: $35,523 — 42,866 households
- New Hampshire: $34,919 — 3,312 households
- Alaska: $32,601 — 4,940 households
- California: $28,209 — 1,807,145 households

Sources: Hispanic Market Connections; U.S. Bureau of the Census, 1990a, 7; 1991c, 4.

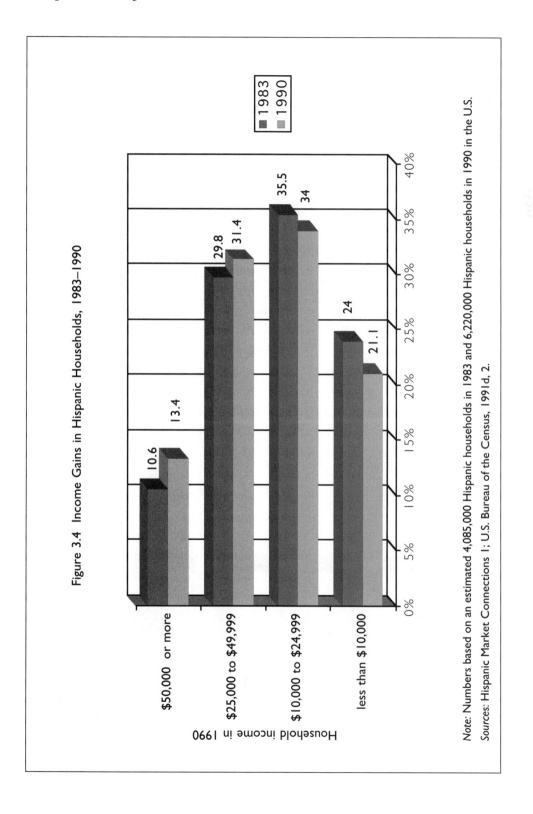

Figure 3.4 Income Gains in Hispanic Households, 1983–1990

Note: Numbers based on an estimated 4,085,000 Hispanic households in 1983 and 6,220,000 Hispanic households in 1990 in the U.S.

Sources: Hispanic Market Connections 1; U.S. Bureau of the Census, 1991d, 2.

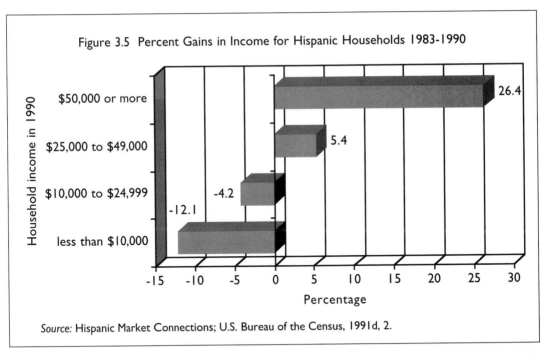

Figure 3.5 Percent Gains in Income for Hispanic Households 1983-1990

Source: Hispanic Market Connections; U.S. Bureau of the Census, 1991d, 2.

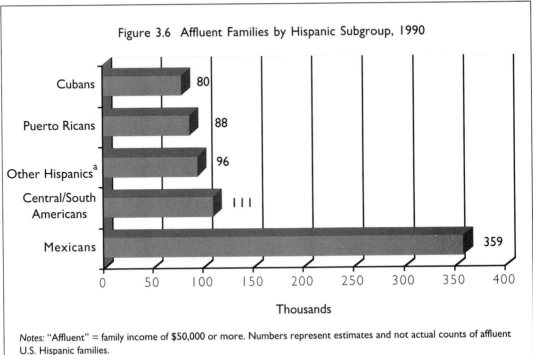

Figure 3.6 Affluent Families by Hispanic Subgroup, 1990

Notes: "Affluent" = family income of $50,000 or more. Numbers represent estimates and not actual counts of affluent U.S. Hispanic families.
[a] Includes people who identify themselves as "Hispanics" from other countries, e.g. Spain.

Source: Hispanic Market Connections; U.S. Bureau of the Census, 1991d, 18-19.

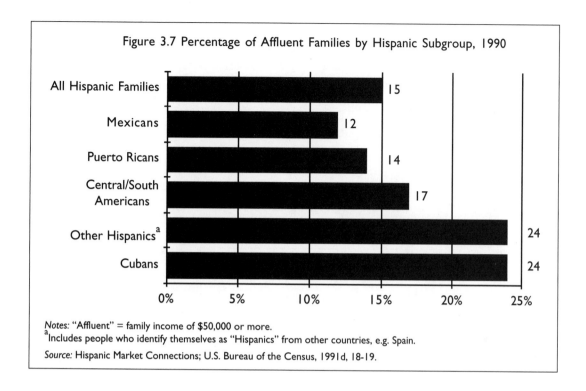

Figure 3.7 Percentage of Affluent Families by Hispanic Subgroup, 1990

Notes: "Affluent" = family income of $50,000 or more.
[a] Includes people who identify themselves as "Hispanics" from other countries, e.g. Spain.

Source: Hispanic Market Connections; U.S. Bureau of the Census, 1991d, 18-19.

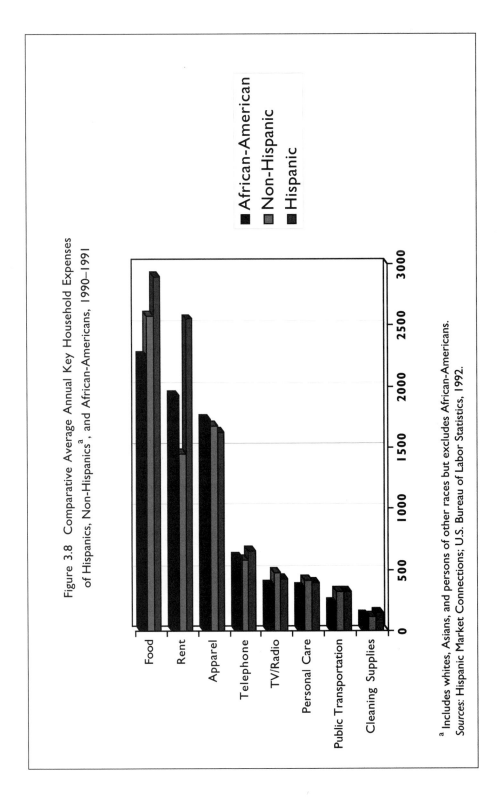

Figure 3.8 Comparative Average Annual Key Household Expenses of Hispanics, Non-Hispanics[a], and African-Americans, 1990–1991

[a] Includes whites, Asians, and persons of other races but excludes African-Americans.
Sources: Hispanic Market Connections; U.S. Bureau of Labor Statistics, 1992.

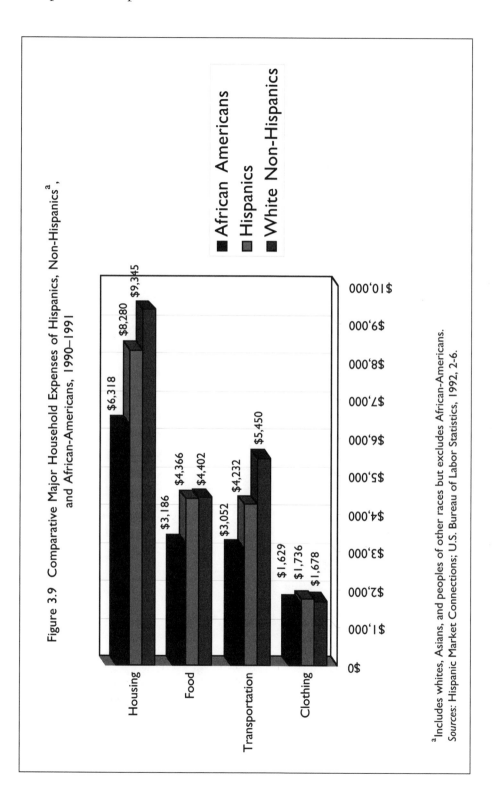

Figure 3.9 Comparative Major Household Expenses of Hispanics, Non-Hispanics[a], and African-Americans, 1990–1991

Housing: African Americans $6,318; Hispanics $8,280; White Non-Hispanics $9,345
Food: African Americans $3,186; Hispanics $4,366; White Non-Hispanics $4,402
Transportation: African Americans $3,052; Hispanics $4,232; White Non-Hispanics $5,450
Clothing: African Americans $1,629; Hispanics $1,736; White Non-Hispanics $1,678

Legend: African Americans, Hispanics, White Non-Hispanics

[a]Includes whites, Asians, and peoples of other races but excludes African-Americans.
Sources: Hispanic Market Connections; U.S. Bureau of Labor Statistics, 1992, 2-6.

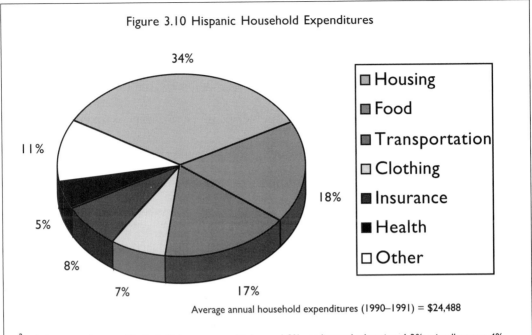

Figure 3.10 Hispanic Household Expenditures

Housing
Food
Transportation
Clothing
Insurance
Health
Other

Average annual household expenditures (1990–1991) = $24,488

[a]Includes entertainment, 4%; alcoholic beverages and tobacco, 1.8%; reading and education, 1.3%; miscellaneous, 4%.

Sources: Hispanic Market Connections; U.S. Bureau of Labor Statistics, 1992, 2-6.

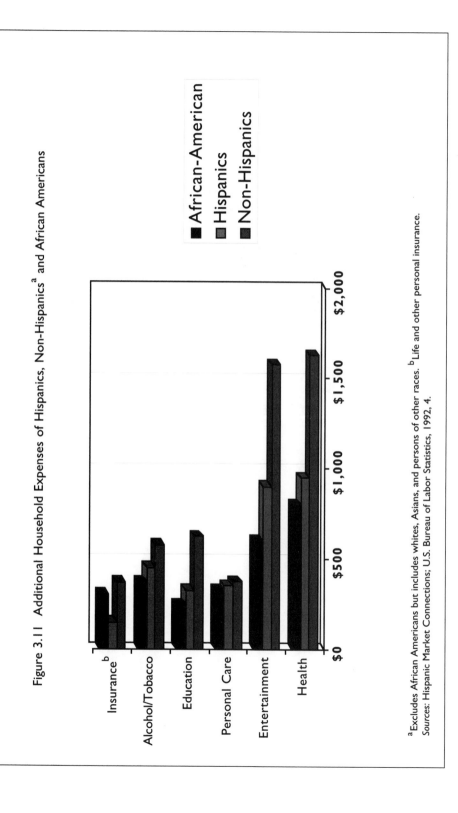

Figure 3.11 Additional Household Expenses of Hispanics, Non-Hispanics[a] and African Americans

[a]Excludes African Americans but includes whites, Asians, and persons of other races. [b]Life and other personal insurance.
Sources: Hispanic Market Connections; U.S. Bureau of Labor Statistics, 1992, 4.

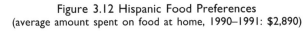

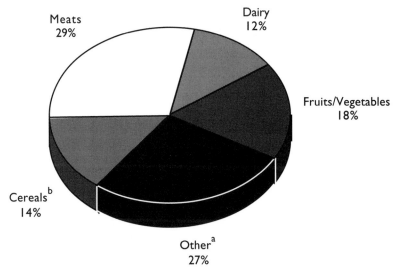

Figure 3.12 Hispanic Food Preferences
(average amount spent on food at home, 1990–1991: $2,890)

Meats
29%

Dairy
12%

Fruits/Vegetables
18%

Cereals[b]
14%

Other[a]
27%

[a]Includes sugar, other sweets, fats and oils, miscellaneous items, non-alcoholic beverages, and food prepared by consumer.

[b]Includes cereal, cereal products, and bakery.

Sources: Hispanic Market Connections; U.S. Bureau of Labor Statistics, 1992, 2.

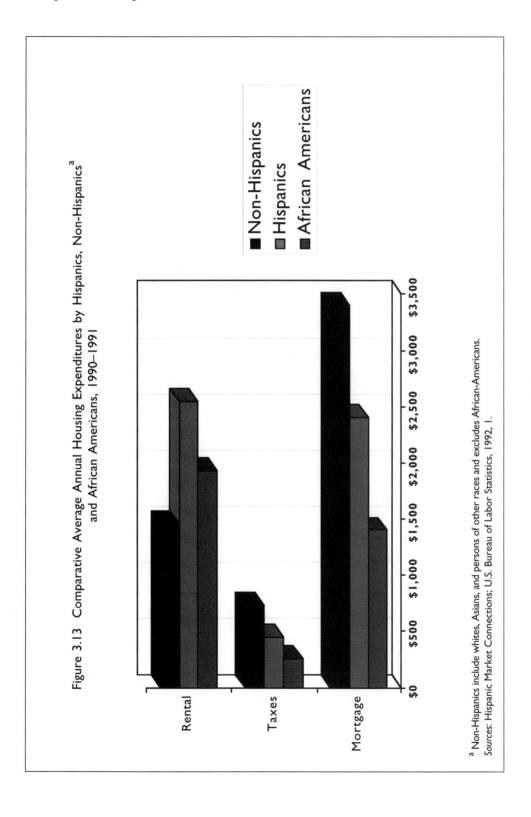

Figure 3.13 Comparative Average Annual Housing Expenditures by Hispanics, Non-Hispanics[a] and African Americans, 1990–1991

[a] Non-Hispanics include whites, Asians, and persons of other races and excludes African-Americans.
Sources: Hispanic Market Connections; U.S. Bureau of Labor Statistics, 1992, I.

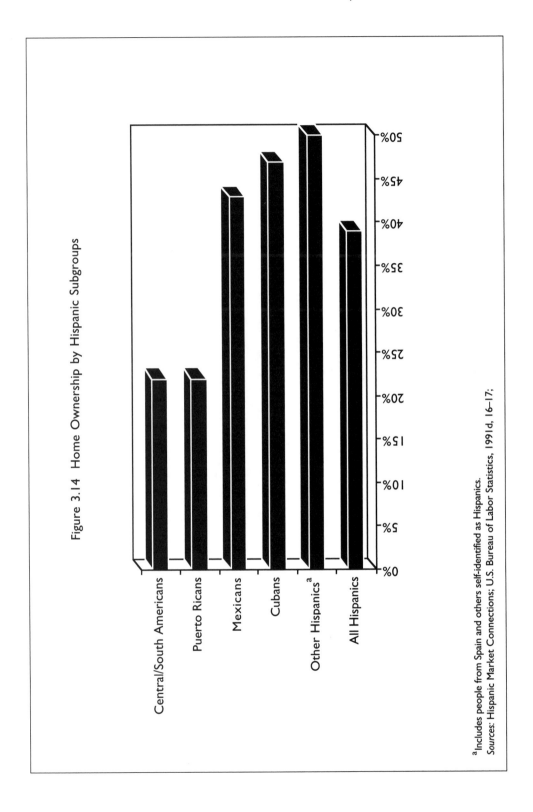

Figure 3.14 Home Ownership by Hispanic Subgroups

[a]Includes people from Spain and others self-identified as Hispanics.
Sources: Hispanic Market Connections; U.S. Bureau of Labor Statistics, 1991d, 16–17;

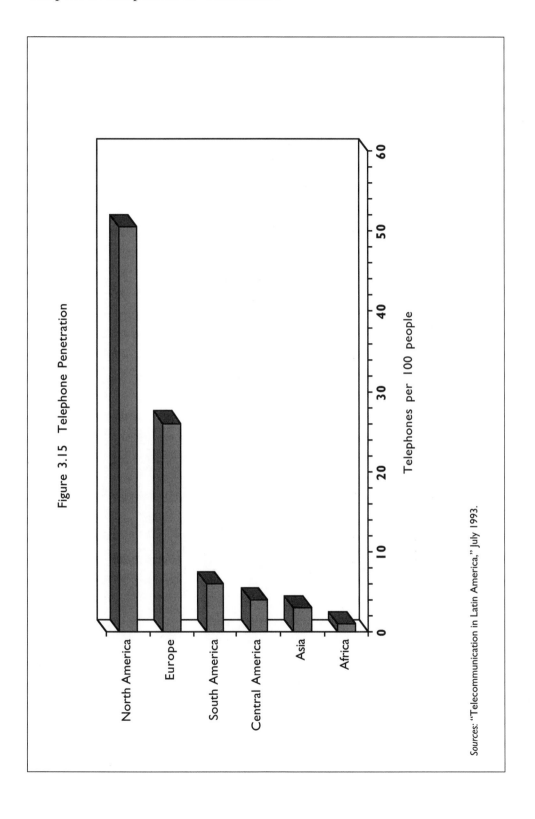

Figure 3.15 Telephone Penetration

Telephones per 100 people

North America

Europe

South America

Central America

Asia

Africa

0 10 20 30 40 50 60

Sources: "Telecommunication in Latin America," July 1993.

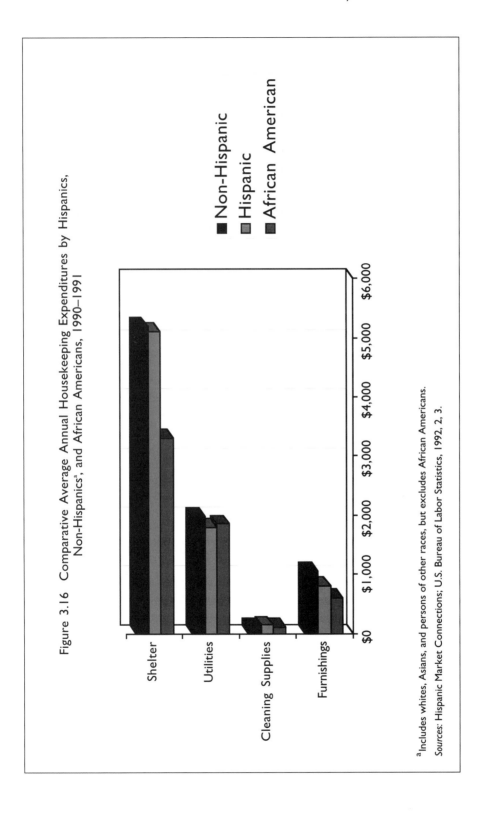

Figure 3.16 Comparative Average Annual Housekeeping Expenditures by Hispanics, Non-Hispanics[a], and African Americans, 1990–1991

[a]Includes whites, Asians, and persons of other races, but excludes African Americans.

Sources: Hispanic Market Connections; U.S. Bureau of Labor Statistics, 1992, 2, 3.

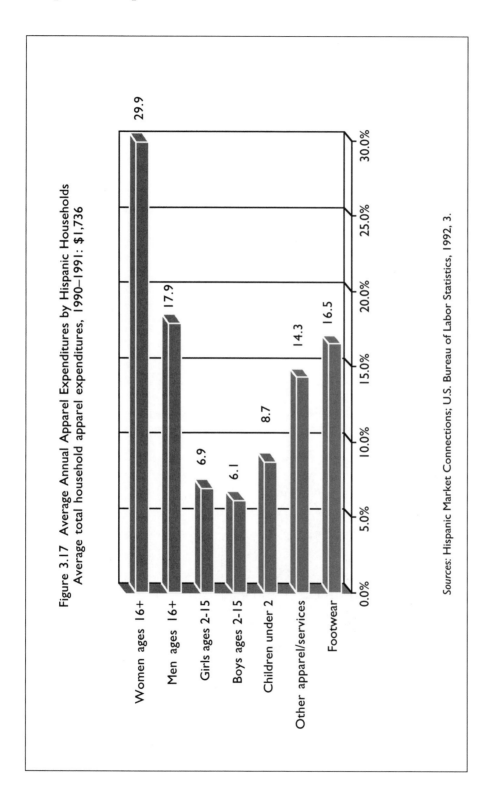

Figure 3.17 Average Annual Apparel Expenditures by Hispanic Households
Average total household apparel expenditures, 1990–1991: $1,736

Sources: Hispanic Market Connections; U.S. Bureau of Labor Statistics, 1992, 3.

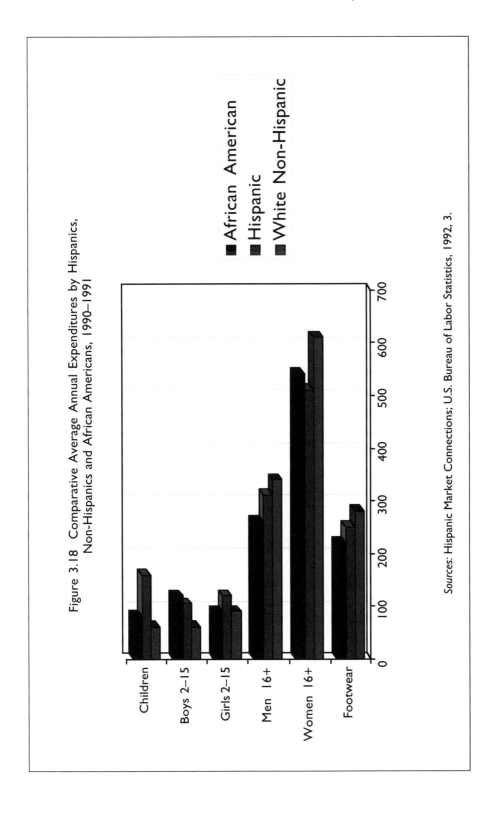

Figure 3.18 Comparative Average Annual Expenditures by Hispanics, Non-Hispanics and African Americans, 1990–1991

Sources: Hispanic Market Connections; U.S. Bureau of Labor Statistics, 1992, 3.

Table 3.1 Hispanic Income by Country, 1990

	Income Per Capita (1991 U.S. $)
U.S. Hispanics	$8,662
Honduras	6,330
Puerto Rico	2,610
Venezuela	2,860
Uruguay	2,870
Mexico	2,780
Argentina	1,930
Costa Rica	2,160
Chile	1,070
El Salvador	930
Guatemala	570

Sources: U.S. Bureau of the Census, *Statistical Abstract of the United States,* 1992a, 454; Population Reference Bureau, 1993.

Table 3.2 States with Hispanic Household Incomes above the U.S. Median

	Hispanic Median Income (1989)	Number of Hispanic Households (thousands)
Maryland	$37,300	33,364
Virginia	35,523	42,866
New Hampshire	34,919	3,312
Alaska	32,601	4,940
Hawaii	31,153	19,495
New Jersey	30,140	207,689
Vermont	29,145	1,126
Maine	28,870	1,865
Georgia	28,351	27,939
California	28,209	1,807,145
Delaware	28,062	4,206
Indiana	28,019	27,022
Illinois	27,945	221,029
Michigan	26,939	50,888
Missouri	26,838	17,868
Nevada	26,582	34,921
District of Columbia	26,295	10,313
South Carolina	25,795	8,013
Connecticut	25,116	58,798
Minnesota	25,295	12,338
Ohio	25,053	38,422
Florida	24,501	505,350

U.S. Hispanic median: $24,156
Total number of Hispanic households: 5,872,040

Sources: Hispanic Market Connections; U.S. Bureau of the Census 1990a, 7.

Table 3.3 Household Income of Hispanics, Non-Hispanics, and African Americans

	Average Annual Household Income for 1990–1991		
	Hispanics	Non-Hispanics	African Americans
Income before taxes	$25,686	$34,717	22,046
Wages and salaries	20,746	26,002	17,797
Self-employment income	1,692	2,724	406
Social security, private and government retirement	1,334	3,848	2,063
Interest, dividends, rental income, other property income	387	1,282	132
Unemployment and workers' compensation, veteran's benefits	346	226	119
Public assistance, supplemental/security income, food stamps	846	231	1,220
Regular contributions for support	170	296	128
Other income	165	108	101
Personal taxes	1,700	3,332	1,670
Federal income taxes	1,360	2,588	1,228
State and local income taxes	311	629	400
Other Taxes	29	115	41
Income after taxes	23,986	31,385	20,376

Note: Non-Hispanic category includes all groups except African Americans.

Sources: Hispanic Market Connections; U.S. Bureau of Labor Statistics, 1992a.

Table 3.4 Hispanic Household Income, 1983–1992

	1992	1983	% change
Total Households	6,626,000[*]	4,085,000[*]	62.2
Household Income			
Less than $10,000	20.4	24.0	-13.7
$10,000 to $24,999	33.4	33.5	7.0
$25,000 to $49,999	30.7	29.8	3.0
$50,000 or more	15.5	10.6	46.2

[*]Estimated number of households.

Sources: Hispanic Market Connections; U.S. Bureau of the Census, 1991d, 2, and 1994, 16.

Table 3.5 Affluent Hispanic Households in States with Largest Hispanic Population[a]

	Number of Affluent Hispanic Households	Percentage of Total Hispanic Households
California	373,456	39.4
Texas	106,086	11.2
New York	105,435	11.1
Florida	86,540	9.1
New Jersey	48,108	5.1
Illinois	39,079	4.1
Arizona	19,807	2.1
New Mexico	16,132	1.7
Washington, D.C. area[b]	25,468	2.7
Colorado	15,059	1.6
Ten State Total	835,170	88.0
U.S. Total	948,764	100

[a]Affluent = incomes of $50,000 or more.

[b]Includes Washington, D.C. and counties of Maryland and Virginia.

Sources: Hispanic Market Connections; U.S. Bureau of the Census, 1990a, 7.

Table 3.6 California's Affluent Hispanic Households by Metropolitan Areas, 1990

	Total Hispanic Households	Hispanic Households with $50,000+ Incomes	Percentage of Total Hispanic Households
Southern California			
Los Angeles-Long Beach	784,171	151,192	19.28
Anaheim-Santa Ana	121,474	35,867	29.53
Riverside-San Bernardino	164,172	33,451	20.38
San Diego	124,588	22,477	18.04
Oxnard-Ventura	38,597	11,199	29.02
Santa-Barbara-Santa Maria-Lompoc	23,451	4,325	18.44
Total	1,256,453	258,991	20.60
Northern California			
San Jose	77,710	24,506	31.54
Oakland	76,295	22,262	29.18
San Francisco	64,564	17,856	27.66
Sacramento	49,227	9,558	19.42
Fresno	59,261	5,727	9.66
Stockton	27,957	4,462	15.96
Bakersfield	17,094	3,928	11.03
Vallejo-Fairfield-Napa	15,165	3,836	25.30
Salinas-Seaside-Monterrey	26,029	3,857	14.82
Modesto	19,468	2,980	15.31
Santa Cruz	10,711	2,379	22.21
Visalia-Tulare-Porterville	27,900	2,143	7.68
Merced	13,732	1,224	8.91
Yuba City	4,345	418	11.68
Redding	1,584	185	11.68
Total	491,042	105,291	21.4

Sources: Hispanic Market Connections; Donnelley Marketing Information Services.

Table 3.7 New York's Affluent Hispanic Households by Metropolitan Area, 1990

	Total Households	Households with $50,000+ Income	Percentage of Total Households
New York	583,596	83,033	14.23
Rochester	8,990	1,135	12.63
Buffalo	6,873	498	7.11
Orange County	5,270	1,290	24.48
Troy	4,473	873	19.52
Syracuse	2,520	327	12.98
Poughkeepsie	2,155	738	34.25
Utica-Rome	1,282	127	9.91
Jamestown-Dunkirk	1,134	51	4.50
Binghamton	808	146	18.07
Niagara Falls	652	101	15.49
Glens Falls	251	36	14.34
Total	618,004	88,346	14.29

Sources: Hispanic Market Connections; Donnelly Marketing Information Services.

Table 3.8 New Jersey's Affluent Hispanic Households by Metropolitan Area, 1990

	Total Households	Households with $50,000+ Income	Percentage of Total Households
Jersey City	59,884	10,684	17.84
Phildalephia, PA-NJ	47,903	6,527	13.63
Monmouth-Ocean	10,154	3,206	31.57
Bethlehem, PA-NJ	8,216	1,003	12.21
Atlantic City	5,120	769	15.02
Trenton	5,112	1,110	21.71
Wilmington, DE-NJ-MD	3,936	707	17.96
Total	140,325	24,006	17.10

Sources: Hispanic Market Connections; Donnelly Marketing Information Services.

Table 3.9 Texas' Affluent Hispanic Households by Metropolitan Area, 1990

	Total Households	Households with $50,000+ Income	Percentage of Total Households
Houston	186,816	23,281	12.46
San Antonio	178,442	17,186	9.63
El Paso	107,558	9,383	8.72
Dallas	94,531	12,468	13.19
Brownsville-Harlingen	52,554	3,519	6.7
Corpus Christi	51,416	4,771	9.2
Austin	47,386	5,285	11.15
Laredo	31,300	2,847	9.1
Lubbock	13,838	728	5.26
Galveston-Texas City	9.224	1,151	12.48
Odessa	9,805	488	4.98
Brazoria	8.430	1,354	16.06
Killeen-Temple	8,294	499	6.02
Victoria	7,286	631	8.66
San Angelo	7,088	466	6.57
Amarillo	7.056	478	6.77
Waco	6,479	355	5.48
Midland	6,070	449	7.40
Abilene	4,630	214	4.62
Beaumont-Port Arthur	4,626	576	12.45
Bryan-College Station	4,562	328	7.19
Wichita Falls	2,917	212	7.27
Tyler	2,152	90	4.18
Longview-Marshal	1,320	59	4.47
Sherman-Denison	747	43	5.76
Total	854,527	86,861	10.16

Sources: Hispanic Market Connections; Donnelly Marketing Information Services.

Table 3.10 Florida's Affluent Hispanic Households by Metropolitan Area, 1990

	Total Households	Households with $50,000+ Income	Percentage of Total Households
Miami-Hialeah	319,803	56,630	17.7
Ft. Lauderdale-Hollywood-Pomano	35,368	7,304	20.6
Tampa-St. Petersburg-Clearwater	46,606	7,026	15.1
Orlando	29,335	4,191	14.3
Jacksonville	7,331	1,324	18.06
Naples	5,050	492	9.8
Winter Haven	4,535	465	10.3
Fort Myers	4,215	493	11.7
Daytona Beach	3,895	385	9.9
Fort Pierce	2,859	368	12.9
Gainesville	2,497	352	14.1
Bradenton	2,340	180	7.7
Pensacola	1,983	256	12.9
Sarasota	1,931	349	18.0
Ocala	1,845	123	6.67
Tallahassee	1,719	271	15.7
Fort Walton Beach	1,220	158	12.9
Ranata City	675	68	10.1
Total	473,207	80,435	16.9

Sources: Hispanic Market Connections; Donnelly Marketing Information Services.

Table 3.11 Illinois' Affluent Hispanic Households by Metropolitan Area, 1990

	Total Households	Households with $50,000+ Income	Percentage of Total Households
Chicago	188,785	31,202	16.53
Aurora-Elgin	10,250	2,182	21.29
Lake County	8,811	2,081	23.62
Joliet	4,876	1,424	29.20
Rockford	2,620	402	15.34
Peoria	1,025	154	15.02
Springfield	430	60	13.75
Kankakee	469	60	12.79
Decatur	158	41	25.95
Bloomington-Normal	465	36	7.74
Total	217,889	37,642	17.3

Sources: Hispanic Market Connections; Donnelly Marketing Information Services.

Table 3.12 Arizona's Affluent Hispanic Households by Metropolitan Area, 1990

	Total Households	Households with $50,000+ Income	Percentage of Total Households
Phoenix	90,408	11,051	12.22
Tucson	47,029	4,885	10.39
Yuma	11,242	838	7.45
Total	148,679	16,774	11.28

Sources: Hispanic Market Connections; Donnelly Marketing Information Services.

Table 3.13 New Mexico's Affluent Hispanic Households by Metropolitan Area, 1990

	Total Households	Households with $50,000+ Income	Percentage of Total Households
Albuquerque	57,721	6,555	11.36
Santa Fe	16,458	2,909	17.68
Las Cruces	21,252	1,271	5.98
Total	95,431	10,735	11.25

Sources: Hispanic Market Connections; Donnelly Marketing Information Services.

Table 3.14 Colorado's Affluent Hispanic Households by Metropolitan Area, 1990

	Total Households	Households with $50,000+ Income	Percentage of Total Households
Denver	65,594	10,118	15.43
Colorado Springs	10,514	1,059	10.07
Pueblo	14,286	949	6.64
Greeley	7,588	658	8.67
Boulder-Longmont	4,491	629	14.01
Fort Collins-Loveland	3,535	440	13.07
Total	106,008	13,853	12.45

Sources: Hispanic Market Connections; Donnelly Marketing Information Services.

Table 3.15 Consumer Housing Expenditures by Market Segment, 1990–1991

	Hispanic[a]	Non-Hispanic[b]	African American
TOTAL HOUSING EXPENDITURE	8,280	9,345	6,318
Shelter	5,094	5,199	3,380
Owned dwellings	2,423	3,375	1,388
Mortgage interest and charges	1,635	2,010	877
Property taxes	443	764	262
Maintenance, repairs, insurance, and other	346	601	250
Rented dwellings	2,566	1,441	1,908
Other lodging	105	384	84
Utilities, fuels, and public services	1,727	1,972	1,809
Natural gas	232	245	288
Electricity	611	804	696
Fuel oil and other fuels	29	114	42
Telephone services	661	600	614
Water and public services	194	210	168
Household Operations	335	485	204
Personal services	208	226	126
Other household expenses	127	259	78
Housekeeping supplies	341	435	288
Laundry and cleaning supplies	140	112	119
Other household products	119	191	109
Postage and stationary	82	133	60
Household furnishings and equipment	783	1,254	637
Household textiles	78	107	49
Furniture	272	318	186
Floor covering	28	113	72
Major appliances	109	145	118
Small appliances, miscellaneous housewares	50	85	31
Miscellaneous household equipment	247	485	181

Notes: Total average annual expenditures for all items: Hispanics, $24,488; non-Hispanics, $30,474; African Americans, $19,398.

Totals within household expenditure categories may not add due to rounding.

[a]Expenditures determined from survey sample of Hispanic households, also referred to as consumer units.

[b]Excludes African Americans

Sources: Hispanic Market Connections; U.S. Bureau of Labor Statistics, 1992.

Table 3.16 Consumer Food Expenditures by Market Segment, 1990–1991

	Hispanic[a]	Non-Hispanic[b]	African American
FOOD	4,366	4,402	3,186
Food at home	2,890	2,578	2,258
Cereals and bakery products	393	394	313
Cereals and cereal products	156	137	125
Bakery products	237	258	187
Meats, poultry, fish, and eggs	847	660	826
Beef	292	216	237
Pork	164	129	201
Other meats	117	99	104
Poultry	135	109	148
Fish and seafood	82	80	99
Eggs	57	28	36
Dairy products	338	302	195
Fresh milk and cream	188	135	93
Other dairy products	149	168	102
Fruits and vegetables	521	417	359
Fresh fruits	171	130	102
Fresh vegetables	165	121	103
Processed fruits	109	95	86
Processed vegetables	76	71	68
Other food at home	792	804	566
Sugar and other sweets	89	101	77
Fats and oils	77	70	63
Miscellaneous foods	350	368	252
Nonalcoholic beverages	249	222	165
Food prepared by consumer unit on out-of-town trips	27	43	8
Food away from home	1,476	1,825	927

Note: Total average annual expenditures for all items: Hispanics, $24,488; non-Hispanics, $30,474; African Americans, $19,398.

Totals within food expenditure categories may not add due to rounding.

[a] Expenditures determined from survey sample of Hispanic households, also referred to as consumer units.

[b] Excludes African Americans.

Sources: Hispanic Market Connections; U.S. Bureau of Labor Statistics 1992.

Table 3.17 Miscellaneous Consumer Expenditures by Market Segment, 1990–1991

	Hispanic[a]	Non-Hispanic[b]	African American
TRANSPORTATION	4,232	5,450	3,052
Vehicle purchases (net outlay)	1,596	2,290	1,018
Cars and trucks, new	736	1,219	508
Cars and trucks, used	860	1,045	508
Other vehicles	–	25	–
Gasoline and motor oils	950	1,063	709
Other vehicle expenses	1,374	1,783	1,116
Vehicle finance charges	199	307	216
Mantainance repairs	566	628	398
Vehicle insurance	487	621	385
Vehicle rental,leases, licenses, etc.	123	228	117
Public transportation	312	313	208
PERSONAL INSURANCE AND PENSIONS	1,914	2,866	1,713
Life and other personal insurance	148	372	304
Pensions and Social Security	1,766	2,494	1,408
APPAREL AND APPAREL SERVICES	1,736	1,678	1,629
Men and boys	417	414	381
Men 16 and over	311	345	259
Boys 2–15	106	69	122
Women and girls	632	700	635
Women 16 and over	510	610	543
Girls 2–15	121	91	92
Children under 2	152	69	80
Footwear	286	221	307
Other apparel products and services	249	274	226

(continued next page)

Table 3.17 Miscellaneous Consumer Expenditures by Market Segment, 1990–1991
(*continued*)

	Hispanic[a]	Non-Hispanic[b]	African American
HEALTH CARE	951	1,645	808
Health Insurance	384	666	370
Medical services	401	606	256
Drugs	114	275	147
Medical supplies	52	97	35
ENTERTAINMENT	911	1,586	619
Fees and admissions	211	417	124
Television, radios, and sound equipment	411	479	339
Pets, toys, and playground equipment	152	302	109
Other entertainment supplies, equipment, and services	137	389	47
OTHER	1,613	2,570	1,585
Miscellaneous	592	910	520
Personal care products and services	362	389	332
Cash contributions	358	962	569
Alcoholic beverages	301	309	164

Note: Non-Hispanics exclude African-Americans.

Totals within expenditure categories may not add due to rounding.

[a] Expenditures determined from a survey sample of Hispanic households, also referred to as consumer units.

[b] Excludes African Americans.

Sources: Hispanic Market Connections; U.S. Bureau of Labor Statistics, 1992, 3, 4.

Table 3.18
Home Ownership among U.S. and Foreign-Born Hispanics in California and Chicago Areas
(**In thousands**)

	Total	(%)	Foreign-Born	(%)	U.S.-Born	(%)
Northern California	797	(100)	154	(19)	643	(81)
Southern California	331	(100)	85	(26)	246	(74)
Chicago area	261	(100)	78	(30)	183	(70)

Source: Hispanic Market Connections, 1992; 1993; 1994.

C H A P T E R

■ "It's Not Only a Matter of Language"

■ What is Culture?

■ Communicating in a Bicultural Context

■ "To Sell Me Is to Know Me"

■ Understanding and Thinking in a Different Culture

■ Managing Acculturation and Diversity

■ Cultural Diversity among U.S. Hispanics

Culture and the Hispanic Consumer

■ "It's Not Only a Matter of Language"

In 1987 Hispanic Market Connections, a marketing research company, adopted the slogan, "It's not only a matter of language." At the time, the practice of advertising to Hispanics via Spanish-language television and radio had already been established. The Hispanic population was growing at unprecedented speed. For companies with an eye on the Hispanic market, it made good business sense to advertise their products in a language that their target audience could understand. After all, companies like Kraft, General Foods, Colgate, and Goya Foods, which had traditionally held large shares of the Hispanic market, had been doing it for years with enormous success. So why the slogan?

Advertisers were certainly on the right track in their strategy to use the Spanish language, but in many cases something was missing. The Spanish-language messages that were being sent to consumers lacked "cultural attunement," the background and experiences with which Hispanic people could identify. It was akin to showing Chinese people using knives and forks, or Westerners using chopsticks, to eat their meals. The Spanish-language messages were not reaching as many consumers and were not as effective as they should have been. Even though the language was right, the images, symbols, and experiences were wrong.

It was clear that while the use of the Spanish language was essential to reach a very large share of the U.S. Hispanic market, by itself it was insufficient to gain customers. Different cultures have distinct ways of perceiving, organizing, relating to, and interacting with society. What is perfectly acceptable in one culture may not be acceptable in another. The message needs to fit the cultural context and the mind-set of the audience being targeted. Imagine, for instance, a situation in which people from the same part of the world converse with dear friends. In most societies language is a common cultural bond, but it is only one element among many. There are other things, including customs, friends, dress codes, salutations, and protocol that may be typical of one group but not another. The attitudes, behaviors, and values vary among cultures so what makes sense (or is "in consonance") to members of one group may mystify others.

For example, in many European countries it is acceptable for males to greet each other with a kiss, whereas this would be unacceptable for most Americans. This behavioral difference in greeting protocol is the result of the meaning of the kiss in each society. In European culture the greeting kiss between males means deep, dear affections, while in the United States it has an erotic connotation. This simple example illustrates the relevance of learning to "manage" culture as well as language differences. To communicate successfully with consumers from another culture, it is necessary to do more than just speak the language—one must speak the culture.

Since World War II, the United States has undergone dramatic sociodemographic changes. Women have come into their own; older Americans are growing in number and in political visibility; nontraditional life-styles have achieved near-parity with traditional ones; "domestic partners" has become an acceptable alternative for "married couples"; and having children outside marriage has become more acceptable, particularly in the large urban areas in the country.

Many marketers had only just adjusted to these social changes when along came the 1990 census figures to warn them of another transformation. The latest count for the continental Hispanic population was 24 million. If the noncontinental Hispanic population of Puerto Rico (3.5 million) is added, the conservative count is over 27 million, a very dramatic change in the marketplace. The 1994 U.S. Census Population update places the U.S. continental Hispanic population at 26.6 million (TGE Demographics, 1994). Hence, the 30-million mark will be reached well before the end of the decade.

Thus, Hispanic consumers, who for the most part had been of marginal importance to the general market for more than a century, suddenly became the center of attention. Marketers and advertisers had paid limited regard to Hispanics and knew very little about their culture and social fabric. Unlike the transformations in the general market, marketers lacked cultural insight for the Hispanic market. When it came to targeting Hispanics, general market marketers lacked a point of reference. They could not draw directly from personal experience or look back to previous marketing efforts in order to make the necessary decisions, as they did with the general market. In order to communicate with this new audience, these marketers had to begin with only little knowledge and the most easily available cultural components: Spanish language, popular beliefs about the Hispanic culture, and stereotypes. But, as in advertising and marketing effectively to the general market, the right language was not enough and stereotypes defied reality; thus the slogan, "It's not only a matter of language." Marketers still need to find the right images and context with which Hispanics identify. Because culture is the strongest bond between Hispanics, utilizing cultural values and culturally driven processes to understand, interact, and communicate with the Hispanic market is probably the safest and soundest means to bridge the cultural gap between traditional American and Hispanic cultures. This chapter explains the acculturation process and the many issues surrounding it. We also describe tools for managing the acculturation process and diversity within the Hispanic market.

■ What is Culture?

There are numerous definitions of culture, and explanations of what culture means have been redefined since the concept was first introduced. Yet it can be almost universally agreed that culture is at the core of an individual's behavior and has a profound effect on the individual's degree of assimilation into a particular environment. For the purpose of discussing Hispanics, acculturation, and marketing, a broad definition is in order. Culture, in broad terms, may be defined as "the system of social institutions, traditions, values, and beliefs that characterize a particular social group or country and which are systematically transmitted to succeeding generations" (adapted from Hamburg, 1975, 19). In other words, culture describes the life strategy in all its various components—aspirations, dreams, and emotional, physical, and metaphysical behavioral traits (McGuill, 19). Culture encompasses everything a person has seen and heard from the day of birth—parents, grandparents, siblings, friends, schoolteachers, radio and TV programs, the clergy, etc. It is the deposit of knowledge, experiences, beliefs, meanings, notions of time, spatial relations, concepts of the universe, and other elements acquired in the course of generations through individuals, groups, and mass media.

ACCULTURATION When people immigrate to the United States, they bring with them the cultural aura that reflects both their personal lives and that of their home country. Their thoughts and actions start to mingle little by little with the culture of the host country, in this case the United States. This is what is referred to as the acculturation process, the process of integration of native and traditional values with the dominant culture's values (adapted from Falicov, 1982).

There are several factors affecting the acculturation process, and these can be either external or internal. External factors include, for example, environment, community, and geographic location. Internal factors include an immigrant's degree of formal schooling and availability of a support system.

The U.S. Hispanic market is composed of consumers in different stages of acculturation to American culture. Because waves of Hispanic immigrants have moved from a variety of countries into different geographic regions at different times, the level of acculturation has varied from region to region as well. In addition, within a family unit there may also be different rates of acculturation; for example, Hispanics who arrived in the United States as children or adolescents usually acculturate faster than their parents or other adults.

Many factors affect the means and the speed with which individuals acculturate into the new culture. There are numerous external factors—circumstances over which the person has little or no control. For example, the size of the Hispanic community or neighborhood in which the person lives may either accelerate or slow the acculturation process. If the Hispanic community is large, chances are the transition will be slower than if the newly arrived immigrant lived in a predominantly Anglo neighborhood. In other words, high Hispanic population density tends to slow down the integration process. If the individual lives and works in a predominantly Anglo environment, then he or she will probably adopt some cultural traits faster. Acculturation also varies according to age. Children and adolescents have an easier time than adults adapting to new circumstances. Another external factor that affects the degree of acculturation is the attitude of the community toward the immigrants, the level of acceptance or rejection. If Hispanics are accepted and integrated into American society, rather than ostracized, their chances for a faster acculturation process are higher.

Acculturation Factors

Other factors affecting the nature and speed of acculturation are internal to the individual and include psychological characteristics, educational level, economic status, and the presence or absence of personal and family networks. When immigrants are educated, financially stable, surrounded by friends and family, and familiar with the language, they acculturate faster. Finally, some cultural aspects can be assimilated faster than others. For example, learning a new language is easier than learning new values. Core cultural values and beliefs are more difficult to change, even for highly educated or affluent Hispanics who have resided in the United States for generations (Gordon 1964; Teske and Nelson, as cited in Falicov and Karrer, 1986, 389–390).

Acculturation and Individual Traits

Attitude, personality, and reasons for migration also affect a person's transition from one culture to another. For instance, the expectations and aspirations of an immigrant who came to the U.S. to escape poverty or unemployment will differ from those of the professional immigrant who fled political persecution. The former chose to leave friends, family, and a known world behind for better working opportunities, whereas the latter might have preferred to stay in his or her home country but was compelled to leave for survival reasons. Similarly, the immigrant child brought to the United States by the his or her parents may have a very different set of expectations and experiences than someone who is older and immigrated alone.

The individuals or families who first moved to the United States, first-generation immigrants, tend to be the pioneers, more innovative and less passive than the relatives who come to join them later or the siblings who are born in the United States (second generation).

DOMINANT THEMES WITHIN HISPANIC CULTURE

The cultural divide between Hispanics and other Americans is wide. A significant number of Hispanic men and women arrive in the United States as adults, bringing with them the experiences, life-styles, expectations, values, legends, and dreams acquired in their Latino non-Anglo-Saxon societies. A recent survey found that "almost two thirds of Mexicans and 80 percent of Cubans [interviewed] emigrated to the U.S. as adults" (de la Garza, 1992, 154). The extent to which these newly arrived immigrants participate in American society affects their interpretation and perception of advertising messages and images.

Lack of "cultural affinity" can diminish the effectiveness of an advertising message. Certain products, brands, and services and how to use them may be common knowledge to the general market, but this does not mean that foreign-born or newly arrived Hispanic consumers have the same knowledge. For example, studies by Hispanic Market Connections have shown that unlike most consumers in the general market, a few Hispanics in the West and Southwest prefer to wash their hair with soap rather than shampoo because it is the way they used to do it "back home" and "it works." Studies on infant care revealed that some Hispanic women in these areas continue to wrap their newborn babies tightly with a cloth to "make sure the belly button heals safely"; others do not bathe their infants until their belly button has healed. Other studies show that many new immigrants don't know about new developments in the telecommunications industry and hence, they see no difference between purchasing a rotary phone or a digital phone. So, when telephone companies want to market "call forwarding" or "three-way calling" services to Hispanic customers, they need to market not only the service, but also the whole concept of digital phone lines and why old rotary phones do not work with these new advanced phone services. These are but a few examples illustrating how people from different cultures can relate to or use a product, and the importance of cultural affinity in targeting consumers. Messages, creative strategies, visuals, and symbols must be selected with the consumer's sociocultural marketing background in mind. The point is not that marketers and advertisers should promote old behavior practices (e.g.: not bathing an infant), but they should be aware that differences exist and then decide on a strategy appropriate to that culture. (See Chapter 7 for further information on this subject.) In addition, anyone attempting to reach a Hispanic market should be aware of dominant Hispanic cultural traits, for example, the importance of family, the attitude toward children, and the traditional role of men.

The pillar of Hispanic culture is the family, which includes the extended family of grandparents, uncles, aunts, and cousins. This emphasis Hispanics place on family relations has been called *familismo*. The family's needs and welfare take precedence over the individual member's needs. The family, as a group, is usually the first and only priority. This is reflected in the educational process within the family as well as family members' expectations of each other. "Parents are viewed as being obliged to make all sorts of sacrifices for the children. As a response, the child is expected to show gratitude, for example, assuming responsibility for younger siblings and for the parents in old age. . . . The child internalizes at an early age the overwhelming and powerful role of the parents and the family; the mother tends to define herself as an individual mostly in terms of her family. The father enjoys more freedom but he is responsible for the respectful behavior of his children and feels morally responsible for the behavior of the whole family" (Falcon, 1972, 40).

Familismo

It is not surprising, then, that so much Spanish-language advertising strategy revolves around the family, either explicitly or implicitly.

Children   A major difference between mainstream American and Hispanic cultures is in child-rearing orientations. "Children [in Hispanic families] are not believed to be capable of acting independently until they reach maturity . . . regardless of the physical and emotional development of the child. This leads to parental overconcern for keeping the child close and attached to the family" (Falcon, 1972). This dependency affects the child's decision-making process in purchases and, hence, the marketing and advertising strategy. Even the most basic children's products, such as cereals and toys, need to include the mother (or another adult) in the creative strategy in order to "close the sale more effectively." This is explained in greater detail in "Marketing to Hispanic Youth," beginning on page 334 in Chapter 7.

Machismo   *Machismo* is a complex set of beliefs, attitudes, values, and behaviors pervasive in Hispanic culture that define the role of men. The concept refers to the roles men fulfill according to societal rules and how men view themselves with respect to their environment and other people. It goes beyond treating women in stereotypically dominating ways, or being "macho." It involves men's functioning as providers, protectors, and representatives of their families to the outer world. They have obligations and responsibilities to uphold the honor of family members, to deal effectively with the public sphere, and to maintain the integrity of the family unit. *Machismo* also refers to having socially acceptable manly characteristics, such as being courageous, strong, and virile. The manly image includes being seen as the head of the household, but listening to and being respectful of women. This traditional role provides much more freedom for men than women with regard to sexual activity and public-social interactions.

CULTURAL CHARACTERISTICS AT A GLANCE...   The following traits tend to be prevalent among Hispanics, particularly foreign-born adults. Variations do exist among the various Hispanic subgroups.

✧ Speak Spanish at home.

✧ Mostly Catholic, but Protestants increasing; other religious practices include Santeria and Espiritism (very limited).

✧ Status-oriented—professionals like to be addressed by their title (e.g., doctor, architect, professor, minister or padre).

✧ Family-oriented.

✧ Group-oriented.

✧ Family stratified by sex and age—father, mother, children.

✧ Generational hierarchy—grandparents, children, grandchildren.

✧ Social interaction based on authority and familiarity of the parties involved.

✧ Amicable but formal in business situations—last names preferred; addressing a new client by his or her first name is rarely welcome.

✧ Social graces are important, especially with regard to women and the elderly. A pecking order exists; in a business situation, first shake hands with the man, then offer a chair first to the oldest person, then the wife.

✧ Tend to focus on the present rather than the future, and live the phrase, *¡Dios Dira!* (God will tell!)

Cultural Differences vs. Socioeconomic Differences: A Caveat

"Culture" is an abstract concept that is too broad and oversimplified when applied to an entire group of people, as it is to "Hispanics" in this book. It is often true that a greater difference is found when the various socioeconomic classes are compared than when ethnic groups are compared within each class. It has been suggested to the authors that many working-class Americans would be more closely aligned with the Hispanic value orientation than that of middle-class Americans (Table 4.1). Similarly, international researchers find that the "average U.S. Hispanic" culture is closer to that of the working-class culture in other areas of the world where Spanish or a Latin-based language is spoken, such as Central and South America, Mexico, Spain, Italy, France, and Portugal, than to that of the middle-class in those countries. Again, this suggests that some of the differences observed may be more socioeconomic in nature than ethnic. In other words, for purposes of discussing differences between the two groups, "Hispanic" and "Anglo" are used as catchalls to refer to the "average" or most common value orientation of each ethnic group in the U.S.

Broader cultural differences reflecting the traits of the "average U.S. Hispanic" and the "average, middle-class American" are listed in Table 4.2.

RETRO-
ACCULTURATION

Retroacculturation, a term coined by marketing researcher Carlos E. Garcia, refers to the conscious search for ethnic identity or roots, especially by second-, third- or fourth-generation Mexican-Americans who have lost some or most of their cultural traits. These individuals tend to be highly assimilated into mainstream American culture yet are interested in enjoying and recovering the culture of their parents and grandparents. A well-known example is the singer Linda Ronstadt, who performed traditional Mexican *corridos* in her album, *Songs from My Father.*

Hispanics who choose retroacculturation typically want to learn Spanish and have their children learn Spanish and to appreciate their cultural heritage (values, music, arts, food, and so on). They are proud of their heritage and welcome ethnic recognition in advertising and promotion of brands and services. As consumers, they may patronize brands that target Hispanics or may watch Spanish-language TV and listen to Spanish-language programming. They also tend to support Hispanic-related activities, purchase Spanish-language newspapers, and vote for Hispanic candidates. A sense of ethnic identity and pride tends to motivate these behaviors.

In typical marketing studies, a wide range of attitudes and practices regarding Hispanic culture can be found. Some Hispanic consumers show very low Spanish-language proficiency scores yet consume at least some Spanish-language media regularly. In contrast, there is a small group of highly assimilated Hispanics who dislike being identified as or associated with the Hispanic culture. They identify with mainstream American culture and lifestyle.

■ Communicating in a Bicultural Context

Scholars in the field of communication have found that successful communication takes place if and only if the message generator/sender (the advertiser, the marketer, any communicator) utilizes the same codes (language, symbols, images) as the decoder/receiver (the customer, client, patient, voter).

Regardless of the size of the audience—ten people or a million— the message is always decoded, received and understood on an individual basis. In today's message-cluttered world, marketers and advertisers cannot expect their audiences to work hard at decoding and understanding their messages. Instead, the message must be culturally and linguistically fine-tuned, delivered within a context and tonality that is acceptable and familiar to the receiver, so that it is transparent and understood without any interference.

Communication, and hence advertising, marketing, and promotion, always takes place within a cultural, social context. Therefore, effective bicultural communication and marketing recognizes and utilizes cultural awareness, cultural sensitivity, and an understanding the mind-set of the consumer from the conceptualization stage of the message to strategic planning, final implementation and execution.

Message meaning can change drastically in a bicultural environment. There is a feeling of "communications safety" that people acquire from having lived in the same country and having shared cultural experiences. For example, in the United States, most people know about Babe Ruth—the symbol of American baseball— and why he became so famous. Anywhere in the country, one American can say to another, "My son is the next Babe Ruth" and the other person would understand the message. No explanations are needed. But if the same remark were made to a Mexican or South American, that person would most likely stare at the other wondering who this babe named Ruth is. Chances are that more "acculturated" Hispanics, and certainly Puerto Ricans or Cubans, who have made substantial contributions to American baseball, would understand the full meaning of the comment.

The basic principles used in communicating with consumers apply to any market. If messages in the general market are continually refined to convey clarity of expression and to match the emergent images in American culture, the same approach can and should be used to target Hispanics, or any other ethnic group. A culturally attuned approach should be followed each step of the way — from conceptualization and strategic planning through final implementation and execution, as indicated in Table 4.3.

The cultural approach to marketing to Hispanics is not new; it has been used in the past. Specialists in the Hispanic market, usually Hispanics themselves, implemented successful marketing campaigns that have made hefty contributions to the bottom line of their clients. Unfortunately, budgets are often too small to reap the great potential offered by the Hispanic market. What is needed now is a new look at business opportunities and budgetary reallocations to meet the marketing challenges of this rapidly growing market.

THE DANGERS OF TRANSLATION

Lack of cultural affinity is evident in many translations found in print ads, radio and TV spots, and billboards. It is common to find literal or academic translations of ads or signs from English into Spanish in which the words are correct, but the meaning is not. A good example of a translation that failed is that of a well-known airline that tried to lure passengers with the phrase *"Sentado en cuero."* The original message was intended to emphasize the comfort of sitting on leather seats, but the translation encouraged consumers to "sit naked" (*San Francisco Chronicle*, 1987).

Anybody can learn another language, but learning the culture is much more difficult and demanding process. For one to successfully translate a message in a 30–second TV or radio ad, a print campaign, a brochure, or an outdoor sign, the message must be culturally attuned — tailored specifically to its intended audience. This is easier to do when the culture of the message writer or creative is that of the target audience.

■ "To Sell Me Is to Know Me"

To position a product or service effectively, one must ensure that the message is clear and free from stereotypes, myths, preconceptions, ambivalence, and potentially negative interpretations. In other words, the message must be perceived by the receiver as if he or she had designed it. The portrayal of a Mexican riding a burro and wearing a sombrero is an example of poor cultural sensitivity and lack of factual information. The burro and sombrero may well communicate Mexico to a non-Mexican audience, but not to a Mexican or Mexican-American one. Anyone of Mexican descent will most certainly perceive this image as an indirect insult, one that says "you and your countrymen are backward." Such popular stereotypes regarding Hispanic consumers should be eschewed to avoid delivering negatively charged messages.

A stereotype is a set of generalizations about a group or category **STEREOTYPES** of people that is usually unfavorable, exaggerated, and oversimplified. Most stereotypes tend to emphasize people's negative aspects, are emotionally charged, and are difficult to change even in the face of empirical evidence (adapted from Theodorson and Theodorson, 1970). Stereotypes, such as the Mexican wearing the sombrero and riding a burro, have the potential to irritate and disrupt the flow of healthy and effective communication between marketers and consumers and should be eliminated from any marketing strategy. Hispanics, like most people, dislike being labeled and placed in cubbyholes. When a consumer perceives being portrayed unfavorably, his immediate response is that the message was not created or executed by someone like him. At that instant, the golden rule of successful communication—the message must be perceived to have come from "someone like me"—is broken. In a matter of seconds, the viewer's attention is diverted from the core message to the false or stereotyped image presented in the ad. As the viewer becomes trapped in a tangle of communication nuances, he is certain not only to miss the core message but also to walk away from the product and the sponsor.

The symbols that are used in stereotypical messages, be they images, music, slang, or talent, are not the ones the people being stereotyped would use to define themselves. As difficult as it may be, marketers need to walk away from such stereotypes. Hispanics are a diverse population. To avoid the problem of stereotypes marketers must be aware that some of the perceptions people hold about others who may not look or speak like them fail in the face of reality. A "reality check" is recommended at all stages of the marketing plan.

Most stereotypes about Hispanics tend to stress issues dealing with money or the lack of it. If these stereotypes were accepted at face value, then one might ask, Why bother targeting consumers that have no money or no potential to make money?

✧ Stereotype 1: *Hispanics are farm workers with no money, no future, and no ambition.*

U.S. Hispanics are the wealthiest Latin American consumers in the Americas. As illustrated in Table 4.4, the income per capita of U.S. Hispanics is several times that of the oil-exporting Latin American countries of Mexico ($2,490) and Venezuela ($2,560). By all criteria, the more than 24 million U.S. Hispanics present a stronger and better opportunity for businesses.

In addition, contrary to popular belief, U.S. Hispanics are far more likely to live in metropolitan areas and central cities than non-Hispanics. Only .06 percent of Hispanics live in farm areas, whereas 1.8 percent of non-Hispanics do (U.S. Bureau of the Census, 1991a, 16–17; 1992a, 6). The vast majority (72 percent) reside in urban areas, as discussed in Chapter 2, page 50.

Although Hispanics are over-represented in craft, labor, and farm occupations, the vast majority work in nonfarm activities. In 1990, for example, only about 8 percent of employed Hispanics in California were farm laborers, with the rest employed in managerial and professional positions (11.7 percent); sales, administrative, and technical support areas (21.8 percent); service jobs (19.4 percent); precision and craft workers (13 percent); and operator and laborer positions (25.8 percent) (Center for Continuing Study of the California Economy, 1992, 69).

Hispanics work hard and frequently work in more than one occupation. Like much of the general population, many U.S. Hispanics fix their own cars and repair their own dwellings. Hispanic

Market Connections' research has consistently shown that regardless of the type of job, a great number of Hispanics work very long hours and are willing to sacrifice family and social life in order to succeed in the United States. Thus the notion of Hispanics as lazy or lacking ambition is a wild generalization that bears no resemblance to reality. Hispanic households and families pour billions of dollars each year into the marketplace ($214 billion dollars were projected for 1994). In fact, based on 1991 household income data, Hispanic households had over $21 billion in discretionary income (TGE Demographics, 1994). The figures are substantial enough to dispute the notion that aggressively marketing to Hispanics is "not worth the investment."

That Hispanics earn on average less than non-Hispanic whites and that some still live below the poverty level should not blind marketers and other business decision-makers to the great variation in income levels among Hispanics. As indicated in Chapter 3, there has been a significant increase in the percentage of Hispanic families with incomes above $50,000 and a decrease in the percentage with incomes below the $25,000 mark. Recent reports on Hispanic income indicate that in some regions Hispanic household income is higher than that of non-Hispanic whites: "In well over half of all counties in California, minorities have higher average incomes than whites" (*San Francisco Examiner*, 1993, B-1).

❖ Stereotype 2: *Hispanics do not wish to participate in American society.*

Again, contrary to popular belief, Hispanics are becoming more and more entrenched in American society. Their participation is reflected in the growing number of Hispanic associations, libraries, research centers, and businesses throughout the United States. Furthermore, Hispanics are increasingly active in government at the federal, state, county, and city levels. Hispanics have also made significant contributions to American art, theater, literature, film, music, and sports. Recent studies indicate that Hispanics are willing to be part of "the American way of life." For example, when Yankelovich's Hispanic Monitor, a longitudinal survey study which tracks Hispanic values and beliefs, asked a representative sample of U.S. Hispanics to respond to the statement, "Hispanic immigrants to the U.S. should be prepared to adapt to the American way of life," 73 percent agreed with the statement (Braus, 1993, 58).

     ✧ Stereotype 3: *Hispanics do not acculturate.*

As discussed previously in this chapter, the rate of acculturation of immigrant groups into the dominant society is influenced by many factors. There are a number of reasons why many Hispanics preserve their cultural values and traditions longer. The most salient one being the on-going rate of migration of Hispanics to the U.S., replenishing and reinforcing the culture on an on-going basis. In addition, relative to other immigrant groups, most Hispanics in the United States are a short distance away from their countries of origin. Proximity, freedom to cross borders, air travel, and modern means of communication facilitate contact with families and relatives back home. It is not unusual, for example, for Hispanics in the United States to travel to their country of origin during the Christmas holidays or the South American summer. Mexicans and Puerto Ricans have been traveling between the United States and their homelands for a century. Presently, Cubans and some Central Americans are an exception, because their freedom to return to their countries may be hindered by political restrictions there.

Hispanic media also contribute to strengthening the cultural bond by keeping the Spanish language alive and keeping all generations of U.S. Hispanics abreast of the political and social developments in their Latin American homelands and in the U.S. Hispanic community.

Among first-generation Hispanics there may also be a desire to return to one's homeland when political or economic stability permits. For example, it is not unusual for Hispanics to come to the United States to work for several years in order to save enough money to make a difference to their families back home, where they later return. Many native Mexicans living in the United States for many years have never bought a home here because they are always thinking about returning to "Mexico Lindo" (Pretty Mexico).

Another factor influencing the rate of acculturation is the fact that the majority of the U.S. Hispanic adult population immigrated to the U.S. as adults, hence their formative years took place in a Hispanic country and society. Their mind-set, values, and attitudes are often difficult to change. Obviously this will change with subsequent generations.

All of these elements reinforce cultural and family ties and impinge on the urgency to settle down and blend in culturally with the dominant society. One fact to remember, however, is that most immigrants undergo some type of acculturation whether they are motivated to do so or not.

■ Understanding and Thinking in a Different Culture

Understanding and thinking in a different culture is a challenge, but it is not impossible. Certainly, the first step is curiosity and an unbiased attitude. One must be open to learning where cultural differences lie and how these impact the reception of your specific product or service in the target market. Building a cultural base will give you the basic tools to identify the key cultural issues; you can then manage them to develop and implement successful strategies and programs. The following section describes how to build a U.S. Hispanic market cultural base.

BUILDING A CULTURAL BASE

How can a marketer, advertiser or employer avoid making major blunders in campaign ads? The only safe way is to get close to the Hispanic consumer. Start from scratch—gather as much background information as possible on the sociocultural aspects of the group you are targeting. Some Hispanics have lived in the United States for many generations, others for a few years, and others are recent arrivals. Learn about their origins. Learn about the culture of each segment of the Hispanic market (see the section on cultural diversity among Hispanics, beginning on page 189). Learn about people's motivations for coming to the United States. Become knowledgeable about your audience's political, religious, and social background. If the target group is primarily foreign-born, learn how they lived at home. Did they have credit cards in their native country? Do they know what credit cards are and how to use them? Credit cards are available everywhere in the world, but they are not as pervasive in other countries as they are in the U.S. Therefore you need to learn if your target consumers owned and used credit cards. Did they have a telephone at home in their native country? If not, why not?

Become familiar with the contributions Hispanics have made to American culture. Make a point of finding out the do's and don'ts of their society. For example, when addressing Hispanic adults, you should refer to them as Mr. or Mrs. and avoid using first names unless you consider yourself a personal friend of the family.

When communicating with Hispanics, pay attention to their specific forms of interaction such as body language, tone of voice, and expressions, which carry great emotional value in face-to-face communications. Be aware of differences in places of origin, social class, income status, gender roles, and age, which are critical to the success of interethnic communications. These issues are of particular relevance when addressing consumers who have recently immigrated. A Puerto Rican from New York, a Cuban from Miami, and a Mexican from San Jose, California, may read and interpret a message differently depending on his or her background. In other words, build a general knowledge base about the overall culture of the group being targeted by becoming familiar with the everyday (micro) aspects as well as the larger (macro) aspects of their culture (Lappin, 1983, 127). This may sound overwhelming at first, but you will find that there are only a few basic issues, many of which are obvious, e.g. if somebody just moved to a new country, chances are they have to learn everything from the basics to the more complex aspects of society.

"Taste the Soup to Know the Soup" To learn about current or potential customers, you should do more than read a few books. You should gain firsthand experience with the target audience and take the time, in this case, to tour Hispanic neighborhoods, stores, restaurants, and movie theaters and to attend Hispanic cultural events. It would be extremely valuable to be a guest in a Mexican, Puerto Rican, Cuban, or Salvadoran household—to sit down with the family, eat what they eat, and share their experiences. Travel and vacation in Latin America. If this is too difficult to do, try Hispanic-specific trade show seminars and cultural crash-courses. In other words, go out into the community: "Taste the soup to know the soup" (Minuchin, 1981, 81).

One of Hispanic Market Connections' most successful seminar and trade show presentations is a slide show portraying Hispanic families. The visuals capture Hispanics of different regions, acculturation levels, countries of origin, legal status, and socioeconomic status. The slides contain pictures of U.S. Hispanic homes, including kitchens, dining rooms, bathrooms, gardens, and garages. One reason for the great appeal of this show, *Visiting Hispanic Households* (1986), is that it opens a window for the audience, enabling them to see what Hispanic consumers are really like. The vignettes offer viewers a "reality check," allowing them to confront their preconceptions and discover a different reality.

For example, one slide takes the audience to the house of a family of illegal aliens to discover a neat apartment where special pride is taken in well-groomed children and clean and shiny floors. Although it is a humble dwelling, the level of care, the pride of the household members, and the confidence of the wife in providing a comfortable home are readily apparent. This slide helps dispel the prevalent notion that undocumented Hispanic immigrants live in crowded conditions.

Other photos portray more sophisticated Hispanic households, homes displaying an array of electronic goods, art, and a definite Latin taste in the decor. Again and again, seminar participants have praised the "visits" to typical Hispanic households simply because the experience allowed them to clear their minds of stereotypes and myths that limited their ability to truly see Hispanics for who and what they are. The visuals helped marketers understand the importance of the theme, "To sell me is to know me."

In summary, to effectively communicate with the Hispanic market, get to know Hispanics consumers by learning as much as possible about who they are, how they live, and what they are like. Recognizing and dealing with stereotypes is the starting point. Coming to terms with personal biases provides the framework for an image change, ensuring the product or company will be viewed favorably by the Hispanic market.

To understand cultural differences, another helpful technique is for marketers or advertisers to take an imaginary trip to another

Play the Role of the Consumer

country where the culture, language, and even the alphabet are different from their own. For example, imagine yourself trying to catch a cab on the streets of Japan or Russia. Picture yourself looking for a job there and trying to learn Japanese or Russian. Imagine looking for a pharmacy to buy medicine for your sick child or trying to locate a hospital in case of an emergency. Or visualize yourself shopping in a store or supermarket—trying to find a product with no one available to help you. Chances are, you would feel miserable, inadequate, and ill-prepared in the new environment. In these new surroundings, all the survival skills accumulated over the course of a lifetime fall flat, and you feel the need for a helping hand. The pressure and the stress can be overwhelming, but you must go on.

Under these circumstances, wouldn't you welcome a toll-free number that you could call for basic information and hear a friendly English-speaking operator respond to your questions? Wouldn't you favor signs reading "We Speak English" or "Welcome"? Wouldn't you feel comforted if there were a friend or a familiar face to give you a helping hand while you learn the ways of the new country?

Although marketers and advertising agents are not substitutes for friends, they do play an important role in assisting U.S. immigrant populations with some of their needs. They can help by advertising in Spanish, providing toll-free numbers, and giving Hispanic viewers useful information about the availability and benefits of their products and services.

■ Managing Acculturation and Diversity

Given the complexity of the U.S. Hispanic market, how should you as a business executive, marketer, or advertiser manage the different levels of acculturation and the cultural diversity of Hispanics in the marketplace?

What is needed is a framework—a point of view—that will allow you (and your company) to approach Hispanic consumers from within their own culture, background, and socioeconomic characteristics. You need a frame of reference that will let you handle with confidence what it is that makes U.S. Hispanic consumers "tick" and allows marketers and advertisers to successfully develop the ads, images, and messages that will communicate with the audience—that will captivate consumers by conveying "I know you."

Such a conceptual model will help build the cultural sensitivity and awareness that will ensure that your ads do not backfire and distract the consumer from the message. When targeting consumers across cultures, what is often lacking is a cultural awareness that can guide you, for example, in choosing which sports to feature for which Hispanic group, so that a commercial featuring a soccer or boxing superstar would be aimed at a Mexican audience and one featuring a leading baseball player would be aimed at Puerto Rican viewers. Similarly, a commercial having *salsa* or *merengue* as its musical background would be aimed at Caribbean Hispanics who now live on the U.S. East Coast, rather than at Mexicans living in Texas, for whom you would perhaps want *conjunto*. The following sections provide concrete examples to help you deepen your knowledge and build a framework for working with the Hispanic culture.

As mentioned earlier, a practical way to understand someone from another culture is to learn to recognize the ways in which their culture and yours differ. You may have noticed, for example, differences in greeting protocol between Hispanics and Anglo-Americans. Americans have a tendency to be more informal in their initial contacts. Hispanics on the other hand, tend to be more formal on first encounters and to address people by their last names, e.g., "Señor y Señora Gutierrez" (Mr. and Mrs. Gutierrez).

There are language differences, subtle nuances, between English and Spanish that help maintain the dichotomy between the cultures. The English pronoun *you*, for example, is neutral with respect to familiarity. It can be used to address a friend, a child, or the president of the United States. Such neutrality is absent from the Spanish language, where the pronoun *tu* conveys informality and the pronoun *usted* is formal and suggests respect and dis-

A FRAMEWORK FOR CULTURAL DIFFERENCES

tance. It would be unthinkable for Hispanics to make use of *el tuteo,* the act of using the *tu,* when addressing a public figure.

Ideally, someone communicating with persons of a different culture would want to think and feel from the perspective of that culture. There are two very useful models for doing this: the life cycle model and ecosystemic model. They will help you understand the basic differences between Anglo-American and Hispanic cultures and help you visualize how these differences may affect consumer behavior, therefore allowing you to modify your approach to Hispanic consumers. Both models were originally presented by Celia J. Falicov and Betty M. Karrer (1986, 389–422) to explain behavioral patterns among traditional Mexican-American families living in a rural environment. The constructs were intended to aid family counselors dealing with clients whose family lives were disrupted in the process of adapting to American society. These models helped family counselors understand family dynamics in a bicultural context, which allowed practitioners to meet the needs of their clients. The models are important for marketing for the very same reason: they provide marketers and advertisers with a framework—a perspective from which to operate, target, and meet the needs of their consumers.

Suppose you are designing a commercial for a Hispanic audience and the commercial requires the presence of a minor or a woman. Can you show a Hispanic child playing alone and unsupervised in a nonfamily environment? Or can you show a young adult Hispanic woman living by herself? Can you show a Hispanic woman drinking an alcoholic beverage alone? A yes to any of these questions might well result in a commercial that could backfire.

Why could they backfire? Frequently, commercials designed for Hispanic viewers will mistakenly reflect the life-styles and idiosyncrasies of Anglo-American viewers, the prevalent attitude among advertisers being that a few adjustments here and there will suffice to elicit the responses of a Hispanic audience. Unfortunately, these minor adjustments overlook cultural nuances. These variations may not be readily apparent to the creative team or management in a company and frequently are not detected with standardized survey questionnaires, such as those used in large quantitative testing. But the variations will surface if the commercials are subjected to in-depth, unstructured qualitative studies such as focus groups or one-on-one interviews with target Hispanic consumers. The following models provide ways to check how close your thinking or strategy is to that of the core Hispanic customer.

THE LIFE CYCLE MODEL

We may find ourselves entertaining thoughts such as "By now I should have finished college, or should be married, or should have children"; "I have a good executive position even though I am still young; my father got his when he was much older"; "My daughter is dating; soon she will be married, leave home, and have children; I will become a grandparent and have a house full of empty rooms." Thoughts such as these reflect people's lifecycle related expectations as they move through different stages in their lives. Most of us have been unconsciously "programmed" to expect certain events to take place at certain particular times in our lives. These programmed lifecycle landmarks are "culturally" driven and, hence, vary between cultures. Therefore the various events that mark the transition from one stage to another in the life cycle should be taken into account in order to develop effective marketing campaigns in another culture. For each stage there is a preconceived set of expectations in the viewer's mind; a commercial should match those expectations.

The life cycle is determined by the social arrangements of the culture to which a person belongs. For example, the age a child begins school, the age at which traditional Hispanic families free their daughters of the presence of a chaperon, or the time that an oldest son begins caring for his elderly parents are socially determined.

The life cycle models of traditional Mexican-American and Anglo-American families are quite different. As illustrated by the life cycle model in Figure 4.1, relationships among traditional Mexican families tend to have longer histories, as it is customary to date the same person for a long time before marriage; couples tend to stay married longer; and children tend to separate from their parents much later than do most Anglo-American children, usually not until they get married. For Mexican-American families, these arrangements allow for greater parental intervention in their children's lives. In Mexican-American culture, courtship is less frequent, there is greater emphasis on romance, and the pressure for the families to know the bride or groom and their families is greater. To many Hispanics, courtship is a long and intense lifetime event. Hispanics also tend to divorce less than non-Hispanics.

As a marketer, your familiarity with the events of the target audience life cycle will enhance your understanding of their attitudes and beliefs. Such awareness will improve your ability to select the themes that will best appeal to Hispanic sentiments. By choosing situations that fit into their everyday life, you thereby gain the minds, hearts and approval of your audience. For example, Hispanic families, on average, tend to send their children to school later than the general market. Hispanic mothers want to keep "baby" at home for as long as possible. Therefore, a manufacturer of toys may want to capitalize on the fact that this mother will need to keep the child entertained and busy while she takes care of the household chores without the traditional help of the extended family. This mother will welcome learning how to go about being practical, taking care of both the child and the household. Many ready-to-serve-foods and products may also be promoted to this particular growing market segment, the Hispanic mother in child-rearing years.

THE ECOSYSTEMIC MODEL

Unlike the life cycle model, which views Hispanics from the perspective of the individual in his or her long-term relation to life and family, the ecosystemic model approaches consumers from the perspective of the individual and his or her relationship to society. As the name implies, the ecosystemic model looks at the individual from an ecological perspective, in which all levels or layers of society in which we operate are taken into consideration. This model is a tool that allows one to examine how individuals from different cultures interact between and within the different layers of society. It also identifies where there is room for "dissonance," that is, where the forms of interaction in a particular social layer of one culture are different from that in another culture, opening the doors for confusion, frustration, and/or misinterpretation. The model helps explain those areas in which Hispanics are changing and adopting to different forms of interaction with their new society.

Psychologists Falicov and Karrer adapted the ecosystemic model from one by U. Brofenbrenner (1977) to help understand and explain the cultural and social difficulties Mexicans encounter when moving to the United States. Even though the model was designed to represent Mexican working-class people, the authors have successfully applied it to explain and uncover behavioral traits of Hispanics from other countries and socioeconomic groups. The model includes a diagram representing traditional working-class Mexican-Americans and modern middle-class Anglo-Americans. The diagrams in Figure 4.2 place the individual at the center of the circle in the area labeled the "microsystem." This first circle represents the individual's home or family and his or her forms of interaction at the core of the family. The next layer explains how individuals interact in the "mesosystem"—the layer rooted in the work place, neighborhood, school, peer group, or extended family. Moving outward, the next level in the circle is the "exosystem," which includes the institutions responsible for organizing people's lives, such as government, business, banks, utilities, schools, and media. The last circle is the "macrosystem" and refers to the larger, broader, intangible layer where shared values, beliefs, attitudes, norms, and aspirations common to people sharing a distinct culture lie (Falicov and Karrer, 1986, 391).

How does the ecosystemic model work? As a businessperson, think of the many Hispanic immigrants who will arrive in the United States during the next twenty years. Think about the Hispanic immigrants who are already here. Have you ever wondered why so many of them make their purchases on a cash basis and do not have checking accounts? Relative to Anglo-Americans, Hispanics tend to have fewer checking accounts, makes less use of financial institutions, and have fewer real estate loans. Have you ever considered why Hispanics spend as much money in rent as they do in mortgages or why home ownership is lower among Hispanics than in the general market? Do you know why proportionately very few Hispanics own investment funds or life insurance?

The ecosystemic model provides a framework for dealing with these types of issues. Figures 4.1 and 4.2 show how traditional working-class Mexicans relate to institutions vis-à-vis middle-class Anglo-Americans. Hispanics tend to rely less on institutions than do middle-class Anglo-Americans. Lack of trust in major institutions is a common trait among many Latin Americans.

Why should Hispanics rely less on institutions such as government and banks? Years of unstable currencies, high inflation, frequent devaluations, and even political instability in their native countries have engendered a "no-trust" attitude toward banks, institutions, and most forms of government. Why put money away that will be worthless tomorrow? Better to spend it on tangible items such as jewelry, appliances and furniture than have it evaporate from the bank's coffers. In most Latin American countries, currency changes denominations frequently. In Argentina during the late 1980s and early 1990s, inflation reached heights of more than 3,000 percent. In Argentina as well as in many other Latin American countries, devaluation eats up savings so fast that parents would not dream of opening a savings account at the birth of a child, since it is likely that they would have nothing to show for it by the child's eighteenth birthday.

In addition to a dearth of trust, a substantial number of people in Latin America have never been familiar with or had access to a bank. In many countries of Latin America, checking accounts are only common among the wealthy, the upper-middle class, businesses, and corporations. Unlike in the United States, where the requirements are minimal and opening a checking account takes a matter of minutes, in most Latin American countries the requirements are very strict and opening a checking account may take months. Therefore, it is not unusual for Latin Americans to conduct their transactions in cash all the time. In the non-affluent classes, it is not unusual for an individual to buy a house and pay for it in cash or borrow the funds from friends or relatives. Because Latin American consumers deal primarily in cash, their knowledge of how banks function is very limited, and they bring this lack of familiarity with them when they move to the United States. This prevents many recently arrived Latin immigrants from making contact with banks.

Any business seeking to attract Hispanic consumers should take into account what the consumers' previous relations were to that type of institution, service, or product. Another example using the ecosystemic model can be situated at the "microsystem" level. The usual forms of interaction inside the Hispanic family tend to be different than those at the heart of the American middle-class. Hispanics tend to stress interdependence within the family while Americans tend to stress autonomy (see Figure 4.2). This affects, for example, how children in both cultures obtain cash to buy things they like. In the American family, it would be perfectly acceptable for the child to find a job and earn his or her money for personal use, savings, etc., and it is actually encouraged. American children can be seen distributing newspapers, selling lemonade or cookies, and engaging in other means of earning spending money. These activities would be unthinkable for non-acculturated, traditional Hispanic families, in which a child is encouraged to earn money only when the family is under severe financial stress. In the Hispanic model, the parents are expected to provide for the children until they are young adults, contributing in this way to the base for long-term family interdependency. Family interdependency can help to explain why some Hispanic mothers continue cooking for their adult children, why Hispanics tend to stick together on weekends, and why parents tend to encourage their children to stay with them for as long as possible.

Certainly, many of these traits change with acculturation to American culture and the pressure to function in a society where the extended family is not present or there is no affordable help for hire as in Latin America. These behaviors and forms of interaction must be taken into consideration when marketing to non-acculturated Hispanics and should be recognized and used in the creative development process.

The ecosystemic model can be very valuable to marketers, advertisers, businesses, or any organization attempting to unravel the social differences that exist between Hispanics and Anglo-Americans. This model helps to illuminate the ongoing acculturation process Hispanics and others start to go through from the moment they arrive in the U.S.

BUSINESSES AND ACCULTURATION

Eventually—usually within three to four generations—immigrant groups become fully integrated into the dominant society. In the interim, immigrants go through a process of cultural transition—acculturation—in which their beliefs, attitudes, and customs gradually blend with those of the new society. Acculturation is not without cost to the individual or to society, since it demands adjustment by both. For the immigrant who used to feel a correspondence between his values and actions and those of his society at large, the cultural transition fills him with ambivalence and uncertainty. (This dissonance, or inner conflict, is shown in Figure 4.2 where the stars meet the levels shown on the right.)

There are a multitude of situations for which the immigrant is not prepared. For example, the recent immigrant lacks a framework that will entice him or her to enter a bank and open a checking account or apply for a loan. There was no need in their home country for a checking account, so why should they have one now? Why can't he or she carry $500 or $1,000 in his or her pocket? Acculturation and adaptation are constant companions to immigrants. To do business with non-acculturated Hispanics or any other immigrant group, you must put yourself in their shoes and try to understand their background and the cultural differences that affect the way your company should do business with them.

Culture, Values, and the Ecosystemic Model

Anyone who has lived in the United States since birth is probably imbued with the values and beliefs underlying Anglo-American culture. Success, individualism, freedom, equality, competition, a strong work ethic, are some of the values that are central to the American character. Compare and contrast these values with those that are typical of Hispanic culture. These core values are characteristic of most Latin American cultures: group orientation, authority, class distinction, religion, respect, faith, fate, and family loyalty. These values vary from country to country, and within a country between rural and urban centers, but in general they are common across Latin American culture. These values are passed from one generation to the next, but may change or weaken as Hispanics integrate into mainstream American culture.

Understanding the differences in infrastructure between Latin American countries and the United States helps explain differences between how Hispanics and Americans organize their daily lives. For example, in the United States, not having a telephone is almost unthinkable. Moreover, having to wait as long as an entire week for telephone service to be connected would be considered totally outrageous. In Latin America, getting a telephone can be an unrealistic proposition, because of either lack of telephone lines or bureaucratic red tape. A similar distinction is evident when it comes to owning a car. In places like California, where distances between home and work can be great and public transportation is limited, owning a vehicle is a matter of livelihood. By contrast, in most of Latin America owning a car is a luxury, and public transportation is the way most people commute to their jobs.

Organizational differences between Latin and Anglo cultures exist at all levels of transportation, news, banking, health, merchandising, education and so on. Thus, business people need to be familiar with the backgrounds of Hispanics. It is surprising how different their experiences are from those of the general market.

■ Cultural Diversity among U.S. Hispanics

What is the difference between *fruta bomba* and *papaya*? None; both terms refer to the same tropical fruit. But to western Cubans the word *papaya* is taboo because it also refers to a part of the female anatomy, whereas for the rest of Latin Americans it is just a fruit. Both Mexicans and Spaniards eat "tortillas." But the Mexican tortilla is a corn cake, whereas the Spanish tortilla is a cousin of the omelette. Mexicans and Mexican-Americans eat "tortas" as part of the main course, but Chileans, Argentines and Peruvians have them as dessert: torta is a sandwich and sometimes a cheeseless omelette for Mexicans but is a sweet cake for the other two groups.

Beans are a very important staple in the Caribbean, Mexico, Central America, and South America. But each country may refer to them and cook them quite differently. Puerto Ricans refer to beans as *habichuelas* and Mexicans call them *frijoles*. Nicaraguans like to eat *gallo pinto* (rice and beans), Puerto Ricans eat *arroz con gandules* (rice and beans), Cubans eat "Christians and Moors" (beans with rice), and Spaniards eat *paella* (a rice dish). Chileans and others in the southern zone call beans *porotos* and prepare them as a soup dish. To get to the restaurant Cubans and Puerto Ricans ride the *gua-gua,* Mexicans the *camion,* Chileans the *micro,* Peruvians the *bus,* and Argentines the *omnibus.* The fact is, each group travels by bus. Peruvians, Argentines, and Spaniards drive *coches* (cars), Mexicans, Cubans, and Venezuelans drive their *carros* (cars), and still other nationalities drive the *automovil.*

These examples illustrate some cultural variations found among Hispanics from different countries. Hispanics also tend to differ from one another in the sports they favor, the music they listen to, the art they produce, and the theater they prefer. The list that follows is a compilation of attributes that differ among the three major U.S. Hispanic groups: Mexicans, Cubans, and Puerto Ricans. Although comprehensive, the list is by no means exhaustive. It must be kept in mind that some of the differences listed are merely tendencies. This list includes characteristics that reflect historical patterns, cultural affinity and diversity, immigration patterns, self-identification, social relationships with other Hispanics and with Anglos, socioeconomic differences, and differences in health habits and religion.

U.S. MEXICANS

✧ The largest of all U.S. Hispanic groups.

✧ The majority reside in the southwestern United States (California, Colorado, Arizona, New Mexico, Texas). Growing Mexican populations in Chicago, Illinois, and Miami, Florida.

Presence in the United States

✧ Except for the colonial Spaniards, Mexican presence in what is today the United States precedes that of other Hispanic groups.

✧ Mexicans were already present in California, Texas, Arizona, and New Mexico prior to American independence. By about 1850, the Mexican population in New Mexico alone was approximately 60,000 according to some sources (Kanellos, 1993, 23).

Immigration- Related Events

✧ Labor migration to the United States precedes that of Puerto Ricans, Cubans, and other Hispanic groups. Mexicans have greater restrictions on immigrating to the United States than the other two groups.

✧ American immigration initiatives to attract low-wage earners, such as the Bracero Program, enticed Mexicans to join the U.S. labor force in 1880.

✧ Motivation to migrate: poor economic conditions in Mexico, desire to improve standard of living, and family reunification (National Association of Latino Appointed Officials, 1992, 2).

✧ Larger undocumented immigration than Puerto Ricans and Cubans.

✧ Aztec civilization, Spain, Mexico, and the United States.   **Cultural Influences**

✧ Indigenous influence greater than in Puerto Rico.

✧ Mexican Spanish influenced by American indigenous   **Language**
elements, for example, *tomate, aguacate, chocolate, chile.* Most of the borrowing refers to flora, fauna, and rustic instruments found in rural Mexico.

✧ Mexican Spanish tends to pronounce all the consonants (unlike Caribbean Spanish, where the final consonants are "swallowed").

✧ Some of the most prevalent indigenous words found among Mexicans and Mexican-Americans are *zacate* (grass, lawn), *elote* (corn), *papalote* (toy kite), *quajolote* (turkey), and *tecolote* (owl).

✧ U.S. Mexicans identify themselves as Mexican, Latino,   **Self-Identification**
Mexican-American, Chicano, La Raza.

✧ Strong identification with own cultural heritage.

✧ Limited contact with individuals from other Hispanic groups.

✧ Tendency to think of themselves as being somewhat similar "culturally" and "politically" to other Latinos.

✧ More likely to report discrimination in the United States than other Hispanic groups (de la Garza, 1992).

✧ Report to have positive relations with Anglos (de la Garza, 1992).

Socioeconomic Characteristics

✧ Higher household income than Puerto Ricans but lower than Cubans, Central and South Americans, and other Hispanic groups.

✧ Younger than Puerto Ricans, Cubans, and other Hispanics.

✧ Larger households than Cubans or Puerto Ricans.

✧ More U.S. Mexicans tend to own their homes than Puerto Ricans and Central and South Americans, but not Cubans and other Hispanic groups.

Values

✧ Strong family values. Family ideology requires individual sacrifice for the good of the family. More group-oriented than other Hispanic groups.

✧ Largest families of all U.S. Hispanic groups.

✧ Extended families (residing with relatives) are more prevalent among immigrants.

✧ Recent immigrants tend to rely more on family kinship and social networks than U.S.-born Mexican-Americans.

✧ Strong tendency to intermarry. Women of Mexican origin are more likely to marry non-Hispanics than are men.

✧ Divorce is less socially acceptable among U.S. Mexicans than U.S. Puerto Ricans, Cubans, and Central and South Americans (Kanellos, 1983, 171–2; U.S. Bureau of the Census, 1992b, 68).

Political Issues

✧ More active politically and have greatest Hispanic political representation in U.S. society. Cubans follow.

✧ Defend cultural heritage, equal rights, and bilingual education.

✧ U.S. Mexicans tend to seek medical care less often and **Health** postpone doing so more often than other groups.

✧ They appear to rely more on vitamins, mineral supplements, and medicinal herbs than other U.S. Hispanics.

✧ Children (age 5 and under) have lower exposure to cigarette smoking (40 percent) before and after birth than all other Hispanics (44 percent) and non-Hispanics (51 percent).

✧ U.S. Mexicans are less open to discussing sexually transmitted diseases than any other Hispanic group. For example, Mexican-American parents are much less likely to have ever discussed AIDS with their children (50 percent) than mainland Puerto Ricans (74 percent) or other Hispanic adults (64 percent) (Biddlecom and Hardy, 1991, 3, 13; Overpeck and Moss, 1991, 3; U.S. Bureau of the Census, 1992b, 134).

✧ Most U.S. Mexicans are Catholic. Regard the Virgin **Religion** Mary as Our Lady of Guadalupe and Our Lady of San Juan de los Lagos.

✧ Fewer are Protestant.

✧ Growing number of Pentecostals.

✧ Nonformal spiritual practices: European Spiritism, the practice of evoking the spirit of the dead through mediums; it is considered a pseudoscience.

✧ Spiritualism, a cult that developed in Mexico among practicing Catholics. Spiritualists act as agents for great religious figures for the purpose of healing. Also present in other parts of South America.

✧ Other practices involve *yerberias* (specialty stores selling medicinal herbs and plants) and the *yerbero* (an herb specialist knowledgeable about the medicinal qualities of plants). *Curanderismo,* the practice of healing by invoking the forces of good and evil.

✧ U.S. Mexican art is strongly influenced by Catholicism **Art** and the sociocultural experience of Mexicans in the United States. The following types of art are prevalent:

Religious Art. Religious art is common in the southwestern United States (New Mexico, Texas, Arizona). It focuses essentially on religious themes such as the Virgin de Guadalupe, *santos* (saints), churches, and altars. Modern religious art originated as a response to a popular demand for private oratories, altars, and shrines. As such, religious art is usually conceived, produced, and marketed by families as opposed to single artists.

Mexican-American Art. Mexican-American art was part of mainstream American art between from about 1920 to 1950. Unlike religious art, Mexican-American art draws essentially on American and Hispanic regional themes. During the 1960s, murals, one of the main modes of expressions of Mexican-American art, took various forms—figurative, abstract, pop funk, and destructive.

Chicano Art Movement. Prominent in California, Texas, New Mexico, and the Great Lakes region, Chicano art focuses on pre-Columbian, Mexican, and Chicano motifs and themes depicting historically controversial relations between Anglos and Mexicans. Popular themes include politics, feminism, barrio life, street life, farm-worker communities, Chicano culture and identity, and religion. Art media include murals, sculpture, drawings, silk screens, photography, graphics, and ceramics. Since the 1970s Chicano painters, print-makers, sculptors, and poster artists have increasingly displayed their work in local and regional events and major exhibitions.

Chicano Murals. Contemporary mural painting became popular in the 1970s. Muralists use walls of housing projects, alleys, concrete stairways, grocery stores, pharmacies, and cultural centers in Mexican communities. Many of the murals address social concerns.

Music   ✧ U.S. Mexican music, prevalent in Texas, New Mexico, Arizona, and California, is unique for its cultural context and Mexican heritage. Partly for this reason it is much less eclectic than musical forms found among other U.S. Hispanic groups. U.S. Mexican music has been less influenced than that of other groups by African culture and the type of instrumentation found in the music played by Caribbean Hispanics. The following types are commonly recognized:

Música Norteña. Also known as the *conjunto,* música norteña was developed by Mexican-Texans as a vocal expression of intercultural conflict between the U.S.-Mexican working-class and Anglo establishment as well as between the Mexican working-class and more acculturated, upwardly mobile Mexican-Americans. This type of music has deep cultural roots.

Orquesta Tejana. Orquesta tejana is an orchestral musical form representative of acculturated, upwardly mobile Mexican-Americans.

Grupos cumbieros or *tropicales modernos.* A variant of *música tropical/moderna* (or Afro-Caribbean music), grupos cumbieros originated with Mexican immigrants in the United States during the 1960s (Kanellos, 1993, 595–603; 617–18).

There is a revival of Latin American music to which first-and second-generation Hispanic artists are contributing. There is a crossover from a strictly Spanish-speaking to a broad English-speaking audience. Cubans have been instrumental in revitalizing Latin jazz, which has great appeal to second-generation Hispanics who speak English and understand Spanish. This new trend has triggered music mail clubs, such as the Club Musica Latina, that offer ready access to current and classical Hispanic music (Holston, December 1992).

An example of this revival is the success of band music and *guebradita* (music and dance). Both are very popular in California and the Southwest. These rhythms have emerged as new expressions of popular Mexican music from different provinces.

Literature

✦ Massive production in English and Spanish. Major emphasis on Mexican heritage and Anglo-Mexican conflicts.

✦ Leads all other U.S. Hispanic groups in literary production.

✦ Rich in poetry, drama, the novel, autobiographies; also *corridos* (ballads) and short stories.

Theater

✦ The U.S. Mexican theater is another cultural expression of the Mexican working class in the U.S. Employs Spanish or

Spanish and English, is rural oriented, and has a strong pre-Columbian heritage. Portrays social issues affecting Chicanos in the United States, such as life among farm workers, Vietnam War participation, bilingual education, community control, and drugs.

✧ *El Teatro Campesino.* A very popular Mexican-American Theater group that emerged as a support group during the farm workers' strike in California during the 1970s.

Sports

✧ Equestrian sports including horse racing, bullriding, and rodeo; soccer; boxing.

Food

✧ Mexican-Indian, native American, and Spanish influences.

U.S. PUERTO RICANS

✧ Second-largest Hispanic group in the United States.

✧ Most U.S. Puerto Ricans live on the East Coast (New York, New Jersey, and Florida).

Legal Status

✧ Puerto Ricans are U.S. citizens and move freely in and out of the commonwealth.

Migration

✧ Economic considerations; family reunions.

✧ Frequent travel between the United States and the island of Puerto Rico.

✧ 1944: Government program Operation Bootstrap designed to stimulate industrialization on the island and to fill U.S. labor shortage stimulates a major wave of worker migration to the United States.

Dominant Cultural Influences

✧ Afro-Antillana (Caribbean, French), Spanish, and Anglo.

✧ Puerto Rican indigenous culture wiped out by disease in 1580s; replaced by African slaves.

Language

✧ Puerto Ricans share language elements of Caribbean Spanish with Cubans and Dominicans (see "Language" section in discussion of U.S. Cubans, page 199).

✧ There is a tendency among Puerto Ricans to pronounce the *rr* sound as *h*, as in *ham.* The tendency is rather prevalent among Puerto Ricans from rural regions and has become a symbol of cultural identification.

✦ The replacement of *r* by *l* at the end of words or after consonants is also prevalent, *trabajar* (work) becomes *trabajal.*

✦ Puerto Ricans (Nuevo Ricans) and *Nuyoricans* (Puerto Ricans born in New York).

Self-Identification

✦ Strong identification with other Puerto Ricans even among U.S.-born generations.

✦ Lower identification with other Hispanic groups and with Anglos. As with Cubans and Mexicans, Puerto Ricans tend to socialize among themselves.

✦ Feelings of discrimination among Puerto Ricans tend to be lower than among Mexicans but higher than among Cubans.

✦ On average lower socioeconomic status than other Hispanic groups.

Socioeconomic Characteristics

✦ Older than U.S. Mexicans but younger than other Hispanic groups.

✦ Smaller households than U.S. Mexicans and Central and South Americans, but larger than U.S. Cubans.

✦ Home ownership is the lowest among all Hispanic groups (U.S. Bureau of the Census, 1991a, 16–17; Schick and Schick, 1991, 59).

✦ Strong family ideology and reliance on the extended family.

Values

✦ Patriarch still important but decreasingly so as more Puerto Rican women head households and join the labor force. Matriarchy present in some groups. Nuclear family formation continues to be preferred.

✦ Most Puerto Ricans tend to feel ambivalent regarding Puerto Rico's sociopolitical relationship with the United States.

✦ Have smaller average families (3.5 members) than U.S. Mexicans (4 members) but larger than U.S. Cubans (3.2 members). More variation in family types than in other Hispanic groups. Divorce is more socially accepted. Puerto Ricans have the second highest divorce rate (8.9 percent) of Hispanic subgroups.

Political Issues	✧ Increased political power in United States.
	✧ Independence movement on island of Puerto Rico (Augenbraum and Stavans, 1993, xv–xxii). Also, statehood movement on island of Puerto Rico.
Health	✧ Medicinal herbs and home remedies are usual practices.
	✧ Have a higher consumption of vitamin and mineral products than U.S. Cubans or Mexicans.
	✧ Puerto Ricans tend to be more open about discussing AIDS with their children than do Mexicans or other Hispanic adults (Biddlecom and Hardy, 1991, 3–13; U.S. Bureau of the Census, 1992b, 134).
Religion	✧ Mostly Catholic. Virgin Mary regarded as Our Lady of Providence.
	✧ Non-Christian cults, including *santeria.* (See "Religion" section under discussion of U.S. Cubans, page 201.)
Music	✧ See "Music" section under discussion of U.S. Cubans, page 201.
Literature	✧ U.S. Puerto Rican literature is more recent and less abundant in general. Notable poetry and drama.
	✧ Written primarily in English (Augenbraum and Stavans, 1993, xv–xxii).
Theater	✧ *Nuyorican (New York Puerto Rican) Theater* began with Puerto Rican artists born in New York. It includes collectively created street theater and works by individual playwrights. Major plays are associated with Puerto Rican working-class culture. The term *nuyorican* has not always been well received by Puerto Rican artists themselves (Kanellos, 1993, 527–28).
Sports	✧ Baseball.
Food	✧ African and Spanish influence; tropical cuisine.
U.S. CUBANS	✧ Third-largest Hispanic group in the United States.
	✧ Largely concentrated in the state of Florida.

✧ During Cuba's first attempt at independence from Spain (1868), large number of Cubans left for the United States and Europe.

✧ 1898: Spain and the United States sign the Treaty of Paris and Spain grants Cuba and Puerto Rico to the United States.

✧ 1901: Under Platt Amendment, Cuba is made a protectorate of the United States.

✧ 1934: Cuban sovereignty is unrestricted after U.S. abrogation of Platt Amendment.

✧ 1959: Fidel Castro ousts Fulgencio Batista as leader of Cuba and declares Cuba a Communist state (1961), resulting in a "closed" U.S.-Cuban border.

✧ 1980: "Marielitos," a brief wave of immigrants arrives in the Mariel boatlift.

✧ 1994: "Balceros," people use rafts to cross Florida straits and migrate to the U.S., fleeing the severe deterioration of the economic conditions of Cuba.

✧ Cuban immigrants have political refugee status.

✧ Unlike Puerto Ricans, Cubans cannot commute freely between the United States and Cuba and are not U.S. citizens.

✧ Historically, political and economic instability has been the main factor in Cuban-U.S. migration.

✧ Travel restrictions exist between the United States and Cuba.

✧ Spain and Africa. Also some Chinese and French.

✧ Pronunciation is the most salient difference between Caribbean Spanish and Mexican Spanish. There is a habit among Cubans, Puerto Ricans, and Dominicans to omit the final consonants. Reportedly, the "swallowing" of consonants contributes to the popular impression that Caribbean Spanish is spoken faster than other forms of Spanish.

Presence in the United States

Legal Status

**Migration
Dominant Cultural
Influences**

Language

✧ Cubans prefer the diminutive *ico* as opposed to the Spanish *ito* as in *momentico, chiquitico,* and so on. (Kanellos, 1993, 210–11).

Self-Identification

✧ U.S. Cubans identify themselves primarily with their national origin and only somewhat with other Hispanic groups. They tend to mingle little with individuals from other Hispanic groups. Cubans are more likely than Mexicans or Puerto Ricans to think of themselves as being different from Latinos.

✧ Cubans report feeling less discriminated against than Mexicans or Puerto Ricans and report having closer relation to Anglos than to other Hispanic groups in general.

✧ Cubans in New York are perceived by Dominicans and Colombians as the most prejudiced group among Latinos.

Socioeconomic Characteristics

✧ U.S. Cubans are older, wealthier. In proportion, more of them are professionals and they have more years of schooling than any other Hispanic group except for South Americans. Recent immigration waves (1980 "Marielitos" and 1994 "Balceros") are changing this socioeconomic profile.

✧ U.S. Cuban households are smaller than any other Hispanic group and smaller than those of white non-Hispanics.

✧ In the United States, more Cubans own their homes than do Mexicans and other Hispanics, (Schick and Schick, 1991, 59; U.S. Bureau of the Census, 1993c, 16–17).

Values

✧ Strong family ideology, kinship, and social network. Favor paternalism within the nuclear family.

✧ Value system closer to American than any other Hispanic group. Favor individualism and upward mobility.

✧ U.S. Cubans have smaller families than Mexicans or Puerto Ricans.

✧ U.S. Cubans tend to marry within the group. But among those who do not, Cuban men tend to marry non-Hispanics more than do Cuban women, Mexicans, and Puerto Ricans, but less than do Central and South Americans and other Hispanic women.

✧ Divorce is socially acceptable among U.S. Cubans (and in Cuba under Castro as well). Together with U.S. Puerto Ricans, Cubans have the highest divorce rate of all Hispanic groups, and it is as high as the non-Hispanic population.

✧ Cubans in exile; the return to Cuba; and the fall of Fidel Castro.   **Political Issues**

✧ Increased representation in U.S. politics.

✧ Cubans may use household remedies and herbs that   **Health**
were used in Cuba.

✧ They seek medical advice with greater frequency than other Hispanic groups.

✧ Cuban adults rely less on vitamin-mineral supplements than any other Hispanic group, less than whites, and as little as blacks (U.S. Bureau of the Census, 1992a, 134).

✧ As with other Caribbean Hispanics, U.S. Cubans tend to   **Religion**
be Catholic.

✧ Cults are prevalent among Afro-Cubans. *Santeria* practice incorporates elements of Catholicism and Yoruba African cults. Belief is that *santeria* controls the forces of nature.

✧ *Santeros* and *babalaos* (terms used in Miami, Tampa, and New York City) are equivalent to the *curanderos* in Mexico. They are spiritual healers or witches of African cults that were brought to the Caribbean during the nineteenth century.

✧ Other differences among Christian U.S. Hispanic groups include variations in the image of the Virgin Mary (Kanellos, 1993, 367–86). Cubans worship La Caridad del Cobre.

✧ U.S. Cubans, like Puerto Ricans, Dominicans, and Afro-   **Music**
Cubans, share musical forms having Spanish and African roots. The *salsa* is the major component of Caribbean music.

✧ The *dazon, rumba-guaguanco, charanga, mambo, guaracha, son, bolero,* and *cha-cha* all originated in Cuba.

✧ The *salsa* combines the styles of *son, rumba,* and *guaguanco* music. The style is known for its call-and-response patterns between the soloist and the chorus. The *salsa* underwent more development in the United States with the infusion of jazz elements. The *salsa* has a strong cultural appeal to Caribbean Hispanics in the United States, as it is associated with religious performances in their homeland.

✧ Latin jazz and Latin rock lack the Cuban cultural roots of *salsa*. It is said to be a creation of the commercial market. It has a great appeal to second-generation bilinguals (U.S.-born Hispanics).

Literature   ✧ Has a long tradition in the United States but is more recent and less profuse than Mexican-American literature.

✧ Written mostly in Spanish. Most recent prose is characterized by its nostalgic and political content.

Theater   ✧ U.S. Cuban theater is more eclectic than Mexican theater. It incorporates several styles and genres, such as vaudeville, Broadway music, bedroom farce, drama, Spanish versions of classics, and themes of anticommunism and Castro. Second-generation Cuban-American playwrights in New York seem to be less traditional than Miami playwrights.

Sports   ✧ Baseball.

✧ Large contribution of Cuban ball players to U.S. leagues.

Foods   ✧ African and Spanish influences; tropical cuisine.

■ *References*

Augenbraum, H., and Ilan Stavans, eds. *Growing Up Latino: Memoirs and Stories.* Boston: Houghton Mifflin, 1993.

Berry, J. W. "Acculturation and Adaptation in a New Society." *International Migration.* Quarterly Review 30 (1992).

Biddlecome, A. E., and A. M. Hardy. "AIDS Knowledge and Attitudes of Hispanic Americans: United States, 1990." *Vital and Health Statistics.* Advanced Data, no. 207. Hyattsville, Md.: National Center for Health Statistics, 1991.

Braus, Patricia. "What does `Hispanic' Mean?" *American Demographics* 15, no. 6 (June 1993).

Brofenbrenner, U. "Toward an Experimental Ecology of Human Development." *American Psychologist,* July 1977, 513–30.

Calbert, Susan, and Peter Calbert. *Argentina: Political Culture and Instability*. Pittsburgh: University of Pittsburgh Press, 1991.

Center for the Continuing Study of the California Economy. *California Economic Growth, 1993 Edition*. Palo Alto, Calif.

Cuellar, José, "Hispanic Elders." Stanford Geriatric Education Center. Working Paper Series no. 5, Ethnogeriatric Reviews (1990).

de la Garza, Rodolfo O., Louis DeSipio, F. Chris Garcia, John Garcia, and Angelo Falcon. *Latino Voices: Mexican, Puerto Rican & Cuban Perspectives on American Politics*. Boulder, Colo.: Westview Press, 1992.

Edmonston, Barry, and Jeffrey S. Passel. *The Future Immigrant Population of the United States*. Washington, D.C.: The Urban Institute, 1992.

Falcón, L. *Diagnóstico de Puerto Rico*. Rio Piedras: Editorial Edil, 1972.

Falicov, Celia J. Paper presented at the Migration and the Family—A Multigenerational Perspective Conference. University of Southern California, March 6–7, 1982.

Falicov, Celia J. and Betty M. Karrer. "Cultural Variations in the Family Life Cycle: The Mexican American Family." In *Family Transitions, Continuity and Change Across the Life Cycle*, edited by Falicov. New York: Guilford, 1986.

Fennell, Geraldine, Joel Saegert, Francis Piron, and Rosemary Jimenez. "Do Hispanics Constitute a Market Segment?" *Advances in Consumer Research* 19 (1992): 28–33.

Gonzalez, J. L. *El Pais the Cuatro Pisos*. San Juan, P.R.: Ediciones Buracan, 1989. (Reprinted in *Hispanic*, December 1992.)

Gordon, M. *Assimilation in American Life: The Role of Race, Religion, and National Origins*. New York: Oxford, 1964.

Guernica, Antonio. *Reaching the Hispanic Market Effectively*. McGraw-Hill, 1982.

Hamburg, B. A. "Social Change and the Problems of Youth," in *American Handbook of Psychiatry*, 2nd ed., edited by S. Ariefi. New York: Basic Books, 1975.

Hispanic Business, July 1993.

Hispanic Market Connections. *Language and Media Planning for the Hispanic Market: Northern California*. Los Altos, Calif.: HMC, 1992.

———. *The National Hispanic Database: Northern California, 1992*. Los Altos, Calif.: HMC, 1992.

Holston, M. "Latino Beat." *Hispanic*. December 1992, 14–22.

Institute for Puerto Rican Policy. *Datanote*, no. 8 (January 1992).

Kanellos, Nicolás, ed. *The Hispanic-American Almanac. A Reference Work on Hispanics in the United States*. Detroit: Gale Research, 1993.

Lappin, J. "On Becoming a Culturally Conscious Family Therapist." In *Cultural Perspectives*, edited by J. C. Hansen and C. J. Falicov. Rockville, Md.: Aspen Publications, 1979.

Marin, G. and B. V. Marin. *Research with Hispanic Populations*. Applied Social Research Methods Series, vol. 23. Sage Publications, 1991.

McGuill, David. "Cultural Concepts for Family Therapy," in *Cultural Perspectives in Family Therapy*, edited by J. C. Hansen and C. J. Falicov. Rockville, Md.: Aspen Publications, 1983, 108–21.

Minuchin, S., and C. Fishman. *Family Therapy Techniques*. Cambridge, Mass.: Harvard University Press, 1981.

Mulhern, Francis J., and Jerome D. Williams. "Hispanic Shopping Behavior: A Look at Actual Purchases and Income." Unpublished paper. April 2, 1993.

National Association of Latino Appointed and Elected Officials. "Mexicans, Cubans and Other Latinos: Variation in Immigration Experiences." *NLIS Research Notes* 1, no. 2. Washington, D.C.: NALEO Educational Fund, 1992.

Ogilvy, D. *Confessions of an Advertising Man.* New York: Atheneum, 1963.

Overpeck, M. D. and A. J. Moss. "Children's Exposure to Environmental Cigarette Smoke Before and After Birth: Health of Our Nation's Children, United States, 1988." *Vital and Health Statistics.* Advanced Data, no. 202. Hyattsville, Md.: National Center for Disease Control, 1991.

Palmeri, Christopher and Joshua Levine. "No Habla Español." *Forbes,* December 23, 1991, 140–42.

The Rose Institute. *California's Latinos, 1988: An Opinion Survey.* Claremont, Calif.: Claremont McKenna College, 1988.

San Francisco Chronicle, February 6, 1987.

San Francisco Examiner, April 25, 1993, p. B-1.

Schick, L., and R. Schick. *Statistical Handbook on U.S. Hispanics.* Phoenix: Oryx Press, 1991.

Sluzki, Carlos E. "The Latin Lover Revisited." In *Ethicity and Family Therapy,* edited by Monica McGoldrick, John K. Pearce, and Joseph Giordano. New York: Guilford, 1982, 492–97.

Soruco, Gonzalo R., and Timothy P. Meyer. "The Mobile Hispanic Market: New Challenges in the '90s." *Marketing Research* (winter 1993).

Standard Rate and Data Service. *Hispanic Media and Markets.* Wilmette, Ill.: SRDS, 1993.

Steward, Edward C. *American Cultural Patterns: A Cross-Cultural Perspective.* Washington, D.C.: Society for Intercultural Education, Training and Research, 1971.

TGE Demographics. "Hispanic Income Growth and Spending: Where Do the Dollars Go?" Paper presented at the Se Habla Español Conference, New York, November 1, 1994.

Tylor, Edward B. *Primitive Culture.* Vol. 1. London: John Murray, 1871.

U.S. Bureau of the Census. Census Special Tabulations. CPH-L-91. Washington, D.C.: Government Printing Office, 1990a.

———. *Hispanic Americans Today. Current Population Reports,* series P-23, no. 183. Washington, D.C.: Government Printing Office, 1992a.

———. *The Hispanic Population in the United States: March 1991. Current Population Report,* series P-20, no. 455. Washington, D.C.: Government Printing Office, 1991a.

———. *The Hispanic Population in the United States: March 1992,* by Jesus Garcia. Current Population Reports, series P-20, no. 465RV. Washington, D.C.: Government Printing Office, 1993.

———. *Languages Spoken at Home and Ability to Speak English for United States, Regions and States: 1990.* CPH-L-133. Washington, D.C.: Government Printing Office, 1990b.

———. *Official 1990 U.S. Census Form.* Form D-61. Washington, D.C.: Government Printing Office, 1990c.

———. Special Tables. Washington, D.C.: Government Printing Office, 1990d.

———. *Statistical Abstract of the United States: 1992,* 112th ed. Washington, D.C.: Government Printing Office, 1992b.

———. *Technical Documentation.* Summary Tape File 3. Washington, D.C.: Government Printing Office, December 1991b.

Valdés, M. Isabel. "Acculturation and Media Usage: Findings from the Hispanic Database©" Paper presented at the 1992 Advertising Research Foundation, New York, June 30, 1992a.

————. "Hispanic Consumer Psychographics." Paper presented at Se Habla Español conference, November 1992b.

————. "Managing Diversity: Hispanics." Paper presented at *American Demographics* 11th Annual Conference on Consumer Trends and Markets, New York, June 10–12, 1990.

————. "To Communicate or Not to Communicate in Spanish: Is There a Question?" Paper presented at the annual meeting of the Advertising Research Foundation, March 1993.

————. "Understanding Hispanic Consumers." In *Marketing Insights*. New York: American Demographics, 1991, 1–14.

Veltman, Calvin. *The Future of the Spanish Language in the United States.* New York: Hispanic Policy Development Project, 1988.

Figure 4.1 The Mexican-American and the Anglo-American Family Life Cycle Cultural Variations

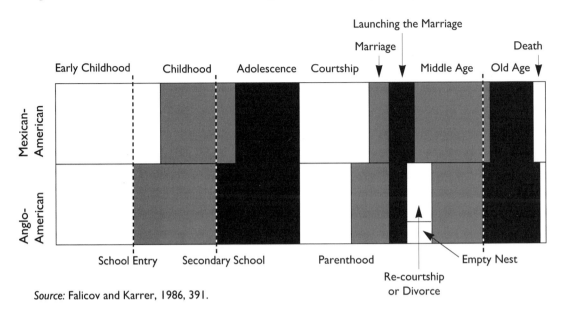

Source: Falicov and Karrer, 1986, 391.

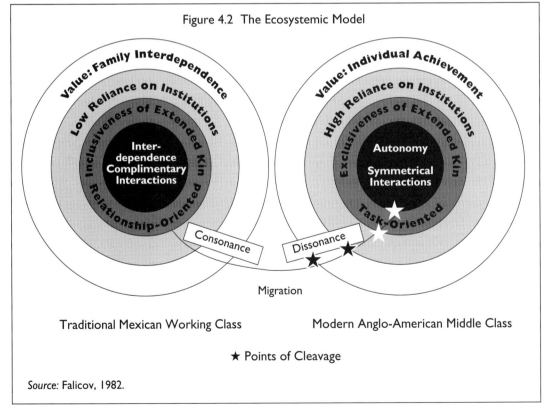

Figure 4.2 The Ecosystemic Model

Traditional Mexican Working Class   Modern Anglo-American Middle Class

★ Points of Cleavage

Source: Falicov, 1982.

Table 4.1 Value Orientation Differences between Hispanics and the American Middle Class

	Hispanics	Anglos
How we see and define ourselves	As part of a family clan or group	Within ourselves, as individuals
Whom we rely on for help	Family, friends, community (Hispanic "social security")	Ourselves and institutions
What we value in people	Stress differences, show respect	Minimize differences, everybody's the same
What we stress in relationships	Respect, cooperation, formality	Symmetrical interpersonal relationships, informality, competition
Children	Dependence, obedience	Independence, egalitarian
Family	Defined roles, hierarchy, old men know more than young men	Role diffusion, "democracy," younger men have a say
Sex roles in social relationships	Male dominance, machismo	Sex equality

Source: M. Isabel Valdés, 1990–1994.

Table 4.2 Broad Cultural Differences between Hispanics and the American Middle Class

Hispanics	Anglos
Group oriented ("for my family")	Self oriented ("for me")
Larger families	Smaller families
Lean toward collectivism	Lean toward individualism
Success means family, group satisfaction	Success means personal possessions, individual satisfaction
Stress hierarchies, social class, social stratification, authority, interdependence	Stress equality, "equal rights," democracy, symmetrical relationships, individual autonomy
Doctors and any established source of authority are much respected and trusted, never questioned	Doctors and other established sources of authority may be respected and trusted but many times questioned
At least one daily meal involves elaborate food preparation	Daily meals are usually not prepared from scratch
Believe in fate; pessimists	Believe in self-determination; optimists
Accept delayed gratification	Look for immediate gratification
"High-touch," physical closeness, hugging, affectionate	"High-tech," more physically distant
Spontaneous	Planners
Overt emotions are part of the culture	Hiding emotions is encouraged
Relaxed about time	Adhere to schedules
Very sensitive to fashion	Relaxed about fashion
Pay careful attention to clothing, appearance, hairstyle	Far more relaxed and casual about clothing, appearance, and hairstyle
Longer social protocols, indirect	Brief, to the point, and direct
Adapt to environment	Change the environment

(continued next page)

Table 4.2 Broad Cultural Differences between Hispanics and the American Middle Class (*continued*)

Hispanics	Anglos
Spiritual, religious things are more important than material things	Material things are more important than spiritual things
Low reliance on institutions	High reliance on institutions
Very decorative in homes	More casual about home decorations
Buy American products	Tend to buy imports
Value highly personal or personalized service	Value fast, efficient service at arm's length
Appreciate being given all the needed time (the more the better) when interacting with service providers	Appreciate concreteness, to the point
Rely more on mutual, implicit understanding	Rely more on explicit language
Tend to prefer prestige brands	Less likely to prefer prestige brands
Tend to live in larger households	Tend to have smaller households
Stress cooperation, participation, being a part of the group	Stress competition, achievement, motivation, self-competence
Huge collection of selves; hide behind a different one depending on the occasion	Reward oriented, straightforward, and moralistic transactions
Pets are not perceived as "family members"	Pets are treated as "family members"

Source: M. Isabel Valdés, 1990–1994.

Table 4.3 Checklist for a Culturally Attuned Communication Process

Message Sender ("Coder")

All elements in a culturally attuned message should be in consonance with the receiver's culture:
- Ad's text (copy)
- People shown (talent)
- Music
- Setting or location
- Interaction between people
- Acting (body language, speech, accent, apparel)
- Pace and tonality
- Product and message context
- Emotional codes

Medium

Language (English or Spanish) and frequency should be that which is closest to the target audience's everyday behavior. If they watch, listen, or read in Spanish most of the time, the number of ads or commercials should be in that specific language.

Message Receiver ("Decoder")

If all elements are in consonance with the receiver's culture, receiver will perceive the message as "talking to me, in my own culture," (Ogilvy, 1963) and the message will not draw attention to itself.

Source: M. Isabel Valdés, 1990–1994.

Table 4.4 Hispanic Income Per Capita, 1990 (Selected Countries and Puerto Rico)

U.S. Hispanics	$8,424
Puerto Rico	6,470
Venezuela	2,560
Uruguay	2,560
Mexico	2,490
Argentina	2,370
Costa Rica	1,910
Chile	1,940
El Salvador	1,100
Guatemala	900
Honduras	590

Sources: U.S. Bureau of the Census, *Statistical Abstract of the United States: 1992*, 1992, 454; Population Reference Bureau, *World Population Data Sheet*, 1992.

C H A P T E R 5

■ Information Overload

■ The Role of Language

■ Language and Translations

■ Spanish in the United States

■ The Isolated or Spanish-Dominant Hispanic Consumer

■ Spanish and Hispanics

■ Bilinguals

■ Communicating with Acculturated Hispanics

■ Managing Language Diversity

Language and the

Hispanic Consumer

The issue of language choice, Spanish or English, when communicating with Hispanic consumers has been at the center of debate for the past decade. The question commonly asked is, Why should companies spend millions of dollars on Spanish-language media when Hispanics can be reached through English-language communication channels? This is the main issue raised by opponents of Spanish-language advertising. In addition, they also ask, why should they address bilingual Hispanics in Spanish if they understand English perfectly? Theoretically, all consumers, regardless of English-language ability or national origin, are exposed to television, radio, and print in English. The question is, Can a consumer for whom English is not the primary language understand, identify with, and be motivated by the English-language creative message? How *effective* is that message? Can verbal or visual messages "coded" in a culture other than the receiver's entice and change his or her purchasing behavior in the direction of the product being sponsored?

Extensive language usage research by Hispanic Market Connections, a marketing research company, shows that when it comes to choosing between English- or Spanish-language media, many Hispanics turn to English-language media for information or entertainment or for educational reasons, to improve their vocabulary, understanding, or auditory capabilities. Many others with less proficiency or no knowledge of English at all may turn to English-language TV in search of entertainment, but their English-language skills are too limited and only visual material overcomes their language barrier. This type of viewer is able to capture only a portion of the full intended message. Whether the goal of these viewers is to be entertained or educated, one thing is certain: While he or she is busy "decoding" the English message—dealing with unfamiliar sounds, interpreting new or different visual cues, and trying to make sense of what he or she sees or hears—there is a very good chance that some or all of the message conveyed will vanish into thin air, escaping the consumer completely. In other words, if the message is an advertisement, that advertising dollar will fly over the audience's head even when the message is heard or seen. Add to the language barrier the visuals and cues that are required of a commercial to capture the viewer's attention, then ask yourself, Will viewers recall the featured brand or be enticed to try the product while their senses work to scan the screen, matching actions with words, words with sounds, and mentally attempting to translate these from one language to another? Will viewers remember what they see, hear, or read if they are forced to *think* about the meaning of every single word they encounter? Will they remember what the message was about? Should they?

This chapter addresses these questions. First, we discuss information overload and the role of language from a cultural and psychosociological standpoint. Next we examine the relevance of Spanish-language advertising in light of the current size and distribution of the Spanish-speaking population in the United States. Then we address the issues of marketing to bilinguals and communicating with acculturated Hispanics. The chapter closes with a discussion on how to manage language diversity in the U.S. Hispanic market.

■ Information Overload

A problem that affects non-native English-speakers, regardless of their country of origin, is information overload. In fact, to one extent or another, everyone suffers from this glut of information. After all, there is only so much information the human brain can absorb, process, and retrieve. In the case of non-native speakers and bilinguals, the risk of information overload is much higher and more severe because the same information needs to be followed, understood, and processed in two languages. Studies show that commercials created and communicated in a language other than that of the non-native speaker adversely affect advertising effectiveness and the consumer's decision-making process. Messages cannot be expected to be properly decoded when the receivers lack some or all of the linguistic and cultural elements that make them proficient in a second language. Such barriers limit the viewers' understanding and work against the communication of the best ad or commercial. However, when messages filled with interest and appeal are delivered in the consumer's native language and in a cultural context that makes sense to the person, the likelihood of recalling ads and trying the product or service is much higher (Dolinsky and Feinberg, 1987).

Those marketers seizing opportunities to increase their sales to Hispanics are gradually becoming aware of the language challenges they face when targeting this group. For instance, major drug chains such as Walgreens have begun to accommodate Hispanic consumers by providing bilingual signs for the products they carry, and many retailers are designing ads that cater specifically to Hispanic consumers (1993). Similarly, major California banks are adapting their informational resources to provide Hispanics access to a wide array of financial services. Bank of America has been a leader in this area. It responded to Hispanics' informational needs by advertising in Spanish, making available flyers and brochures in Spanish, with text specific to the informational needs of these consumers and with designs reflecting Hispanic art and culture. In addition, Bank of America spearheaded the bilingual automated teller machine (ATM) screens with extraordinary results (see page 419). Bank of America managers understood that some Hispanic

One of Bank of America's ads targeting the Hispanic market — this time the small business-owner. The slogan is "Va con América" (Go with America).

consumers needed basic, introductory *information* in Spanish, whereas others needed more complex financial information.

It seems logical to target consumer groups in a language and culture they readily understand; one that does not demand a major effort to follow, especially when that particular language — Spanish in this case — is the principal means of communication in their daily lives.

■ The Role of Language

Language is the essence of culture. It is the point at which individuals interact with families, friends, and society at large. Word selection, meaning, association, and origin are central to the study and understanding of the human mind. In a bilingual marketing environment it is even more important to select the right language.

For example, a German living in the United States expresses his feelings to his American girlfriend by saying, *"Ich liebe dich."* In response she says, "I love you." Literally both expressions have identical meanings, but expressions of affection (emotional messages) in the non-native language arouse different or no emotions and feelings. The meaning of each word that we use to convey a message, and the emotion it elicits, is deeply rooted in the subconscious. Much like us, words have a life of their own; they evolve and develop as people do. Words, experiences, and events are internalized together. They are bonded in the subconscious in such a way that only those words said or heard in the native language *and no other* can express the exact thoughts or emotions in a given situation. For instance, when one hears the words "I love you" said in a foreign language (*"Ich liebe dich,"* or *"Te amo"*), one does not *feel* quite the same as when they are said in the native language. Something seems to be missing. What is absent is the depth, the tonality, and the full emotional *significance* of the phrase, which has been replaced by its underlying rational or intellectual meaning.

In addition, there is added pleasure and advantage when people who speak the same language communicate their feelings or thoughts to each other. In the case of the two lovers, there is pleasure in the certainty that the chosen words and intonation will communicate the emotional message exactly as it was intended from one to the other. There is also an advantage in intuitively knowing that the emotional stimulus encoded in the message will elicit the desired response. In contrast, when people speak different languages, both sender and receiver are at a disadvantage because there is less pleasure in expressing precious sentiments in a non-native language. There is also the uncertainty as to whether the expressed sentiment fully reaches the other person. (From a marketing, sales, or communications viewpoint, the "sale" was not "closed.") Language, in other words, does much more than convey rational meaning; words communicated in a particular language go straight to the mind but also touch a very special chord in people's hearts.

Messages, editorials, and ads produced in Spanish free Hispanic consumers from unnecessary thinking, misunderstandings, and awkward translations. They also provide the Hispanic audience with added emotional pull that allows them to appreciate more fully the information or the advantages and merits of the product or service being advertised.

In television, culturally attuned vocal sounds, accents, pitch, inflection, cadence, and rhythm must be reflected in facial expressions and body movement. Language must convey the emotions associated with a particular product, brand, or service. Take, for example, the commercial promoting "Brand X" of a breakfast cereal in a family situation where the child eating "the other leading brand" will use language conveying disgust or disappointment while frowning or pouting as he is forced to eat the undesired product. On the other hand, when a second child is served the "target brand," his use of language and facial expressions will reflect the joy and excitement aroused by the "proper brand." The child's facial expressions and reactions are also subject to cultural variations. In all likelihood, the Hispanic or the Italian child will wave hands more forcefully than the American child while speaking.

Associating language, emotions, and body movements with the correct and appropriate physical and cultural surrounding is a challenge for non-Hispanics communicating with a Hispanic audience. Modern psychologists place great emphasis on understanding the human mind through language, on the selection of words people use to express themselves, as well as on the explicit and implicit meanings, suggested associations, and origin of the words. Jacques Lacan took the link between language usage and the psyche to its ultimate conclusion when he said, "The unconscious is structured like a language" (Lacan, 1990, 62). The challenge then, when communicating with Hispanic consumers, goes far beyond the simple choice of language, English or Spanish; the real job is to "speak the culture."

■ Language and Translations

Literal translations from English into Spanish add to the challenges of successful communication between Hispanics and non-Hispanics. The prevalent tendency is to translate or adapt a given text from English into Spanish, as opposed to creating a separate text in Spanish. Understandably, in advertising in a second language or culture, the ideas, thoughts, and conceptualization are largely conceived and developed by professionals who rarely *think* in the language and culture in question. This results in mistranslations, and/or mis-communications. Translations that are grammatically incorrect have, on occasion, resulted in "market blunders." One example is that of a Spanish translation for "Budweiser: The King of Beers," which used the masculine instead of the feminine gender for the noun *beer* (*cerveza*). In Spanish, Budweiser would be "the queen," not "the king," of beers (Valencia, 1983–1984, 19).

Poor translations also permeate the myriad legal and public documents that are published in Spanish. The words in the text conform to an English syntax and frame of mind, both of which make it very difficult to convey the underlying ideas to non-English or non-native speakers. As a result, they are useless. Reading becomes stressful and difficult, and the reader is lost. Even if translations are "grammatically correct" in a strict academic sense, the resulting text may not be colloquially correct in the target Hispanic market segment, or in the U.S. Hispanic barrios, where a new form of Spanish, "Spanglish" (a mix of Spanish and English), has developed. It always pays to test the material on target Hispanic consumers. Sometimes it is better to use a less grammatically correct, more colloquial version of Spanish in lieu of a literally correct translation that does not communicate the intended meaning.

■ Spanish in the United States

Whether or not to advertise in Spanish would not be so important an issue if it were not for the enormous size of the U.S. Spanish-speaking population, the business opportunity they present, and the growing number of Spanish-language media available (see Chapter 6). According to the 1990 census, Spanish was the language most spoken in the United States after English, the leading second language in thirty-nine states, and the most popular Indo-European language in each region of the country. For more than 17 million people age 5 and older, Spanish was the primary language spoken at home; and the numbers are growing. Four states alone accounted for 70 percent of the U.S. Spanish-speaking population. California led the nation with 5.5 million people, followed by Texas (3.4 million), New York (1.8 million), and Florida (1.4 million) (Table 5.1; Figure 5.1).

One factor contributing to the increase in Spanish-speakers is "retroacculturation"—a wave of Hispanic pride, heritage, and identity that has rekindled the desire to learn and speak Spanish among third- and fourth-generation Hispanic Americans. According to some reports, Spanish is gaining momentum among Hispanic adults, some of whom perceive the language as more important now than in the past (Braus, 1993, 47), and also among some Hispanic youths. For example, Mexican-American children were reported more likely than other groups to speak their parent's language (*New York Times*, June 29, 1993). Around the country in communities overwhelmingly Hispanic such as those found in Miami, New York, and parts of southern California, Spanish is the dominant language. As Spanish is spoken more often and in some communities exclusively, many Hispanics remaining are somewhat isolated from mainstream English-speaking America. This fact is so pervasive today in the United States that the Bureau of the Census started tracking English-language proficiency in the 1990 census.

■ The Isolated or Spanish-Dominant Hispanic Consumer

Imagine trying to advertise, communicate, or sell to a household where no one speaks your language. Or the other way around. Picture consumers who may be interested in your merchandise or service but who are unable to cross the language barrier, keeping them away from your product or service. The number of households and consumers fitting this situation reaches into the millions. There were 6.8 million Spanish-speaking households in 1990, and about 1.6 million of these, or 23 percent, fit the census definition of "linguistically isolated" (U.S. Bureau of the Census, 1990b, 1), or Spanish-dominant, households. The official figures underscore the true number of Hispanic households where nobody speaks English. According to the Census Bureau, a linguistically isolated household is one in which "no person aged 14 and older speaks only English, and no person residing in the household age 14 or over who speaks a language other than English, speaks English 'very well'" (p. B 25). Under this definition the presence of a teenager age 14 or older who speaks English very well would make that household not linguistically isolated — even if no adult speaks English.

Although the presence of an English-proficient fourteen-year-old in any household provides a communication link with the community at large, and can act as an interpreter for the other household members, the teenager cannot fully compensate for the linguistic and cultural shortcomings of the adults in the household. Marketers know that they cannot view children and teenagers as substitutes for the parent(s) when it comes to making household purchasing decisions. Regardless of how mature or smart a teen may be, he or she cannot replace the parents. As with any family, Hispanic teens can influence parents' decisions to purchase some products or services, but not all, and certainly not those that do not interest the teen. For example, it would be easier for a teenager to influence the purchase of household goods than the selection of a bank, clinic, or dental plan.

In nonfamily households, the adult or teenager claiming to speak English very well is often not related to the other household members. It is not uncommon for recent immigrants unrelated to each other to share living arrangements in order to minimize expenses. In such situations it would be unrealistic to expect that the one household member proficient in English would be present for every purchase that the other household members make. Furthermore, the tastes and needs of one individual are not necessarily those of the group.

■ Spanish and Hispanics

In addition to the 1.6 million Spanish-dominant or linguistically isolated households, the 1990 census counted 4.5 million Spanish-speakers age 5 and over who spoke English "not well" or "not at all" and were also considered linguistically isolated (Bureau of the Census, 1990b, 1). At last census, Hispanics accounted for over half (59 percent) of all linguistically isolated persons residing in the United States; Mexicans alone accounted for 37 percent (Figure 5.2). Among Hispanics, Mexicans have the lowest percentage (24 percent) but because of their large U.S. population, the highest number of people living in linguistically isolated households (2.7 million). Of the other Hispanic groups, 41 percent of Central Americans, 39 percent of Dominicans and 27 percent of Cubans reported not to speak English very well (Bureau of the Census, 1992). Mexicans also have the largest number (8.8 million) of Hispanics living in English-speaking households or in households where at least one person age 14 or older speaks English (Bureau of the Census 1993, 81).

The concentration of Spanish-dominant or linguistically isolated Hispanics varies by region. For instance, more Mexicans, Puerto Ricans, and Dominicans are linguistically isolated in the New York/New Jersey area than in California; and Cubans tend to be more English-proficient in New York than in Florida (Figure 5.3). Among the total Spanish-speaking population, the incidence of Spanish-dominant (those who speak English not well or not at all) persons was higher in California (32.5 percent) than in any other part of the country (Bureau of the Census, 1990a, 4).

■ Bilinguals

According to the 1990 census, the Hispanic market is overwhelmingly bilingual, including more than 9 million Spanish-speaking people age 18 and older who at the time of the 1990 census claimed to speak English "well" or "very well." Seventy-four percent of those who spoke Spanish at home claimed to speak English well or very well (Figure 5.4). With three out of four Spanish-speakers claiming to speak at least some English, which makes them bilingual, why not reach them through English media, or with English language publications only?

Although at first glance the sheer size of this bilingual market may strongly speak in favor of English-language media, a closer look into the dynamics of language usage shows this group as a major communications challenge, one not so easy for marketers and advertisers to target. Why? First, there is the question of how people determine how well they speak English. Responses to the language questions asked on the 1990 census (Table 5.2) reflect respondents' self perception with regard to personal language abilities. People differ considerably on their assessment of what it means to speak a second language "well" or "very well" and on the standards they use to measure their own proficiency. Some people, for example, may think they speak English very well, although they may have very limited vocabulary and speech ability. And there are those who may claim to speak English well, and probably do so in a face-to-face encounter, but are not able to maintain a coherent telephone conversation because clues such as sight, body movements, hand motions, and facial expressions and the opportunity to lip-read are absent. Also, there are those who for myriad other reasons either overstate or understate their own bilingual abilities.

Second, "ability to speak" is just one measure of language proficiency. By itself "ability to speak" may overstate the true capabilities of the individual to function with a second language. For example, a study among Latino immigrants found that when various parameters are used to measure proficiency, such as the ability to understand, write, read, and translate statements, "actual" English ability overstates or understates "self reported" ability (National Association of Latino Elected and Appointed Officials, 1992, Vol. 1). Similar discrepancies were found in the many studies with Hispanic consumers conducted by Hispanic Market Connections, all of which led to the development of a standard set of questions to measure Hispanics' degree of bilingualism and monolingualism, as described later in this chapter (see page 230).

The 1990 census did not ask respondents whether they could read or write in English. If these questions had been asked, the results would be probably different. For example, the number of linguistically isolated or Spanish-dominant households would have probably been higher. Without such information and further analysis one could hardly consider the number of bilinguals counted at the census to be functional bilinguals who can interact fully in both languages. In all probability the number of functional bilingual adults is much lower than the 9 million figure cited. Finally, the census data on undercounted Hispanics suggests that those who did not participate in the census are more likely to be Spanish-dominant or linguistically isolated.

English proficiency among Hispanic bilinguals varies according **DIVERSITY** to gender, geographical location, age at time of arrival in the United States, length of residency in the United States, citizenship status, and place of nativity. A Hispanic Market Connections study (1992b, 10) found that foreign-born Spanish speaking women tend to be far less fluent in English than men (see "Marketing to Women," beginning on page 330 in Chapter 7). Other studies have found that Mexican immigrants are less fluent in English than Cuban or other Latino immigrants (Veltman, 1988,

77–79) and that non-U.S. citizens tend to be less bilingual than naturalized ones (partly because some English proficiency and a minimum length of stay of five years are required to become a citizen, which enhances learning opportunities) (National Association of Latino Elected and Appointed Officials, 1992).

LANGUAGE USAGE AND STRATEGIES

Targeting Hispanic bilinguals is a challenge in and of itself. To many, being fluent in two languages means that person functions equally well intellectually in two cultures, which is not necessarily the case. First, there are ranges of bilingualism in which consumers may be more inclined to communicate in one language than the other. Second, among Hispanic bilinguals fluent in English, there is a segment whose behavior and beliefs are molded along traditional Hispanic rather than Anglo-American cultural values, and there is also a segment whose behavior and values are molded along Anglo-American beliefs. Frequently in the bicultural or multigenerational Hispanic household, English is the language spoken but Hispanic is the culture taught.

It is not uncommon for second-generation Hispanics fluent in both English and Spanish to live or have grown up in households with relatives with varying degrees of English-language proficiency, in which one parent prefers to speak Spanish, another parent prefers to speak English, and a grandparent can speak only Spanish. Also common are two-generation Hispanic households in which the parents are immigrants who prefer to or are able to speak only Spanish and the children speak English fluently. It is not out of the ordinary in these households for a child, teenager, or adult to shift the conversation from one language to the other depending on the situation. Usually the speaker switches to Spanish when the subject of the conversation is emotional in nature, and then switches back to English when the conversation is less emotionally involving (Sluzki, 1983, 75).

This switching phenomenon has to do with the actual process of language acquisition. Often in bilingual households, children who are brought up by predominantly Spanish caregivers first learn to deal with and verbalize their emotions and sentiments—such as love, happiness, anger, sadness, frustration—in Spanish. It is in this context that Spanish is to many Hispanics the "emotional" language. English, on the other hand, is the bridge, the "rational" language that "connects" and links the child and the household with the outside world in general—the school, the job, the marketplace, and so on. Psychologists have observed that bilingual individuals unconsciously choose to communicate in the language most likely to provide security, providing contact with affect and emotions, whereas the second language is used to emphasize intellectualization (Bamford, 1991, 13). In other words, bilinguals tend to switch automatically to Spanish when emotions play a role.

The choice of one language over another thus carries an inherent symbolic value. If the primary language is the one to connect a person's emotions with past memories, experiences, life events, and relationships, it will be the language of choice when the time comes to communicate (send or receive) an "emotional" message. On the other hand, if the message is more rational in nature, the individual will tend to choose the second, or rational, language. The decision to speak one language or another will also depend on the particular circumstances and at times may define the tone or climate of a given event. Bilingual couples, for example, may show a tendency to quarrel and settle their disputes in one language and to converse about more neutral matters in another. Why is this relevant to effective advertising? Because ads work better if the *emotions* are engaged in the communication process. A final decision usually *is* an emotional rather than a rational act.

Expert advertisers familiar with this language dynamic are quick to capitalize on the emotional pull that the Spanish language has on bilingual Hispanics. One highly successful ad campaign was launched a few years ago by Pacific Bell, a telephone company searching for the patronage of first- and second-generation Hispanics. To enhance the emotional content of the message, Pacific Bell made skillful use of bilingual switching. In the first ten seconds, the commercial depicts a young Hispanic girl named Laura, who is embarrassed when her mother calls her name with the Spanish pronunciation in front of her teen friends. Later the ad shows Laura as a mother with her newborn baby. In a role reversal, Laura's mother calls her grandson Eddy, and Laura informs her mother that the child's name is "Eduardo, not Eddy." This is a situation where the symbolic meaning of language switching

Un Momento así Sólo en McDonald's

McDonald's goes after new arrivals. Here a young man shows off pictures of his daughter, "mi princesa," to another, older man who has already succeeded in bringing his family to the U.S.—"A Moment Like This Only [Happens] in McDonald's."

communicates part of the core advertising message: Pacific Bell is a part of the Hispanic family's tradition, and Pacific Bell is with you to help you communicate and bridge generations. Campaigns and media programs targeting Hispanic bilinguals can, if carefully planned, convey messages in a context that uses both emotional and rational language.

■ Communicating with Acculturated Hispanics

Pacific Bell shows its understanding of the Hispanic community again with this ad offering better service—Spanish-language service.

In some markets there is a growing segment of Hispanics highly proficient in English, but whose ability to speak Spanish is limited or practically nil. These consumers may be classified as English preferred and English dominant. This is a group with unique socio-demographic characteristics. They tend to have been born in the United States or to be longtime residents. They tend to have high incomes and more years of formal schooling than less acculturated Hispanics. They are also likely to be immersed in American society much more than other Hispanics. They feel established in America and have adopted many of its cultural values. English-preferred Hispanics tend to be proud of their heritage and usually remain sensitive to Hispanic cultural issues. (U.S.-born and foreign-born Hispanics are compared in more detail in Chapter 7—see pages 326–328.)

English-dominant and English-preferred Hispanics speak in English all or most of the time and most have limited command of Spanish. As a group, acculturated Hispanics tend to be more active in political and community grass-roots organizations. Studies show that acculturated Hispanics are much more likely to recognize and name U.S. political figures at the national and regional levels.

From a marketing and advertising standpoint, the more acculturated Hispanics tend to watch, listen to, and read mostly English media. Exposure to Spanish-language media tends to be minimal or nonexistent. They usually shy away from Spanish-language media, yet they tend to support bilingual publications, teach Spanish to their children, and encourage them to learn about and enjoy traditional Hispanic food, music, arts, and theater. Why then favor English over Spanish media and then turn around and teach Spanish culture to their children? Most English-preferred/dominants were born in this country or have lived here for many years. Most of them were brought up speaking English, and were strongly motivated to assimilate and belong in American society. English became their primary language at home, at work, and in conducting business. English became the practical language. Under these circumstances it would seem reasonable for them to choose English media more often.

Most English-speaking Hispanics, however, reside in the United States-Mexican border states of Texas, Arizona, and New Mexico. And as stated in Chapters 2 and 4, these states not only share a long history with Spain and Mexico, but they have recently sustained a steady increase in the number of Hispanics. All of these factors—proximity, history, density, and cultural heritage—rekindle the process of retroacculturation mentioned earlier.

Advertisers may find it beneficial to target Hispanic yuppies using English or bilingual material with a Hispanic cultural angle or content. McDonald's, for example, was one of the first companies to use the English-language/Hispanic heritage approach when it aired a commercial on mainstream TV showing a father and daughter visiting a McDonald's restaurant. In the ad, the situation, body language, and tonality between father and daughter were purely Latino. The dialogue was warm and encouraging, and there was abundant eye contact between them. The conversation focused on a very traditional rite of passage in Hispanic culture—*la fiesta de la Quinceañera*, or turning sweet fifteen. There was no room left for doubt—the McDonald's commercial was targeting an English-speaking, acculturated, yet *culturally* Hispanic audience. Much like McDonald's, many other companies use culturally attuned publications and campaigns to advertise their products to this lucrative and growing segment of the Hispanic market.

■ Managing Language Diversity

A simple and cost-effective marketing tool to manage language diversity—and to some extent the degree of acculturation—is language-based segmentation. Developed by Hispanic Market Connections (HMC) in the 1980s, language-based segmentation has become an industry standard and an indispensable marketing tool to successfully target the U.S. Hispanic consumer.

In this technique language segmentations are used to classify Hispanic consumers according to certain language characteristics such as ability, proficiency, and language preference for speaking, reading, and writing. This classification permits the marketer or advertiser to correlate the Hispanic consumer's language profile with his or her purchasing habits, media usage, and other important marketing variables.

Variations and differences in brand or product usage can be partly tied to the consumer's language profile. These variations are usually intimately related to acculturation, brand heritage, and media exposure patterns. The language segments provide marketers and advertisers with valuable insight to target a specific market segment in one or another language with campaigns specifically designed to appeal to that segment. In this manner marketers can visualize the market, track and understand the changes taking place in the Hispanic marketplace, and adjust their targeting strategies to the various segments accordingly.

HMC'S LANGUAGE SEGMENTATION   In developing its language segmentation, HMC conducted several major marketing studies in which over 6,000 Hispanic adults were interviewed throughout the country. The findings on language usage and preferences were very useful in developing a segmentation that accurately predicts factors relating to the respondent's degree of acculturation, product and service awareness, product usage, and product-switching behavior. The language segmentation has also been very useful in tracking studies to follow behavior changes and responses to ad campaigns by language segment.

In the studies responses to a battery of twelve language proficiency questions and media usage patterns were used to cluster the U.S. Hispanic market into five segments: "Spanish Dependent," "Spanish Preferred," "No Preference, or true Bilinguals," "English Preferred," and "English Dominant." Because of the small number of people in the two latter groups, they were collapsed into one group, "English Preferred/Dominant."

The first studies consisted of more than 3,000 one-hour interviews conducted with Hispanic consumers in California. Respondents were qualified to participate in this survey if they (1) defined themselves as being of Hispanic, Latino, or Spanish origin and (2) were at least eighteen years old (Hispanic Market Connections, 1992a, b).

Later on, several national studies based on the findings of these first seminal investigations were conducted (Hispanic Market Connections, 1993, 1994).

Each of the five language segments presents a different sociodemographic and psychographic profile.

LANGUAGE SEGMENTS

For example, in southern California, Spanish-dominant and Spanish-preferred tend to be foreign-born and average respectively 10 years and 14 years of residence in the United States, tend to use Spanish-language media, and have lower formal educational achievement and annual incomes than those classified as English-dominant/preferred (Table 5.3).

On the other hand, true-bilinguals—English-preferred/English-dominants—tend to be U.S.-born, or foreign-born. Respectively they average 18 and 28 years of residence in this country. They depend heavily on English-language media and have the highest household incomes of all four segments. A demographic profile of the language segments in southern California is presented in Table 5.3; a recent demographic profile for Chicago is presented in Table 5.4. The findings were quite consistent.

The proportions of each language segment for various areas of dominant influence are shown in Figure 5.5. The Hispanic populations in Miami and New York tend to be from the Caribbean islands, including Cuba, Dominican Republic, and Puerto Rico, and language proficiency and bilingualism vary greatly depending on the market. Hispanics in San Antonio, Texas, tend to be the most acculturated and hence the most English preferred/English dominant. In California these two segments combined represent more than 80 percent of the California Hispanic market and are composed mostly of Mexicans and Central Americans. Data analyzed by segment reflect how acculturation rates have an impact on media usage and value orientation, as well as on shopping behavior, as discussed in more detail below.

Tables 5.5 and 5.6 illustrate the speaking and reading proficiency in English and Spanish of four of the language segments in southern California and in Chicago. As expected the correlation between language proficiency and preference is very high. Spanish dominants are by definition highly proficient in Spanish and not proficient in English. To communicate with this language segment, the largest in the U.S. Hispanic market, the language used must be Spanish.

Psychographic Profile of Segments

In addition to demographic differences, attitudinal, cultural, and value-based differences can be observed between the different language segments. Spanish dominants are the most "traditional" in their beliefs; the English dominant/preferred are the least traditional, closer to the Anglo-American culture. Responses to value-oriented questions by language segments are shown for southern California Hispanics in Table 5.7.

Because consumers in different language segments may have different values as well as language usage patterns, messages and campaigns should be created keeping these variations in mind.

For example, differences in terms of shopping behavior, product usage, couponing, and other variables can also be tracked by language segment. Spanish dominants primarily consult family and friends for information on places to shop for clothing (Table 5.8). Other groups rely on other sources of information, such as print and broadcast media. At the time of the southern California study (1992), very few department stores advertised in Spanish-language media. Therefore, it is not surprising that the more dependent a consumer is on the Spanish language, the higher the dependency on personal networks.

Media Usage and Language Segments

In addition to language preference, one of the most challenging factors when marketing to Hispanic consumers in the United

States is the English and Spanish media mix usage patterns. This country has little in common with monolingual societies, where media are tracked, purchased, and rated in one single language. Until the advent of Nielsen's Hispanic Television Index in 1992, no ongoing reliable data were available about Hispanic language usage and their media mix usage. Hispanic TV ratings data are also tracked by language segment, which mirror Hispanic Market Connections' language segments described earlier in this chapter.

Media usage patterns by language segment for southern California Hispanics and Chicago Hispanics are presented in Tables 5.9 and 5.10. The consumers who are Spanish dominant or Spanish preferred tend to use predominantly Spanish broadcast and print media, and those with no preference and those who are English dominant/preferred tend to use English media most often. As might be expected, Spanish dominants indicated significantly higher preference for television shows and radio programs in Spanish and significantly less interest in English-language programs than other groups. But language crossover is present in all language segments. The acculturation continuum can be observed and tracked based on the different language segments.

Marketers and advertisers who want to capitalize on the opportunity presented by the $200 billion Hispanic market must take into consideration the acculturation process and how this affects the language, media, and communication strategy to be employed for each particular language segment.

Marketing and advertising strategies and research studies based on language proficiency and usage segmentations are efficient tools for targeting and tracking the Hispanic consumer. They provide direction to fine-tune creative strategies with culturally relevant messages in the most effective language and media mix.

■ *References*

Bamford, Katheryn W. "Bilingual Issues in Mental Health: Health Assessment and Treatment." *Hispanic Journal of Behavioral Sciences* 13, no. 4 (1991): 384–385.

Berry, J. W. "Acculturation as Varieties of Adaptation" in *Acculturation: Theory, Models and Some New Findings*, edited by A. M. Padilla. Boulder, Colo.: Westview Press, 1980, 9–25.

————, and R. C. Annis. "Acculturative Stress: The Role of Ecology, Culture and Differentiation." *Journal of Cross-Cultural Psychology*, 5,5, 382–406.

Braus, Patricia. "What Does 'Hispanic' Mean?" *American Demographics* (June 1993); 46–49, 58.

Drug Store News (August 16, 1993).

Hispanic Market Connections. *The Hispanic Database. Northern California.* Los Altos, Calif.: HMC, 1992.

———. *The Hispanic Database. Southern California.* Los Altos, Calif.: HMC, 1991.

———. *Language and Media Planning for the Hispanic Market,* Northern California (1991), Southern California (1992).

———. *The National Hispanic Database.* Los Altos, Calif.: HMC, 1993.

Kanellos, Nicolas, ed. *The Hispanic-American Almanac: A Reference Work on Hispanics in the United States.* Detroit: Gale Research, 1993.

Lacan, Jacques. *Une Saison chez Lacan.* Translated into Spanish from the French by Pierre Rey. (Spanish-Language translation, Editorial Seiz, Barral, Argentina, 1990.)

National Association of Latino Elected and Appointed Officials (NALEO). "Mexicans, Cubans and Other Latinos: Variations in Immigration Experiences." *NLIS Research Notes.* Washington, D.C.: NALEO Educational Fund, 1992.

New York Times, June 29, 1993. As cited in *Minority Markets Alert.* "Immigration Youth Assess Assimilation." August 1993.

San Francisco Chronicle, February 1987.

Schick, L. and Schick, R. *Statistical Handbook on U.S. Hispanics,* Oryx Press, Phoenix, Arizona.

Sluzki, Carlos E. 1983.

U.S. Bureau of the Census. 1990a. *Language Spoken at Home and Ability to Speak English for United States, Regions and States: 1990.* CPH-L-133.

———. 1990b. *1990 Census of Population and Housing.* Summary Tape file 3 (corrected) California Data Center.

———. 1990c. *Official 1990 U.S. Census Form.* Form D-61.

———. 1991. *1990 Census of Population and Housing.* Form B-26, December.

———. 1992. *1990 Census of Population and Housing.* Public Use Microdata Samples.

———. Press Release, 1990.

———. *Current Population Reports,* Series P-25, No. 995 and Series P-20, No. 431.

Valdés, M. Isabel. "Acculturation Process: Which Audience to Reach," paper presented in conjunction with Telemundo at the "Se Habla Español" Fifth Annual Conference, Los Angeles, November 1992.

———. "Acculturation, Value Orientation and Media Usage in the U.S. Hispanic Market." Paper presented at ESOMAR, Mexico City, Mexico, June 1993 (printed in the proceedings of the conference).

Valencia, Humberto. "Point of View: Avoiding Market Blunders." *Journal of Advertising Research.* Vol. 23, no. 6 (December 1983–January 1984): 19–22.

Veltman, Calvin. *The Future of the Spanish Language in the United States.* New York: Hispanic Policy Development Project, 1988.

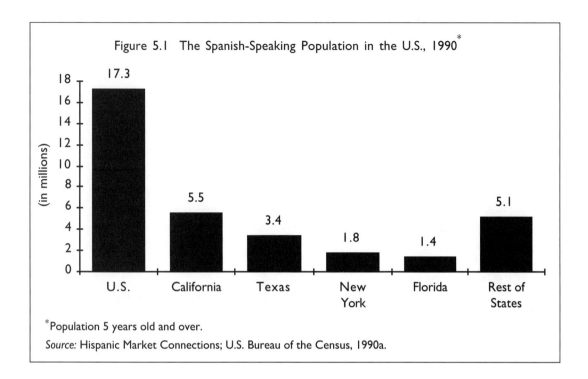

Figure 5.1 The Spanish-Speaking Population in the U.S., 1990[*]

*Population 5 years old and over.

Source: Hispanic Market Connections; U.S. Bureau of the Census, 1990a.

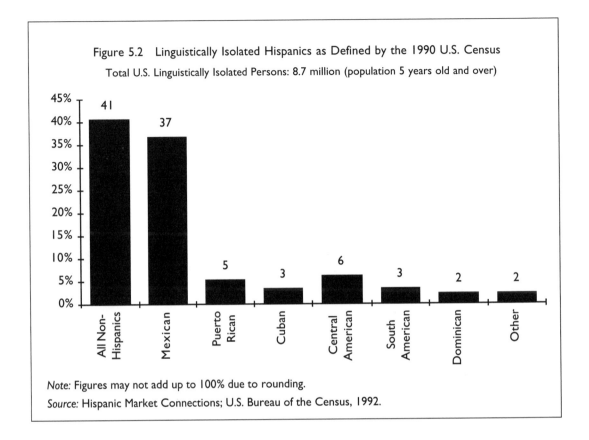

Figure 5.2   Linguistically Isolated Hispanics as Defined by the 1990 U.S. Census

Total U.S. Linguistically Isolated Persons: 8.7 million (population 5 years old and over)

Note: Figures may not add up to 100% due to rounding.

Source: Hispanic Market Connections; U.S. Bureau of the Census, 1992.

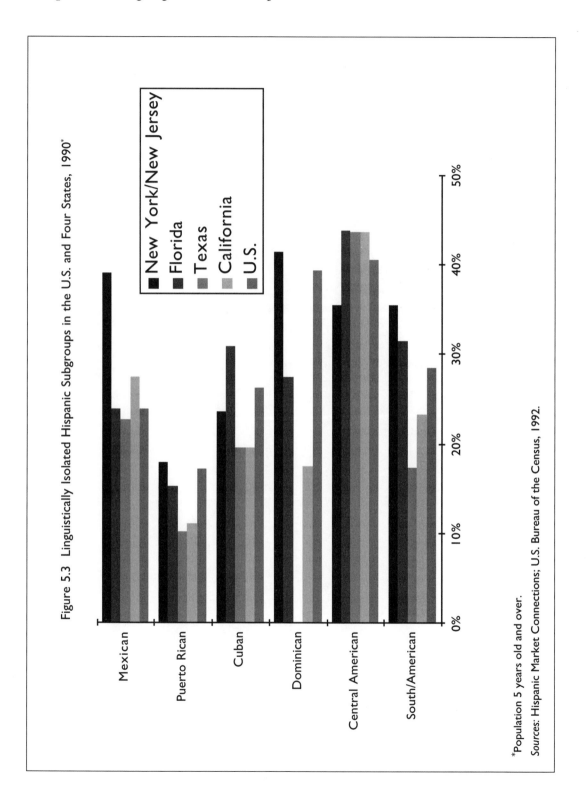

Figure 5.3 Linguistically Isolated Hispanic Subgroups in the U.S. and Four States, 1990*

*Population 5 years old and over.

Sources: Hispanic Market Connections; U.S. Bureau of the Census, 1992.

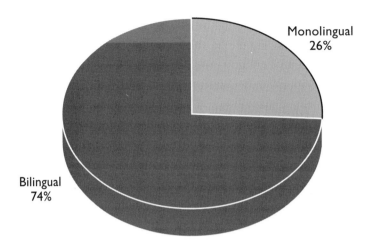

Figure 5.4 U.S. Spanish Monolingual and Bilingual Population 5 Years Old and Over
Total Spanish-speaking population = 17.3 million

Monolingual
26%

Bilingual
74%

Note: Monolingual: speaks English not well/not at all. Bilingual: Speaks English well/very well.

Source: Hispanic Market Connections; U.S. Bureau of the Census, 1990a.

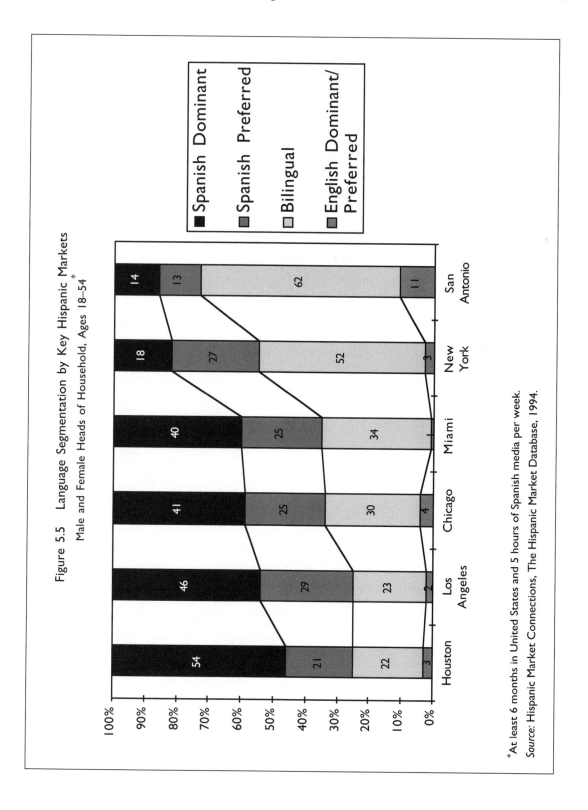

Figure 5.5   Language Segmentation by Key Hispanic Markets
Male and Female Heads of Household, Ages 18–54 *

Legend:
- Spanish Dominant
- Spanish Preferred
- Bilingual
- English Dominant/Preferred

Houston: 54, 21, 22, 3
Los Angeles: 46, 29, 23, 2
Chicago: 41, 25, 30, 4
Miami: 40, 25, 34, 1
New York: 18, 27, 52, 3
San Antonio: 14, 13, 62, 11

*At least 6 months in United States and 5 hours of Spanish media per week.
Source: Hispanic Market Connections, The Hispanic Market Database, 1994.

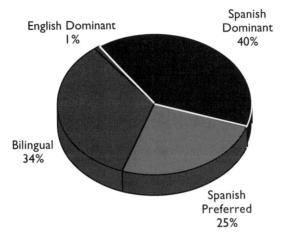

Figure 5.6 Language Preference - New York ADI
Male and Female Heads of Household, Ages 18–54[a]

English Dominant
1%

Spanish
Dominant
40%

Bilingual
34%

Spanish
Preferred
25%

[a]At least 6 months in the United States and 5 hours of Spanish media per week.

Source: Hispanic Market Connections, 1994.

Table 5.1 Census Data on Bilingual and Monolingual Spanish-Speakers Age 5 and Older (United States and Selected States, 1990)

	Speaks Spanish at Home		
	Total (In Thousands)	Monolingual	Bilingual
U.S.	17,339	4,501	12,838
California	5,475	1,780	3,695
Texas	3,442	747	2,695
New York	1,848	472	1,377
Florida	1,447	427	1,020
Rest of states	5,127	1,075	4,051
Percentage of Total U.S. Spanish-Speakers			
California	31.6	39.5	28.8
Texas	19.9	16.6	20.9
New York	10.7	10.5	10.7
Florida	8.3	9.5	12.4
Rest of states	29.5	23.9	27.2

Notes: Monolingual: Speaks Spanish at home and claims to speak English "not well" or "not at all." Bilingual: Speaks Spanish at home and claims to speak English "well" or "very well."

Source: U.S. Bureau of the Census, 1990a.

Table 5.2 Language Questions on the 1990 U.S. Census

15.a. Does this person speak a language other than English at home?

✧ Yes

✧ No—Skip to 16

b. What is this language? (For example: Chinese, Italian, Spanish, Vietnamese)

c. How well does this person speak English?

✧ Very well

✧ Well

✧ Not well

✧ Not at all

Source: U.S. Bureau of the Census, 1990c.

Table 5.3 Demographic Profile of Language Segments: Southern California, 1992
In Percentages

	Total Sample	Spanish Dominant	Spanish Preferred	No Preference	English Dominant/Preferred
Language Usage	(2014)	(962)	(664)	(267)	(117)
	a	b	c	d	
Country of Birth					
United States	16	2	10a	48ab	89abc
Foreign-born (net)	84	98	90	52	11
Mexico	73	88bcd	75cd	42d	7
El Salvador	4	5	5	3	–
Guatemala	3	3	4	2	–
Other Central/ South America	2	6	5	4	–
Years Lived in U.S. (Foreign-Born)					
10 years or fewer	46	62bcd	42cd	14d	–
Average # years in U.S.	12	10	14a	18ab	28abc
Educational Achievement					
Attended/completed grade school	38	54bcd	30cd	15d	4
Attended/completed high school	38	32	43	46a	42
Attended/completed college	22	10	26a	39a	54ab
Income (US$)					
Avg. household annual income (thousands)	$23	$17	$23	$30	$48

Note: Letters in the table denote differences between subgroups that are statistically significant at the 95% level of confidence.

Source: Hispanic Market Connections, 1992, 28.

Table 5.4 Demographic Profile of Language Segments: Chicago, 1994
In Percentages

	Total Sample	Spanish Dominant	Spanish Preferred	No Preference	English Dominant/Preferred
Language Usage	(600)	(212)	(138)	(198)	(52)
	a	b	c	d	
Country of Birth					
United States	22	1	5a	41ab	83abc
Foreign-born (net)	78	99bcd	95cd	59d	17
Mexico	60	90bcd	70cd	33d	6
Caribbean (net)	10	4	9	17a	6
Puerto Rico	9	4	9	16a	4
Cuba	1	1	–	–	2
Central America (net)	5	5	9	4	–
Guatemala	3	2	4	3	–
El Salvador	1	1	2	1	–
South America (net)	3	1	7a	5a	–
Years Lived In U.S. (Foreign-Born)					
Base: Foreign-born	(468)	(211)	(131)	(117)	(9[*])
10 or fewer	42	58cd	44cd	12	–
Avg. # yrs. in U.S.	14.5	10.9	13.7a	21.5ab	21.9a

Note: Letters in the table denote differences between subgroups that are statistically significant at the 95% level of confidence.

[*]Extremely small base size.

Source: Hispanic Market Connections, 1994.

Table 5.5 English and Spanish Language Proficiency Segments: Southern California, 1992 In Percentages

	Total Sample	Spanish Dominant	Spanish Preferred	No Preference	English Dominant/Preferred
Language Usage	(2014)	(962)	(664)	(267)	(117)
	a	b	c	d	
Claimed Ability to Speak Spanish					
Very well/well	97	100d	100d	100d	40
A little/very little	2	–	–	–	36abc
Not at all	–	–	–	–	24abc
Claimed Ability to Read Spanish					
Very well/well	87	89d	94acd	86d	26
A little/very little	10	9b	5	11b	40abc
Not at all	3	2	1	3	34abc
Claimed Ability to Speak English					
Very well/well	33	–	43a	100ab	100ab
A little/very little	27	18cd	57cd	–	–
Not at all	–	82bcd	–	–	–
Claimed Ability to Read English					
Very well/well	33	1	43a	97ab	99ab
A little/very little	25	15cd	54cd	2	–
Not at all	42	84bcd	3	1	1

Note: Letters in the table denote differences between subgroups that are statistically significant at the 95% level of confidence.

Source: Hispanc Market Connections, 1992, 27.

Table 5.6 English and Spanish Language Proficiency Segments, Chicago[*], 1994
In Percentages

	Total Sample	Spanish Dominant	Spanish Preferred	No Preference	English Dominant/Preferred
Language Usage	(600)	(212)	(138)	(198)	(52)
	a	b	c	d	
Can speak Spanish	97	100d	100d	100d	67
Base: Can speak Spanish	(583)	(212)	(138)	(198)	(35[**])
Claimed Ability to Speak Spanish					
Very well/well	92	96d[**]	99d[**]	100d	–
A little/very little	6	–	–	–	100abc
No answer	2	4	1	–	–
Claimed Ability to Read Spanish					
Very well/well	81	84d	94cd	81d	6
A little/very little	17	16	6	15	74abc
Not at all	3	–	–	4	20abc
Can speak English	73	25	100a	100a	100a
Base: Can speak English	(440)	(52)	(138)	(198)	(52)
Claimed Ability to Speak English					
Very well/well	56	–	–	99ab	100ab
A little/very little	43	100cd	100cd	–	–
Claimed Ability to Read English					
Very well/well	56	4	8	92ab	100ab
A little/very little	38	77cd	83cd	7	–
Not at all	6	19cd	9c	1	–

Note: Letters in the table denote differences between subgroups that are statistically significant at the 95% level of confidence.

[*]Adults 18 and Older

[**]A few respondents did not answer this question, but were classified into these language segment groups due to meeting other criteria which qualified them to be defined as ``Spanish dominant'' or ``Spanish preferred.''

Source: Hispanic Market Connections, 1994.

Table 5.7
Value Orientation Differences between Language Segments: Southern California, 1992
In Percentages

	Total Sample	Spanish Dominant	Spanish Preferred	No Preference	English Dominant/Preferred
Language Usage	(2014)	(962)	(664)	(267)	(117)
	a	b	c	d	
% Agreeing that...					
Children should always follow their parents' beliefs	69	77bcd	64	61	55
Parents should sacrifice to send their children to college/university	86	90cd	87cd	78	74
The child who doesn't show respect for the family loses respect in the community	82	84d	81d	81d	65
It is important that known American brands be advertised in Spanish	89	91cd	92cd	83d	67

Note: Letters in the table denote differences between subgroups that are statistically significant at the 95% level of confidence.

Source: Hispanic Market Connections, 1992, 32.

Table 5.8 Retail Information Sources by Language Segments: Southern California, 1992
In Percentages

	Total Sample	Spanish Dominant	Spanish Preferred	No Preference	English Dominant/Preferred
Language Usage	(2014)	(962)	(664)	(267)	(117)
	a	b	c	d	
Source of Store Information					
Family/friends	33	44bcd	29cd	18d	4
Television	16	11	22ab	21ab	10
Coupon mailers	14	12	19acd	9	8
Flyers	11	10	13	8	8
Newspapers	8	6	11a	8	3
Local shopping guides	8	6	10a	9	3
Catalogs	8	6	10a	8	4
Window signs	8	7	11ac	5	8
Radio	7	4	12ad	9a	3
Magazines	6	5	9a	6	1
Yellow pages	5	2	7a	5	3

Note: Letters in the table denote differences between subgroups that are statistically significant at the 95% level of confidence.

Source: Hispanic Market Connections, 1992, 30.

Table 5.9 Media Usage Profile by Language Segments: Southern California, 1992
In Percentages

	Total Sample	Spanish Dominant	Spanish Preferred	No Preference	English Dominant/Preferred
Language Usage	(2014)	(962)	(664)	(267)	(117)
	a	b	c	d	
Avg. Hrs. TV Watched					
Spanish TV on weekdays	3.4	4.1bcd	3.1	2.5	0.7
Spanish TV during weekends	4.9	6.1bcd	4.5	3.2	1.1
English TV on weekdays	2.0	1.2	2.4a	3.3ab	4.1
English TV during weekends	2.8	1.6	3.4a	4.2ab	7.4
Avg. Hrs. Radio Listened To					
Spanish radio on weekdays	2.4	2.9bcd	2.4	1.8	0.6
Spanish radio during weekends	2.4	2.7bcd	2.3	1.9	0.6
English radio on weekdays	1.1	0.5	1.3a	2.4ab	2.7
English radio during weekends	1.2	0.5	1.4a	2.6ab	3.0
Percentage Saying They Read					
Spanish newspapers	47	48cd	56d	36d	10
Spanish magazines	33	32cd	41acd	30d	9
English newspapers	35	12	48a	63ab	87abc
English magazines	20	4	23a	46ab	78abc

Note: Letters in the table denote differences between subgroups that are statistically significant at the 95% level of confidence.

Source: Hispanic Market Connections, 1992, 29.

**Table 5.10 English and Spanish Proficiency Language Segments: Chicago, 1994
In Percentages**

	Total Sample	Spanish Dominant	Spanish Preferred	No Preference	English Dominant/Preferred
Language Usage	(600)	(212)	(138)	(198)	(52)
	a	b	c	d	
Avg. Hrs. TV Watched					
Spanish TV	13.1	17.4cd	15.7cd	9.4d	2.1
English TV	10.6	4.9	9.4a	14.5ab	21.9abc
Avg. Hrs. Radio Listened To					
Spanish radio	12.2	14.2cd	16.1cd	9.5d	3.7
English radio	6.1	1.4	3.8	10.2ab	15.4abc
Percentage Saying They Read					
Spanish newspapers	57	57d	70acd	55d	29
English newspapers	60	24	63a	88ab	94ab

Note: Letters in the table denote differences between subgroups that are statistically significant at the 95% level of confidence.

Source: Hispanic Market Connections, 1994.

C H A P T E R

■ Dynamics of Hispanic Media Use

■ An Overview of the U.S. Hispanic Media

■ Multi-Media Strategies and the Hispanic Consumer

■ Language Segmentation and Media Preference: California

Hispanic Media

in the U.S.

The Spanish-language media industry has a long history of public service in the United States. It first emerged as a response to the informational needs of Hispanics living in the Mexican border states during the 1800s. Since those early days when the first newspapers brought local news in Spanish to Mexicans living and working in southwestern Texas, the Hispanic communications industry has grown into a sophisticated system reaching a mostly Spanish-speaking population across the country. Every single medium is available in Spanish — television and radio, community newspapers, consumer magazines, business publications, outdoor and direct mail listings, and special events. With the advent of satellite communication technology in the 1960s, major television and radio networks began transmitting Spanish-language programming originating in the United States and abroad to their stations and affiliates across the nation. As of March 1994 there were 1,645 media organizations serving the needs of the Hispanic market listed in the Standard Rate and Data Service book, a comprehensive advertising and marketing industry directory (Table 6.1).

The U.S. Hispanic media have a long history of accomplishments and public service; despite this, awareness of the media's strengths, advantages, and potential for marketing has come slowly to most Americans businesses. This lack of awareness is partly because of unfamiliarity with the Hispanic market in general, and partly because Hispanic media have traditionally targeted a Spanish-speaking audience while attempting to draw financial support from non-Spanish speakers, such as corporate advertisers.

Traditionally, corporate America has been skeptical and slow to embark on major Hispanic advertising campaigns. For the most part, budget allocations earmarked for these purposes have proportionally been way below those for the general market. In other words, advertising expenditures have historically not kept pace with the growth of the Hispanic population—an attitude that is reversing itself as more and more information flows to marketers and advertisers, making them aware of the Hispanic population's characteristics and dollar potential.

The first challenge in marketing to Hispanics is choosing the proper medium or best combination of media for an effective advertising campaign. Rapid market growth, large size, and diversity are forcing companies into making difficult decisions about splitting advertising dollars between types of media, geographical areas, and English- and Spanish-language media. Regardless of which specific Hispanic group is being targeted, knowledge of Hispanic media behavior is of the essence. Following are some questions that marketers need to ask in order to successfully select the appropriate media to reach a specific Hispanic audience.

✧ Is the Hispanic target group watching television, listening to the radio, or reading? In English, in Spanish, or both?

✧ What types of programs do they tune to and when? What magazines or newspapers do they read?

✧ How frequently are they tuned to their television or radio sets—in a particular language, according to age, and by gender?

✧ What is the best media language mix?

In this chapter the U.S. Spanish-language media and their potential for targeting Hispanics are covered. We begin with a discussion on the dynamics of Hispanic media use. Next is an overview of some of the major accomplishments and contributions of Hispanic television, the increasing relevance of radio, the various forms of print media, and the role of the leading agencies that monitor them: Nielsen, Arbitron, and the Traffic Audit Bureau for Media Measurement. The next section focuses on the dynamics of Hispanic media usage. Then we move on to explore the strengths and weaknesses of each medium and the advantages of using multiple-media strategies in the Hispanic market. Finally, we discuss the role acculturation plays in Hispanics' choice of medium.

■ Dynamics of Hispanic Media Use

The cultural diversity within the Hispanic market is reflected in its use of the media. For an immigrant population, the media can play a very relevant emotional and informational role. For example, for the foreign born, the Spanish-language media provide a link with their past, their country of origin, and their culture, in addition to companionship. The media are also the means for these consumers to become more active and informed participants in the United States. For the Spanish-dominant group, Spanish-language media is like a lifeline, a major source of information and education, that helps them deal with their often severe information gaps, a godsend that helps ease the transition between countries and cultures. For the Spanish-preferred and bilinguals, Spanish-language media is also a source to practice their native language, and help their children learn and practice the language of their ancestors. An important cultural value that helps ensure the inter-generational bond. For U.S.-born and bilingual Hispanics, the Spanish-language media provide the value of cultural or ethnic identification, much the same way as specific programming targeting the African-American community does for that population segment.

HISPANIC CONSUMERS Research shows that Hispanics consume every type of media although they seem to have a special attraction to television and radio. With two languages and cultures from which to choose, many Hispanic consumers can exercise an option generally unavailable to the rest of the population: they can choose between English- or Spanish-language media. Again, research shows however, that Hispanics, particularly Spanish-dominants and Spanish-preferred, tend to lean heavily toward Spanish language media. This pattern is expected to continue for the foreseeable future because of the emotional and informational benefits that Spanish-language provides to these consumers. One can envision, however, that as the number of bilingual and bicultural Hispanics increases, so will the competition between the major English and Spanish media for this market.

Regardless of what the future holds, what is clear now is that marketers targeting Hispanic consumers cannot afford to dismiss Spanish-language advertising. The evidence is clear. English media alone provide insufficient coverage to target this market.

■ An Overview of the U.S. Hispanic Media

The general mass media and Hispanic media function side by side. Both are part of a vast communication system of electronic and printed information specifically designed to meet the cultural, linguistic, informational, and marketing needs of the U.S. population. The Hispanic media differ from those of the general market in that the Hispanic media provide entertainment, cultural events, political news, sports, and social developments of interest to Hispanics, about and from countries in the Spanish-speaking world, in addition to mainstream information. These events are only sporadically covered by mainstream English media and sometimes are completely absent from those sources.

Over the years the Spanish-language media have become indispensable and heavily utilized sources of public information about Hispanic culture in general, and especially about Latin America.

The U.S. Spanish-language media have become principal sources of information for events taking place in the Spanish-speaking areas of the world and the main vehicles to keep Hispanics abreast of local and national U.S. events.

A critical function of the Hispanic media is to provide a friendly informational and entertainment milieu for Spanish-speaking immigrants to enjoy the Hispanic culture. Another important but less noted function is the role the media play in the acculturation and economic integration of Hispanics into U.S. society. Spanish-language corporate and government advertisements and Spanish-language television, radio, and print media in all forms bring American culture to wide segments of the Hispanic population that otherwise is linguistically and culturally isolated from American society.

For marketers, advertisers, and government agencies, Spanish-language media are the best available means to reach Spanish-speaking consumers and constituency. There are millions of Spanish-dominant consumers in the United States who depend on Spanish-language media for their daily informational needs. Members of this particular consumer group, comprising one-fifth of the entire U.S. Hispanic population, are active participants in the American economy. They pour billions of dollars into the marketplace while simultaneously consuming American goods and services that are advertised in Hispanic media. Hence, the best strategy to reach over 23-million-total U.S. Hispanic audience is one that includes Spanish-only media or a combined strategy of Spanish and English channels.

TELEVISION

Gone are the days of the 1950s and 1960s when part-time Spanish television and radio served relatively few Hispanic viewers in New York and west Texas. With the advent in 1961 of Spanish International Communication Corporation (SICC) and its sister company, Spanish International Network (SIN)—the two of which later became the Univisión Group—a new chapter began in the history of the U.S. Hispanic media. U.S. Spanish-language media development reflects the accomplishments and vivid imaginations of a few people with the vision, foresight, financial power, and opportunity to embark on the global business of entertaining and informing Hispanic viewers in the United States and Latin America.

The oldest networks—SICC and SIN—remained unchallenged for nearly 25 years, until in 1986 a new network, the Telemundo Group, came into being. Then in 1988, Galavisión, at the time a small cable-operated Spanish network, was transformed into an advertising-based basic cable service offering 24-hour-a-day programming via networks fed by satellites. In October 1993, Music Television (MTV) network launched its Hispanic operations. MTV airs a customized 24-hour music video network for Spanish-speaking viewers in Latin America and the United States. In October 1994, Fox entered into an independent production deal with Nely Galán, a young Hispanic producer and TV station manager, to create and produce programming aimed at the English-dominant, second generation U.S. Hispanic segment. The new production company will also create original programming for distribution throughout Latin America (*Hispanic Media and Market* Update, October 31, 1994, 2).

Historically, about one-half of Hispanic networks' operations have originated in Latin America and Spain. *Novelas* (soap operas), movies, plays, and other forms of entertainment are transmitted to the United States directly from Mexico and other countries in South America. More recently, however, there has been a rise in the number of Spanish-language TV programs being produced in the United States—a trend that is expected to accelerate in the next few years, as the Fox deal shows.

The addition of three television networks in less than 15 years revolutionized the Hispanic media scene in the United States. Programming once restricted to a few broken hours on English-language stations is now continuously transmitted by Spanish-language stations. Currently the three major Spanish television networks—Univisión, Telemundo, and Galavisión—transmit to 64 cities across the country via 95 stations (Table 6.2).

A major accomplishment of Spanish-language television was the pioneering of modern communication technology in the United States. In 1976 SICC preceded the leading English networks— CBS, ABC, and NBC—in distributing programming directly through satellite. In 1993 the Telemundo Group leased from Hughes Communications, the largest private commercial satellite operator, two C-band transponders. Together in 1993 Univisión and Telemundo had close to 1 million cable and satellite connections.

With a blossoming Hispanic audience here and abroad, the stakes in the television industry have become high. When it comes to television, almost every U.S. Hispanic household owns a set. And there are over 6.7 million Hispanic households in the United States according to *Hispanic Business* (Lopes, February, 1993, 36). Together the two leading Spanish networks operating coast to coast reach on average 6 million households, or 89 percent of the total Hispanic market. Galavisión, serving California, Texas, and Arizona, reaches over 3 million households, up from 160,000 in 1988.

A favorable climate of openness in Latin America brought about by democratization, privatization, improved economies, and the spirit of free market competition has encouraged a major move to make television more accessible to Latin American audiences. New business deals and acquisitions in several Latin American countries (Venezuela, Argentina, Chile) by Univisión and its Mexican co-owner, Televisa, make it possible for the Hispanic media to reach significant segments of the Latin American audience. In time the mega-television network could reach over 460 million Spanish-speakers in Latin America alone.

In addition, the cable industry is branching out aggressively to reach Spanish-speakers in this country and Latin America. For example, in the United States the new cable channel HBO En Español brings sporting events and Hollywood movies in Spanish to major U.S. Hispanic markets. In Latin America, Fox television network in 1994 launched 24-hour general entertainment cable television programming in Spanish, Portuguese, and English for audiences from Mexico to Argentina. Cable television is also targeting specific audiences within the Hispanic market. GEMS Television in Miami is the "first and only cable service with programming for women in Spanish." Entertainment includes novelas, comedies, musicals, and movies, which are aired daily for 16 hours.

The rapid expansion of Hispanic cable television in such a brief period of time reflects an increasingly positive and enthusiastic Hispanic response to the medium. The 1993 MTV Hispanic Audience Survey, reported in *Se Habla Español* (Hispanic Business, 1994, 1–3), showed that

✧ 33 percent of Hispanic non-subscribers would like to subscribe to cable if MTV Latino were offered by the operator.

✧ 62 percent of Hispanic subscribers expressed high interest in the new channel, as well as 55 percent of non-subscribers.

✧ 46 percent would be more satisfied with their cable service if MTV Latino were included.

The expansion in cable television will open up tremendous opportunities for advertisers and cable operators.

Despite a leading role, the Spanish-language networks are not alone in their quest for a larger Hispanic audience. Unlike the old days when Univisión and Telemundo had only each other to compete with, now the major English-language networks have joined the race to capture a larger share of the growing bilingual Hispanic audience. To measure up to the competition, two Spanish-language networks in a recent and unprecedented historical shift joined forces to upgrade their rating system. To do this they commissioned Nielsen Media Research to provide the industry with standard viewer ratings data—the "what," "which," "when," and "how long"—of Hispanic television viewers. Because of Nielsen's reputation for reliable ratings within the industry, the move has earned the Spanish-language networks added credibility among advertisers.

The international scope of Spanish-language television operations, which allows the networks to reach millions of people in the United States and across the border, simultaneously gives companies in the United States and the rest of the world the greatest marketing tools for promoting their products and services.

Nielsen Hispanic Television Index (NHTI)

November 1992 marked a turning point for Univisión and Telemundo. At that time, Nielsen Media Research revolutionized networks, advertisers, TV stations, program producers, cable systems, and networks by introducing a new service designed to measure television viewing in Hispanic households nationwide. Although Nielsen had always measured Hispanic households, it had done so only as part of its overall total television viewing. The new service, known to the television industry as Nielsen's Hispanic Television Index, or NHTI, is the counterpart to the National Television Index (NTI), which measures the viewing habits of the entire nation.

To ascertain what Hispanics living in more than 6.2 million households across the nation are watching and on which channels, Nielsen gathers its data from a scientific sample consisting of a panel of over 800 Hispanic households representing approximately 3,000 people. The sample is designed to represent the Hispanic household population in its proper proportion according to geographical dispersion and language spoken at home (the sample does not include those Hispanics living in institutions or group quarters). The data collected from the sample are then projected to achieve TV viewership results for the entire U.S. Hispanic household population (Nielsen Media Research, 1993, 8–15).

To collect the data, Nielsen uses a sophisticated measuring device known as the People Meter, the same instrument used to measure viewing patterns for the general national television audience. The meter, which is attached to each household TV set, is specifically designed to retrieve the personal input of each household member—and also of visitors—at the exact time a program is being viewed. The unique design of the meter and its accompanying remote control unit allows Nielsen to collect information on when the set is turned on or off, which channel is viewed, and when a channel is changed, for any TV set in any room in the house. The information is then stored daily in the in-home metering system and retrieved by Nielsen's computers in Dunedin, Florida (Nielsen Media Research, 1993a, 14). This sophisticated mode of viewing data collection allows Nielsen's professionals to monitor and interpret results on a daily basis.

A major advantage of Nielsen's method of data collection is the ability to record the audience's viewing behavior as it happens, thus bypassing errors that occur with day-after recall interviews. Limitation of the method, however, is its ability to maintain the original sample size, which largely depends on the willingness of the household members to consistently push the button connecting each viewer to the overall system. Reluctance to do this occurs because some participants feel uncomfortable with in-home meter technology and also with a long-term commitment to NHTI as well. These factors, which are more common among the less acculturated Hispanic viewers and recent arrivals, hinder the representativeness of this particular segment. Hence, Nielsen's management carefully monitors NHTI's drop-outs as well as the changes in the demographic composition of the sample, to ensure its accurate representativeness of the total Hispanic market.

Once the data are collected and analyzed, NHTI subscribers— Telemundo and Univisión, major ad agencies, corporations like Anheuser-Busch and Clorox, and others—are able to obtain monthly information on the viewing habits for the total Hispanic household sample and for those households in the sample in which Spanish is the dominant language. The results are then extrapolated to represent the viewing habits of the total U.S. Hispanic population. In this fashion, subscribers can determine which programs are viewed most frequently; the extent to which they appeal more to some demographic segments than others; and, most importantly, the extent to which Spanish and English television are adequately serving the Hispanic audience. The availability of NHTI's ratings data has increased dramatically the accuracy of the media planning task.

The hiring of an independent agency with high standing among corporate America gave Spanish-language television a credibility it had not experienced in the past. In bringing Nielsen in to measure Hispanics' television-viewing habits relative to those of the general population for each major U.S. television network, both Univisión and Telemundo achieved the much-needed legitimization and respect of their own subscribers and advertisers at large.

Legitimization and recognition were essential aspects of the Nielsen's Hispanic Television Index revolution. What really startled the Spanish-language networks, as well as the entire television industry, was the new rating service findings. The new television index showed that contrary to prevalent beliefs, all Hispanics watch some English-language media, but they were not watching the mix of Spanish- and English-language TV that was previously assumed. The new system also showed a big drop, about 70 percent, in the ratings of some of the Spanish network programs that were thought to be the most popular (Wool, 1993). In other words, Nielsen found that fewer viewers than previously reported by other media research services were watching what were thought to be the leading Hispanic programs, such as "Siempre en Domingo" and "Sabado Gigante." Still, the data showed that these are highly watched programs, but not to the extent believed before Nielsen's rating. What appeared to be a shift in viewing habits was actually a methodological change that essentially affected the sample design and the data collection. According to some sources, the previous methodology tended to over-represent Spanish-dominant viewers and to use methods of data collection thought to be less reliable for rating purposes, for example memory recall about programs aired the day before the interview (Wool, 1993).

According to the Nielsen Hispanic Television Index (1993), the four major English-language television networks—ABC, CBS, NBC, and FOX—under-deliver by a great margin Hispanic viewers. During prime-time television, for example, the rating for all Hispanic viewers averages 43 percent lower, and for Spanish dominants 75 percent lower, than for the general audience (Figure 6.1). Compared with the total population, relatively few Hispanics tune into English-language television. According to Nielsen's media rating indices, over 60 percent of all men (Figure 6.2) and 70 percent of all women (Figure 6.3) tend to watch television during prime-time hours, and 66 percent of all women watch over a 24–hour period (Figure 6.4). Compared with Spanish-dominant men, Spanish-dominant women watch more prime time Spanish-language television and less cable and English-language television programming.

Television Viewing Patterns

How often the target audience watches television, listens to the radio, reads a newspaper, or looks at a billboard makes a great difference in the effectiveness of the ad campaign. As a rule of thumb, fewer than two exposures is considered ineffective. Ten to seventeen exposures is considered excessive and deemed to bring negative results. But two to ten exposures is usually considered adequate (Figure 6.5). Given these exposure parameters, it is obvious that to target Hispanics today, Spanish-language TV, and radio for that matter, deliver a greater share of the Hispanic market. Figures 6.6 and 6.7 show viewing patterns for Spanish-dominant adults and California households.

Viewership of Top-Rated General Market

Hispanic viewers and general market audiences have different viewing tastes. Ratings for shows in English reflect the tastes of the general market rather than that of the Spanish-speaking audience. The top-rated general market shows usually under-deliver Hispanic adults in general and Spanish-dominants in particular by a wide margin (Tables 6.3 and 6.4). For example, in February 1993, viewing patterns show that "60 Minutes" was a favorite of the general market but not of the Spanish-dominant audience. In contrast, "Rescue 911" was a favorite of Spanish dominants but not of the general audience (Tables 6.5 and 6.6). Table 6.7 shows the ten top-rated general market programs for Spanish-dominant women and their respective ratings for general audience women.

RADIO

Spanish radio broadcasting in the United States began service to the public in the 1920s. From a few isolated stations transmitting live and only a few hours a week, Spanish-language radio developed into a system of AM and FM stations transmitting via wire stations and satellite. Standard Rates & Data Service (March 1994, 64, 87–89) lists 9 radio networks groups (Table 6.1) and over 500 radio stations transmitting over 10 hours a week. Also listed are 271 AM and 99 FM spot radio stations. While some stations produce their own programming, others utilize outside agencies for newscasts or full-service programming. Spanish language radio provides U.S. Hispanics with a cultural forum of their own while connecting them with the larger society. Programming includes news, talk shows, sports, and music, mainly from and about Latin America, other Hispanic countries, and to a lesser extent the United States (Standard Rates and Data Service, March 1994, 87–89). Another important fact for advertisers is that many Hispanics prefer Spanish-language over English-language radio not only because they can understand the language but because radio offers a unique cultural forum with which specific Hispanic groups can identify.

The accelerated pace in the rise of Spanish-language radio stations around the country sends strong messages to the marketing industry. Not only are there more Hispanics in the country, but more can be reached via radio. Note, for example, that in less than a decade the number of AM and FM stations owned or represented by Spanish Katz Radio Group more than doubled in the eastern United States and quadrupled in the West. On the local level, in Los Angeles KLAX-FM radio, owned by Spanish Broadcasting System, reported that "during an average week, about 895,000 people 12 years of age and over tune in to KLAX for at least five minutes," making KLAX (or "La X") a star in the national radio industry, regardless of language of broadcasting.

The success story of KLAX-FM, which almost overnight surpassed English-language radio in popularity by becoming the number-one station in Los Angeles (*Mendose Hispanic Magazine*, April 1993, 24–26), speaks to this issue. Located in the middle of Los Angeles' large Mexican immigrant population, KLAX-FM began broadcasting musical themes that were already popular in the regions from which these potential listeners originated. Once the station began to play the familiar sounds, the audience followed. The familiar sounds offered a cultural refuge to an audience that was in the midst of change. Population density, size, language, and cultural sensitivity were all factors that entered into the marketing plan of this radio station.

The KLAX story also illustrates the fundamental significance of radio for advertisers in this particular market. Once a station has captured an audience, the audience can be followed just about anyplace. Those who listen to radio will do so everywhere—at home, in any room in the house, at work, in their cars, at the beach, or while exercising. People will listen to it alone or in the company of others, to party or just to relax, or listen to the news. The continuity and intimacy of radio provides advertisers with the opportunity to promote their products and services closer to the moment when they will most likely be used.

The transportability of radio is a prime reason why programming varies markedly between stations, locations, AM and FM, and English- or Spanish-speaking audiences. Different Hispanic subgroups have different musical backgrounds and tastes (see Chapter 4, page 189). For this reason, more and more Spanish-language stations are adapting their programs to suit a particular segment of the Hispanic audience. The popularity of Mexican music in the Southwest reflects the preferences and tastes of a large Mexican audience and its affinity for themes such as *ranchero*—the equivalent to American country music, *norteña*—a form of country typical of northern Mexico, or *banda*—a blend of country and western music and contemporary Spanish. Hispanic radio is also leading in the "language switching" format, which uses both English and Spanish in a conversation, reflecting acculturation's impact on language usage (see Chapter 5, page 226). Switching between languages is common among bilingual Hispanics and those for whom English is the dominant or preferred language. In Texas, where switching languages is more pervasive, the switching has been called *Tejano*, which derives from the older term *Chicano* (del Castillo, 1994, 4). Language switching radio stations have enjoyed tremendous popularity in the recent past, both in Texas and California, since switching is more prevalent among Mexicans and Mexican-Americans.

Radio reaches well over 90 percent of Hispanics of most ages. Ninety-nine percent of all U.S. households, 95 percent of all cars, 61 percent of adults, and 84.3 percent of walk-along players include a radio (Radio Association of Broadcasters, *RAB/Facts Book*, cited in Katz Hispanic Radio Research 1992, 5). Hispanics are great radio listeners, tuning in on an average of 26 to 30 hours a week and listening about 13 percent more than the general population (Arbitron cited in Gerlin, 1993, *Wall Street Journal* B-1, and Arbitron, 1993a, 6). They listen to radio at home, in the car, and at work, and according to several HMC regional studies, more on weekdays than on weekends (Figures 6.8 and 6.9; Table 6.8) (Hispanic Market Connections, 1992a, 1992b, 1993, 1994, Arbitron, 1993b, 8). It is clear that radio is an effective choice for advertisers interested in targeting Hispanic consumers.

Hispanic Listening Habits

Hispanics have unique listening habits. According to Arbitron, Spanish-language radio is the format preferred by Hispanics age 12 and over (43.1 percent). Hispanics' affection for Top 40 music (15 percent) is greater than that of the general population (10 percent) as well as that of African-Americans (6 percent). Urban music, a combination of Hip-Hop, Rhythm, Blues, and Rap, and a big favorite among African Americans (54.5 percent), is not popular among Hispanics (4.2 percent) (Arbitron, 1993a, 7).

Also, according to Arbitron, Spanish-language radio is unaffected by seasonality or time of day. This unique characteristic, not found among other population segments, gives advertisers an edge. They can target specific Hispanic groups any time of the day or any time of the year. Audience share will not vary whether it is summer or winter, 6:00 a.m. or 12:00 midnight. Monday through Sunday large segments of the Hispanic market will be tuned to their radios all day long, all year round. As shown in Figure 6.10, every single demographic group age 12 and older listens to radio, although most listeners cluster around ages 25–64 (Arbitron Ratings, 1987, 22).

Because radio can cater to very defined audiences, this medium gives advertisers opportunities not yet fully realized, for example, using Spanish language radio to specifically target women in specific age groups: teens, young adults, mature women. Hispanic women tend to listen to radio more than Hispanic men (Arbitron, 1993a, 7). Radio offers the perfect opportunity to speak one-on-one to the members of this rapidly emerging market.

Arbitron is to radio what Nielsen is to television. Arbitron has been measuring Hispanic listening since 1967, when the first Spanish-language diaries were introduced. Diaries are booklets or notebooks that keep track of the time, stations, place, day of the week, and demographics of the listeners. Participants are asked to fill these out on a weekly basis. In 1985 a bilingual review board was created, and currently Arbitron uses bilingual interviewers, survey materials, and diaries in forty markets with significant Hispanic populations.

Arbitron

Since 1989, when the first large study of Spanish radio was conducted, Arbitron has considerably improved its data collection methodology. Still, the diary system has several disadvantages: It relies on the willingness of individuals to keep the diary, the accuracy of the entries and memory recall, and the ability of the respondents to record the entries. In addition, the task of recording information depends on the person's ability to follow the instructions properly. Some of these are tasks that may be cumbersome for less literate listeners, recent immigrants, or for those individuals coming from countries not familiar with this information-gathering method. This may well result in under-reporting of the number of Spanish-dominant and Spanish-preferred listeners.

Primary Hispanic Radio

✧ Caballero Radio Network: 79 AM/FM non-interconnected stations in Arizona, California, Colorado, Connecticut, District of Columbia, Florida, Georgia, Illinois, Louisiana, Massachusetts, Nevada, New Mexico, New Jersey, Pennsylvania, Texas, and Washington.

✧ Cadena Radio Centro: 53 AM/FM interconnected stations via satellite in Arizona, California, District of Columbia, Florida, Georgia, Idaho, Illinois, Louisiana, Massachusetts, Missouri, Nevada, New Mexico, New York, Oklahoma, Oregon, Pennsylvania, Rhode Island, Texas, Utah, and Washington.

✧ CBS Hispanic Radio Network: 50 interconnected stations via satellite in Arizona, California, Colorado, Connecticut, Florida, Georgia, Illinois, Massachusetts, Nevada, New Jersey, New Mexico, New York, Oklahoma, Oregon, Rhode Island, Texas, and Washington.

✧ CNN Radio Noticias: 40 AM/FM interconnected stations via satellite in Arizona, California, Colorado, Connecticut, District of Columbia, Florida, Georgia, Illinois, Louisiana, Massachusetts, New Hampshire, New Mexico, New York, Texas, Utah, and Washington.

✧ Hispanic Radio Network: 82 AM/FM interconnected stations in Arizona, California, Colorado, Connecticut, District of Columbia, Florida, Illinois, Louisiana, Massachusetts, Nevada, New Jersey, New Mexico, New York, Pennsylvania, Rhode Island, Texas, and Washington.

✧ Lotus Hispanic Radio Network: 74 AM/FM non-interconnected stations in Arizona, California, Colorado, Connecticut, Florida, Illinois, Nevada, New Jersey, New Mexico, Oklahoma, Puerto Rico, Texas, and Utah.

✧ Katz Hispanic Media: 49 AM/FM non-interconnected stations in California, Colorado, District of Columbia, Florida, Illinois, New Mexico, New York, Pennsylvania, Texas, Washington, and Puerto Rico.

✧ Spanish Information Service: 44 AM/FM interconnected stations via satellite in Arizona, California, Colorado, Florida, Massachusetts, Nevada, New Mexico, New York, and Texas.

✧ Tichenor Spanish Radio Group: 14 non-interconnected stations by tape and interconnected live by wire stations in Illinois, Florida, New York, and Texas.

(*Source:* Standard Rate and Data Service, 1993, 87–89.)

PRINT

The Hispanic print media include Spanish, bilingual, and English-language newspapers, magazines, publications, outdoor listings, and direct mail advertising. The first Hispanic community newspaper, *El Misisipi,* began circulation as early as 1808 in New Orleans, and the first Hispanic commercial use of posters dates back to the first quarter of the twentieth century. Today there are more than 300 newspapers, magazines, and business publications, and 37 organizations for outdoor listings.

As it did in television and radio, modern communication technology has swept through the print media, dramatically improving the way news and information are gathered and distributed. Today satellites, computers, fax machines, special phone lines, and home information systems are the principal tools used by newspapers and magazines servicing this growing market segment. The increase in Spanish-language newspapers and magazines could not have been possible without the continuous growth and participation of professional Hispanic bilingual journalists, reporters, copy editors, and others working in the industry (The Dow Jones Newspaper Fund, 1993, 4, 11, 15–17). This is a trend that will surely persist as the Hispanic newspaper industry matures and grows in an effort to better represent and voice the needs, ideas, and concerns of the growing Hispanic communities they serve.

As expected, the major daily Spanish-language newspapers are found in areas where the Hispanic concentration is highest, for example, in Los Angeles (*La Opinión*), Miami (*El Nuevo Herald and El Diario de Las Américas*), and New York (*El Diario-La Prensa and Noticias del Mundo*), whereas smaller local newspapers are spread over a wide range of localities. Clearly, Hispanics have a strong preference for reading in Spanish; otherwise, it would be difficult to explain why their use of Spanish-language newspapers far exceeds that of bilingual and English-language papers. Of the newspapers listed in *Hispanic Media and Market* for 1993, 102 were printed in Spanish, 36 were in Spanish and English, and 6 were in English (Standard Rate and Data Service, 159–89). Similarly, most Hispanic magazines also cater to the Spanish-speaking population.

Readership among Hispanics

The publication of hundreds of newspapers and magazines serving Hispanics defies the perception often conveyed by the media that as a group Hispanics do not, cannot, or will not read. This image continues to be reinforced because most times Hispanics are compared with the general market, which on average has higher readership levels. Depending on the source, readership for Spanish-speaking persons ranges from 60 percent (Hispanic Market Connections, 1993, 51) to 72.4 percent, compared with 85 percent for whites (U.S. Bureau of the Census, 1992, 551).

In all societies readership levels are largely determined by socioeconomic conditions. Research shows that ethnicity plays a minor role or no role at all in how much or how well Hispanics read (Burgoon and Burgoon, 1986, 7; Greenberg et al., 1986, 91). Much as with the rest of the population, Hispanics with more formal education, higher incomes, and white-collar occupations tend to read more than those at the lower end of the socioeconomic scale.

For example, according to Standard Rate and Data Service (1993, 165, 167), Miami's Spanish-language newspaper *El Nuevo Herald* has a circulation on Sundays (126,398) that is about twice the circulation of Los Angeles' *La Opinión* (63, 382). Yet the size of the Hispanic population of Miami is about half the size of Los Angeles'. So why the difference? Cubans are the Hispanic majority in Miami, they are also relatively older, and better educated and tend to have higher incomes than Mexicans, the largest group in Los Angeles. Thus, Cubans would be more likely than

Mexicans to buy newspapers and other publications. Per capita newspaper readership in Los Angeles is much lower than in Miami even when differences in the age composition of both groups are taken into account. Since the frequency with which people buy newspapers, magazines, and other reading materials increases with education, income, and age, a larger consumption of print media among Hispanics in Los Angeles can be projected to increase as Hispanics there mature and move up the educational and income ladders.

Different readership levels among Hispanic groups calls for different marketing and advertising strategies. For example, in areas of lower readership there is a greater need for using a combination of print media. Supplementing newspapers and magazine advertisement with outdoor advertising, posters, couponing, pictorials, and visual images allows marketers to widen their target group by reaching Hispanic consumers of various socioeconomic levels.

Research shows that although proportionally fewer Hispanics read than general market consumers, those who do read spend as much time as Anglos in a given day reading a newspaper (Greenberg et al., 1986, 89). Predictors associated with increased Hispanic readership are shown in Table 6.9. As discussed later in this chapter, print media play a unique role for immigrant populations in the communicative strategy (see page 275).

OUTDOOR ADVERTISING

Because of its unique marketing strengths, outdoor advertising is an excellent option for targeting Hispanics. In addition to being less costly than any of the other media, which makes it more affordable to small businesses, it is highly visible and can be used to convey a message of strength and permanence. This is particularly relevant for a large segment of Hispanics who need psychological confirmation that brands, products, or services are strong, important, and well-known in order to gain trust.

Ads can also be placed inside public transportation, where a captive audience has time to read and concentrate on the ad. This can be especially helpful to those Hispanics who have lower readership skills and limited knowledge of English.

For Spanish-speaking consumers, outdoor advertising has several advantages: the print on posters and billboards is big and the information can be looked up as often as needed. Best of all, such large print images give the impression of being "tangible" and permanent, both of which enhance product recognition and recall.

Outdoor advertising catering to a Spanish-speaking population should be directional. For example, to promote a clinic, it should include an 800 number and/or an address where the clinic is located. Since the benefits of outdoor advertising depend on traffic and the number of people circulating in a particular spot, this type of advertising is very valuable in Hispanic neighborhoods.

The outdoor advertising industry is monitored by the Traffic Audit Bureau—an independent, nonprofit organization whose primary mission is "to authenticate circulation for out-of-home media in an unbiased and objective manner" (*Outdoor Advertising Magazine* 1993, 2:4).

■ Multi-Media Strategies and the Hispanic Consumer

Two main types of mass media are discussed in communication theory. One consists of the dynamic media, such as television, radio, electronic billboards, and interactive television, and the other consists of the still, or nondynamic, media, which include all forms of print, such as newspapers, magazines, coupons, leaflets, bill inserts, outdoor billboards, posters, and public transportation boards. Each type of medium has its own strengths and weaknesses (Valdés, 1976). Multiple-media combinations—that is, when both dynamic and still media are involved in a communications campaign—offer the most effective means to get a message across and move the consumer to action.

From a marketing perspective, communication through television or radio is similar to face-to-face communication in the sense that either medium can capture the audience's attention as if the person were "there." A picture paints a thousand words; the right tone of voice or the proper music can touch an audience's heart.

Both television and radio can have a tremendous impact on the way the audience perceives a particular product or service. They can raise awareness to new heights or change the image of the product forever.

One of the greatest assets of dynamic media is the potential to capture in a brief moment the mind of the person who is watching or listening to the ad. Contact with the viewer, however, is short-lived. The ad is powerful insofar as it is actively present for the audience. Once it is gone, however, not even the power of freeze-frame technology can keep the message alive. This "touch-and-go" characteristic is a major limitation of broadcast media, for a message is only effective while it is on the air. Once the message is over and the images and sounds are gone, there is nothing tangible for the audience to hold on to—no pictures, no visuals, no music. Viewers are left cold, forced to rely on their own memories. Attaining a good message or brand recall rate is hard enough for consumers who are free from linguistic and cultural constraints, but it is much, much harder for those who are not, such as immigrants or less acculturated Hispanic consumers. Increased advertising frequency and culturally attuned ads help offset these limitations.

The ephemeral relationship that exists between radio and television advertising and the consumer is a major handicap for immigrant populations, which frequently need substantially more time to understand foreign-language brand names or addresses and more repetition to grasp the full impact of the messages being aired. Because these consumers may also suffer from informational gaps, their need for product or service information reinforcement surpasses that of the general population. In this sense, a piece of paper in their hands showing and describing the product they saw being promoted on television or radio is a greatly valued and effective communication device.

That "piece of paper," be it a newspaper or a magazine ad or a coupon describing the product or service of interest, is the one thing an eager consumer can carry along with them to the store. With this aid, the consumer will be able to recognize the product and buy it. The printed ad also offers other advantages for Spanish-dominant consumers. It helps them avoid having to say the product's name in a language they are not fluent in, and so save face when confronted with what they think is an embarrassing situation, such as having to ask the store clerk the same question repeatedly, or not being able to say what product they are looking for or is on sale. In other words, that ad on a "piece of paper" also helps consumers keep their pride and personal comfort. In sum, it helps them to shop at ease for the particular product or brand they saw advertised in a television commercial or heard about on a radio broadcast.

For example, researchers from Hispanic Market Connections (HMC) (based on qualitative research conducted in Los Angeles and Miami with young Hispanic males, 1991) observed this need for visual or auditory repetition and reinforcement among young Hispanic males during a qualitative "communications check" of a television commercial that advertised several styles of athletic shoes. After the TV commercial was shown the first time, the young men in the focus groups kept asking the moderator to replay the ad. When asked why, they responded that they were very interested in the product but that the commercial "had not shown the shoe brand and styles long enough" for them to find the ones they liked at the store. What they wanted from the commercial was more than just knowing that the product exists — they wanted a very clear image of the product, which would help them recognize the shoes later in the store.

When television or radio commercials are reinforced with printed material, the situation changes. For example, if, in addition to a television commercial, a coupon or print ad is also available, the Hispanic consumer needing more detailed information about the product can look at the ad for any length of time and internalize the subtleties and characteristics of the product, all of which would help him or her with the in-store search.

The foregoing example highlights two crucial elements in the Hispanic communication strategy and media-planning process. First, if more air time is spent focusing on the unique identifiable characteristics of the product, the unfamiliar consumer viewing or listening to the commercial has a greater chance to recall the brand and find it in the store. In the example, the air time to identify the product's characteristics was too brief and too incomplete to be effective. The "sale" was not closed. Second, if, in addition to raising brand and product awareness the same ad had also directed the consumer to the local newspaper or a magazine to obtain additional information, then it would have provided the consumer with written information about where the product could be found. The combination of broadcast and print information thus makes it possible to "close the sale." The combined action of the dynamic and nondynamic (still) media is what generates truly effective advertising.

Multi-media strategies can be even more powerful in the Hispanic market than in the general market because of the different roles advertising and media play in mature markets and in young ones.

COMMUNICATIVE STRATEGY

In a mature consumer market, one in which all or most of the consumers have an established, historical relationship to the specific brand, product, or service being advertised, the communicative strategy, that is, the message to be communicated, may be identical for the various media. In a mature market consumers already know the product or service and certainly are aware enough of the product to know where to find it. The same key messages communicated in a print campaign can be used in a TV or radio campaign. For a young or unevenly developed market, where consumers are at various stages of awareness and familiarity with products, services, and marketing, such as the U.S. Hispanic market, the communicative strategy should be complementary across media. That is, whereas the dynamic media raise brand benefit, product awareness, and image, the still media should provide the more practical and operative information. For example, the still media or print ad should mention or show on a map the name of the street where an establishment is located, or perhaps indicate the section of a store where a product is displayed, and prominently mention how long a sale will last.

For the Hispanic market, television, radio, and print play complementary informational roles. Each medium contributes one part to the total communication story, one piece to effectively solving the sales and marketing puzzle. In addition, each medium can bring to Hispanic consumers important information not made available to them in the others or in the general market media. The degree to which media and communications strategy diverges from that of the general market will depend on which Hispanic market segment is targeted—U.S.-born Hispanics or foreign-born Hispanics. Foreign-born Hispanics, particularly the newly arrived, often require the complementary multi-media strategies just described. U.S.-born Hispanics certainly have product and market historical background like any other U.S.-born consumers and can be targeted with more traditional (but culturally attuned) methods. (Specific strategies for both segments are discussed in Chapter 7—see page 325.)

REACHING NEW ARRIVALS

Recently arrived Hispanic consumers are usually curious to know what is out there in the marketplace. A wealth of products they have never seen or heard of are available, and there are many others with which they may be familiar but that were not available to them in their home country. Thus, even well-established brands may require a communication strategy introducing the brand or product to the new consumers. A popular technique currently used on Spanish-language television is "product integration." This approach was quite popular on English-language television during the 1950s and 1960s, when actual products were shown and promoted on live TV shows.

Product integration responds to the informational needs of consumers by introducing several products that are repeatedly displayed and described in a live television show. Univisión introduced this approach to U.S. Spanish-language television through its popular "Sabado Gigante," hosted by Don Francisco. Currently Univisión and Telemundo have several programs with similar formats.

During the TV show, the audience participates by singing jingles associated with the products and the host describes the products' benefits and attributes. In addition, the same products are advertised during commercial breaks. Celebrities also give testimonials, which enhance the advertisers' claims. The entire show is similar to a gigantic classroom where learning occurs through visuals, repetition, reinforcement, and active participation.

Another more novel approach is the "infomercial." Infomercials in Spanish have taken a unique route. For example, in 1991–92 NutraSweet aired a 60–second ad campaign on Spanish-language

TV. The first 30 seconds of airtime informed the audience about health issues such as the dangers of high cholesterol and the need to exercise daily. The latter 30 seconds were used to promote NutraSweet. This was a subtle yet very valued connection. Recall of the ad campaign and the NutraSweet brand was very high long after the campaign aired.

Spanish-language radio and print ads were also used to support the television infomercial. NutraSweet's management understood and used the informational needs of the Spanish-dominant and Spanish-preferred consumer segment. They capitalized on that understanding to cement NutraSweet in the minds of these mostly foreign-born Hispanics who were unfamiliar with the product before.

Innovative, creative approaches always pay off with the Hispanic consumer, particularly when there is integration of product information and attributes and a well-thought-out multi-media strategy.

■ Language Segmentation and Media Preference: California

Hispanic Market Connections' language segmentation research (Chapter 5, page 230) and media preference studies of Hispanics nationwide consistently show that when it comes to choosing between English and Spanish media, and between broadcast and print, factors such as the consumer's language, country of birth, formal education, income, and years lived in the United States play a major role.

For example, most Spanish-dominant and Spanish-preferred consumers with foreign ancestry tend to have different socio-demographic characteristics than bilingual or English-preferred/dominant consumers. Spanish dominants tend to favor Spanish-language media much more than English-language media. The opposite was found to be the case among English dominants, who rely almost exclusively on English-language broadcast and print.

Given the size of the Hispanic market and its growth in the state during the past two decades, California provides the best example of the media preferences of Spanish-dominant and Spanish-preferred consumers, the largest Hispanic market segments.

BROADCAST MEDIA   To illustrate the strength of each medium in the Hispanic market and the dynamics of Hispanic acculturation and diversity, the following sections will review in detail the California market, media usage and its Hispanic consumers. As previously stated, Spanish-dominant and Spanish-preferred consumers have a much stronger preference for Spanish- than English-language television. HMC found that in California, as in other Hispanic market regions, the total adult Hispanic population on average views more Spanish-language TV on weekdays (3 hours and 23 minutes) and on weekends (4 hours and 33 minutes) than English-language TV (2 hours and 14 minutes on weekdays and 2 hours and 53 minutes on weekends) (Figures 6.6 and 6.7; Table 6.10).

When media preferences are broken down by language segments, as shown in Figures 6.6 and 6.7, it becomes clear that every segment watches Spanish-language television and that the more Spanish-dominant or less acculturated viewers watch much more Spanish- than English-language television. The results indicate that Spanish-dominant consumers spend roughly three times more viewing this medium than they do English-language TV. Unquestionably, California's Spanish-dominants are avid Spanish-language TV viewers. When the figures for television viewing in Table 6.10 television viewing are converted from weekly to annual, out of approximately 2,166 hours a year Spanish dominants spend watching television, 1,664 hours (76 percent) are spent on Spanish-language television and the remaining 502 hours are spent on English-language TV.

RADIO   According to Hispanic Market Connections' studies, California Hispanics spend on average less time listening to radio than watching television, but they spend twice as much time listening to Spanish- than to English-language radio. This preference was observed in HMC's findings for the state (Table 6.8) as well as for the Los Angeles area (Table 6.11).

Spanish-dominant and Spanish-preferred listeners in California are tuned to their stations somewhat more during the week than on weekends, whereas the opposite holds for those who feel as comfortable in either language. On average, even Hispanics who prefer to use English still listen to Spanish radio daily.

Among Hispanics in the Los Angeles area there is a strong preference for Spanish or Latino music. Mostly of Mexican origin, Hispanics in this area prefer folk music, ballads, and the sounds of northern Mexico (Figure 6.11).

PRINT MEDIA

Regardless of what language California Hispanics speak, newspaper readership among them tends to be low. Certainly this varies from area to area in California and correlates with socioeconomic factors. If a Spanish-language newspaper is available in a region, such as *La Opinión* in Los Angeles, readership frequency is much higher among the Spanish dominant/Spanish preferred. A study for the State of California shows 61 percent of the respondents reported they never read Spanish-language newspapers, and 60 percent claimed they never read English-language papers (Hispanic Market Connections, 1992a, 1991). However, the study also showed that readership increased with English-language proficiency (Tables 6.12 and 6.13). Curiously, and despite low reported readership levels, Spanish-dominant shoppers claimed to rely extensively on a wide array of printed media (Table 6.14). These results point to the importance of print media when targeting this group. When asked to identify which media vehicles were most frequently used in either language, in order to select a retail shop, Spanish dominants cited newspapers more often than broadcast media. As an informational source for shopping, coupons were almost as popular as television. The yellow pages were relied on more than were families, friends, magazines, catalogs, flyers, or window signs.

Among English dominant/preferred Hispanics, newspapers also scored as the number-one medium of choice for shopping-related information. Flyers were reported to be used more frequently than window signs, radio, catalogs, magazines, or local shopping guides. Referrals from families and friends were placed as the last resource. The Hispanic print media has shown major growth in the past few years and its coverage continues to increase (Table 6.15).

ADVERTISERS   Despite increasing success at supplying information and entertainment to a distinct population growing in size and purchasing potential, the Hispanic media have been slow at matching dollar for dollar consumer growth with advertising billings. Figures for 1991 indicate that advertisers spent only a fraction of their advertising budgets on the Hispanic media. Dollars spent on Hispanic advertising account for one-half of one percent of what is spent for general market advertising ($750 million and $130 billion respectively) (Soruco and Meyer, 1993, 7).

In 1993 gross advertising expenditures in the Hispanic market totaled $720 million, of which 28 percent, or $198.6 million, was accounted for by the top 50 Hispanic market advertisers. Of the 50 companies, 22 increased spending, and 2 made it to the list for the first time. Together, the 2 new companies, led by California Lottery, spent $3.3 million, representing one-third of the $10 million advertising dollar increase among the top 50 between 1992 and 1993 (Table 6.16). The top 20 advertisers and their gross media expenditures in the Hispanic market since 1991 are listed in Table 6.17. With the exception of Philip Morris, which spent the most in 1991, all of the advertisers spent more or about the same money each year reaching the Hispanic market.

Television was the medium of choice for advertisers in 1993 followed by radio, print, and other forms of advertising (Table 6.18). Spending on local television and local radio alone accounted for 42 percent of total net advertising expenditures, and the most money was spent in the heavily Hispanic Los Angeles ADI. Except in three instances television advertising led every other medium in the leading ADIs (Table 6.19). The biggest exception was San Antonio, where radio spending outweighed that for television by $3 million. Dollars spent on television in Los Angeles took a disproportionate amount relative to other forms of advertising when compared to New York and Miami. In Chicago almost as many dollars were spent on television as on radio (11.7 million and 12 million respectively).

■ *References*

Arbitron. *The Arbitron Radio Hispanic Market Report.* 1989.

———. "Arbitron . . . the standard for radio audience information." 1993.

————. "How Hispanics Listen to Radio" in *Beyond the Ratings/Radio.* Laurel, Maryland: 1993.

Arbitron Ratings. *Radio Year-Round. The Medium for All Seasons.* New York, 1987.

————. *Radio Ratings: Your Diary.* Week of Thursday, January 10 through Wednesday, January 16, 1991.

Broadcasting and Cable. "Reebok, Univisión Strike World Cup Deal." July 26, 1993.

Burgi, Michael. "Univisión Hispanic Network Signs a Pair of Blue-Chip National Advertisers." *Mediaweek.* March 15, 1993.

Burgoon, Michael, and Judee K. Burgoon. "Media Use Among Minorities: Assumptions, Misunderstandings and Myths" in Virginia Dodge Fielder and Leonard P. Tipton, eds. *Minorities and Newspapers. A Survey of Readership Research.* New Jersey: Ables Publishing Corporation, 1986.

Galavisión. Press releases and promotional material, 1993.

Greenberg, Bradley S., Michael Burgoon, Judee K. Burgoon, and Felipe Korzenny. *Mexican Americans & the Mass Media.* New Jersey: Ablex Publishing Corporation, 1986.

Hispanic Business. March 1993.

Hispanic Market Connections. *Language and Media Planning for the Hispanic Market, Northern California.* Los Altos, California: HMC, 1992.

————. *The Hispanic Database.* Los Altos, California: HMC, 1992.

Kanellos, Nicolás, ed. *Hispanic-American Almanac.* Detroit: Mich: Gale Research, 1993.

Katz Hispanic Radio Research. *Why Spanish Language Radio?* October 12, 1992.

The Media School. "Media Concepts." Los Angeles, 1987.

Nielsen Media Research. *Pocket Guide to TV Terms.* New York, 1992.

————. *What TV Ratings Really Mean,* 1993.

Nielsen News Media Services. *Nielsen Media Research News* (various press releases).

Nielsen NHTI Newsletter. Volume 3 (no date).

Outdoor Advertising Association of America, Inc (OAAA). *Outdoor: It's Not A Medium, It's A Large.* New York, 1993.

Outdoor Advertising Magazine. July-August 1993, Vol. 2, issue 4.

Soruco & Telemundo. *Unedin,* winter 1993.

————. Various press releases, promotional material and viewing data, 1993.

The Traffic Audit Bureau for Media Measurement. "Doing it by the Numbers: The Role of TAB in Media Research." New York (no date).

Univisión. Various press releases and promotional material, 1993.

U.S. Bureau of the Census. *Statistical Abstract of the United States: 1992* (112th edition). Washington, D.C., 1992.

Valdés, M. Isabel. "Mass Media and Their Communicative Roles." Unpublished paper. Buenos Aires, Argentina, 1976.

Wool, Abbott. "Hispanic Ratings Get Real." *Mediaweek,* April 19, 1993.

At a Glance. . .
On a typical weekend:

Spanish-dominants and Spanish-preferred spend more time watching Spanish television than listening to Spanish radio: 5 hours, 40 minutes v. 2 hours, 44 minutes and 4 hours, 20 minutes v. 2 hours, 13 minutes.

English-dominant/preferred spend less time watching Spanish television than listening to Spanish radio: 1 hour v. 36 minutes

Spanish-dominants spend more hours watching Spanish than English television: 5 hours, 40 minutes v. 1 hour, 42 minutes.

Spanish-dominants tend to spend fewer hours watching English television than Spanish-preferred: 1 hour, 42 minutes v. 3 hours, 19 minutes.

Spanish-dominants spend more time with English television than English-dominants spend time with Spanish broadcast: 2 hours, 53 minutes English television vs. 1 hour Spanish TV and 36 minutes of Spanish radio.

Source: See Figures 6.6–6.9, pages 291–92.

At a Glance. . .
Univisión Network Profile

Television Network Headquarters
    605 Third Ave., 12th Floor, New York, N.Y. 10158–0180

Network Operations Center and Production Studios"
    9405 NW 41 Street, Miami, Fl; (305)471–4174

Coverage: markets and over 6.3 million Hispanic Households

Stations: 9 television channels, 607 affiliate stations (19 full power stations, 18 low power stations, 570 cable stations).

Satellite Transmission: Univisión Television Group, Inc. operates the dominant Spanish-language television stations in nine major Hispanic markets covering 56 percent of Hispanic USA. Galaxy I, Transponder 6

Programming: 24 hours a day, seven days a week

Program Production: Majority of programming is produced by Televisa, Mexico

Ownership: Owned by three limited partners:
    A. Jerrold Perenchio, United States
    Televisa, Mexico
    Venevision, Venezuela

At a Glance. . .
Telemundo Network Profile

Headquarters:
   2440 West Eighth Ave., Hialeah, FL 33010

Coverage:
   59 markets, 6 million Hispanic TV households

Stations:
   U.S. full-power TV stations, 11 low-power TV stations, 500 (approximate) cable affiliates, and 58 affiliate stations.

Satellite Transmission:
   Distribution via GM Hughes communication satellite of Spanish-language programming to TV stations and cable TV affiliates.

Program Production:
   50 percent United States and 50 percent abroad

Other:
   Noticiero Telemundo—24–hour TV news service in association with Reuters and British Broadcasting Corporation (BBC).

Ownership:
   Apolo Advisors, Los Angeles
   Reliance Group Holdings, Inc., New York

At a Glance. . .
Galavisión Network Profile

Headquarters:
   6701 Center Drive West, Sixth Floor, Los Angeles, CA 90045

Ownership:
   Univisa—the U.S. division of Mexico's Televisa.

Coverage:
   United States, Central and South America, Western Europe and northern Africa 4.6 million total U.S. cable households 1.4 million U.S. Hispanic cable households Over 222,000 households in the Houston market

Satellite transmission:
   In the U.S. via Galaxy 1 Transponder 20, 24 hours a day
   From Mexico to the rest of the world via four satellites

Programming Format:
   Movies, news, sports, novelas, comedy, and variety

Landmarks in Galavisión:
   October 1979. starts operations as a pay service.
   June 1986. Makes service available to advertisers and begins conversion to basic cable.
   September 1988. ECO (Empresas the Comunicaciones Orbitales) news and entertainment service is introduced.
   December 1989. Galavisión joins the international network when ECO news is introduced to the European market.

At a Glance. . .
Viewing by Spanish-Dominant Households

Hours of television watched Monday through Sunday, 7:00 p.m. to 11:00 p.m. December 1992

Among women 18 to 49, those in Spanish-dominant households watch more Spanish-language TV than women of the same age in all households: 7 hours, 25 minutes versus 4 hours, 17 minutes

Women ages 18 to 49 in Spanish-dominant households watch more Spanish-language TV than men in the same type of households: 7 hours, 25 minutes versus 5 hours, 32 minutes

Children in Spanish-dominant households watch more Spanish-language than general market TV: 5 hours, 14 minutes versus 2 hours, 10 minutes

Children in Spanish-dominant households view more general market television than men and women ages 18 to 49. 2 hours, 10 minutes versus 1 hour, 34 minutes (men) and 1 hour, 44 minutes (women)

Source: NHTI Newsletter, Nielsen National Hispanic Television Index, (1993), 7–9.

At a Glance. . .
Multimedia Audiences Summary: 1991

Total Population:
    White 158,153; Black 20,734; Other 4,926; Spanish speaking 13,949

Television viewing/coverage:
    White 92.4; Black 95.8; Other 92.5; Spanish speaking 94.8

Television prime time viewing/coverage:
    White 78.6; Black 85.2; Other 79.6; Spanish speaking 82.9

Cable viewing/coverage:
    White 58.1; Black 44.9; Other 41.0; Spanish speaking 39.4

Radio listening/coverage:
    White 84.8; Black 84.5; Other 80.1; Spanish speaking 87.9

Newspaper reading/coverage:
    White 85.5; Black 76.3; Other 64.4; Spanish speaking 72.4

Note: In percent, except as indicated. As of spring. For persons 18 years old and over. Based on sample and subject to sampling error.
Source: U.S. Bureau of the Census, *Statistical Abstract of the United States: 1992.*

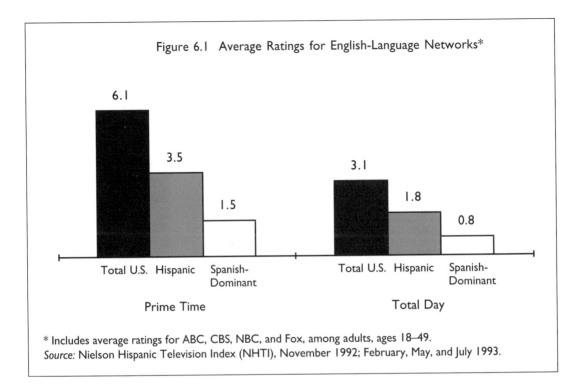

Figure 6.1 Average Ratings for English-Language Networks*

Prime Time

Total Day

* Includes average ratings for ABC, CBS, NBC, and Fox, among adults, ages 18–49.
Source: Nielson Hispanic Television Index (NHTI), November 1992; February, May, and July 1993.

Figure 6.2 Television Auduence Shares among Men 18 and Over

Monday–Sunday Prime Time

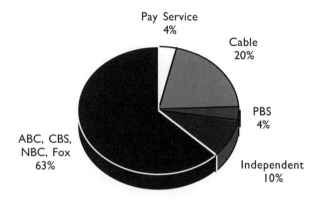

Total U.S. Men 18 and Over*

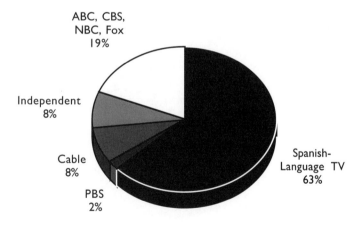

Spanish-dominant Men 18 and Over*

* Numbers may not add up to 100% due to rounding.
Source: National Television Index (NTI), and National Hispanic Television Index (NHTI), February 1993.

Figure 6.3   Television Auduence Shares among Women 18 and Over

Monday–Sunday Prime Time

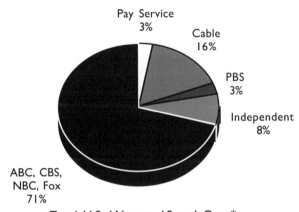

Total U.S. Women 18 and Over*

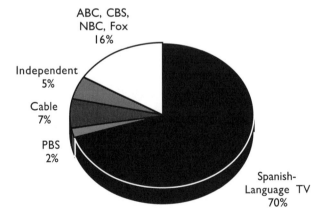

Spanish-dominant Women 18 and Over*

* Numbers may not add up to 100% due to rounding.
Source: National Television Index (NTI), and National Hispanic Television Index (NHTI), February 1993.

Figure 6.4 Television Auduence Shares among Women 18 and Over

Monday–Sunday 24-Hour Total

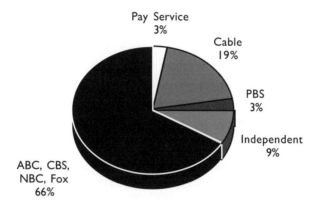

Total U.S. Women 18 and Over

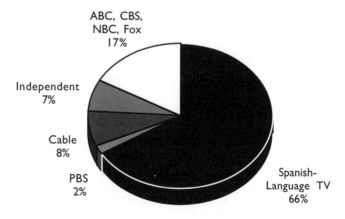

Spanish-dominant Women 18 and Over

Source: National Television Index (NTI), and National Hispanic Television Index (NHTI), February 1993.

Figure 6.5 Effective Frequency and Effective Reach

Effective Frequency: The frequency level that is deemed minimal for producing a positive response in awareness, attitude or purchasing action toward the brand.

Effective Reach: The percentage of people reached by a media schedule at the desired level of frequency.

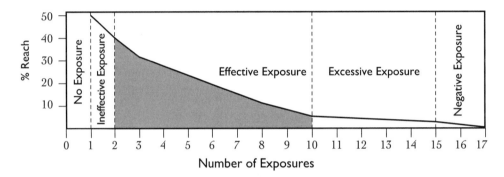

There is no definitive study which provides the optimum frequency levels required for all products or campaigns. Data from a number of studies taken as a whole, however, suggests that the range is between 2 and 10 exposures over a specified period of time that can vary by product.

Source: The Media School, 1987.

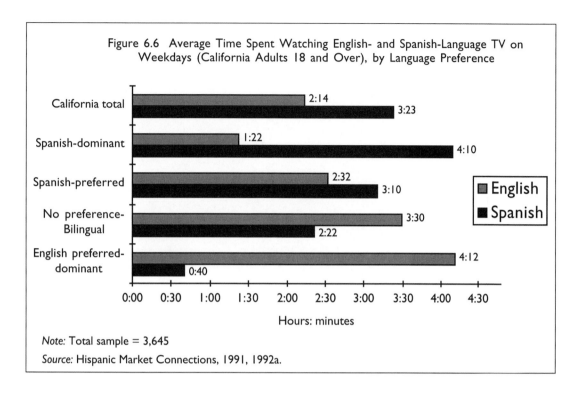

Figure 6.6 Average Time Spent Watching English- and Spanish-Language TV on Weekdays (California Adults 18 and Over), by Language Preference

Note: Total sample = 3,645

Source: Hispanic Market Connections, 1991, 1992a.

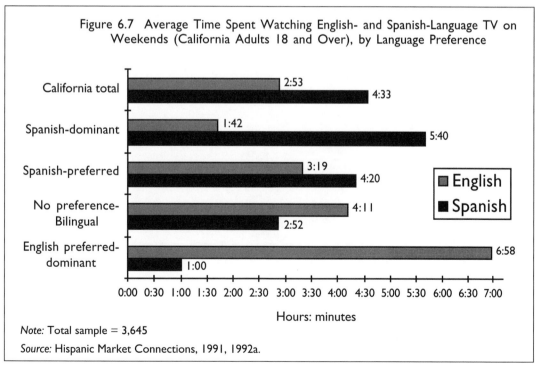

Figure 6.7 Average Time Spent Watching English- and Spanish-Language TV on Weekends (California Adults 18 and Over), by Language Preference

Note: Total sample = 3,645

Source: Hispanic Market Connections, 1991, 1992a.

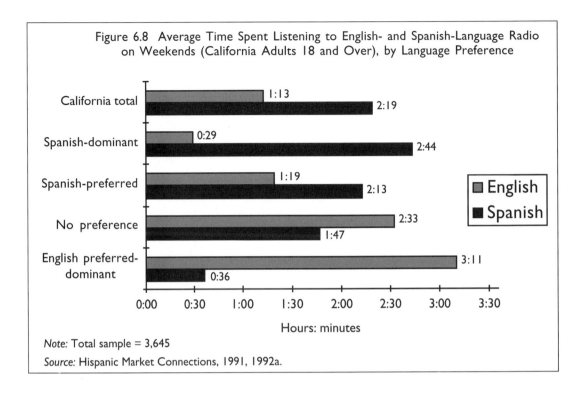

Figure 6.8 Average Time Spent Listening to English- and Spanish-Language Radio on Weekends (California Adults 18 and Over), by Language Preference

Note: Total sample = 3,645

Source: Hispanic Market Connections, 1991, 1992a.

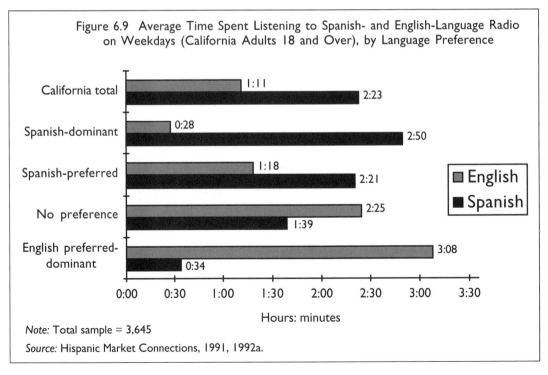

Figure 6.9 Average Time Spent Listening to Spanish- and English-Language Radio on Weekdays (California Adults 18 and Over), by Language Preference

Note: Total sample = 3,645

Source: Hispanic Market Connections, 1991, 1992a.

Figure 6.10 Spanish-Language Radio Listenership by Season, Time of Day, and Sex and Age

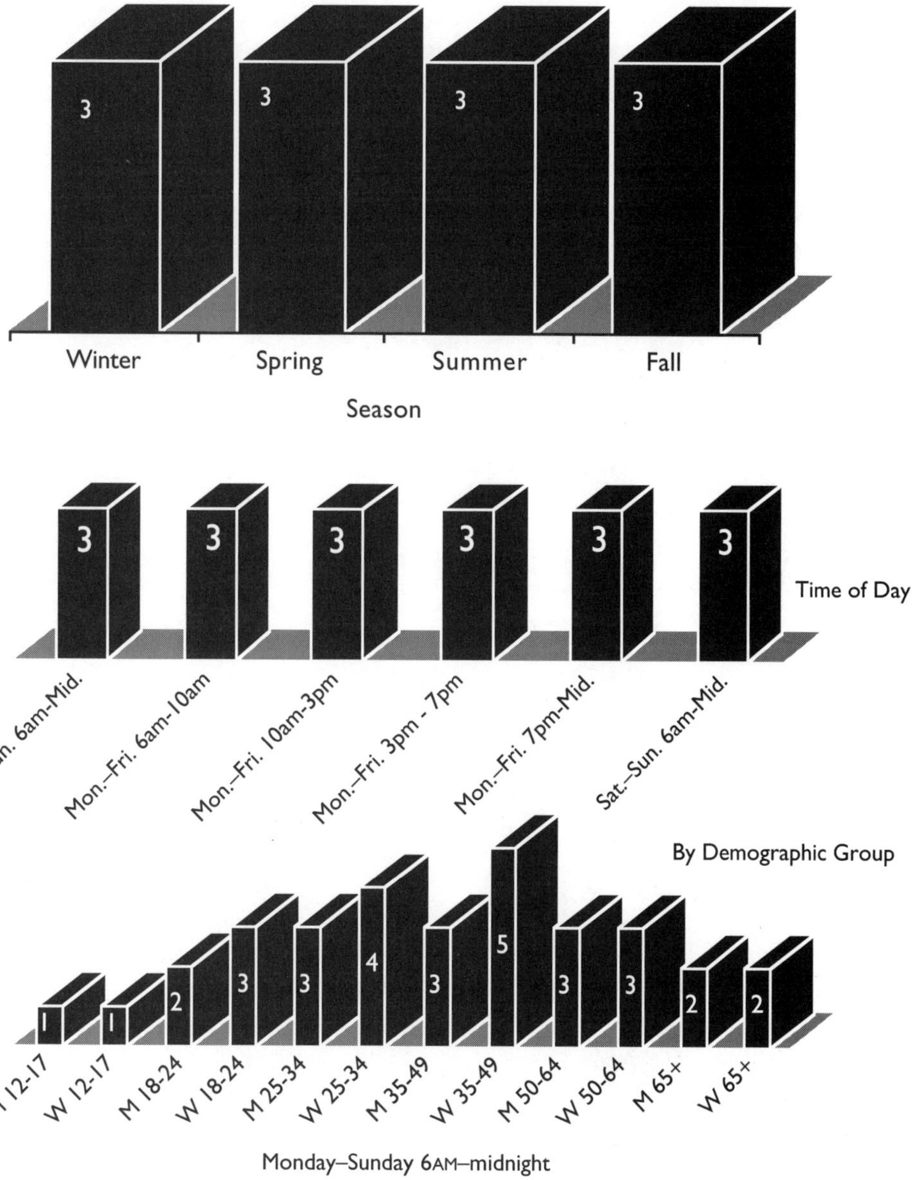

Note: The numbers (1–5) are indices based on audience levers for entire year. The indices show seasonal variations from the average annual audiences.

Source: Arbitron Ratings, 1987, 2, 22.

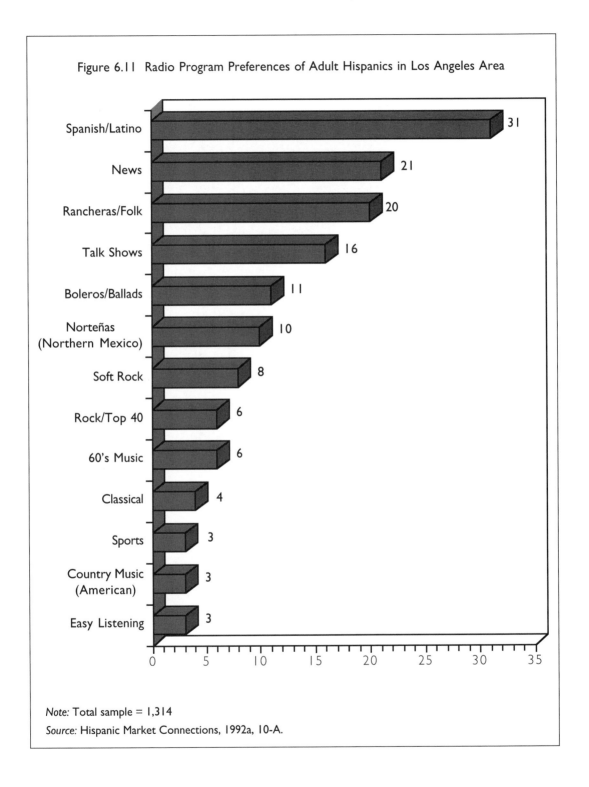

Figure 6.11 Radio Program Preferences of Adult Hispanics in Los Angeles Area

Note: Total sample = 1,314

Source: Hispanic Market Connections, 1992a, 10-A.

Table 6.1 Hispanic Media Organizations, 1994

	Number
Representatives of Hispanic media (negotiating parties between ad agencies and media)	40
Radio syndication format	4
Radio networks	9
Radio stations	376
Limited radio stations	122
TV and cable networks	4
TV stations	71
Daily newspapers	15
Community newspapers	130
Consumer magazines	83
Business publications	116
Outdoor listings	37
Direct mail listings	231
Special events	238
Supplies and services (ad agencies, PR, and marketing firms)	209
Total	1,645

Source: Standard Rate and Data Service, March 1994, A9–A12, 87–318.

Table 6.2 Spanish Network Coverage by Market[a]

Rank by Household Reach 1992	Area of Dominant Influence (ADI)	Univisión Stations	Telemundo Stations	Galavisión Stations
1	Los Angeles, CA	KMEX/34*	KVEA/52*	KWHY/22
2	New York, NY	WXTV/41*	WNJU/47*	–
3	Miami, FL	WLTV/23*	WSCV/51*	–
4	San Francisco, CA	KDTV/14*	KSTS/48*	K22DD/22
5	Chicago, IL	WCIU/26	WSNS/44	
6	San Antonio, TX/	KWEX/41*	KVDA/60*	K17BY/17
	Eagle Pass, TX	–	KVAW/16[b]	–
7	Houston, TX	KXLN/45	KTMD/48*	KTFH/49
8	Albuquerque, NM/	KLUZ/41*	K59DB/59	–
	Santa Fe, NM	–	K52BS/52*	
9	Dallas/Ft. Worth, TX	KUVN/23*	KFWD/52	–
10	McAllen/Brownsville, TX	KNVO/48	XHRIO/2	–
11	El Paso, TX	KINT/26	XHIJ/44	–
12	San Diego, CA	K19BN/19	XHAS/33	–
13	Fresno, CA	KFTV/21*	KMSG/59	–
14	Phoenix, AZ	KTVW/33*	K64DR/64	K67FE/67
15	Sacramento, CA/	KCSO/19	K47DQ/47*	
	Stockton, CA/	–	K52CK/52*	–
	Modesto, CA	–	K65IFI/61*	–
16	Denver, CA	KCEC/50	KUBD/59	–
17	Philadelphia, PA	W42BI/42*	WTGI/61	
18	Corpus Christi, TX/	KORO/28	K66EB/66	K22BH/22
	Alice, TX/	–	K08LQ/8	–
	Kingsville, TX	–	K13WE/13	–
19	Boston, MA/	–	WHLL/27	–
	Worchester, MA	–	W19AH/19	–
	Providence, RI	–	WHLL/27[c]	–
20	Washington, DC	WMDO/48[b]	W42AJ/42	–
21	Tucson, AZ	K52AO/52*	KHRR/40	K43CW/43
22	Tampa/St. Petersburg, FL	W61BL/61	W57BA/57	–
23	Austin, TX	KCFP/54[b]	K11SF/11*	–
24	Orlando, FL/	W63BH/63	W07BZ/07	–
	Altamonte Springs, FL	–	W12CD/12	–
25	Hartford, CT	W47AD/47*	W13BF/13	–
26	Salinas/Monterey, CA	KSMS/67	K15CU/15*	–
27	Bakersfield, CA	K39AB/39*	–	K58DJ/58
28	Laredo, TX	–	KLDO/27	–
29	Odessa, TX/	–	K60EE/60*	–

(continued next page)

Table 6.2 Spanish Network Coverage by Market[a] (*continued*)

Rank by Household Reach 1992	Area of Dominant Influence (ADI)	Univisión Stations	Telemundo Stations	Galavisión Stations
	Midland, TX	–	K49CD/49*	–
31	Colorado Springs, CO	K27DU/27	K49CJ/49*	–
32	Santa Barbara, CA/	–		KSTV/57[d]
	Santa Maria, CA/	K09UF/09[e]	–	K39CO/39
	San Luis Obispo, CA	K07TA/07	–	
33	Lubbock, TX	K51BX/51	K46CS/46	–
	Plainview, TX	–	K44DA/44	–
34	El Centro, CA/	–		–
	Yuma, AZ	–	KSWT/13	–
35	Las Vegas, NV	K27AF/27	–	–
36	Detroit, MI	–		–
44	Palm Springs, CA	K04NT/4	–	K06MB/6
45	Milwaukee, WI	W46AR/46	–	–
48	Yakima, WA	–	K17CJ/17	–
49	Springfield, MA	–	W65BX/65	–
	Reno, NV	KREN/27	–	–
	St. Louis, MO	K52AY/52	–	–
	Victoria, TX	–	K51BG/51	–
	Syracuse, NY	–	W35AQ/35	–
	Cheyenne, WY	–	K49AY/49	–
	South Bend, IN	W69BT/69	–	–
	Rockford, IL	W33AR/33	–	–
	Cable/satellite connections	269,932	717,637	
	Households reached	6,102,665	5,745,000	3,025,838
	Total Hispanic households	6,761,400		
	Percentage coverage	90.3%	85.0%	44.8%

*Network owned.

[a]Includes all full-power and low-power owned and operated and affiliated stations. Only ADIs were at least one network is represented are included. Top 50 ADIs are ranked by Strategy Research Corp.

[b]Operating as a low-power station in spite of its call letters.

[c]WHLL in Boston reaches Providence market.

[d]Stabon is in Oxnard, CA, with a repeater, K38DK/38 in Santa Barbara.

[e]Stabon is in Morro Bay, CA.

Sources: Hispanic Business, Inc. (360 S. Hope Ave., Ste. 300C, Santa Barbara, CA 93105), February 1993, 36. Based on data provided by Univisión, Telemundo, and Galavisión.

Table 6.3 Viewership of Top-Rated General Market Programs[a] by Total Adults and Hispanic Adults (18–49)

	Total U.S. Adults 18–49	Hispanic Adults 18–49	Index (%)
Cheers	15.0	5.4	36
Home Improvement	13.9	5.6	40
Roseanne	12.9	6.4	50
Coach	12.3	4.7	38
Seinfeld/9:30–10 pm	11.4	3.3	29
Wings	11.3	3.4	30
NFL Monday Night Football	10.4	7.5	72
Knots Landing	9.9	4.2	42
Jackie Thomas Show	9.8	4.5	46
Seinfeld/9–9:30 pm	9.6	2.5	26
Murphy Brown	9.5	2.2	23
CBS NFL Football Sunday	9.4	7.2	77
Love and War	9.3	2.2	24
Northern Exposure	8.7	2.2	25
Simpsons	8.7	6.5	75
15-Program Average	10.8	4.5	42

[a] Top 15 programs on ABC, CBS, NBC, and FOX, 1993.

Source: Nielsen (NTI and NHTI), November 1992; February, May, and July 1993.

**Table 6.4 Viewership of Top-Rated General Market Programs[a]
by Spanish-Dominant Adult Hispanics**

	Total U.S. Adults 18–49	Spanish-Dominant Hispanic Adults 18–49	Index (%)
Cheers	15.0	1.9	13
Home Improvement	13.9	1.7	12
Roseanne	12.9	2.2	17
Coach	12.3	1.3	11
Seinfeld/9:30–10 pm	11.4	1.2	11
Wings	11.3	1.0	9
NFL Monday Night Football	10.4	3.7	36
Knots Landing	9.9	0.7	7
Jackie Thomas Show	9.8	1.4	14
Seinfeld/9–9:30 pm	9.6	0.9	9
Murphy Brown	9.5	0.8	8
CBS NFL Football Sunday	9.4	3.2	34
Love and War	9.3	0.6	6
Northern Exposure	8.7	0.7	8
Simpsons	8.7	3.5	40
15-Program Average	10.8	1.7	16

[a]Top 15 programs on ABC, CBS, NBC, and FOX, November 1993.

Source: Nielsen (NTI and NHTI), November 1992; February, May, and July 1993.

Table 6.5 Viewership of Top-Rated General Market Programs for Women[a]

	Total U.S. Women 18 and Over	Spanish-Dominant Hispanic Women 18 and Over	Index (%)
60 Minutes	18.4	1.7	9
CBS Sunday Movie	17.9	1.6	9
Home Improvement	16.0	2.2	14
Murder, She Wrote	16.0	0.3	2
Roseanne	15.0	3.0	20
CBS Tuesday Movie	14.2	3.0	21
Dr. Quinn Medicine Woman	13.4	0.6	4
Evening Shade	13.2	1.0	8
Murphy Brown	13.2	1.0	8
Coach	13.1	1.1	8
Rescue 911	13.0	3.7	28
20/20	12.6	3.2	25
Cheers	12.3	1.3	11
Matlock	12.1	0.9	7
Hearts Afire	11.9	1.0	8
Northern Exposure	11.7	0.8	7
Seinfeld	11.6	0.6	5
Love and War	11.4	0.7	6
Primetime Live	11.1	1.9	17
NBC Sunday Night Movie	11.0	2.1	19
20-Program Average	13.5	1.6	12

[a]Top 20 programs on ABC, CBS, NBC, and FOX, February 1993.

Source: Nielsen (NTI and NHTI), 1993.

Table 6.6 Viewership of Top-Rated General Market Programs for Men[a]		
	Total U.S. Men 18 and Over	Spanish-Dominant Hispanic Men 18 and Over	Index (%)
60 Minutes	16.5	1.2	7
Home Improvement	12.7	2.2	17
Cheers	11.8	1.1	9
Seinfeld	11.0	1.1	10
Coach	10.4	1.4	13
Rescue 911	10.2	3.4	33
Roseanne	10.1	1.4	14
Murphy Brown	9.7	0.9	9
Primetime Live	9.7	1.8	19
Northern Exposure	9.6	0.9	9
20/20	9.5	2.3	24
CBS Tuesday Movie	9.3	2.8	30
American Detective	9.2	1.6	17
CBS Sunday Movie	9.2	0.9	10
Murder, She Wrote	9.2	0.3	3
Evening Shade	8.8	0.8	9
Unsolved Mysteries	8.7	2.1	24
Dr. Quinn Medicine Woman	8.5	0.4	5
Matlock	8.5	0.9	11
Love and War	8.4	0.6	7
20-Program Average	10.1	1.4	14

[a] Top 20 programs on ABC, CBS, NBC, and FOX, February 1993.

Source: Nielsen (NTI and NHTI), 1993.

**Table 6.7 Top-Rated Programs of Spanish-Dominant Women and
Their Respective Ratings by General Audience Women, February 1993**

	Spanish-Dominant Women 18 and Over	General Audience Women 18 and Over
Rescue 911	1	11
20/20	2	12
Roseanne	3	5
CBS Tuesday Movie	3	6
Home Improvement	4	3
NBC Sunday Night Movie	5	20
Primetime Live	6	19
60 Minutes	7	1
CBS Sunday Movie	8	2
Cheers	9	13
Coach	10	10

Source: Compiled from Nielsen (NTI and NHTI), 1993.

Table 6.8 Average Time Spent Listening to Radio by Hispanic Adults 18 and Over in California, 1991 and 1992[*]

	Spanish-Language Radio		English-Language Radio	
	Weekday	Weekend	Weekday	Weekend
	(hours:minutes)		(hours:minutes)	
California total	2:23	2:19	1:11	1:13
Spanish dominant	2:50	2:44	0:28	0:29
Spanish preferred	2:21	2:13	1:18	1:19
No Preference	1:39	1:47	2:25	2:33
English preferred/dominant	0:34	0:36	3:08	3:11

Note: Total sample = 3,645.

[*]Combined data.

Source: Hispanic Market Connections, 1991, 1992a.

Table 6.9 Factors Associated with Increased Hispanic Readership

Predictors	Relationship to Readership
Age	As age increases, reading time increases
Sex	Males spend more time than females
Frequency of newspaper readership	As frequency increases, reading time increases
Time spent reading magazines	As magazine time increases, newspaper time increases
Time spent watching TV news	As TV time increases, newspaper time increases

Source: Adapted from Greenberg, et al., 1986, 92.

Table 6.10 Average Time Spent Watching Television by Hispanic Adults 18 and Over in California, 1991 and 1992[*]

	Spanish-Language Radio		English-Language Radio	
	Weekday	Weekend	Weekday	Weekend
	(hours:minutes)		(hours:minutes)	
California total	3:23	4:33	2:14	2:53
Spanish dominant	4:10	5:40	1:22	1:42
Spanish preferred	3:10	4:20	2:32	3:19
No preference	2:22	2:52	3:30	4:11
English preferred/dominant	0:40	1:00	4:12	6:58

Note: Total sample = 3,645.

[*]Combined data.

Source: Hispanic Market Connections, 1991, 1992a.

Table 6.11 Hispanic Listening Habits in Los Angeles Area

	Spanish-Language Radio		English-Language Radio	
	Weekday	Weekend	Weekday	Weekend
	(hours)		(hours)	
Total Los Angeles area	2.7	2.4	1.1	1.2
Spanish dependent	3.2	3.0	0.5	0.6
Spanish preferred	2.4	2.3	1.3	1.4
No preference	1.9	1.6	2.3	2.3
English preferred	0.7	0.4	3.4	2.9

Source: Hispanic Market Connections, 1991.

Table 6.12 Hispanic Reading Habits in California:
Readership of Spanish-Language Newspapers, Adults 18 and Over, 1991 and 1992[*]

	California Total	Spanish Dominant	Spanish Preferred	No Preference	English Preferred/Dominant
Base: total sample	(3645)	(1688)	(1196)	(565)	(189)
	%	%	%	%	%
Daily	5.2	4.4	7.4	4.2	0.5
Several times a week	4.6	4.2	6.3	3.9	0.5
About once a week	8.1	8.2	10.6	5.1	1.6
Only on Sundays	1.8	2.0	1.6	1.9	0.5
Less than once a week	3.1	3.3	3.3	2.7	0.5
Rarely	16.0	17.7	16.5	13.8	5.3
Never	61.0	60.3	54.1	68.0	89.9

* Combined data.

Source: Hispanic Market Connections, 1991, 1992a.

Table 6.13 Hispanic Reading Habits in California:
Readership of English-Language Newspapers, Adults 18 and Over, 1991 and 1992[*]

	California Total	Spanish Dominant	Spanish Preferred	No Preference	English Preferred/Dominant
Base: total sample	(3645)	(1688)	(1196)	(565)	(189)
	%	%	%	%	%
Daily	15.8	3.4	18.1	36.1	50.3
Several times a week	6.0	2.1	7.9	11.0	12.7
About once a week	5.3	2.3	8.1	6.9	10.6
Only on Sundays	2.5	0.7	1.6	2.5	1.6
Less than once a week	1.3	0.7	1.6	2.5	1.6
Rarely	8.8	6.3	11.7	9.9	7.9
Never	60.3	84.4	48.4	29.7	12.2

* Combined data.

Source: Hispanic Market Connections, 1991, 1992a.

Table 6.14 Source of Retail Store Information and Language Segmentation in Northern California, 1991

	Total Sample	Spanish Dominant	Spanish Preferred	No Preference	English Dominant/Preferred
Base: Language proficiency/usage	(1631)	(726)	(532)	(298)	(72)
		a	b	c	d
Source of Store Information					
Family/friends	11	14bc	7	8	22bc
Television	42	39	45	46	42
Coupon mailers	33	32	34	27	49ac
Flyers	18	14	19	19	39abc
Newspapers	55	44	61a	65a	74a
Local shopping guides	15	12	16	16	26a
Catalogs	19	15	19	23a	32a
Window signs	16	14	15	18	38abc
Radio	23	23	20	23	35b
Magazines	19	15	21a	20	26
Yellow pages	34	25	36a	46ab	63ab

Source: Hispanic Market Connections, 1991, 30.

Table 6.15 Coverage of Hispanic Print Media, Top 10 Areas of Dominant Influence (ADI), 1993

Market ADI	% Hispanic by Households	1993 Hispanic Households (thousands)	Number of Publications	Primary Circulation (thousands)	Issues per Week (thousands)	Issues/ Household per Week	Estimated 1993 Ad Expenditures $ (thousands)	Ad $ per Hispanic Household
Los Angeles	23.2%	1357.6	20	2294.7	2664	2.0	$46,470	34.2
New York	12.9%	941.6	9	418.0	787	0.8	$16,830	17.9
Miami	29.5%	414.5	9	406.0	1360	3.3	$14,360	34.6
San Francisco	11.6%	276.3	7	166.0	164.5	0.6	$3,330	12.1
Chicago	8.1%	260.8	11	473.0	538.3	2.1	$9,435	36.2
San Antonio	39.9%	253.2	2	130.0	130	0.5	$3,750	14.8
Houston	15.7%	240.6	7	574.0	480.3	2.0	$4,800	20.0
Dallas	9.2%	170.9	7	232.0	232	1.4	$2,740	16.0
Lower Rio Grand Valley	75.5%	161.5	3	167.7	207.9	1.3	$1,300	8.0
San Diego	14.8%	141.4	7	201.0	175.5	1.2	$1,640	11.6
Top 10 Total		4218.4	82.0		6739.5		$104,655	
U.S. Total (all markets)		6626.0					$111,455	
Top 10 as Percent of U.S. Total		63.7%					93.9%	

Notes: Nearly two-thirds of all Hispanic households are in the top 10 area of dominant influences (ADIs). Issues per week is calculated by multiplying the circulation of each paper times its frequency of publication.

Source: Hispanic Business, December 1993, 42.

Table 6.16 The 50 Leading Hispanic Market Advertisers, 1993
Gross Media Expenditures ($ millions)

Rank	Company	1992	1993
1	Procter & Gamble	$30.2	31.6
2	Anheuser-Busch Inc.	9.6	9.9
3	McDonald's Corp.	9.0	9.0
4	Coca-Cola Co.	8.6	8.9
5	Philip Morris Cos. Inc.	8.5	8.5
6	Colgate-Palmolive Co.	7.6	7.6
7	AT&T	5.8	6.7
8	Ford Motor Co.	6.0	6.3
9	Grand Metropolitan (Burger King)	5.1	5.5
10	PepsiCo Inc.	4.6	5.5
11	Adolph Coors Co.	5.3	5.3
12	Quaker Oats Co.	4.6	5.1
13	Sears, Roebuck, & Co.	5.0	5.0
14	Honda Motor Co. Ltd.	4.0	4.2
15	Goya Foods Inc.	4.0	4.0
16	CPC International Inc.	3.4	3.6
17	Toyota Motor Corp.	3.4	3.5
18	General Mills Inc.	3.5	3.5
19	Warner-Lambert Co.	3.0	3.3
20	Ralston Purina Co.	3.1	3.1
21	American Home Products Corp.	3.1	3.1
22	AMR (American Airlines)	3.0	3.0
23	Johnson & Johnson	3.0	3.0
24	Sprint	2.6	3.0
25	Unilever PLC	2.4	2.4
26	Kimberly Clark Corp.	2.1	2.3
27	Nissan Motor Corp.	2.3	2.3

(continued next page)

Table 6.16 The 50 Leading Hispanic Market Advertisers, 1993
Gross Media Expenditures ($ millions) (*continued*)

Rank	Company	1992	1993
28	JC Penney Co.	2.0	2.3
29	Chrysler Corp.	2.0	2.3
30	MCI Communications Corp.	1.5	2.2
31	Hershey Food Corp.	2.5	2.0
32	Eastman Kodak Co.	2.0	2.0
33	General Motors Corp.	2.0	2.0
34	California Lottery	–	2.0
35	SC Johnson & Sons Inc.	1.9	1.9
36	Western Union	1.8	1.9
37	U.S. Army	1.8	1.8
38	Clorox Co.	1.8	1.8
39	Kmart Corp.	1.8	1.8
40	Miles Labs Inc.	1.5	1.7
41	Polaroid Corp.	1.7	1.7
42	Bacardi Imports Inc.	1.5	1.5
43	Woolworth (Kinney Shoe)	1.5	1.5
44	Mazda Motors	1.5	1.5
45	Helene Curtis Industries Inc.	1.3	1.5
46	UAL (United Air Lines)	1.0	1.3
47	Montgomery Ward	–	1.3
48	Wal-Mart	1.2	1.2
49	Mars Inc.	1.0	1.2
50	General Electric Co.	1.0	1.1
	Total	$187.1	198.6

Source: Hispanic Business, December 1993, 41.

Table 6.17 The 20 Leading Hispanic Market Advertisers, 1991–1993
Gross Media Expenditures ($ millions)

Rank	Company	1991	1992	1993
1	Procter & Gamble Co.	28.8	30.2	31.6
2	Anheuser-Busch Inc.	8.6	9.6	9.9
3	McDonald's Corp.	7.5	9.0	9.0
4	Coca-Cola Co.	7.5	8.6	8.9
5	Philip Morris Cos. Inc.	10.0	8.5	8.5
6	Colgate-Palmolive Co.	7.6	7.6	7.6
7	Ford Motor Co.	5.2	6.0	6.3
8	AT&T	5.0	5.8	6.7
9	Adolph Coors Co.	5.3	5.3	5.3
10	Grand Metropolitan (Burger King)	5.2	5.1	5.5
11	Sears, Roebuck & Co.	4.5	5.0	5.0
12	PepsiCo Inc.	4.2	4.6	5.5
13	Quaker Oats Co.	4.0	4.6	5.1
14	Goya Foods Inc.	3.5	4.0	4.0
15	Honda Motor Co. Ltd.	2.6	4.0	4.2
16	General Mills Inc.	2.7	3.5	3.5
17	Toyota Motor Corp.	3.4	3.4	3.5
18	CPC International Inc.	2.7	3.4	3.6
19	American Home Products Corp.	3.1	3.4	3.1
20	Ralston Purina Co.	2.6	3.1	3.1

Source: Hispanic Business, December 1991; December 1992; December 1993.

Table 6.18 Hispanic Market Net Advertising Expenditures, 1993

Medium	Expenditures ($ millions)
Network and national TV	$198.0
Local TV	126.0
National radio	52.2
Local radio	178.5
National print	35.0
Local print	111.4
Out-of-home	20.4
Total	$721.5

Source: Hispanic Business, December 1993, 41–42.

Table 6.19 Leading Hispanic ADIs, 1993[a]
Net Expenditures by Medium ($ millions)

Rank by 1993 expenditures	Rank by population	ADI	TV	Radio	Print	Total
1	1	Los Angeles	$73.88	$45.00	$46.47	$165.35
2	3	Miami	29.96	30.00	14.36	74.32
3	2	New York	28.36	21.00	16.80	66.16
4	5	Chicago	11.73	12.00	9.44	33.17
5	7	San Antonio	8.85	11.75	3.75	24.35
6	4	San Francisco	10.78	8.75	3.33	22.86
7	6	Houston	8.50	5.50	4.8	18.80
8	10	San Diego	8.50	4.90	1.64	15.04
9	9	Dallas-Ft. Worth	6.55	3.9	2.70	13.2
10	8	McAllen-Brownsville	6.60	4.00	1.3	11.9
		Totals	$193.71	$146.85	$104.59	$445.15

[a]ADI = area of dominant influence.

Source: Hispanic Business, December 1993, 41–42.

CHAPTER

7

- Marketing to Hispanics
- Targeting Hispanic Market Segments
- Marketing to Hispanic Women
- Marketing to Hispanic Youth
- Couponing and the Hispanic Consumer
- Advertising to Hispanics
- Community Marketing

Reaching Hispanics

Effective marketers and advertisers know that the secret of successful business lies in knowing the market and the target consumer. If intimately knowing the target consumer is the key to a successful marketing campaign, how can marketers and advertisers ensure that their campaigns and messages "talk to" consumers from a different culture?

Throughout this book various subjects and components that play a role in successful marketing to Hispanic consumers in the United States have been presented: regional and ethnic demographics, the Hispanic culture, the acculturation process, the cultural and emotional role of language, language segmentation tools, and media usage patterns. This chapter addresses the dynamics of integrating these elements and examines in detail specific topics unique to the Hispanic market.

Because advertising is a key component in marketing communications, we will explore those issues that make or break advertising campaigns, such as conceptualization strategies, purchase and behavior change trigger points, what communication elements work, and what does not work. The chapter also focuses on marketing to specific subsegments of the U.S. Hispanic market: foreign-born Hispanics (new arrivals), U.S.-born Hispanics, Hispanic women, and Hispanic youth. Finally, we review basic issues of marketing research as they relate to the Hispanic market in the United States, concentrating on those aspects that set Hispanic marketing research apart from traditional research.

■ Marketing to Hispanics

Marketers cannot simply transfer directly to the U.S. Hispanic market the conceptualizations or marketing strategies that work with the general U.S. market or even with the Latin American market. Too many factors—historical, contextual, cultural, demographic, financial—place Hispanic consumers in a different category. Hispanic Americans could be viewed as constituting a country within a country. Thus, it is necessary to invest time and resources in the planning stage to develop a sound, unique conceptual framework for targeting Hispanics. Success during the promotional, advertising, and merchandising processes demands a carefully conceptualized and executed marketing plan.

CONCEPTUALIZING The best demographic data in the world will not ensure the right marketing decisions. Developing a sound conceptual framework to devise culturally grounded marketing strategies is the key to avoiding marketing, advertising, or promotional pitfalls. To aid in the development of the conceptual framework and the marketing strategy, theoretical models, reliable market data, demographics, and culturally sensitive research techniques and methods from a variety of disciplines are useful. These provide "handles" to "grasp the market." Relevant disciplines include, for example, ethnography, psychology, anthropology, marketing, communications, and sociology.

It is of paramount importance to develop a Hispanic market-specific conceptualization process at the outset, before deciding on a specific strategy or course of action, such as starting any marketing or advertising program. It is absolutely necessary to get a good handle on the marketing environment by analyzing (1) Hispanic market specific data, gleaned from secondary data such as demographics, volumetrics, and product- or service-specific data, and (2) Hispanic consumer insight data, gathered from the potential Hispanic customer's feedback, providing information about the consumer's mind-set and the usefulness of the product/service to the customer.

The validity of the marketing strategy will be as reliable as the sources of market data used. Thanks to the U.S. Department of Commerce and the ongoing data it generates, Hispanic demographic information is readily available at low cost. Despite some under-reporting, it is the most reliable source of Hispanic demographic data available today. But this is not the case with Hispanic consumer information; the amount of reliable data specific to Hispanic consumers is very limited. Most consumer data sources tend to collect Hispanic market data following traditional general market ratio rules, data-gathering methodologies, and sample plans. As a result, the market data gathered tend to be skewed toward one or another demographic group, depending on the specific method, geographic boundaries, stores selected in the sample, and statistical sampling models that are used.

MARKET DATA

One source of biasing data is found on the consumer end. For example, some companies gather their data by means of self-administered diaries, cards, or lengthy survey forms. The study participant is expected to (1) be fully literate and (2) recognize the names and brands of the products or services in question as they are written in English. Unfortunately, both assumptions are often false when one is talking about the Hispanic market. Familiarity with research instruments is low, Hispanic literacy rates overall are low in comparison to the general market, and English-language literacy rates are significantly lower in most key Hispanic markets. This is particularly the case among women. Therefore, brand names in English will be recognized by only a segment of the Hispanic market, defeating the primary objective of the data gathering function—market data accuracy and market representativeness. Even if the questionnaire is written in Spanish, the brand names of products or services are in English and, because a vast majority of Hispanic consumers tend to verbalize or "call" the brand in a Hispanic version, they may not recognize the English names. As a consequence, if study participants are not probed verbally or visually, a significant number may not be counted as users of a product they consume regularly. This results in ongoing misreporting and under-reporting of product or service usage in Hispanic market data. In a recent study conducted by Hispanic Marketing Connections in New York among Spanish-dominant and Spanish-preferred Hispanic males, the awareness levels for some brands tested varied as much as 40 percent, depending on the survey probing method used—auditory only or visual.

If one adds to the language and literacy limitations the clutter of brands all consumers must deal with in today's market, it is obvious that foreign-born consumers will have even more trouble accurately recalling or identifying brand names they use. In addition, if a study is conducted only by phone, the lack of telephones in a portion of Hispanic households (5 to 19 percent; Figure 7.1) requires additional efforts in order to accurately gather and project product or service usage data (Valdés, 1993).

Other serious market data limitations involve biases introduced by sampling methods, the language and translation of the survey form (English versus Spanish), the language and cultural sensitivity of the interviewer, and the research probing techniques. For example, for years many market data businesses marketed and sold Hispanic market data collected utilizing only English-language instruments or phone conversations with non-Spanish-speaking interviewers. Hence, Spanish-dominant consumers, a very large segment of the market, were systematically excluded.

Another common error involves the sampling and statistical manipulation of data. If the sample design, that is, the process through which it is determined "which" and "how many" consumers will be approached to participate in the study, is not conceptualized within the framework of an "anomalous growth" population, chances are the sample will not include, for example, new immigrants or immigrants residing in lower Hispanic population density areas and hence not represent proportionally the Hispanic market. Instead these sampling methods over-represent some segments of the market and under-represent others. If the demographic growth of the U.S. Hispanic market resembled that of a natural non-immigrant population, and all "types" of Hispanics were distributed evenly across the U.S. territory, measuring, finding, and tracking them would be far less of a challenge than it is today. But the acculturation process, demographic shifts, and uneven immigration, development, and distribution of the Hispanic market in the United States require independent and sometimes very different sampling models and statistical calculations to generate accurate market data. This issue is addressed in detail in Chapter 8 (see page 377).

Some improvements have been made to deal with these problems, including bilingual interviewer training and translating surveys. But until the sampling bias, the cultural context, and the probing methods are modified and changed, the Hispanic market consumer data will continue to be flawed and skewed. As of late 1994, a new Hispanic consumer data service was being developed, the Nielsen Hispanic Household panel. This new service, because of its data gathering system—a scanner placed at the household that "reads" the UPC codes in products purchased—together with careful sampling methods and cultural sensitivity, has the potential to overcome the barriers and limitations of present data services that generate Hispanic market data.

VOLUMETRIC DATA

Hispanic volumetric data (the data measuring actual purchase volume—how many products of a particular brand Hispanics buy in a particular market during a certain week, month, or quarter) also tend to seriously under-report Hispanic market participation. Here the challenge to marketers is of a different nature. If, as research (by Hispanic Market Connections and others) shows, many Hispanics tend to shop not only at traditional store chains but also at small corner stores (*bodegas*) and other retail outlets that are not included in the count by the data-gathering company, how can it be accurately determined what volume Hispanics purchase in a particular product category?

If the stores included in the sample are only those in highly dense Hispanic population areas (over 50 percent population penetration only), how can this data be used to gauge the strength of the entire Hispanic market in a particular product category, such as soap, diapers, cereal or shampoo? What about the stores location in areas with less than 50 percent Hispanic population density? And what about the non-participating stores? Product managers are forced to work with data that consistently under-represents the purchases of Hispanic consumers.

Again, major efforts to correct and manage these biases are now taking place. For example, gathering actual purchase data at the Hispanic household level with bar code scanning systems such as the new Nielsen Household panel could provide the most accurate volumetric data today.

CONSUMER MIND-SET Insight into consumer behavior can be obtained by learning about the consumer's mind-set and gauging the consumer's response to the various features of a product or service. To help form an accurate picture of the Hispanic customer's mind-set, marketers must talk to, observe, and learn directly from the Hispanic consumer. This is the proven and tested approach for selecting the right components of a marketing and advertising campaign, including the attributes and benefits of a product or service. The strategy involves ascertaining the product or service's life cycle (that is, whether it is perceived as a new product or a mature one) and evaluating its context of use (that is, who uses the product; where and when it is used; what its cultural images, beliefs, perceptions, and associations are; and what financial influences may facilitate or delay trying it). These questions will go a long way toward generating the necessary information to conceptualize, define, and fine-tune a successful strategy.

Product or Service Life Cycle: The Hispanic Consumer's Perception When evaluating the consumer's mind-set toward a product or service, the marketer's first task is to conduct a life cycle status check to determine which stage of its life cycle the consumer perceives the product or service to be in. That is, is it perceived as something new? Or is the consumer already quite familiar with the product or service? Everything about the product or service should be evaluated from the perspective of the Hispanic market segment. Variables that were deemed under control in the general market or in Latin America cannot be taken for granted. These and all other assumptions should be questioned. The goal is to ascertain with as much detail and clarity as possible what the consumer knows, expects, likes, or dislikes about the product or service.

A basic consumer product, natural gas, can be used to illustrate this point. A public utilities manager dealing with the U.S. Hispanic customer must ask, How was gas delivered to my foreign-born Hispanic customers? The manager will find out that a large segment of the Hispanic customer base used to purchase gas in tanks in their home countries. Therefore, these customers relate to and visualize natural gas in a quite different manner than U.S.-born customers. Consequently, the manager will need to address gas delivery at an introductory phase. For example, these Hispanic consumers may not understand how gas gets to their heaters or ovens. They may not be aware that pipes with gas run underground. Therefore, as utility customers, they may present different issues and risks, such as gas leaks in unexpected places or lack of awareness of gas shutoff valves. An aboveground gas tank has a given size, and the gas in it has a different smell and weight and a specific price per unit; "running gas" does not. These consumers therefore relate to gas in a different way than those utility customers, Hispanic or otherwise, who are already familiar with pipe gas. They perceive gas as a different product.

If, prior to developing a marketing strategy for a product or service, marketers conduct an exploratory assessment study of the product or service life cycle and its context of use (who uses it, when, where, and so forth), they virtually guarantee a focused, targeted strategy that incorporates the customer's vision of the commodity.

Typically, exploratory information is gathered in focus groups, ethnographic observations, or other forms of qualitative research. Qualitative research allows in-depth unstructured probing about the product or service. The marketer can address issues such as whether or not the product or service was used in the country of origin. If it was, the marketer knows to ask who the key players, brands, and shapes were. What were the main product or service benefits expected within that culture? Why did people use, like, or dislike it? If the product or service is unknown to the consumer, qualitative research provides marketers with the opportunity to test introductory concepts, describe the product or service, or, if appropriate, show or demonstrate the product to get a feeling for consumer reaction.

Product or service life cycle information provides marketers with an understanding of where to start the marketing campaign, and which segment within the Hispanic market is familiar or not with the product or service. The following questions can help managers devise realistic long- and short-term marketing strategies:

✧ In the eyes of the Hispanic market, is the product or service in its introductory stage, requiring "starting from scratch"?

✧ Is the product or service suffering from a negative image or heritage problem and thus in need of repositioning? (e.g.: If the brand was known in another country and had poor quality locally.)

✧ Does the product need to be reintroduced? (e.g.: The product or service category is known to the target market but it needs "revamping.")

✧ Is there a need to build category awareness and familiarity? (e.g.: In the case of a product or service not known in most Latin American countries.)

✧ Should brand recognition and heritage be capitalized on? (e.g.: If the brand is known and enjoys a good image in Latin America.)

✧ Do Hispanic consumers perceive, use, and relate in a different or unique way to the product or service? Should it be repositioned to address their specific cultural context and usage?

✧ Can a national "Pan-Hispanic" campaign that talks to all Hispanics be formulated? What are the common elements across ethnic backgrounds (for Cubans, Dominicans, Mexicans, Puerto Ricans, Salvadorans, and so forth)?

These are preliminary questions that marketers should ask to define the positioning parameters for the brand, product or service and to uncover its cultural context.

CULTURAL CONTEXT To date, the U.S. marketplace has rarely seen manufacturers and businesses develop new products to serve the specific needs of U.S. Hispanics. Most of the time, marketers approach the Hispanic market with an existing product or service they would like to promote to Hispanic consumers. In other words, most marketing efforts to Hispanics are product driven, rather than consumer driven. Therefore, to successfully position and promote the product or service to Hispanic consumers, marketers must first address the *cultural context* of the product or service. Cultural context is the unique set of expectations and experiences that consumers have in different cultural milieus vis-à-vis products or services. The cultural background of the different Hispanic groups often determines how consumers use and relate to a product or service. It also affects how they mentally deal with the negative aspects of a commodity as well as its benefits. Quite often important variations in the Hispanic market are observed. Thus, by examining the various cultural contexts, marketers can determine the differences as well as the common denominators that affect the products' or services' positioning and the strategies to be employed.

For example, American middle-class teenagers tend to relate to food consumption differently than Mexican, Puerto Rican, and Cuban teenagers raised in traditional Hispanic families. An American (or an acculturated Hispanic) teenager will probably fix a sandwich anytime he or she feels hungry. The teen would tend to have greater control and decision-making autonomy over when and what to snack on than the teen's Hispanic counterpart would. In other words, the American teen has a greater locus or sphere of control than the non-acculturated Hispanic teenager, who would tend to involve the mother in some way, for example, by asking permission to snack or by asking the mother to fix the snack.

Therefore, a marketer or advertiser of a food product who desires to target the traditional Hispanic family should ascertain and understand the *forms of interactions* among the Hispanic family in regard to the product. For example, a marketer may decide to use the strong family orientation of the traditional Hispanic family by promoting the product with a complementary marketing strategy that speaks to both the teen and the mother, with one message targeting the teenager with a culturally attuned (yet peer-group-oriented) message and the second targeting the mother as the family decision maker for food purchases and as the food preparer. The teen's campaign could be in Spanish or English, or both, and the mother's in Spanish.

General Mills' Spanish-language ad shows a toddler saying, "I'm happy. I'm old enough to eat Cheerios."

Since marketers know traditional Hispanic mothers enjoy pleasing their children with foods prepared by them "the old fashioned way," and kids and teens are important sources for introducing new food products to Hispanic households (because they see new, different products at their friends' homes and at school), the marketing strategy may be more effective if it focuses on this cultural context by involving both players, directly or indirectly. Spanish-language ads targeting the mother can speak in that cultural context. She wants to please her child, but she is not familiar with peanut butter sandwiches or cereals. However, her child has asked her to buy peanut butter because he wants to "try the stuff his friends eat." So even though she would prefer to fix him something that she knows, she may decide to purchase the advertised brand of peanut butter to please her child.

Analyzing the cultural context vis-à-vis other products and services will provide similar insights into purchasing motivations. Observing Hispanic automobile use patterns would reveal that Hispanic families tend to travel more often with all family members than non-Hispanics. Hence, for the (larger than average) Hispanic family, the car should be perceived as large and roomy and providing great interior comfort if it is going to appeal to them. Many foreign-born Hispanics will purchase their first factory-new car in the United States, and many may not be aware of recent automotive technological developments, such as antilock brakes, new impact-absorbing body structures, and children's remote door locks. Hence, unless they are introduced to these benefits in an explicit, descriptive manner—stating the benefits for the family—a car model's competitive advantage may be totally lost. Because of the strong family orientation of Hispanics, the family's comfort, approval, and safety may weigh more than fuel efficiencies and other technological innovations in the final decision.

DEMOGRAPHIC VARIATIONS

Cultural context of use, discussed above, varies according to the differences between the demographic profile of key market segments and the specific geographic region being targeted (for example, the differences between foreign-born and native-born Hispanics or between lower and higher socioeconomic groups or between the Texas and Miami markets). Consequently, to define or test a strategy the following sociodemographic differences should be taken into account in the conceptualization process:

✦ Country of origin

✦ Length of residence in the United States

✦ Specific market region

✦ Age

✦ Language usage preferences in daily life, including media consumption

✦ Degree of formal education

✦ Marital status (single, married, divorced, widowed)

✦ Household composition (extended family, nuclear family, nonfamily household)

In sum, to ascertain the product's or service's marketing environment and devise a strategy, the marketer needs to:

1) Be cognizant of existing Hispanic market data;

2) Define where the product or service is located in terms of its *life cycle* (Is the product familiar or unfamiliar to the prospective consumer?);

3) Learn about the *cultural context of usage* in which the product or service was used;

4) Devise the best positioning strategy to promote the product or service considering the particular life cycle of the product or service and its Hispanic cultural context.

■ Targeting Hispanic Market Segments

In addition to traditional market segments, such as women, youth, men and seniors, the Hispanic market is segmented by the consumers' immigration-driven sociodemographics. After standard demographic parameters (income, age, sex, education) for marketing, advertising, or merchandising purposes, the *degree of acculturation* or assimilation into mainstream American culture is the most important factor in segmenting U.S. Hispanics (see Chapter 4). Unfortunately, it is difficult, if not impossible, to find readily available data broken down by degree of acculturation. In addition, not every marketing budget allows targeting Hispanics by acculturation segmentation, which is probably the most effective approach today. Still, marketers should make an informed decision as to the acculturative make-up of the target market.

A good alternative to acculturation segmentation involves a two-pronged strategy. First, marketers and advertisers can use a language-based segmentation such as the one described in Chapter 5 (page 230). This approach will give an approximate idea of the size of the different segments (from Spanish dominant to English dominant) in the market and a fairly good description of the demographics and mind-set of each segment. (However, even though language is a good predictor of the degree of acculturation, it reveals only a part of the many cultural variables that can affect the behavior of the different Hispanic cultural segments.)

Second, to better understand how much cultural variation exists between these segments, the advertiser should get to know and visualize the points of difference between those consumers who are at either extreme of the acculturation process. To aid in understanding the differences between these two cultural poles, marketers should learn about foreign-born and U.S.-born Hispanics, because both groups are large and fast-growing segments of the Hispanic market (Figure 7.2). Marketing strategies targeting U.S. Hispanics should always consider at least these two main segments.

THE FOREIGN-BORN U.S. HISPANIC

As Hispanic immigration continues in an upward trend in response to the demands of the U.S. labor market, foreign-born Hispanics continue to appear in all socioeconomic groups. The U.S. economy continues to absorb foreign-born unskilled and semi-skilled laborers in factories and service sectors as it has done historically. In addition, business ties with Mexico and other Latin American countries are booming, fueled by the synergy created by the prosperous U.S. Hispanic market and the potential for business resulting from the North American Free Trade Agreement, the Pacific rim economies, and international global trade in general. These new business opportunities are attracting professionals from Mexico and Central and South America. Professionals, investors and business people immigrating from Latin America, even though constituting a small proportion of overall Hispanic immigrants, tend to be highly educated and belong to the upper and middle socioeconomic groups of their native countries. They may represent businesses from their home countries or join American enterprises or start new business ventures in the United States.

The strong growth trend of the traditional Hispanic immigrant segment (unskilled, semi-skilled, technical, and small service business owner) is predicted to continue if the native economies do not improve enough to offer labor opportunities more appealing than those in the United States, and if the U.S. economy continues to depend on Hispanic immigrants to satisfy its labor demands. Foreign-born Hispanics present a different marketing and consumer profile than their U.S.-born counterparts, as is shown in detail in Table 7.1.

The growth rate of the U.S.-born Hispanic segment is also projected to continue to increase. Hispanics enjoy large families and tend to have on average more children than the average U.S. family. Acculturation does have an impact on Hispanic family size—the more acculturated, the smaller the family. So far, however, this impact has not been strong enough to bring acculturated Hispanic families down to the size of those of the general population. Hence, the ratio of births to deaths will continue to contribute to strong growth in the U.S.-born Hispanic segment (Figure 7.2).

THE U.S.-BORN HISPANIC

U.S.-born Hispanics naturally display many of the same traditional Hispanic cultural traits as foreign-born Hispanics, but as a result of growing up in the United States, their language, social experience, and familiarity with products and services tend to be quite different from that of the foreign-born.

Figures 7.3 through 7.6 illustrate attitudinal and value-related differences between U.S.-born and foreign-born Hispanics and how language proficiency or preference—a gauge for acculturation—has an impact on their value orientation. Traditional Hispanic values are present across the market, but to a lesser degree among U.S.-born and more acculturated consumers. Messages and images should conform to these differences and similarities depending on the campaign.

A DUAL-TIERED STRATEGY

As discussed earlier, as part of any initial marketing analysis and conceptualization, demographic differentiations between foreign-born and U.S.-born Hispanics must be considered and built into the marketing plan, both for short- and long-term goals. Each group's mind-set toward the product or service and their informational needs, interests, degree of acculturation, and language and media usage patterns are, as would be expected, quite different. A two-tiered Hispanic universe or strategy is thus often the best way to manage and reach both these segments.

The foreign-born demographic segment naturally includes a larger proportion of unacculturated Hispanics than the U.S.-born segment. The Spanish-dominant and most of the Spanish-preferred Hispanics comprise this tier. For many corporations this may be the Hispanic market segment where greater business opportunities lie. For example, for marketers promoting mass market consumer goods and products and services, marketing to the Spanish-dominant/preferred foreign-born tier is a must. Personal care products, soft drinks, beer, packaged goods, clothes, shoes, and services such as dentists, insurance policies, eye care

Lowenbräu beer promotes itself as "the international lion" to Spanish-speaking consumers.

services, eyeglasses and contact lenses, savings and loans, money remittance products, credit cards, checking accounts, telephone, water, gas and electricity, entertainment and amusement parks, airline travel and tourism are some examples of categories with great appeal among these Hispanics. Other products that have great acceptance among the Spanish-dominant/preferred are hard durable goods, such as radios, CD players, video players, microwave ovens, sewing machines, pressure cookers, and irons. Another sought-after product among consumers in this foreign-born tier is a brand new car, an attainable American dream for many immigrant Hispanics.

The other tier, the U.S.-born segment, includes the most acculturated Hispanics. Yet contrary to what many would tend to assume, not all U.S.-born Hispanics are fully acculturated, at least from a marketing perspective. For example, it is common to find U.S.-born Hispanics who prefer to communicate in Spanish, or who rank low on the acculturation scale. Presently, these people tend to be older and reside mostly in the West and Southwest. They feel very close to the traditional Hispanic culture. But the great majority of the U.S.-born Hispanics are fluent in English and many are fully bilingual or speak Spanish fluently. The U.S.-born Hispanic tier includes two language segments, the "true bilinguals" and the English preferred/dominants. As Figure 7.2 illustrates, this second tier is composed of 2nd, 3rd and 4th generation Hispanics.

Corporations that target acculturated and U.S.-born Hispanics tend to do so through general market campaigns, occasionally adding an "ethnic touch" to these campaigns, for example, by casting Latin-looking actors in their ads. Others channel their communication projects through English-language publications and magazines, such as *Hispanic Business* and *Hispanic*. Bilingual media are emerging with a stronger advertising voice. Radio and TV are slowly but steadily creating programming that appeals to this market segment, both young (teens and young adults) as well as mature.

As the acculturated Hispanic segment has grown in political power and financial strength, more and more Hispanic-specific marketing programs have been developed. Banks, automotive companies, fast food restaurants, airlines and others are capitalizing on the importance of this group.

■ Marketing to Hispanic Women

Given that *familismo,* or strong family orientation, is at the core of Hispanic culture, it is no surprise that the *Latina* woman is the driving force behind both the desire to move up the socioeconomic ladder and the desire to keep the Hispanic culture at the heart of the family.

In addition to being in charge of the everyday management of the household, child care, cooking, and other chores, the Hispanic woman plays a key role in every decision affecting the family and the family quality of life. She is usually a key player in the financial decision-making process, far beyond grocery shopping and children's clothing. She is the "engine," encouraging her husband to purchase a new car or a new home by asking and learning through friends (*comadres*—godmother, close friends, neighbors) and the media how to apply for a loan. In addition, having joined the labor force in large numbers, Hispanic women make major contributions to the family's household income.

To market successfully to Hispanic women, marketers and advertisers need to address their unique demographic and psychographic characteristics. There is much diversity within the Hispanic women's market, particularly between U.S.- and foreign-born women. Acculturation, country of origin, and socioeconomic factors have tremendous impact in the Hispanic market, and these apply to the Hispanic women's market as well. Cuban and U.S.-born Mexican women tend to be at opposite poles of Hispanic culture, and it is a real challenge to communicate to both women's groups with the same campaign.

DEMOGRAPHICS Hispanic women comprise half of the U.S. Hispanic population. In 1990 there were over 11 million, of which more than 7 million were older than 18 (Table 7.2). The median age is 27 years; the non-Hispanic white woman's median age is 37 years. These figures are projected to continue to hold into the next century, keeping more Hispanic women in the child-rearing age group.

In 1994 alone, Spanish-speaking women were projected to give birth to over 50,000 children in the United States. That so many Hispanic women are of prime child-bearing age, have larger families, and continue to immigrate the United States means the United States is witnessing a 30–year Hispanic baby boom, comparable to the Anglo baby boom that took place between 1946 and 1964 (Lupo, 1993, 4). As a consequence, many product categories related to children and personal care, such as medical care, pregnancy tests, baby furniture, children's toys and apparel, baby food, and child care, will be in increased demand by Hispanic mothers.

In terms of formal schooling, Hispanic women now trail their non-Hispanic counterparts (Table 7.3). Combined with their overall lower English-language literacy rates, this makes them more likely to be linguistically isolated and more dependent on Spanish-language media and resources than Hispanic men. As illustrated in Figure 7.7, Hispanic women tend not to be bilingual and thus are more Spanish dependent. This situation is particularly acute in those areas with a higher influx of recent immigrants, such as California, Miami, and Washington, D.C., and much less so in the Southwest.

HOUSEHOLDS IN TRANSITION

A mental picture of what is happening in the Hispanic household is useful in marketing to Hispanic women. As discussed in Chapter 2 (see page 45), the growth of Hispanic households during the past decades has been dramatic and is projected to continue unabated into the next century (Table 7.4).

As in the general market, the demographic profile of Hispanic households is changing in many respects. For example, the divorce rate among Hispanics is increasing in general, particularly among U.S. Cubans and South Americans, who in 1992 were divorcing at rates of 8.8 and 9.2 percent, repectively. In spite of these changes, Hispanics tend to marry within their own cultural subgroup (Figure 7.8), so their cultural values are likely to be passed on for generations to come. This suggests that the cultural traditions at the core of the Hispanic household should continue to receive close attention from companies marketing to Hispanic women.

A GROWING FINANCIAL FORCE

During the past decades, Hispanic women have joined the labor force in increasing numbers (Table 7.5), particularly in professional, technical/sales, and administrative support/clerical occupations (Figure 7.9), and their earnings have increased significantly as well. Now, more than ever before, they are working or looking for jobs. For example, more than half of those age 16 or older were in the labor force in 1991. Hispanic women's participation in the labor force has increased dramatically, as they became the fastest-growing segment of the labor market between 1980 and 1990. Hispanic women as a group are also making more money than ever before. Those women earning less than $10,000 per year declined from 70 percent to 50 percent from 1985 to 1989, and those earning more than $25,000 per year increased from 4 percent to 12 percent during the same period.

Hispanic women are active buyers in the market. For example, traditional women-driven purchases index higher among Hispanics than other population segments for items such as cleaning supplies, laundry detergents, personal care products, home food, apparel, furniture, and major and small appliances.

THE HISPANIC FEMALE SOUL

When marketing, advertising, or communicating with the Hispanic woman, marketers are talking to a "different female soul." Despite the diversity among Hispanic women, the commonalities outweigh the differences. Hispanic women tend to characterize themselves as "romantic," and romance and courtship tend to occupy a predominant place in their life. Courtship before marriage traditionally lasts several years and is "a family affair." Parents on both sides tend to be quite involved in the couple's social life. This romantic mind-set may help explain the overwhelming popularity of *novelas,* Spanish-language TV soap operas that last a couple of months and invariably portray highly charged romances.

For the foreign-born Hispanic woman, especially if the extended family does not reside in the United States, there is always an important nostalgia factor, reminiscing about a past when a larger family group was always available and present for important dates and holidays.

Hispanic women tend to be "outer-directed" and very conscious of their overall appearance, including fashion and cosmetics. They are very expressive and highly emotional within the socially acceptable parameters of their particular subgroup. Cuban and Puerto Rican women, for example, tend to be the very fashion-conscious and are attracted to a more European high-fashion style. They wear dressier, more elegant clothes in social gatherings, and even their casual clothing tends to be more formal. This European style also tends to be preferred among Mexican, South American, and Central American upper-middle-class women. Younger women and teens follow a more casual American style.

U.S. Mexican women and those from other Central American countries are more traditional in their dressing styles. They tend to prefer simpler clothes that resemble the fashions of the 1950s and 1960s. The "presentation of the self" also tends to be more traditional. Special care and attention is taken with color combinations, dress style, jewelry, makeup, and hairstyle. Most Hispanic women are proud of how they dress and many tend to spend a significant amount of their income on their physical appearance.

In the Hispanic woman's personal milieu, the house, she is "la Reina" (the queen) of the house. This is one of the few individualistic aspects of her personality: generally, her primary and extended family come first. Her cultural- and religious-based values emphasize suffering, obligation, and sacrifice. Pleasing husbands, children, mothers-in-law, friends, and others in her social network is a characteristic aspect of her personality. Certainly this tends to vary considerably with acculturation: the more acculturated the woman, the more "individualistic" she is likely to be. But even among highly acculturated Hispanic women who have resided all their lives in the U.S., the tradition of *pleasing* is present. Being helpful, giving, and a good hostess are values appreciated in the Hispanic culture, and Latin women tend to be proud of them.

The children and the home tend to take up all or most of her daily life even if she is working outside the home in a high-level capacity. Hispanic mothers tend to keep their young children at home longer, postponing school entry for one or two years. Young girls are dressed with traditional feminine dresses while boys battle constantly with the present teenage trend of loose-fitting clothes and their moms' desires to have their shirts "tucked inside their pants." The battle is usually won by the children when they reach puberty, to their mother's chagrin.

A culturally-attuned ad from Kraft appeals to Hispanic mothers with the Spanish slogan, "The care of your family depends on you . . . and you depend on Kraft."

Cooking from scratch and serving fresh foods is a normal, every-day practice. It is not considered a burden, but a pleasure by most. Pleasing their husbands' palate and making every effort to do so on a daily basis often occupies several hours of the day, every day. This trait varies significantly with the degree of acculturation and socioeconomic status. The more acculturated and/or the higher degree of formal education attained, the more the Hispanic woman will lean toward using convenience foods or having household help.

Her body language is very affectionate, even in public. Women hug and kiss upon greeting, even if they saw each other earlier the same day. The Caribbean Hispanic (Cubans, Puerto Ricans, Dominicans) tend to be more verbal and sometimes also quite confrontational; Mexicans and Central Americans tend to be more consenting and go to great lengths to avoid confrontations.

There is a universal focus by Hispanic women on the home, which they tend to decorate carefully and within the traditional taste of their different countries of origin. All these factors that affect their daily lives must be taken into consideration when marketing and advertising to Hispanic women. Good advertising should also mirror who she is—her mind-set, what's important to her, and how she dresses. Again, focus groups can always help fine tune these issues before a campaign is executed.

■ Marketing to Hispanic Youth

The Hispanic youth (under age 20) market is the fastest-growing segment in the nation, and it is expected to grow to 12.7 million by 2005 (from 8.4 million in 1990, a 52 percent increase in 15 years), while the non-Hispanic youth market is expected to decrease in the same period.

According to a recent article in the *Wall Street Journal* (June 15, 1993), "Hispanics are predominantly young; in California alone more than one quarter [of the Hispanic population] are under 15 years old. [These are] much higher proportions than non-Hispanic whites, non-Hispanic blacks, or Asians." In addition, according to 1990 census data, over a third (34.7 percent) of the Hispanic population are under age 17. In comparison, the total U.S. population is on average 7.4 years older with only a quarter (25.6 percent) under age 17 (Table 7.6; Valdés, 1993).

The Hispanic market is expected to grow very rapidly in the future. In 1980 there were 4.6 million Hispanics under age 15. By the year 2000 the number is expected to reach 8.8 million, a 100 percent increase or an average annual growth rate of 3.3 percent in 20 years (Table 7.7; Valdés, 1993). Two factors are contributing to this growth. First, the U.S. Hispanic population is younger than the rest of the population, with a median age of 25.5 years, whereas the median age for the total U.S. population is 32.9. Second, on average, Hispanic couples have more children than non-Hispanic couples.

The Hispanic youth market will thus become increasingly important. Major market players in the toy, apparel, soft drink, food, and media industries have noticed this trend and are targeting Hispanic youth and their parents. Hispanic parents are known for overindulging their children. It is one of the cultural differences between Hispanics and the Anglo middle class. Take, for example, the apparel industry and the expenditures by the three main ethnic market segments: African-American, Hispanic, and non-Hispanic white. Hispanics tend to spend more money on their children, particularly the younger ones (see Figure 3.18, page 144). Hispanic kids and their parents tend to be terrific customers.

What's so different about Hispanic children and teens? Obviously a child or a teenager is a child or a teenager in any culture. Hispanic children and teens follow developmental stages like any other child or teen in the world. Teens want to identify with their

**TARGETING
CHILDREN AND TEENS**

peer group, to look and behave like their friends at school or in the neighborhood, whether Hispanic or American. Young infants and children are as dependent on their parents and their support as any other child or infant in the world. Can one therefore assume that the strategies for targeting Hispanic children and teens closely follow the strategies used to target American youth? For the majority of the Hispanic market, the answer is no. Their unique familial context and ways of social interaction require marketers and advertisers to take an in-depth look into this group's psychographics, media usage, and shopping behavior. As can be expected, these reflect the differences between the two main cultures in question, the "average" Hispanic culture and the Anglo middle-class culture, as described in Chapter 4, page 169.

Depending on his or her socioeconomic background, a young child or teen may respond better to the Hispanic culture's emotional buttons than to those of the American middle class, even if he or she is fluent in English. Hispanic culture stresses child dependency on parents, whereas traditional American culture stresses independence. In traditional Hispanic culture, parents want their children to be at home for as long as possible. As a result, Hispanic children on average tend to start school later than American children (Fuller, 1994, 4). In contrast, in the traditional American family children are introduced much earlier to earning their own money (even in high-income families) through household chores or after-school jobs. The traditional Hispanic mother takes pride in doing the household chores; asking children to earn their own money usually happens among low-income families or in more acculturated Hispanic families.

A strong family orientation is forged and reinforced during childhood, so it plays an important role in children's lives, affecting how they interact with friends, relatives, and the community at large. As a result, the Hispanic parent tends to have a stronger say, for example, in purchases for the child. As a result, marketing and advertising to the Hispanic child always includes the mother and/or father in one way or another. For example, a successful Spanish-language campaign for General Mills promoting cereals talks to the mother regarding the benefits and attributes of the cereal, while targeting the child with messages of fun and entertainment. In contrast, General Mills' English-language campaign targets only children, not the parents. Obtaining the parents' blessings in favor of your product or service will make a difference in the effectiveness of your ad campaign.

The acculturation process adds another dimension to the Hispanic consumer picture. In most cases, children have to live between two cultures, adding new roles and expectations that result in additional pressure and anxiety. This situation is particularly acute among households with Spanish-dependent parents where the child is the bilingual communicator. The child many times has to act as translator and go-between to help in adult decision making. This includes purchases of durable goods, selection of brands and products, and translating at the physician's office for the parents. Currently, Spanish-dependent adults comprise the largest Hispanic adult segment, representing close to 50 percent of Hispanic adults in California alone, which is home to 34 percent of the U.S. Hispanic market.

CHILD REARING BY LANGUAGE SEGMENTATION

Parents in bilingual households often feel at a loss, dependent on their children's help, not able to play their proper parental roles, and not in control of what their children get involved in. For example, Hispanic parents often perceive English-language media as a threat because they cannot control what their bilingual children are watching. Parents in these households may either limit their children's exposure to English-language media or sit through the television shows trying to understand and control what their children are watching. Traditional Hispanic parents are particularly annoyed by some modern-style music video format programs and encourage their children to watch Spanish-language programs where they have more control.

On the positive side, children act as "acculturation factors" and can boost their self-esteem by telling parents about new products and helping them locate the products in the store. In this case children can play an important role in the decision-making process, which should be considered in marketing and advertising strategies.

The differences between acculturated and unacculturated children and teens are striking. For example, the type of chocolate flavor preferred by one group is often disliked by the other; some

ACCULTURATED AND UNACCULTURATED HISPANIC YOUTH

products that enjoy heritage among non-U.S.-born children don't get any points with U.S.-born Hispanic children. The toys and games the recent immigrant child looks for in the United States are those he or she heard about "back home." New American products may not appeal to recent immigrants for some time, especially if they are not promoted via Spanish-language media.

As mentioned throughout this book, consideration of cultural nuances can make the difference between a successful, profitable marketing campaign and one that fails miserably. For targeting Hispanic youth, strategic planning and consumer research should include both parents and children, carefully focusing on cultural differences and how the product, service, or program is perceived in the Hispanic cultural context.

HISPANIC YOUTH AND MEDIA USAGE

Hispanic children and teens watch TV both in English and Spanish. Degree of exposure to one or the other correlates directly with the child's proficiency in English and the degree of bilingualism of the parents.

According to the Market Development, Inc., Hispanic Teen Poll, most Hispanic teens (66 percent) watch TV in both languages, 29 percent watch only English-language shows, and 5 percent watch only Spanish-language shows (MDI Poll, 1992, 4). These numbers may actually under-represent Spanish-dominant teen viewing habits, because the poll is conducted by phone and hence does not include Hispanic families without telephones, which tend to be more Spanish dominant and have larger households.

From an audience share analysis, according to recent data from Nielsen's Hispanic media measurements (*Nielsen Hispanic Television Index*, February 1993), Spanish-dominant/dependent children have radically different viewing habits from their English-dominant counterparts. Spanish-dominant teens devote 41 percent of their viewing time to Spanish-language TV, a higher share of viewing than that for the four major broadcast networks. A similar pattern can be observed among Spanish-dominant teens.

Today's Spanish-dominant/dependent youth market is composed of over 4 million Hispanics ages 5 to 17, according to census data on non-English-language speakers (Macias, F., 1993, 244). These data show that a large percentage of the Hispanic youth market falls in this category, and in order to have an impact, marketing campaigns should be conducted in Spanish.

■ Couponing and the Hispanic Consumer

Until recently it was believed that Hispanic women did not use coupons, for a variety of reasons. A popular explanation was that Hispanic women "thought these were food stamps." Hispanic Market Connections' extensive research on the subject shows conclusively that Hispanic coupon use correlates directly with acculturation and English-language usage (Figure 7.10).

Foreign-born Hispanic women have been slow in catching up with the value and role of coupons. But once they become familiar with these, many will usually collect and redeem them, as they tend to be budget conscious. As a matter of fact, in today's economy, many will clip double coupons and sometimes drive distances to take advantage of a special sale.

■ Advertising to Hispanics

There is no one set way or hard-and-fast rule for advertising successfully to the U.S. Hispanic market. Variety and a creative imagination in addition to cultural insight are the keys to advertising simultaneously to the different segments. A good professional Hispanic creative group can bring culturally attuned, emotional messages to the marketplace, because they are a product of the culture to which they are communicating. The best Hispanic ad campaigns usually come from agencies staffed with Hispanic ad executives, creatives, and media directors who intimately know their audience. Rarely does a non-Hispanic creative come up with a fine-tuned ad campaign for the Hispanic market.

If a company's goal is to achieve big results in the Hispanic market, it should hire Hispanic creative talent, not just translate general market advertising. If the goal is just to get an ad out, with no expectation of impressive results or long-term benefits, then a company might want to consider the translation option, with the consequent risk of an inferior product.

An inferior advertisement or one showing no sensitivity to Hispanic culture may hurt the image of a company or its product. By airing poorly executed or low-budget ad campaigns that are either dubbed or directly translated from an English-language campaign, marketers are communicating to the Hispanic market, "You are not an important customer to me" and "I don't care about you." U.S. Hispanic consumers are accustomed to seeing high-quality, professional advertisements in English and Spanish. Products advertised on "cheap" commercials insult and irritate many consumers, Hispanics included.

Another crippling result of inferior advertising may be the low return on investment and management's consequent decision-making. For example, the financial returns of a poorly executed, low-budget campaign may be low and, as such, the marketer concludes wrongly that there's no money in advertising to Hispanics and abandons further efforts. This is referred to as "the vaccine approach"—one advertises just enough to miss or even kill the business opportunity.

These comments do not necessarily mean only mega-advertising budgets will work. To the contrary, Hispanic advertising has seen excellent regional and local advertising results with moderate budgets, but these ad campaigns have always been created and produced by professional Hispanic talent and Hispanic culturally-attuned testing methods.

DEVELOPING EFFECTIVE ADVERTISING

What is effective in the mainstream American market is not necessarily successful in the Hispanic market. Rational, distant, or indifferent messages are simply not effective. A company's message should be designed with an emotional hook in order to obtain what award-winning creative Norma Orci has called "share of heart." Emotional appeal can be built into even the coldest and most rational type of product or service.

For example, in the case of a mortgage insurance broker who wants to appeal to Hispanics, simply describing in straightforward language what a policy offers ("The policy covers and pays mort-gage payments if the lendee is unable to do so") will not get mas-sive results. It may succeed in informing the audience—which is certainly important—but it will not motivate the majority. In order to raise the Hispanic consumer's purchase interest—and to increase recall—there must be an emotional hook ("With this insurance policy, you can rest assured that your loved ones will not need to worry if you lose your job and cannot make the house payments"). The basic concern of "not being able to make pay-ments" is replaced with an emotional message that touches in a reassuring manner the emotions that are associated with "losing one's job," such as worry, shame, and fear of losing the property and hurting the family.

Non-emotional, distant, detached, or national messages tend to go over the head of the majority of Hispanic consumers. How to uncover that emotional and relevant positioning strategy is described below.

When a company is targeting a Hispanic audience, the strength of the emotional message may vary considerably, often depending on the acculturation level of the audience. As in the general mar-ket, determining the "emotional positioning" strategy, or what message communicates more effectively, should be decided through research—with target consumer input or feedback. The educated guess is always a last resource in advertising or concept testing, especially when advertising cross-culturally. Even a tal-ented creative staff cannot replace a solid awareness of the actual mind-set of the consumer.

POSITIONING

An example of "emotional positioning" in the financial services category is a campaign promoting checking accounts to foreign-born, unacculturated Hispanics. Although checks are a very con-venient form of managing bill payment and purchases, this fact alone would not capture the attention of this Hispanic segment unfamiliar with these services. The ad strategy for this group needs to be completely different from that for the Hispanic mar-ket segment familiar with checking accounts.

How should a company present or position the benefits of conve-nience and practicality to a consumer group not particularly dri-

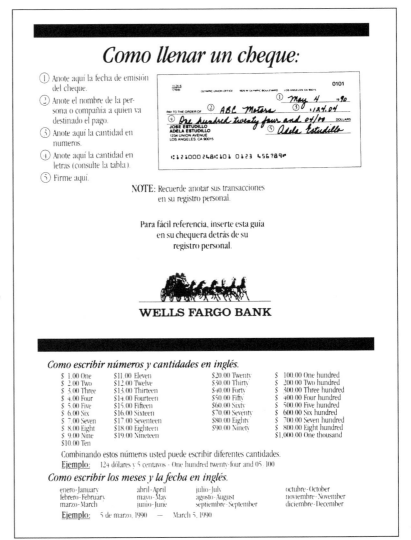

ven at the moment by such abstract notions? How can it entice a consumer who has rarely ventured into a bank, an unfamiliar setting? What kind of emotional handle can be used to communicate the dynamics of a checking account?

The family/group value orientation prevalent in Hispanic culture (see Table 4.1, page 207) provides the central clue as to what this emotional appeal might be. The message has to convey benefit for the group—the family—rather than the individual. If one were to ask the target consumers how the family would benefit from a checking account, then the emotional, family-driven message would emerge spontaneously. Or, to look at the issue from a different angle, one could ask what *not* having a checking account is like. How does it affect family life? Here are two possible responses from Hispanic consumers:

✧ Father or mother spends a lot of time paying the bills, standing in line, or driving a long distance, and this takes away from family life.

✧ Father or mother (or grandfather or uncle) carries cash, and muggers know this. It makes them easy targets for assaults and theft. This affects the family in that there is insecurity and potential loss of money, in addition to potential physical harm during an attack. The family is at the mercy of the muggers, with little or no control.

The same rationale applies to Hispanics households that don't have savings accounts. Money saved in these Hispanic households is many times hidden away, making these dwellings prime theft targets. In addition, if fire, earthquakes, or tornados occur, all savings are gone when the household is destroyed, at a time when the family is financially hurt and severely vulnerable. A checking and savings account could certainly help the family, offering security (of the money and person), more time to spend with the family and friends, and more time for other activities. These are highly valued benefits that, if promoted via a culturally sensitive campaign, can be used to entice non-acculturated or recently arrived Hispanics.

The ecosystem model described in Chapter 4 (see page 184) is a useful tool in the creative brainstorming and conceptual analysis. The above analysis of savings accounts occurs at the first level of the ecosystemic model, the microsystem or household level. The next level of analysis, the mesosystem, entails analyzing the target consumer's interaction with the product or service at the institutional level, that is, how the foreign-born and/or less acculturated Hispanic target group interacts with the bank in this case. Marketers need to look at all the possible points of interaction between the consumer and the bank: services, language of service, signage in Spanish, personal versus non-personal service, the language of brochures and other collateral materials, ease of access to these materials, the waiting place (remember, chances are children will come as well), and parking space.

Once the forms and points of interaction pertaining to the product or service and the Hispanic consumer are considered, a long list of emotionally driven attributes or benefits can be devised. It will become obvious which items on the list could be the ones that get the product or service closer to the Hispanic consumer's needs and wants. Which message is the most moving and enticing? Hispanic creative writers will propose a couple of possibilities, which ideally should be tested with target consumers.

WHAT DOESN'T WORK

Assuming that abstract and rational messages and images influence Hispanics tends to be a very common mistake among advertisers. The majority of U.S. Hispanics tend to be very literal in their interpretation of advertising messages. In consequence, abstract or elaborate metaphors, images, and messages tend to be missed, or even worse, misinterpreted.

One reason marketers make this mistake is that it is sometimes difficult to grasp without consumer feedback the fine level of comprehension and knowledge of consumers vis-à-vis the product or service. People tend to naturally assume that others know and understand as much about basic products and services as they do. Unfortunately, this is not the case.

A second cause of the mistake stems from the hoped-for cross-cultural campaign "umbrella effect." Product managers tend to want their Hispanic ad campaigns to be as close as possible to their general market campaigns, the rationale being to capitalize on increased exposure to the same message (in the case of bilinguals who may be exposed to both the Anglo and the Hispanic campaign) and to maintain consistency of the image of the product or service. Message consistency and frequency of message exposure are both laudable advertising goals—if all other variables that enter into the equation at the campaign design level and the consumer audience are the same, which is not the case here.

It is hard for brand and product managers or other decision makers to accept that a creative strategy that is highly successful in the general market may very well fail when introduced to the Hispanic market. It is even harder to convince these decision makers that the reasons a particular campaign does not work are cultural, social, and demographic.

Other common snafus include: too much information in one ad, lack of focus, product or service not presented at the level of comprehension or mind-set of the consumer, message too abstract, and no emotional pull.

Successful ad campaigns tested by Hispanic Market Communications in the course of ten years tend to have some basic elements in common:

WHAT DOES WORK

✧ The campaigns are emotionally driven and talk to the heart.

✧ The product or service is presented in simple, familiar, and realistic backgrounds.

✧ Copy and key messages are simple, direct, and to the point.

✧ Only one or two product or service benefits or attributes are communicated and repeated.

✧ Clear suggestion of price (if applicable, "Not too expensive for you").

✧ The campaigns show product (with and without packaging, if needed), logo, and/or location — as needed.

✧ The campaigns tell a simple story. There is a beginning and an end. Elements in the ad tend to be related, not independent juxtaposed images à la MTV.

Successful television and radio ads have the following elements in common:

✧ The ads repeat the key message or messages and show the product several times during the ad.

✧ The pace tends to be somewhat slower than for general market material.

✧ Talent and people shown in the ads are "average-looking" Hispanic people, not too dark, mestizo, or Indian looking, not too blond or European-looking either. These "physiological" parameters are correlated with social class; a more light-haired/blond Hispanic is associated with an "upper-class Hispanic." There is much Hispanic consumer sensitivity in this area, and talent testing (with photos or videos) is advised. Consumers in Latin America ten to prefer the "blond and tall" image and talent. This is somewhat different in the U.S. Hispanic market where class structure is more loose and far more dark, or "Latin looking," people are successful.

✧ The ads show (or suggest) a particular person—a mother, father, teenager, baby, child, grandmother, teacher, teller, salesperson—whoever is appropriate for the product or service.

✧ The ads may show children (happy, smiling) and talk about motherhood or fatherhood with tenderness.

✧ Generally, the ads explain or show where to find the product or service.

✧ The ads suggest positive images, such as smiles, accomplishments, family members, or an improved quality of life.

✧ The ads do not show or dwell on negative images or connotations unless strictly necessary for the message to hit home, such as for drunk driving or AIDS themes.

If the visuals or messages are negative or painful, such as a grimacing child receiving shots in the arm or a dentist's drill whirring in the background, the effect will tend to be the opposite of the desired one: denial ("My kids don't need shots" or "My teeth don't hurt"), low recall, anger, and finally, no action. If the message is portrayed with positive emotions (such as a healthy, smiling child in her mom's arms talking to a warm and friendly nurse who administers the shots, or a boy or girl with a beautiful smile to entice oral care), the response tends to be positive and recall much higher. The ad below illustrates this point.

If a marketer must communicate several messages in the same ad campaign, building a story around the campaign will enhance recall and overall receptivity. Experts in the area of memory use and development agree that to facilitate recall, messages or icons must relate to or be attached to a familiar context, word, story, or place, in which actions, benefits, or attributes are connected. In a TV ad, a diaper commercial may talk about the "stay-dry" baby benefit, showing details of the new diaper, or the ad can tell a brief story of a baby that smiles longer because s/he is dry all the time, and the mother uses the baby as the demo to describe and show the specific details of the diaper. The ad should next focus on showing the box of diapers — (or describing it if a radio ad), concentrating on the logo or icon that is original or unique to the brand. This facilitates both message recall as well as brand recognition.

Colgate promotes healthy smiles in the Spanish-speaking world; the tag-line (lower right corner) reads "porque tu sonrisa es para toda tu vida" (because your smile is yours for life).

■ Community Marketing

A highly effective way to market to Hispanics is to link advertising campaigns to strong promotional efforts within the world of Hispanic culture and the Hispanic community. Colgate-Palmolive, PepsiCo, and other companies have built brand awareness and loyalty by sponsoring community programs such as school cleanups and literacy programs in low-income neighborhoods of big cities. For example, Colgate has sponsored "My School Project" and "Clean Block" contests, in which students, parents, local businesses, and other community members pitched in to clean up schools and neighborhoods. Literacy is the area chosen by the Coors Brewing Company; for several years it has sponsored programs, materials, and events to bring literacy to adults and children.

The Catholic church, an icon of Hispanic culture, has been approached many times by corporations wanting it to provide that grass-roots community edge to their Hispanic marketing and promotional efforts: "Recognizing the pivotal role the Catholic church plays in the life of most Hispanics, some 300 food and beverage companies joined together to sponsor more than 100 celebrations and fund-raising activities in Hispanic communities in Texas and California. Called 'Friends of the Community' the programs were anchored by H. E. Butt Grocery Company in Texas and Ralph's Grocery Company in California. The 'Friends' help churches and non-profit groups promote events by donating products and gift certificates. For their help, the sponsors receive recognition on banners and promotional vehicles to get product exposure at the community level and access to influential people in the Hispanic community" (Swenson, 1990, 40–41).

Many local and national businesses also approach local parishes in order to build their image and credibility in the Hispanic community. Community marketing through the church is an American phenomenon that would probably surprise the traditional Catholic churches in Latin America. Yet it seems to work very well and not hinder the relationship of the church with its parishioners or the image of the product or service. On the contrary, it is appreciated by the Hispanic community.

THE AD AGENCY   The Hispanic creative team may be part of a Hispanic-only agency or a department within a large general market agency or corporation. What matters is that there be a professionalism to the Hispanic creative and marketing team and a serious commitment of resources to Hispanic advertising and marketing. When the Hispanic creative team is only a part of a general market ad agency, it is often hard for them to obtain the resources and support that they need, because bottom-line contributions from Hispanic advertising tend to be limited in comparison with those generated by the general market accounts. As a result, management tends to underestimate the resources needed and does not allocate as much to that area. Hence, Hispanic departments in these circumstances tend to suffer from under-staffing and lack of professional support.

This problem does not occur with independent Hispanic advertising agencies, whose sole income is usually generated by advertising to Hispanics. This has led many corporations to choose a

Hispanic-only advertising agency over a general market/Spanish-shop option. But certainly there are exceptions to this point.

One caveat when selecting a Hispanic ad agency: you should not assume that because the names or ethnicity of people in the company are Hispanic this makes the principals or their staff experts in the U.S. Hispanic market or experts in advertising and marketing per se. As with any other business relationship, professional qualifications and track records should be checked.

Ad agencies that target Hispanics can be located through directories and other resources (see Sourcebook, beginning on page 451). In addition, for those searching for a Hispanic ad agency, professional Hispanic trade shows such as Se Habla Español, sponsored by *Hispanic Business Magazine* of Santa Barbara, California, provide an excellent opportunity to tap into the Hispanic advertising and marketing network.

THE ADVERTISING BUDGET

As in the general market, the advertising budget for a promotion targeting Hispanics should reflect a company's desired short- and long-term objectives and, specifically, the business potential for the product or service in the Hispanic target market. These goals may include, for example, the market share a company aims to capture or the image it wants to create for a product vis-à-vis the competition. If the Hispanic market in a target area city represents a substantial segment of the population for your product or service, the Hispanic advertising, marketing, and promotional budget should be allocated accordingly and proportionally. In other words, if the Hispanic target segment has the potential to represent a third or a half, or even 10 percent of the desired consumer base, it is good business sense to budget a third or a half, or 10 percent of the ad and marketing dollars for Hispanic marketing endeavors to see important results and return on investment. How would a company otherwise realize the results it had anticipated? Why should it expect more? It is worth investing and allocating resources to develop an effective advertising and marketing campaign.

■ *References*

Deshpande, R., W. Hoyer, and N. Donthu. "The Intensity of Ethnic Affiliation: A Study of the Sociology of Hispanic Consumption." *Journal of Consumer Research* Vol. 13 (September 1986): 214–220.

Edmonston, Barry, and Jeffrey S. Passel. *The Future Immigrant Population of the United States.* Washington, D.C.: The Urban Institute, February 1992, 7.

Fuller, Bruce, et al. "Rich culture, poor markets: Why do Latino parents choose to Forego pre-schooling?" Harvard University: April, 1994. (Appeared in *School Choice: The Cultural Logic of Families.*)

Hispanic Market Connections. *The Hispanic Database. Northern California.* Los Altos, Calif.: HMC, 1991.

———. *The Hispanic Database. Southern California.* Los Altos, Calif.: HMC, 1992.

———. *Language and Media Planning for the Hispanic Market. Northern California.* Los Altos, Calif.: HMC, 1992a.

———. *Language and Media Planning for the Hispanic Market. Southern California.* Los Altos, Calif.: HMC, 1992.

———. Proprietary research study. New York, 1993.

Intercambios, Vol. 6, no. 2, winter 1994.

Korzenny, Felipe, and Betty Ann Korzenny. "When a Hispanic is Not a Hispanic: Issues in Conducting Hispanic Qualitative Research." In *Quirk's Marketing Research Reviews* (November 1992): 14.

Lupo, Tom. "Hispanic Ethnic Marketing." *Money Maker's Monthly* (May 1993): 4.

Macias, F. "Language Minority Classification." In *Hispanic Journal of Behavioral Sciences* (May 1993): 244.

Marin, G., and B. VanOss Marin. "Research with Hispanic Populations." In *Applied Social Research Methods Series.* California: Sage Publications, 1991.

"MDI Hispanic Teen Poll." Review in *Research Alert* (March 1992): 4.

Nielsen, February 1993. National Hispanic Television Index (NHTI).

Swenson, A. Chester. "How to Speak to Hispanics." In *American Demographics* (February 1990): 40–41.

U.S. Bureau of the Census. *The Hispanic Population in the United States.* By Patricia A. Montgomery. *Current Population Reports,* no. P20–475, March 1994.

———. *Statistical Abstract of the United States: 1992* (112th edition). Washington, D.C.: Government Printing Office, 1992.

Valdés, M. Isabel. "Dual Interviewing Mode." Paper submitted for publication to the *Advertising Research Journal,* 1993.

———. "The Mexican Strategy." Special advertising supplement. *Food and Beverage Marketing* (December 1990): 11–a.

———. "Targeting Hispanic Women." Paper presented at *Se Habla Español* Conference, New York, 1993.

———. "What You Need to Know About the Fastest Growing Segments of the Youth Market: Hispanic Children and Teens." Paper presented at the Advertising Research Foundation, Children's Research Workshop, New York, 1993.

Wall Street Journal, June 15, 1993.

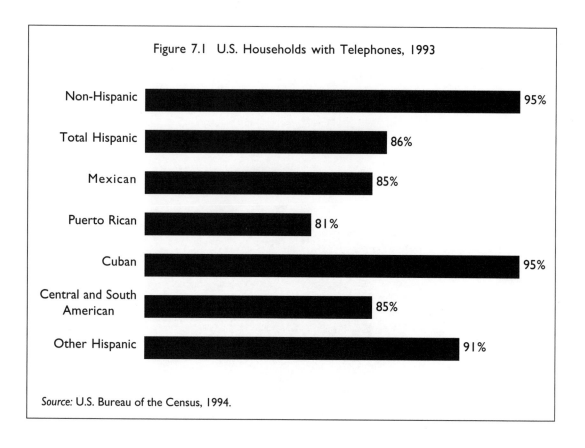

Figure 7.1 U.S. Households with Telephones, 1993

Non-Hispanic	95%
Total Hispanic	86%
Mexican	85%
Puerto Rican	81%
Cuban	95%
Central and South American	85%
Other Hispanic	91%

Source: U.S. Bureau of the Census, 1994.

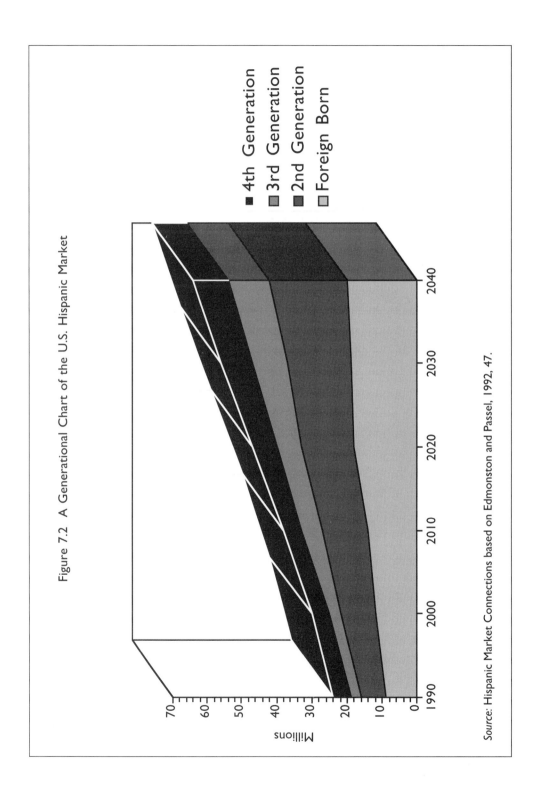

Figure 7.2 A Generational Chart of the U.S. Hispanic Market

4th Generation
3rd Generation
2nd Generation
Foreign Born

Millions

70 60 50 40 30 20 10 0

1990 2000 2010 2020 2030 2040

Source: Hispanic Market Connections based on Edmonston and Passel, 1992, 47.

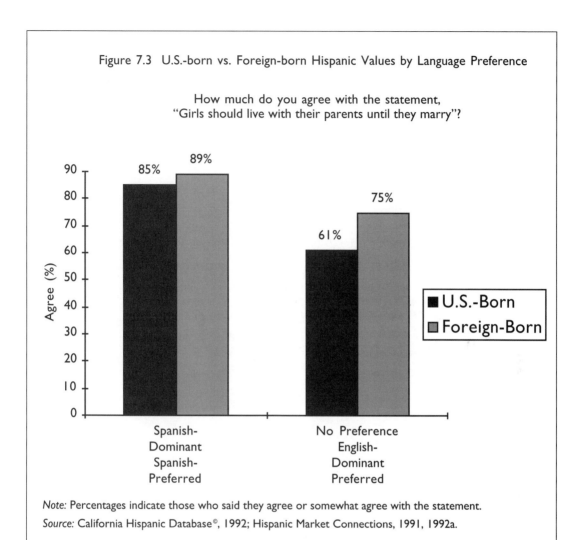

Figure 7.3 U.S.-born vs. Foreign-born Hispanic Values by Language Preference

How much do you agree with the statement,
"Girls should live with their parents until they marry"?

Note: Percentages indicate those who said they agree or somewhat agree with the statement.

Source: California Hispanic Database©, 1992; Hispanic Market Connections, 1991, 1992a.

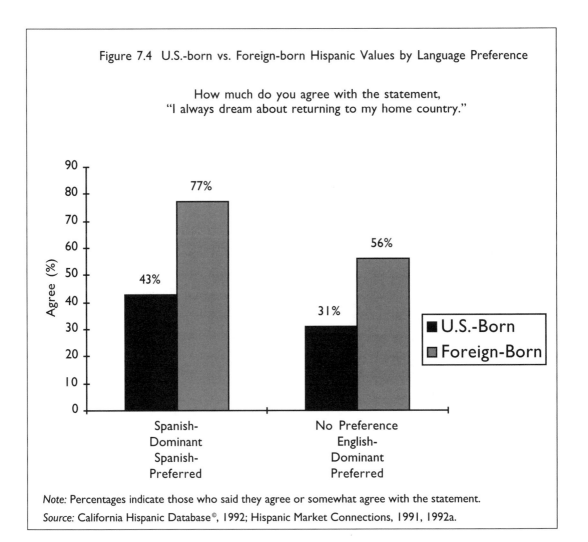

Figure 7.4 U.S.-born vs. Foreign-born Hispanic Values by Language Preference

How much do you agree with the statement,
"I always dream about returning to my home country."

Note: Percentages indicate those who said they agree or somewhat agree with the statement.

Source: California Hispanic Database©, 1992; Hispanic Market Connections, 1991, 1992a.

Figure 7.5 U.S.-born vs. Foreign-born Hispanic Values by Language Preference

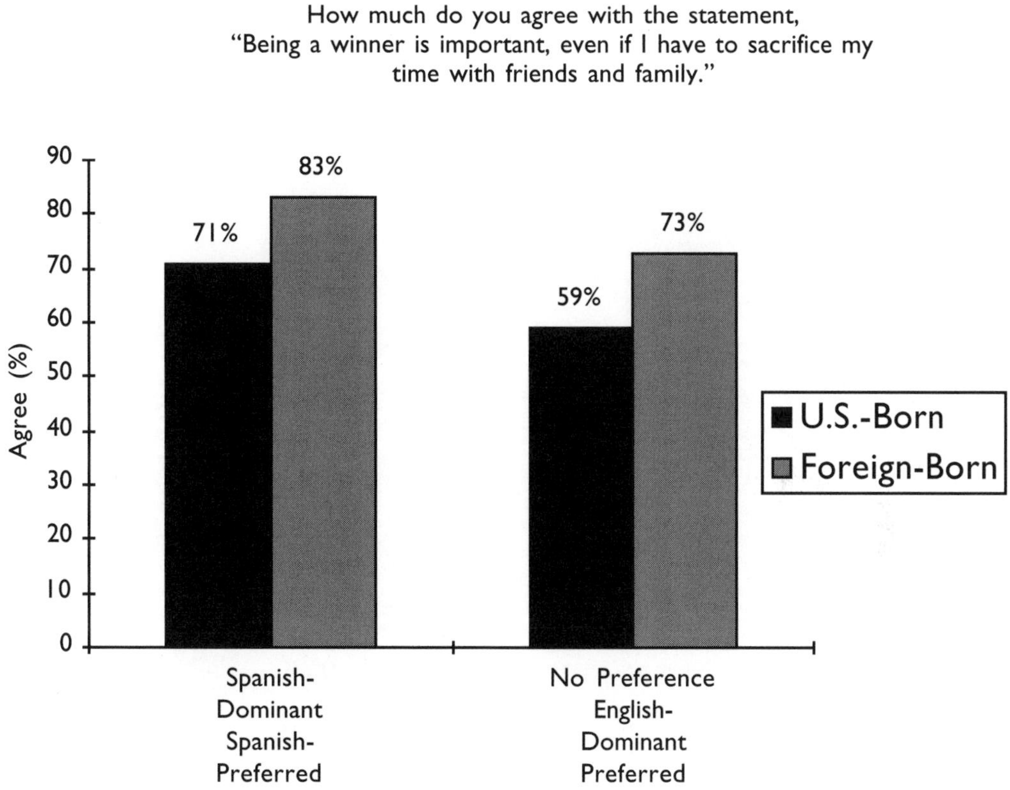

How much do you agree with the statement,
"Being a winner is important, even if I have to sacrifice my
time with friends and family."

Note: Percentages indicate those who said they agree or somewhat agree with the statement.

Source: California Hispanic Database©, 1992; Hispanic Market Connections, 1991, 1992a.

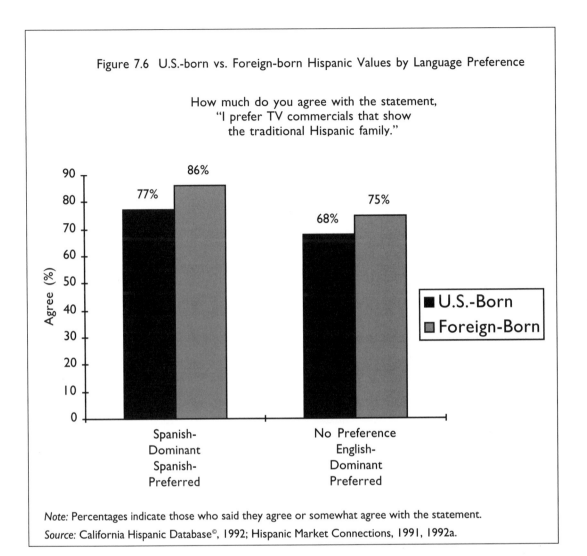

Figure 7.6 U.S.-born vs. Foreign-born Hispanic Values by Language Preference

How much do you agree with the statement,
"I prefer TV commercials that show
the traditional Hispanic family."

Note: Percentages indicate those who said they agree or somewhat agree with the statement.

Source: California Hispanic Database©, 1992; Hispanic Market Connections, 1991, 1992a.

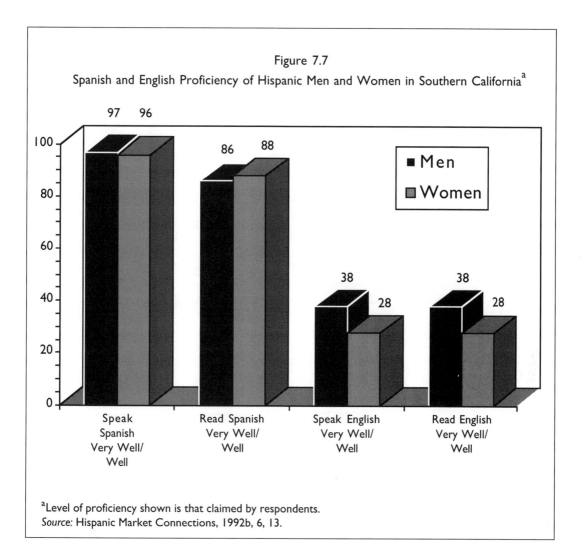

Figure 7.7

Spanish and English Proficiency of Hispanic Men and Women in Southern California[a]

[a]Level of proficiency shown is that claimed by respondents.
Source: Hispanic Market Connections, 1992b, 6, 13.

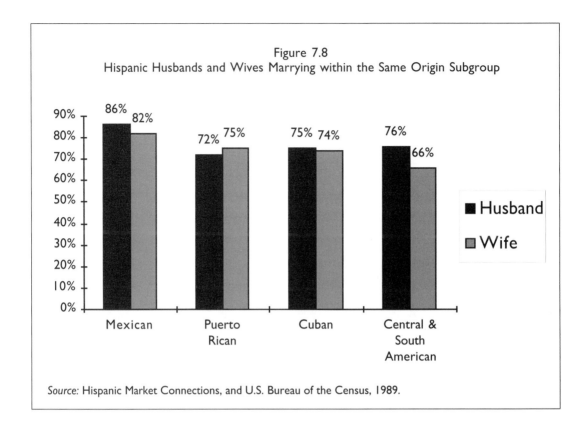

Figure 7.8
Hispanic Husbands and Wives Marrying within the Same Origin Subgroup

Source: Hispanic Market Connections, and U.S. Bureau of the Census, 1989.

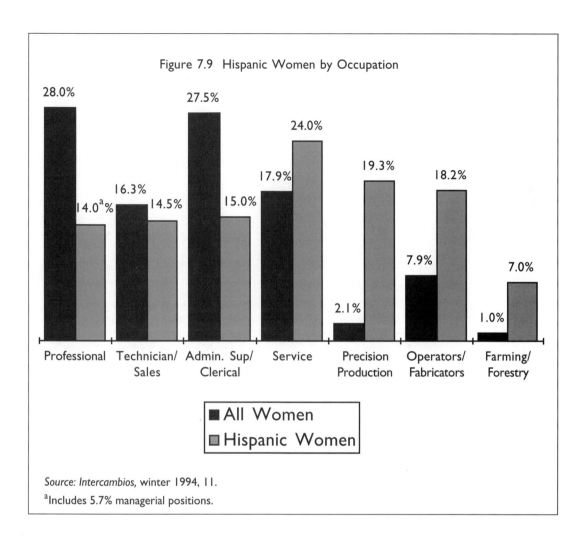

Figure 7.9 Hispanic Women by Occupation

Source: Intercambios, winter 1994, 11.

[a]Includes 5.7% managerial positions.

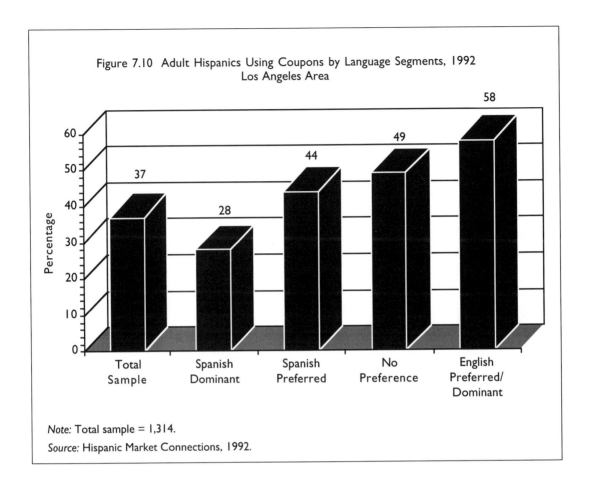

Figure 7.10 Adult Hispanics Using Coupons by Language Segments, 1992
Los Angeles Area

Note: Total sample = 1,314.

Source: Hispanic Market Connections, 1992.

Table 7.1 Consumer Profiles

U.S.-Born Hispanics	Foreign-Born Hispanics "Core Hispanic Consumers"
Tend to be bilingual or English preferred/dominant.	Tend to be Spanish dominant or Spanish preferred.
They may be fully or more acculturated into mainstream culture.	They are less acculturated or nonacculturated into mainstream society.
Familiar with American brands, products, and lifestyles.	Only familiar with American brands and products that were promoted and marketed in their countries of origin but not with those that did not have a presence there.
Have a larger brand set and hence tend to be less brand loyal.	Tend to know a limited number of brands and hence appear as more brand loyal.
Less likely to buy prestige brands.	More likely to buy prestige brands.
English-language media is usually the media of preference.	English-language media is often used to "improve English proficiency," or out of curiosity, not as the core or true source for entertainment or information.
Tend to have a less positive attitude toward advertising.	Tend to have a more positive attitude toward advertising.
Can be reached more effectively via English-language media with Hispanic acculturated, culturally attuned messages and creative strategies.	Can be reached most effectively via Spanish-language media, or serviced better in Spanish utilizing Hispanic culturally attuned messages and strategies.
Spanish-language advertising talks to some of them in terms of ethnic identification, providing emotional and political satisfaction.	For the recent immigrant, Spanish-language advertising is a basic means of learning about new products and how to go about everyday life in their new host country. For long-term bilingual residents, Spanish-language advertising has been shown to be more effective than English-language advertising.

(continued next page)

Table 7.1 Consumer Profiles (*continued*)

U.S.-Born Hispanics	Foreign-Born Hispanics "Core Hispanic Consumers"
Spanish-language media consumption and support often reflects strength of ethnic identification or retroacculturation.	Spanish-language media consumption is the main and many times only source of information, particularly to the shorter-term resident.
Many enjoy receiving bilingual materials. A minority feels uncomfortable and interprets the material as "it is not for me."	Most truly appreciate and prefer being addressed in Spanish and receiving bilingual or Spanish-language materials, coupons, etc. They interpret material as "it is not for me" if it is only in English.
They tend to enjoy traditional American sports—baseball, basketball, football.	They tend to enjoy soccer (Mexicans and South Americans in particular) and baseball (Puerto Ricans, Dominicans, Cubans).
As U.S. citizens, and hence legal residents, they tend to be more aware of and have access to jobs in government institutions. They also tend to use more public services.	Since they are not citizens—and many are slow in obtaining citizenship—they tend not to work in government posts and do not rely on government-sponsored services.
They tend to have, on average, more years of formal schooling and professional degrees. As a consequence, they also tend to have higher household incomes.	They tend, on average, to have fewer years of formal schooling than U.S.-born Hispanics. They tend to have lower household incomes, though this varies drastically depending on personality traits or socioeconomic status upon arrival in the U.S.
Most have a relationship with a financial institution and have several bank accounts, such as checking, savings, and others.	Many don't have checking accounts or credit cards, although this is changing rapidly.
They tend to pay by check and by mail.	Many prefer to pay bills in cash, in person, or by money orders.

(continued next page)

Table 7.1 Consumer Profiles (continued)

U.S.-Born Hispanics	Foreign-Born Hispanics "Core Hispanic Consumers"
They are an integral part of American society. More active in mainstream U.S. society.	They are many times marginal, not active members of mainstream American society.
They are more actively involved in U.S. politics, vote, understand and relate to the national and regional U.S. political and legal scene. In terms of news programs and information, U.S. politics tend to play a more relevant role.	They tend to be distanced from U.S. politics, fewer vote, and many relate in a fragmented form to the U.S. political scene. In terms of news programs and information, U.S. politics tend to play a limited role.
Some groups have an active history of political struggle for recognition of their sociopolitical and economic rights. (This is particularly the case with Mexican Americans and Cuban Americans).	Tend to have no identification with the political struggle of U.S.-born Hispanics, and some openly reject being a part of it. Others identify intellectually and support their cause.
Depending on the generation (second, third, fourth), they tend to have weaker or no emotional ties with their ancestors' country of origin.	Tend to have very strong emotional ties with their countries of origin.
Follow less closely the political and social developments in Latin America and/or their ancestors' country of origin. In terms of news programs and information, Latin American news plays a secondary role.	Tend to follow closely the political and social developments in Latin America, particularly their countries of origin. In terms of news programs and information, country of origin news captures their attention and interest most.
Many feel proud of being "Hispanic" or "Latino," although a few would rather not be identified or singled out as Hispanic or Latino.	Ethnic identification with the country of origin is usually very strong. They may accept the "Hispanic" or "Latino" umbrella term as an American organizing principle to address them.

(continued next page)

Table 7.1 Consumer Profiles (*continued*)

U.S.-Born Hispanics

They maintain different degrees of identifiable Hispanic cultural traits depending on geographic regions and historical backgrounds.

Most like to see Hispanics in higher offices, government, and successful corporate careers. There tends to be a strong brotherhood and support system within the different ethnic subgroups; Mexican-Americans with Mexican-Americans, Cubans with Cubans, but less between Hispanic subgroups.

Foreign-Born Hispanics "Core Hispanic Consumers"

They tend to follow closely the traditional Hispanic cultural values and religious traits.

Most tend to be highly motivated and eager to achieve the "American dream" through hard work and education for their children. The ultimate dream for many is to purchase a home, purchase a new car, support their families, and see their children graduate, at least from high school.

(continued next page)

Table 7.2 Demographic Profile of U.S. Hispanic Women, 1990

- ✧ 11 million total
- ✧ 7,181,000 over age 18
  - ✧ 62% married
  - ✧ 22% single
  - ✧ 7% widowed
  - ✧ 9% divorced

Source: U.S. Bureau of the Census, 1992, 18.

**Table 7.3 Educational Attainment of Hispanic and White Women Age 25 and Older
(In percentages)**

Population Completing	Elementary			High School		College	
	1 to 4 years	5 to 7 years	8 years	1 to 3 years	4 years	1 to 3 years	4 years or more
Hispanic	12.1	14.7	6.5	15.5	30.1	11.7	9.4
White	1.8	3.3	4.5	10.5	41.8	18.8	19.3

Source: U.S. Bureau of the Census, *Statistical Abstract of the United States: 1992,* 1992, 144.

Table 7.4 Projected Number of Households, 1990–2000

	1990	2000	Absolute Change	% Change
Total Households (in thousands)	91,950	103,810	11,860	12.9
White	76,028	79,411	3,383	4.4
Black	10,307	12,441	2,134	20.7
Hispanic	6,365	9,422	3,057	48.0

Source: TGE Demographics, 1993.

Table 7.5 Increase in Hispanic Women Participating in the Work Force, 1980–1990

	1980–1990 (increase)
Hispanic women	54%
Hispanic men	23%
Non-Hispanic women	23%

Source: Hispanic Market Connections; U.S. Bureau of Labor Statistics, 1992, 1.

Table 7.6 Hispanic and General Market Children and Teens

Age	Percent of Total Total U.S. Population	Percent of U.S. Hispanic Population
0–5	8.9	12.7
6–13	11.4	15.0
14–17	5.3	7.0
Total	25.6	34.7

Source: Valdés, 1993.

Table 7.7 Hispanic Youth Growth Trends (in Thousands)

Age	1980	1990	2000	2005
Under 5	1,663	2,388	3,055	3,338
5–9	1,537	2,194	2,945	3,196
10–14	1,475	2,002	2,814	3,147
Subtotal	4,675	6,584	8,817	9,681
15–19	1,606	2,054	2,617	3,058
Total under 20	6,281	8,638	11,434	12,739

Source: Valdés, 1993.

C H A P T E R

8

■ Research

■ Conceptualization, Sampling, and Survey Issues

■ Segmenting the Hispanic Market

■ Door-to-Door *vs.* Telephone Studies

Market Research

The objective of this chapter is not to lecture about marketing research, but to highlight for buyers and users of Hispanic market and consumer data the issues that make research more reliable and culturally attuned.

Whereas previous chapters address key factors relevant to the conceptualization and data analysis processes, in this chapter we focus on those issues specific to conducting research studies with Hispanic consumers, such as developing accurate sampling plans, measuring a consumer market in different stages of acculturation and with different levels of formal education, managing cultural traits that affect the research results, dealing with over-positive or non-critical responses typical of Hispanic consumers, and improving measurement accuracy.

■ Research

Reliable strategic market and consumer data are essential for effective marketing and advertising campaigns. The best marketer or advertiser in the world cannot make up for insufficient or inaccurate marketing data. As the saying goes, "What can hurt you is not only what you don't know, but what you know that ain't so."

If successful marketing is the outcome of reality-based conceptualizations and sound strategies, the same principles apply to reliable, actionable Hispanic market research. The validity and predictability of Hispanic consumer data correlate directly with the quality of the research process in all its stages:

✧   The quality of the *conceptualization process*, that is, the thinking and planning stages, which should incorporate the mind-set of the Hispanic consumer and the differences of the Hispanic marketplace prior to implementation of the research study. The more culturally attuned and informed about the Hispanic market a product manager or research director is, the better the planning and conceptualization stages, and hence the data that are gathered.

✧   The quality of the *research implementation process*, including, for example, the survey questionnaire or the screener instrument for focus groups, the discussion guide, the sample plan, the fielding service, the interviewing technique, and so on.

✧   The quality of the *data analysis process*, that is, the depth of knowledge of Hispanic consumer behavior and the U.S. Hispanic market, along with the standard professional skills needed to conduct marketing research analysis.

✧   The degree of insightfulness into the Hispanic market, which correlates with the quality of the *data extrapolation process*, that is the ability to make sound and actionable recommendations and to bring to the final analysis all the pieces that will have an impact on the successful implementation of the research recommendations.

DEFINING THE RESEARCH UNIVERSE

Over the past decade more than six different indicators have been used to define who is Hispanic in order to draw the research samples, or the people selected to participate in a study. These indicators range from Spanish surname and paternal ancestry to legal status, area of residence, and self-identification. The variety of indicators not only illustrates how disagreements about the nature of Hispanic ethnicity emerge but also explains to some extent the many inconsistencies that are pervasive in the present market data about the Hispanic consumer market in the U.S. today. Given that the definition of "Hispanic" tends to vary with the purpose and type of study in question, it is possible that no consensus can ever be reached. For example, following the growing recognition that "soft" or qualitative aspects of a consumer group's behavior and mind-set (for example, culture and ethnicity in the case of Hispanics) are central to understanding, measuring, and successfully communicating with consumers, anthropologists have concluded that a reliable definition of "Hispanic" in the United States should go beyond the standard demographic variables such as Spanish ancestry, country of origin, or surname. The identification factors should also include behavioral and psychological indicators, such as strength of ethnic identification, that is, how strongly or closely a Hispanic consumer feels or identifies with his or her Hispanic roots. The stronger the ethnic identification, the stronger an individual's Hispanic cultural values.

Defining who is "Hispanic" for marketing purposes is not just an exercise designed to generate a label devoid of actionable meaning. On the contrary, broadening the parameters of ethnic identification can provide richer and more insightful marketing directions. It requires the marketer to ask, How does *ethnicity* impact the marketing and advertising strategy? What specific barriers or benefits may degree of acculturation, ethnic identification, and demographics add? For example, does it may make a difference to the research whether the Hispanic target consumer is U.S. born or foreign-born? Spanish-only or bilingual? Legal or undocumented? A registered voter or not? The latter may be very relevant for federal, state, or local government offices or for some financial services and products that require that customers have legal status and permanent residence in the United States. But for the vast majority of marketers and advertisers, the definition of who is Hispanic varies according to who is included in the market universe specific to their product or service. What counts is which Hispanic consumers can be reached and marketed to. And hence, media usage and language preference become relevant questions:

Can the Hispanic consumer be reached effectively and through which media channels? In other words, the issue of who to include in the Hispanic market universe should be all those consumers that identify themselves as Hispanic, as the U.S. Census Bureau defines it in its question, "Do you consider yourself of Hispanic, Latin or Spanish origin?" In addition, communications and acculturation indicators should be considered. The issues of language and media preferences (English or Spanish) and acculturation ("Anglo" or "Hispanic" value orientation) always shed light on the Hispanic marketing strategy and should carry as much weight in a marketing research study. In sum, who is "Hispanic" for marketing research purposes should go beyond self-identification and incorporate empirical behavioral sociopsychographic variables. Both objective and subjective questions should be asked, for example, language use items (for both English and Spanish), country of origin and number of years of residence in the United States, and media preferences (both English and Spanish), among others. Not only does one need to know whether a consumer is "Hispanic," but more important, how strong the consumer's ethnic identification is and how this should affect the marketing and advertising strategies. As the second, third, and fourth generations of Hispanics acculturate, the strength of ethnic identification shifts. Hispanic marketing research should be able to uncover and track how the cultural shifts affect the marketing strategy and provide new direction (see Chapter 7, page 316).

MANAGING AND AVOIDING RESEARCH ABUSES
A major problem facing Hispanic market and consumer researchers is that to do it right, that is, "by the book," is expensive. Hence, to be competitive and appealing to clients, some researchers reduce costs by cutting corners, usually in crucial yet not explicit areas.

For example, in the case of quantitative studies, little or no control is exercised in the sample plan development process. The data collection process is often unsupervised. Many studies are fielded without instructing survey fielding facilities exactly where and how many interviews should be completed in each zip code or census tract. Little if any control is exerted over the actual execution of a sample plan; hence, interviewers and fielding vendors are free to compromise research integrity. In addition, few—very few — Fortune 500 companies or other buyers of Hispanic research are willing to invest research dollars in good quality control, including the task of meeting with the actual field interviewers or sending a supervisor or trainer to meet with local interviewers in the different markets. The result is interviewers who do not speak Spanish or do not speak it fluently enough to write questions or probe are conducting interviews "in Spanish." Poorly translated questionnaires, impossible to follow, are being sent to the field.

These problems can be avoided through hands-on control of the sample plan development, fielding, coding, validating and editing processes, which can help ensure reliability and quality control in Hispanic marketing research. Although this will mean investing additional dollars, it will pay for itself in reliable data. Buyers should always request from research vendors — regardless of how slick the sales package is — a sample plan in advance, for telephone as well as for door-to-door research projects. Vendors should be asked to explain how the plan was developed (sources, software, weighting, rationale, etc.) and be required to submit proof of quality control measures, including compliance with the sample plan, and the questionnaires. In addition, research buyers might want to conduct a random sample editing of the questionnaires in-house.

Even when editing is conducted properly, however, interviewer cheating may go undetected. For example, interviewing friends or relatives, not collecting the demographic data at the proper predetermined location, or completing the questionnaire at the interviewer's leisure can all render studies invalid. The best deterrent to such abuse is for the research firm to send out a person not only to train and brief interviewers about the study and the questionnaire, but also to detail in advance the quality control procedures. Even then, clients should request demonstration of compliance with the sample plans as well as questionnaire editing and validating proofs. These steps will dramatically reduce abuse and poor field work and will also tremendously increase the quality of the data that are gathered.

If cheating and poor sampling go undetected, how valid is the result of the research? Is it worth saving a few thousand dollars in up-front costs only to lose a small fortune in misdirected marketing efforts because of invalid data? Unfortunately, owing to lack of competition in the field interviewing area, very few businesses offer bilingual interviewers in the different Hispanic markets. Very few good options are available. Therefore, clients need to take control. They must become educated about potential abuses, and they should get involved, shop around, and talk with experienced Hispanic market researchers.

In qualitative research studies similar quality controls are recommended. It should go without question that a field facility that advertises "Hispanic research recruiting" services should have a Spanish-speaking recruiter conducting or intercepting the calls to select focus group participants.

Research buyers should not accept "professional" focus group participants, that is, Hispanic consumers who are not selected randomly, who make a living as focus group participants. In addition, unless the topic of research calls for inclusion of unemployed study participants, it should be specified that group participants be members of an "employed household," that is, a household where at least one adult member is employed full-time or part-time. It is easy to go to unemployment offices and recruit everybody for the groups—at $30 to $40 per person (the current average participant incentive for group participation), it is extremely easy to do this kind of recruiting, yet absolutely against professional marketing research practice. In border area studies, research clients should make it understood that group participants cannot be "imported from Mexico" for the study. Group participants should have resided in the United States for at least a year in order to have some familiarity with U.S. advertisements, consumer goods, and stores, unless otherwise required for the purpose of the study.

With the boom in the Hispanic market, many companies have jumped on the bandwagon to offer Hispanic marketing research services. For many of these companies, hiring "people who speak Spanish" is the only needed investment to bring in the business. Unfortunately, awareness of the cultural complexities and the needed professional expertise we have discussed are absent in many cases. Just because a person "speaks Spanish," whether the person is Hispanic or not, does not mean he or she is a professional researcher. Again, clients are in the driver's seat. By learning about the professional qualifications and expertise of the research team, and about every party involved in a research study, research buyers can find reliable, ethical researchers with whom they can develop long-term relationships. Resource directories are also available from professional Hispanic business organizations. For example, *Hispanic Business* magazine and the SRDS *Hispanic Media and Market Source* are two sources that publish such directories annually.

■ Conceptualization, Sampling, and Survey Issues

Addressing specific issues and questions regarding conceptualization, sampling, and field surveys will help ensure culturally attuned Hispanic research projects and hence facilitate quality control functions and data reliability.

As discussed in detail in chapter 7, the conceptualization process (see page 316) is of paramount importance. The conceptual framework must be thoroughly developed before deciding on strategy or implementing any phase of the research study.

After the conceptualization stage, determining the study's universe, the population that should be included in the sample should follow easily (e.g.: High acculturation and/or low acculturation consumers, or Spanish-only, foreign born consumers, etc.). The following are some of the types of studies and populations frequently targeted in Hispanic market research.

If the advertising or marketing strategy is to target "Hispanic consumers who are best reached via Spanish-language media," the Hispanic consumer segments selected should be those that are more exposed to Spanish-language media than to English-language media, for example, Spanish-dominant and Spanish-preferred consumers. To make sure that those are the Hispanics

SPANISH-ONLY STUDY

being studied, it is essential that all the interactions with the study participants be conducted in Spanish, ideally by Hispanic interviewers, with screener questionnaires and survey instruments developed and tested with these consumers in mind. Since Spanish-dominant/preferred Hispanics tend to reside in inner city barrios, Hispanic neighborhoods can be targeted by zip code. But the sampling plan should include a large number and wide dispersion of zip codes, so that all types of Spanish-dominant/preferred consumers are surveyed. Unfortunately, it is not uncommon to discover that some research vendors, in order to be more competitive, conduct all study interviews in only a few zip codes, usually only those with the highest Hispanic population, thus under-representing the Spanish-dominant/preferred market and generating faulty data for their clients. This common problem can be easily avoided with a sample plan, as discussed on page 380.

BILINGUAL STUDY

If on the other hand, the research goals are to measure and project "the Hispanic market" to develop long-term strategic plans, or to track over time how acculturation is affecting a brand or product category in the Hispanic market, one should include Hispanics in all stages of acculturation. Therefore, the study universe should include Hispanics from all language segment groups from Spanish-dominant to English-dominant.

All research instruments and sample plans, as well as the fielding procedures, must be tested and conducted in both English and Spanish. For quantitative studies, the sample size should be large enough to include enough Hispanics in the smaller language segment groups, such as true bilinguals and English preferred/ dominant persons. In addition, the sample plan must include zip codes with lower incidence of Hispanic population, since more acculturated Hispanics tend to reside in suburbs as well as in inner-city areas.

SPANISH-LANGUAGE TESTING

If the goal is to target a broad spectrum of Hispanics from all ethnic backgrounds (Mexicans, Salvadorans, Puerto Ricans, Cubans, Dominicans) or a specific group only, Spanish-language testing with consumers from each of these groups must be conducted. Even though the Spanish that is spoken throughout Latin America and Spain is similar, there are occasionally different words or discrepancies between the colloquial Spanish of these countries, thus there is room for miscommunicating the intended question or probe. This may sound more complicated than it actually is. A professional Hispanic research vendor usually has on staff (or knows) Hispanics from various Latin American countries and a check on research instruments is done routinely.

If marketing and advertising strategy calls for targeting upscale Hispanics, the sample population should be skewed toward more bilingual Hispanics, including some Spanish-preferreds, true bilinguals, English-preferred/dominant Hispanics. Survey instruments or focus groups should be executed in both English and Spanish as well. Since upscale Hispanics are also found across language segments, quantitative studies for upscale Hispanics should include income-based geographical segmentation to ensure proper representation. Census-based segmentation computer software can easily generate income-based stratified or weighted Hispanic sample plans, selecting only those zip codes or census tracts where upscale Hispanics reside. (See "Hispanic Affluence," page 117, in Chapter 3.)

RESEARCHING "UPSCALES"

Upscale Hispanics may be approached by phone or by mail. The limitations or barriers to their participation will tend to be similar to those encountered when researching more upscale general market consumers, which is to say there will be much lower research participation. Response rates depend to a large extent on the cultural attunement and emotional tone of the survey questionnaire. This is where qualitative testing of mail pieces with target consumers comes into play: It is worth every penny.

The foreign-born Hispanic market segment tends to prefer Spanish as the language of choice, whereas U.S.-born Hispanics tend to prefer English or bilingual interviews, depending on the number of years of residence in the United States and age at the time of immigration. In terms of sampling strategy, foreign-born Hispanics are scattered in all areas where Hispanics reside. Hence, the sample plan must consider a wide dispersion of zip codes, particularly if upscale, foreign-born Hispanics should be targeted. For industries such as telecommunications, travel, and financial services this is particularly relevant.

STUDYING THE FOREIGN-BORN

As to research methods, foreign-born Hispanics' response rate to mailed questionnaires is very low and the answers are often incomplete. The response tends to be skewed toward the bilin-gual, more educated consumer. Response to telephone studies also tends to be skewed to particular population segments (see "Telephone vs. Door-to-Door," beginning on page 392). In other words, the most *representative* method to approach the foreign born Hispanics is the door-to-door study method.

The decision whether to use the telephone or door-to-door method again depends on the category being studied and the pur-pose of the research undertaken. For example, a soft drink study may be conducted by telephone without sacrificing projectability; on the other hand, a restaurant patronage study, financial ser-vices study, health insurance study, or utilities study may exclude base or potential market if conducted only by phone.

DEVELOPING A SAMPLE PLAN

Sample plans are a key component of Hispanic market research studies, but are regularly overlooked under the assumption that the same sampling rules developed and tested for the general market will apply. Unfortunately this is not the case.

Because the Hispanic population is not distributed evenly through-out the United States, by region, by county, or by city, and because where Hispanics live does make a big difference in sociodemo-graphic, language, and economic terms, the sample plan must be carefully drawn to include all the areas or zip codes where Hispan-ics reside. This is especially true if the research results are intended to study and measure the Hispanic consumer in an entire region or city and not only Hispanics living in a few blocks within a high-density Hispanic population area. Unfortunately, the latter is often the case, and the research data gathered are not representative of the Hispanic population in the area or city desired.

To manage the complexities of high-versus-low Hispanic popula-tion density mix and the uneven population distribution, a sample plan should be weighted for these two factors. Computers and census data are very handy here. Any geodemographic software can help generate the sample plan desired, for both telephone surveys and door-to-door surveys.

Table 8.1 is an example of a sample plan stratified or weighted by density of Hispanics per zip-code. This computer model was developed to draw sample plans based specifically on the Hispanic population in the area and their density—that is how many Hispanics reside in a particular zip code or census tract. This determines what percentage of the zip code area is composed of Hispanics, from 1 percent to 100 percent. The computer model is also designed to balance the sample's dispersion, that is, how many interviews are to be conducted in each zip code for census tract or cluster.

The sample plan generated mirrors the existing population in the area of study. The more Hispanics in a particular zip code, the more interviews to be conducted in that area, and vice versa. If desired, the model can limit the "population penetration density," in other words accept all those zip codes with at least 20 percent population penetration. This means that all Hispanics that reside in zip codes that are less than 20 percent Hispanic are automatically excluded from the study. Again, the judgment call here will depend on what product or service is being studied and how expensive it would be to include those low-incidence Hispanic zip codes. Dual interviewing modes, that is, a combination of telephone and door-to-door, can help solve this problem. Those zip codes with lower incidence can be studied by phone, if the research methodology in place can ensure the integrity of the sample plan.

Sample plans can be designed to measure a particular segment of the Hispanic population, say, Hispanics who reside in a three-mile radius of a clinic or restaurant. Or the sample plan may call to select more Hispanics with a particular characteristic, say Mexicans only. In this case, only zip codes in the three-mile radius or where Mexicans reside are selected to run the computer program which will then generate a balanced, well dispersed, and representative Hispanic population sample within the defined area. These samples can be quite complex. Optimal allocation using stratified random samples require careful statistical handing (Fuller, 1993; Waksberg, 1978).

In sum, the sample plan should determine how many zip codes or census tracts are to be included, how many interviews will be conducted in each zip code or census tract, and what the Hispanic population penetration cut-off point is, among other factors. It must be decided whether to include *all* zip codes or census tracts where Hispanics reside or, for example, only those with at least 10 or 20 percent Hispanic population penetration. The sample plan should be drawn at the onset of a tracking study, and the same one should be used for subsequent waves of tracking.

In the case of door-to-door studies, the population penetration cut-off point is usually determined by cost factors. The cost per interview (CPI) to conduct studies in areas with very low Hispanic population density is prohibitive. In the case of telephone interviews, low population incidence affects the morale of the interviewers and field quality can become a serious problem. On the positive side, though, the cost of dialing a number is much lower than that of walking several blocks before identifying a Hispanic household. To maintain the integrity of the sample plan, phone calls should be placed in all the telephone prefixes of the zip codes or census tracts indicated.

With computer-aided telephone interviewing (CATI), it is quite simple to track how many interviews have been conducted in a particular zip code, and in this way comply with the quotas per zip code set in the sample plan. The details of compliance should be discussed and requested at the time of the research bidding process. This allows the research bidders to be more explicit as to the actual work to be undertaken in the field.

Research buyers should request from their research vendors a detailed sample plan *at the time of the research bidding process,* because the actual cost of the study directly correlates with how many interviews will be conducted in different zip codes and how far apart they are in the case of door-to-door studies.

SURVEY TECHNIQUES
Adapting Research Practices to the Hispanic Market

Interviewing Hispanic consumers, be it by phone or door to door, requires special skills and communication techniques. Protocol, the unspoken social forms in which we interact with one another, such as the way we greet others, must be taken into consideration because it differs from that of the general market (for example, in the meaning of silences, voice inflections, or regional slang). In general, Hispanics are inquisitive and talkative, so the interviewing process will take more time. Protocol needs to be respected in order to build rapport and familiarity with the respondent. In addition, there are distinct sales and communication styles that distinguish Hispanics and general market consumers. What may be considered direct, straightforward speaking in the general market may be considered too aggressive and possibly offensive by Hispanic consumers. Hence, the preface of a question may need to be longer and more friendly.

To compensate for the often over-positive responses of many Hispanics, evaluative research should be based on a set of questions rather than an isolated item. For example, when evaluating copy strategy or concepts in focus groups, two or more creative concepts or ideas should be discussed, first individually and then in comparison with each other. This will force participants to verbalize their pros and cons, including those negative aspects, beyond the typical response, *"está bien"* ("I like it"). For example, ask specific questions such as, Which of these two creative concepts *better* communicates the message? And why? Comparisons can open a window into the less-liked aspect of a campaign, which participants may feel uncomfortable voicing in focus groups.

Also, in addressing sensitive issues, a direct, open approach is *not recommended*. Projective research techniques should be used initially until participants feel comfortable and at ease with the discussion topic and talk about themselves spontaneously. For example, during a research study conducted by Hispanic Market Connections (HMC) dealing with AIDS and AIDS prevention, it was necessary to ascertain whether Hispanic males would inform a sex partner that they were HIV positive. To broach the topic yet not talk directly about it, HMC developed a series of vignettes telling the story of several people with AIDS and their dilemma: Should they tell their partner (spouse, girlfriend, boyfriend) that they are HIV positive? At that point, the vignette, which was audiotaped by the moderator, was stopped, and group participants were asked what the men should do. This technique proved highly effective in eliciting discussion and honest responses. HMC learned in the process, for example, that most participants in particular socioeconomic groups would not tell their sexual partner if they were HIV positive, and some would also not use a protective condom because it would "give them away." Their responses confirmed that they felt safe and comfortable enough to talk honestly about their feelings (Forrest, et al., 1993).

As the foregoing example illustrates, Hispanic consumer research often requires a tangential approach to obtain the desired information. A professional and knowledgeable marketing research company that concentrates exclusively on the Hispanic consumer market will naturally devise better research tools and methodologies than those for whom Hispanics are a side interest. Even the simplest research task is affected by the cultural elements that make Hispanic consumers a unique group.

MEASURING ACCULTURATION

Acculturation may be viewed as inversely proportional to ethnic identification. The stronger the Hispanic ethnic identification, the lower the degree of acculturation, and vice-versa. Scientifically or accurately measuring acculturation or strength of ethnic identification is a major task not normally permitted by most Hispanic marketing budgets. Yet an approximation is strongly recommended. An alternative method of measuring acculturation is based on language usage. Language-based questions combined with media usage preferences (Spanish and/or English) and descriptive demographic items (for example, country of birth, number of years of residence in the United States, income) provide a low-cost, efficient tool to group Hispanic consumers and thus manage acculturation. (Use of a language-based segmentation to measure acculturation is discussed in detail beginning on page 230 in Chapter 5.) Research scholars in a variety of fields have developed acculturation scales for their specific needs. Because of the academic nature of much of the work, however, their conceptualizations and questionnaires tend to exclude key issues concerning marketing and advertising, such as language and media usage, and the issue of verbal versus written language usage and proficiency (Table 8.2). The Marin and Marin scale, developed to be applied in the health-care field, is a very useful tool once the media usage questions have been added and included in the final computations. See Table 8.3 for a sample of media questions.

Acculturation measurement scales for advertising and marketing purposes should include questions that address these issues:

❧ *Language proficiency, usage, and comfort*, in both English and Spanish. These questions should separately probe verbal and written communication skills in both languages. This will allow the researcher to group people into distinct segments, such as Spanish-dominant or bilingual. (See "Segmenting the Hispanic Market," page 386.)

❧ *Media preference (Spanish or English)*, probing separately radio, television, and print. More acculturated Hispanics generally consume considerably more English-language radio but considerably less Spanish-language TV than non-acculturated Hispanics. Advertisers targeting acculturated Hispanics would thus do better to consider an English-radio campaign.

❧ *Value-based questions*, budget permitting. (For example, "Girls should live with their parents until they marry.") A multivariate analysis based on such value-based questions will provide a definite picture of the mind-set of each acculturating segment. Each segment will tell the story of a particular group of Hispanic consumers. For example, those whose values are more "traditional" or more "modern." Advertisers can then use this information to create and implement highly targeted campaigns.

As with the general market, the appropriate research methodology to measure Hispanic consumer behavior depends on the research objectives, the research budget, and the types of decisions to be made from analysis of the data.

SELECTING THE RESEARCH METHODOLOGY

However, because of inherent cultural differences between the Hispanic and the general population, researchers should not apply general market research methods directly to the Hispanic market. The research process and methods should first go through a "cultural adaptation and sensitization" process to allow these tools to better measure and grasp the specific reality of this population—in all facets of the research process, from study design, sampling methodology, and survey questionnaire design to scales, probing techniques, survey language, and interviewing method.

The conceptualization process (page 316) must be reality based and culturally attuned before hypotheses can be drawn. That is, consumer input and Hispanic market data should be sought and be the base to delineate hypothesis. The questions to ask will vary drastically in some cases from those one would ask in a typical mainstream marketing study. For example, while reviewing the response data from a pre-test study for a large AIDS prevention study in California, researchers discovered that a small segment of the adult Hispanic male population pre-tested did not know what a condom was, and therefore all the questions related to condom use were completely off-track. The hypothesis based on the assumption that "all Hispanic males in California know what a condom is" had to be rethought.

Therefore, preliminary exploratory qualitative research and thorough pre-testing of complex questionnaires is strongly recommended. It is extremely important to know and understand the Hispanic consumer in the context of the product or service. Only after getting a handle on what issues are to be studied—based on target consumer input—can researchers be sure which Hispanic consumer segment is the most appropriate target and which is the most appropriate interviewing methodology. The choice will usually be between in-person exchanges or telephone interviews. Use of mail surveys is rarely recommended with the Hispanic market given its sociodemographic parameters (lower levels of formal schooling among foreign-born Hispanics, lower levels of familiarity with brands, and so on).

■ Segmenting the Hispanic Market

Throughout this book the need to segment the Hispanic market based along different parameters has been stressed. Segmentation may be based on such elements as language capability as a proxy for acculturation, country of birth, U.S.-born versus foreign-born, psychograhics, values, or ethnic identification. This section will provide a brief introduction to the concept of segmentation and some useful guidelines. For further information on advanced segmentation methods, the reader should refer to specialized literature such as *Introduction of Factor Analysis* by J. O. Kim and C. W. Mueller (1978) and *Multivariate Analysis: Methods and Applications* by W. R. Dillon and M. Goldstein (1984).

Generally, three key reasons move marketers and advertisers to develop market segmentation, that is, to divide the market or their consumer base into different groups or types of consumers. These reasons apply to the U.S. Hispanic market as well:

WHY USE A MARKET SEGMENTATION?

✧ To manage growth and diversity in the marketplace

✧ To gain an edge over the competition

✧ To better serve and respond to specific customer needs

Growing at roughly five times the rate of the total population, the Hispanic market is heterogeneous, with some consumers having arrived just yesterday and others having resided in the United States for several generations. Not only is their culture different from mainstream culture, but there is growing diversity and variation among Hispanics. In other words, the same message would not reach or "speak to" every Hispanic. Hence, marketers and advertisers need to uncover the differences within the Hispanic marketplace (e.g.: degree of acculturation, language usage, psychographics), and then identify their specific target audience within the Hispanic market and fine-tune marketing strategies and media messages to reach the different consumer segments.

Managing Growth and Diversity

Hand-in-hand with growth and business opportunity comes the competition for the Hispanic market. The Hispanic market is becoming increasingly competitive, with new players entering the marketplace every week. The implementation of NAFTA will add to the clutter. In this atmosphere, marketers and advertisers that want to retain or increase market share will not only need better, more reliable demographic and behavioral data, but also more sophisticated marketing tools. Segmenting the market, tracking the behavior of the segments, and developing specific messages to

Beating the Competition

reach those segments that present the greatest business opportunity will provide the marketer with a competitive advantage, capturing a larger share of *that* key market segment.

Responding to Customer and Community Needs

An increasing number of corporations are recognizing their need to commit to the Hispanic market, not only to develop products and services that better meet Hispanic consumers' specific needs but also to help improve their overall quality of life. By communicating better with Hispanics, interacting with their leaders, and supporting their educational programs, these corporations will in return benefit from a better long-term strategy and the consequent growth in sales and loyalty. By creating goodwill these corporations make in-roads in the Hispanic market. A segmentation will open the doors of understanding that will aid a corporation in deciding where to dedicate their communication efforts, public relations dollars, and community activities.

WHAT IS MARKET SEGMENTATION?

A wide array of statistical methods are used to segment consumer markets. They range from simple "crosstabs" to highly complex statistical multivariate analysis. "Crosstabs" help in a straightforward way to look at customers in different lights. For example, a Hispanic marketer can group consumers by how often they speak Spanish, how much Spanish-language TV they view, or how much of a particular product they consume.

Crosstabs can reveal, for example, which segment consumes more of a product or which media are preferred by heavy users of the product, thus giving direction to marketing efforts. Tables 8.4a, b, and c are examples of crosstab tables for southern California. Twenty-two points in the header (or banner) are crosstabbed with the question "Do people in this house speak Spanish?"

Researchers can easily identify how different or similar the responses of specific groups are with regard to how much Spanish is spoken in those particular households. The letters in each column heading, B, D, E, etc., help run statistics between the different data columns to see if there are "real differences" (or statistically significant differences) between the columns.

If differences between the columns are large enough, a small letter appears next to the percentage. These letters then indicate that the groups or columns are indeed different, that the differences observed are not due to chance or statistical error, but to other true factors. For example, go to Table 8.4a, look at the "All of the time" line and run your finger across that line. You will find that the "Mexico" header/banner point intersection with "All of the time" reads 1082, 73.8%B. This means that of all Mexicans interviewed in this study 73.8 percent speak Spanish "All of the time" and that there is a statistically significant difference with people in column B, "U.S.," where only 91 people, or 28.8 percent speak Spanish "All of the time." Table 8.4a would allow you to uncover differences and group your market based on country of origin, Central versus South Americans, number of years resided in the U.S., income, and education. Tables 8.4b and 8.4c look at the study participants from other angles. As a researcher and analyst, your criteria and marketing insight will help determine which tables and information are indeed the relevant ones for your study.

Although crosstabs are simple ways to "group" customers, they are not "true market segmentations," nor the kind of segmentation that helps marketers and advertisers understand the mindset of the different groups of Hispanic consumers or why they behave in particular ways. A true "Hispanic" segmentation is based on more than simple demographics, media, or language usage. It is based on sociocultural, psychographic, and value-oriented information. These "qualitative" factors show how the different consumer segments think and they explain why the consumers behave one way or another. Such nondemographic variables help explain, for example, why some unacculturated Hispanics tend to purchase "traditional type" shoes or clothes rather than the latest trendy designs, or why some acculturated, wealthy Hispanics would decide to spend their time helping the Hispanic community and others would not.

Value-based Hispanic consumer segmentations go several steps beyond the simple crosstabs. They require utilizing advanced statistical methods to uncover segments and also demand in-depth cultural insight and understanding of the consumer. These

advanced market segmentations require both financial commitment and management support to transform the findings into
actionable strategies for the Hispanic marketplace. The following
section describes one such segmentation, Hispanic LIVES©.

Hispanic LIVES©   Hispanic LIVES© (Lifestyles, Interest, Values, Expectations,
and Symbols) is a joint venture between Hispanic Market Connections and American LIVES©. This package is usually applied
on industry-specific bases, such as travel, financial services,
telecommunications, clothing, selected food products, and automobiles.

The following case study illustrates an application of the Hispanic LIVES© segmentation package. The client was a philan-
thropic organization needing specific directions to penetrate the
Hispanic market. The objectives of this case were as follows:

✧ To segment Hispanic donors into types based on the Hispanic LIVES© program

✧ To identify barriers to charitable giving, as well as the
consumer segments with greater giving potential

✧ To provide direction to reach the different donor types

Developing the LIVES© segmentation involved three steps:

1. A set of 40 LIVES© questions were specifically developed
   by a multidisciplinary team to measure values, attitudes,
   and giving-related behavior of Hispanics.

2. From the responses to these and other questions (such as
   demographics), nine LIVES© "dimensions" were created
   by use of multivariate analysis and other market segmentation techniques.

3. From the dimensions developed in step 2, the Hispanic
   "giver types" were generated, again by use of multivariate
   analysis.

Five distinct groups or donor types were identified:

1. Winners

2. Givers

3. Abstract-givers

4. Traditional-young

5. Traditional-old

Each "type" of donor and the percentage of the market they represented were described in actionable, concrete terms. For example, this is a summary of the "winner" type profile:

Winner-Type Donors Profile

  ✦ Are the most acculturated of all five types of donors

  ✦ Tend to be egocentric and tribal

  ✦ Are high in socioeconomic status

  ✦ Tend to be bilingual

  ✦ Watch less Spanish-language TV than the other segments

  ✦ Tend to be men

  ✦ Are well off financially

In regard to their giving behavior the following characteristics were found to apply to those matching the "winner" profile:

  ✦ Not as empathetic as other donor groups

  ✦ Not religious

  ✦ Idealistic

  ✦ Concerned with self and family

  ✦ Not prevented from giving by financial or other constraints

The communications approach appropriate to communicate effectively to the "winner" type was identified as follows:

  ✦ Rational "success language"

✧ Tribal language

✧ Suggestion of "modern" payment methods, to facilitate the giving process

Once the segmentation was completed, two clear communication strategies were developed based on the LIVES© segmentation and presented to the client. One was geared to attract those Hispanic consumers who were already giving to charitable organizations, and the other was designed to motivate those who had the means to give but were not presently giving as much.

What Type of Market Segmentation is Appropriate? Not every product or service lends itself to value-based or psychographic segmentation. Some instead may benefit more from other types of customer groupings, such as geographical segmentation (for direct-mail targeting) or simple language-based segmentations. Because some products and services do not reflect the values of those who use or consume them, they are not good candidates for psychographic or value-based segmentation studies. For example, the purchase of tomato sauce or canned chili beans as they are marketed today would probably not be affected by one's self-image. But the purchase of other, more personal products and services are often very much affected by self-image. The most dramatic example of this is the purchase of a car. Other products or services highly value sensitive are homes, insurance, clothes, shoes, beers, ethnic foods, hospitals, and banks.

■ Door-to-Door *vs.* Telephone Studies

Telephone interviewing is often the method of choice in Hispanic survey research, owing largely to lower costs and improved sampling techniques such as stratified random digit dialing and higher quality name lists. Moreover, some studies show few differences between this mode of research and door-to-door interviewing. There are concerns, however, that telephone interviewing may carry substantial nonresponse bias when surveying particular population subgroups, such as minorities and low-income households.

It is obvious that many advantages presented by telephone interviewing in the general market do not apply to particular subgroups of the U.S. population. A study by Thornberry and
Thornberry (1988) found that 22 percent of Hispanic households
did not have a phone; the rate varied considerably between ethnic
subgroups. Even though telephone penetration rates have
improved, this is still an issue among Hispanics. Other high non-
telephone rates were reported for unemployed respondents (16
percent), heads of households that have low formal education
levels (18 percent), and low-income households (13 percent and
higher for under $10,000 per year). Households without phones
have different socioeconomic characteristics from those with telephones, but since as a whole telephone penetration rates are high,
it is usually assumed that a Hispanic telephone sample would not
necessarily be unrepresentative of Hispanic households overall,
depending on the product or service being studied.

In reality these issues pose a question about the validity of surveys of the Hispanic market that rely exclusively on telephone
interviews. The most damaging flaw is the high rate of households without telephones among certain Hispanic groups, which
results in only partial coverage of the whole Hispanic market.
Known as "nonresponse," this is a problem to the extent that non-
respondents might have responded differently from those who
did participate in a study. Statistics based on this data alone will
give biased estimates of the full population parameters (Groves
and Lyberg, 1988).

Using door-to-door interviews corrects some of these pitfalls, but
a growing trend is to conduct studies using dual interviewing
modes, combining telephone and personal or door-to-door interviews. The face-to-face interview adds the advantages of lower
refusal rates, higher completion rates, and the added value of
showing products or visuals, which can dramatically reduce poor
measurement of brand or product familiarity and usage among
unacculturated Hispanics (Aneshensel, et al., 1989; Goyder,
1985; Valdés, Torres, 1994). Joint use of more than one method
may mitigate, if not eliminate, certain limitations of individual
methods (Dillman and Tarnai, 1988).

Based on several dual-interviewing mode studies conducted by

Hispanic Market Connections in four regions of the country, the profile of participants reached via the different interviewing methods can be drawn. Each sample population resulting from each interviewing method is somewhat different. The *door-to-door* sample tends to display the following characteristics:

✦ Younger

✦ More males and singles

✦ More Spanish dominant and less English proficient

✦ Fewer years in the United States

✦ Larger households

✦ Lower literacy rates

✦ Lower financial sophistication

✦ Stronger preference and value for Spanish-language advertisements

✦ Higher purchase interest in many categories

The *telephone* sample presents the contrasting profile:

✦ Older

✦ More acculturated

✦ Somewhat better English-language skills

✦ More years in the United States

✦ Smaller households

✦ Higher literacy rates

✦ Higher financial sophistication

✦ More products and goods

Economically, the door-to-door interview group owned far fewer consumer products, but a correspondingly larger percentage who plan to buy in the next year. Here is a group of product-poor consumers at the beginning of a growth curve for increased spending and who want to buy a wide variety of goods—a large potential market. Studies of this population might retrieve opinions when brand loyalties are still forming (Saegert et al., 1985). The same growth potential is there for many financial and utilities services, particularly telephones.

The *door-to-door* study sample shows Hispanic consumers who have lower familiarity with American products and way of life and not only value, but need and depend on Spanish-language media. It can be hypothesized that these consumers would be more strongly motivated by Spanish-language ad campaigns.

It also seems plausible that since these consumers are on average less "financially sophisticated" and because fewer maintain checking or savings accounts, they can or should be interviewed by phone only. However it can also be argued that these are consumers that offer greater opportunity to marketers *because* they do not currently own many consumer products or use financial services. Specifically targeting them with a culturally attuned campaign might thus be very lucrative.

The telephone interview, although providing a cost advantage, tends to over-represent more acculturated Hispanics and those with spending patterns and financial standing closer to the general market population. Since the telephone interview method elicits more responses from Hispanics who are more financially mature and who own more consumer products, it might be more appropriate for middle-class consumer surveys. A study of banking habits or credit cards, for instance, would be better addressed by the telephone sample. Telephone respondents are more literate and better versed in English, so products or services that require English fluency might make better use of the telephone method alone. Other areas where the telephone method alone may be more effective are homeowners, buyers of telephone products, or English-newspaper readers (Valdés, 1993).

For those using phone books or lists to generate names for telephone studies, it is important to note that there is a high percentage of Hispanic households with unlisted numbers. GENYSYS conducted a national random digit study of more than 22,000 households to examine demographics between households with listed and unlisted telephone numbers. Demographic groupings with the highest unlisted rates were found to be:

- ✦ Hispanics (62%)

- ✦ African Americans (Non-Hispanic) (61%)

- ✦ Other Races (56%)

In addition, they found that a listed household sample frame will create a bias that under-represents the non-White population, families with children, and groups with high mobility rates, such as young adults, renters and singles, all of which are important segments in the Hispanic market. Finally, and most important, is the finding that "the biggest difference (among unlisted households) occurred among those with less than $10,000 annual income and those with incomes over $100,000" (GENYSYS News, March 1993, 1).

■ *References*

Adams-Esquivel, H., and Darryl A. Lang, "The Reliability of Telephone Penetration Estimates in Specialized Target Groups: The Hispanic Case." *Journal of Data Collection* 27, no. 1 (spring, 1987): 35–39.

Aneshensel, Carol S., Rosina M. Becarra, Eva P. Fielder, and R. H. Schuler. "Participation of Mexican American Female Adolescents in a Longitudinal Panel Survey." *Public Opinion Quarterly* 53, no. 4 (winter 1989): 548–62.

Aquilino, William S., and Leonard A. Lo Sciuto. "Effects of Interview Mode on Self-reported Drug Use." *Public Opinion Quarterly* 54, no. 3 (fall 1990): 362–95.

Cassady, Robert J., and Monroe Sirken. "Sampling Variance and Non-response Rates in Dual Frame, Mixed Mode Surveys." In *Telephone Survey Methodology*, edited by R. M. Groves, et al. New York: John Wiley, 1988.

Collesano, Stephen P. "Personal and Telephone Interviews: Comparison for Trend Data." *Dissertation Abstracts International* 47, 1–A (July 1986): 329.

De Leeuw, Edith D., and Johannes van der Zouwen. "Data Quality in Telephone and Face to Face Surveys: A Comparative Meta-Analysis." In *Telephone Survey Methodology*, edited by R. M. Groves, et al. New York: John Wiley, 1988.

Deshpande, R., Wayne D. Hoyer, and Naveen Donthu. "The Intensity of Ethnic Affiliation: A Study of the Sociology of Hispanic Consumption." *Journal of Hispanic Research* 13 (September 1986).

Dillman, Don A., and John Tarnai. "Administrative Issues in Mixed Mode Surveys." In *Telephone Survey Methodology,* edited by R. M. Groves, et al. New York: John Wiley, 1988.

Dillon W. R., and M. Goldstein. *Multivariate Analysis Methods and Applications.* New York: John Wiley, 1984.

"Examining Case Studies in Ethnic Marketing," *Minority Markets ALERT,* June 1993.

Forrest, A. Katherine, M. Michael Austin, M. Isabel Valdés, Efrain Fuentes, Sandra Wilson. "Norms and Beliefs Relevant to HIV/AIDS Prophylaxis among California Hispanic Men: Results from Focus Groups." *Family Planning Perspectives,* 25 January 1993, 1–21.

Fuller, Steven J. "Selection of a Stratified Random Sample," *Quirk's Marketing Research Review,* October 1993, 12–17.

Garcia, Carlos E., "Sampling, the Key to Projectability of Hispanic Research," unpublished paper, 1992.

GENYSYS News, March 1993, 1.

Goyder, John. "Face-to-Face Interviews and Mailed Questionnaires: The Net Difference in Response Rate." *Public Opinion Quarterly* 49, no. 2 (summer 1985): 234–52.

Groves, Robert M., and Lars E. Lyberg. "An Overview of Non-Response Issues in Telephone Surveys." In *Telephone Survey Methodology,* edited by R. M. Groves, et al. New York: John Wiley, 1988.

Herzog, A. Regula, and Willard D. Rodgers. "Interviewing Older Adults: Mode Comparison Using Data from Face-to-Face Survey and Telephone Resurvey." *Public Opinion Quarterly* 52, no. 1 (spring 1988): 84–99.

Kim, J. O. and C. W. Mueller. *Introduction to Factor Analysis.* Beverly Hills, CA: Sage Press, 1978.

Kormendi, Eszter. "The Quality of Income Information in Telephone and Face to Face Surveys." In *Telephone Survey Methodology,* edited by R. M. Groves, et al. New York: John Wiley, 1988.

Korzenny, F., and B. A. Korzenny. "When a Hispanic Is Not a Hispanic: Issues in Conducting Hispanic Qualitative Research." *Quirk's Marketing Research Review* 6, no. 9 (1992): 14–27.

Mann, William C. "Survey Methods." *American Journal of Occupational Therapy* 39, no. 10 (October 1985): 640–48.

Marin, G., and B. V. Marin. *Research with Hispanic Populations, Applied Social Research Methods Series.* Vol. 23. Sage Publications, 1991.

Reese, Stephen, et al. "Ethnicity-of-Interviewer Effects among Mexican-Americans and Anglos." *Public Opinion Quarterly* 50, no. 4 (winter 1986): 563–72.

Saegert, Joel, Robert J. Hoover, and Marye T. Hilger. "Characteristics of Mexican American Consumers." *Journal of Consumer Research,* 12, no. 1 (1985): 104–9.

Smith, Michael D. "Woman Abuse: The Case for Surveys by Telephone." *Journal of Interpersonal Violence* 4, no. 3 (September 1989): 308–24.

Soruco, R. Gonzalo, and P. Timothy Meyer. "The Mobile Hispanic Market," *Marketing Research,* winter 1993, 6–11.

SRDS, *Hispanic Media and Market Source,* Boulder, Colo. Quarterly Reports.

Thornberry, O. T. and J. T. Massey, "Trends in United States Telephone Coverage across Time and Subgroups." In *Telephone Survey Methodology,* edited by R. M. Groves, et al. New York: John Wiley, 1988.

Valdés, M. Isabel. "A Dual Mode Study in the Hispanic Market." Unpublished paper.

———, and Jannet Torres. "The Use of V.I.P.©, (Visual Icon Probing) Technology to Improve Cross Cultural Awareness and Usage Measures." Unpublished paper.

Waksberg, Joseph. "Sampling Methods for Random Digit Dialing," *Journal of the American Statistical Association,* 73, no. 361, Applications Section (March 1978): 40–46.

Table 8.1 Weighted Sampling Plan by
Hispanic Population Density of the Houston Metropolitan Area

Zip Code	City	Hisp Pop	%Hou	%Grp	Cum	%Hou	Cum			# Cs	N=
77003	Houston	6,307	1.0%	3.0%	6,307	1.0%	5,073	1	7,474.85	1	5
77007	Houston	12,929	2.0%	6.1%	19,236	3.0%	18,002	1	36,218.85	0	5
77009	Houston	28,744	4.4%	13.7%	47,980	7.4%	46,746	3	25,560.4	3	15
77011	Houston	20,923	3.2%	9.9%	68,903	10.6%	67,669	2	24,087.1	2	10
77012	Houston	19,581	3.0%	9.3%	88,484	13.6	87,250	2	17,103.8	2	10
77017	Houston	14,071	2.2%	6.7%	102,555	15.8%	101,321	1	23,054.65	1	5
77020	Houston	16,478	2.5%	7.8%	119,033	18.3%	117,799	2	27,009.35	2	10
77023	Houston	25,009	3.9%	11.9%	144,042	22.2%	142,808	2	25,163.05	2	10
77081	Houston	19,208	3.0%	9.1%	163,250	25.1%	162,016	2	20,683.75	2	10
77087	Houston	16,565	2.6%	7.9%	179,825	27.7%	178,591	1	31,602.6	1	5
77093	Houston	21,446	3.3%	10.2%	201,271	31.0%	200,037	3	9,293.15	3	15
77587	S. Houston	9,272	1.4%	4.4%	210,543	32.4%	209,309	0	15,600.15	0	0
	Houston Total	649,400						20		19	100

Start	1234	
#Clusters	20	
Interval	10,527.15	
Sample size	100	
Interviews per cluster	5	

#Cs = number of clusters; N = number to be interviewed.

Source: Hispanic Market Connections, 1995.

Table 8.2 Short Acculturation Scale

A. English Version

In general what language do you read and speak?

Only Spanish	1
Spanish better than English	2
Both equally	3
English better than Spanish	4
Only English	5

What language do you usually speak at home?

Only Spanish	1
Spanish better than English	2
Both equally	3
English better than Spanish	4
Only English	5

In which language do you usually think?

Only Spanish	1
Spanish better than English	2
Both equally	3
English better than Spanish	4
Only English	5

What language do you speak with your friends?

Only Spanish	1
Spanish better than English	2
Both equally	3
English better than Spanish	4
Only English	5

(continued next page)

Table 8.2 Short Acculturation Scale (*continued*)

B. Spanish Version

¿Por lo general, qué idioma(s) lee y habla usted?

Sólo Español	1
Más Español qué Inglés	2
Ambos por igual	3
Más Inglés qué Español	4
Sólo Inglés	5

¿Por lo general, qué idioma(s) habla en su casa?

Sólo Español	1
Más Español qué Inglés	2
Ambos por igual	3
Más Inglés qué Español	4
Sólo Inglés	5

¿Por lo general, en qué idioma(s) piensa?

Sólo Español	1
Más Español qué Inglés	2
Ambos por igual	3
Más Inglés qué Español	4
Sólo Inglés	5

¿Por lo general, qué idioma(s) habla con sus amigos?

Sólo Español	1
Más Español qué Inglés	2
Ambos por igual	3
Más Inglés qué Español	4
Sólo Inglés	5

Source: Marin and Marin, 1991, 62–63.

Table 8.3 Media Questions, Hispanic Database©, Hispanic Market Connections, 1990

[Questions 1–12 omitted]

Television

Now, I would like to ask you about the programs you watch on TV, not taped programs or rented videos, but broadcast programs.

13. How many hours of Spanish/English TV do you watch on a typical weekday?
    (Probe: Total number of hours)
How about during the weekend? (Saturday and Sunday combined)

	Weekday	Weekend
Spanish	_____ hrs.(24–27)	_____ hrs. (28–31)
English	_____ hrs (32–35)	_____ hrs. (36–39)

(If all 4 are 0, then go to Q.24)

(If watch Spanish TV—Q.13—continue)
(If not, go to Q.17)

14. What time do you watch Spanish television on weekdays?
    (Probe if needed) (Probe: Weekends)
    (Circle all that apply)

	Weekday (40)	Weekend (41)
Before 9 a.m.	1	1
9 a.m. to 3 p.m.	2	2
3 p.m. to 5 p.m.	3	3
5 p.m. to 8 p.m.	4	4
8 p.m. to 11 p.m.	5	5
After 11 p.m.	6	6
Doesn't watch TV	7	7
All day long	8	8

15. How many hours of Spanish TV did you watch yesterday? _____ hrs. (42–45)
(If Watch English TV—Q.13—continue)
(If not, go to Q.20)

[Question 16 omitted]

17. What time do you watch English television on weekdays?
    (Probe if needed) (Probe: Weekends)
    (Circle all that apply)

(continued next page)

**Table 8.3 Media Questions, Hispanic Database$^{©}$,
Hispanic Market Connections, 1990 (*continued*)**

	Weekday (48)	Weekend (49)
Before 9 a.m.	1	1
9 a.m. to 3 p.m.	2	2
3 p.m. to 5 p.m.	3	3
5 p.m. to 8 p.m.	4	4
8 p.m. to 11 p.m.	5	5
After 11 p.m.	6	6
Doesn't watch TV	7	7
All day long	8	8

18. How many hours of English TV did you watch yesterday?_____ Hrs. (50–53)
    (Doesn't remember ... X)

[Question 19 omitted]

20. Which Spanish TV stations do you get in your home?

[Questions 21–27 omitted]

Cable Section

28. Have you heard of cable TV?
    Yes   1 (12)
    No   2—Go to Q.34

29. Do you currently have cable TV?
    Yes   1 (13)—Go to Q.33
    No   2
    (Don't know   3)

30. Have you ever subscribed to it?
    Yes   1 (14)
    No   2
    (Don't know   3)

31. Why haven't you subscribed/resubscribed to cable?

[Question 32 omitted]

33. Are you subscribed to any of the following premium (extra cost) channels?
    (Read list)

(*continued next page*)

Table 8.3 Media Questions, Hispanic Database©,
Hispanic Market Connections, 1990 (*continued*)

	Yes	No	D/K
HBO	1	2	3 (20)
Showtime	1	2	3 (21)
The Movie Channel	1	2	3 (22)
The Disney Channel	1	2	3 (23)
Cinemax	1	2	3 (24)
Other (Specify)			
_____	1	2	3 (25)

(Do not read the following Alternatives)

MTV	1 (26)
ESPN	2
Cable Vision	3
Galavision	4

Radio

This section refers to your radio and music preferences.

34. How many hours of Spanish/English radio do you listen to on a weekday?
    (Probe: Total number of hours) How about on a weekend?

	Weekday	Weekend
Spanish	_____hrs. (27–30)	_____hrs. (31–34)
English	_____hrs (35–38)	_____hrs. (39–42)

        (If all 4 are 0 then go to Q.43)
        (If listens to Spanish radio in Q.34—continue)
        (If does not listen to Spanish language radio, go to Q.38)

35. What time do you listen to Spanish language radio on weekdays?
    (Probe if needed) (Probe: Weekend?)

	Weekday (43)	Weekend (44)
Before 6 a.m.	1	1
6 a.m. to 10 a.m.	2	2
10 a.m. to 3 p.m.	3	3
3 p.m. to 7 p.m.	4	4
7 p.m. to midnight	5	5
After midnight	6	6

(continued next page)

**Table 8.3 Media Questions, Hispanic Database©,
Hispanic Market Connections, 1990 (*continued*)**

Varies	7	7
All day	8	8
(N/A	0	0)

36. How many hours of Spanish radio did you listen to yesterday?_____hrs. (45–48)
    (Doesn't remember   X)
        (If Listens to English Radio in Q.34—continue)
        (If does not listen to English radio go to Q.40)

[Question 37 omitted]

38. What time do you listen to English language radio on weekdays?
    (Probe if needed) (Probe: Weekends)

	Weekday (51)	Weekend (52)
Before 6 a.m.	1	1
6 a.m. to 10 a.m.	2	2
10 a.m. to 3 p.m.	3	3
3 p.m. to 7 p.m.	4	4
7 p.m. to midnight	5	5
After midnight	6	6
Varies	7	7
All day	8	8
(N/A	0	0)

39. How many hours of English radio did you listen to yesterday? _____hrs. (53–56)

40. Where do you usually listen to the radio? (OK if more than one)
        At home   1 (57)
        At work   2
        In the car   3

41. What kind of program(s) do you prefer to listen to:
    (Probe: Any other?) (Probe if needed)
        News   1 (58)
        Talk shows/Call-in shows   2
        Sports   3
        Classical music   4
        Jazz   5
        Soft rock   6
        Religious programs/gospel   7
        60's music   8
        Heavy metal   9

(continued next page)

**Table 8.3 Media Questions, Hispanic Database©,
Hispanic Market Connections, 1990 (continued)**

Country music (American)   0
"Easy listening"   X
Rock/Top-40/   Y
Spanish or other Latin music 1
Requests   2
Rancheras   3
Nortenas   4
Boleros   5
Other (Specify)
_____   6

42. How often do you listen to the news on the radio?
    (Probe: Number of days per week)
    Everyday   1 (60)
    4–6 days a week   2
    2–3 days a week   3
    1 day a week   4
    Only on weekends   5
    Rarely   6
    Never   7

Newspaper

Now I would like to ask you about newspapers.

43. How often do you read the newspaper in Spanish? And in English?

	Spanish (61)	English (62)
Daily	1	1
Several times a week	2	2
About once a week	3	3
Only on Sundays	4	4
Less than once a week	5	5
Rarely	6	6
Never	7	7 (If rarely or never for both Eng. & Span. go to Q.51)

44. Which newspapers do you read regularly? (Probe: Spanish/English)
Spanish _____(63)
        _____(64)
        _____(65)
        (Doesn't remember. Y)

(continued next page)

**Table 8.3 Media Questions, Hispanic Database©,
Hispanic Market Connections, 1990 (*continued*)**

English   _____(66)
           _____(67)
           _____(68)
           (Doesn't remember. Y)

45. Which sections do you read regularly in the weekday edition of the paper?
        And in Sunday's edition?
        (Do not read list. Probe if needed)
        Any other?

[Questions 46–50 omitted]

Magazines

Now, I would like to ask you some questions about magazines.

51. Do you read magazines in Spanish? (Probe in English)

	Yes	No
Spanish	1	2 (36)
English	1	2 (37)

(If does not read magazines go to Q.52)

55. What magazines do you read? (Probe: Spanish/English)
    Any other?

Spanish   _____(38)
           _____(39)
           _____(40)
English   _____(41)
           _____(42)
           _____(43)

[Question 53 omitted]

54. When was the last time you read a magazine?
        Today   1 (45)
        Yesterday   2
        A few days ago   3
        About 3–4 days ago 4
        A long time ago   5

55. What magazine(s) did you read?
    (Probe: English or Spanish)

(*continued next page*)

**Table 8.3 Media Questions, Hispanic Database©,
Hispanic Market Connections, 1990 (*continued*)**

	English	Spanish	DK
_____(46)	I	2	3 (50)
_____(47)	I	2	3 (51)
_____(48)	I	2	3 (52)
_____(49	I	2	3 (53)

(Doesn't remember....X)

56. What types of magazines do you read regularly?
   (Probe with the list if necessary)

Table 8.4a

HISPANIC MARKET CONNECTIONS, INC. - HISPANIC DATABASE - SOUTHERN CALIFORNIA - MAY 1992

1. Do the people in this house speak Spanish?

	TOT	U.S. (B)	PRTO RICO P.R	U.S/ P.R ICO (D)	MEX-ICO (E)	EL SALV ADOR (F)	CUBA	TOT CENT AMER (H)	TOT STH AMER (I)	0-5 (J)	6-9 (K)	10-19 (L)	20+ (M)	LESS THAN 12,4 (N)	12,4 TO 23,9 (O)	24,0 TO 34,9 (P)	35,0 TO 49,9 (Q)	50+ (R)	GRDE SCHL (S)	HIGH SCHL (T)	HIG-HER EDUC (U)
										← TIME RESIDED IN THE U.S. →				← ANNUAL INCOME (*$1000) →					← EDUCATION →		
TOTAL (count)	2014	316	13	1682	1467	87	13	167	19	493	316	541	322	386	472	200	136	92	761	765	420
(%)	100.0	100.0	100.0	100.0	100.0	100.0	100.0	100.0	100.0	100.0	100.0	100.0	100.0	100.0	100.0	100.0	100.0	100.0	100.0	100.0	100.0
No Answer (count)	4	-	-	4	3	-	-	1	-	1	1	2	-	-	1	1	-	-	2	1	1
(%)	0.2			0.2	0.2			0.6		0.2	0.3	0.4			0.5	0.5			0.3	0.1	0.2
Any Response (count)	2010	316	13	1678	1464	87	13	166	19	492	315	539	322	386	472	199	136	92	759	764	419
(%)	99.8	100.0	100.0	99.8	99.8	100.0	100.0	99.4	100.0	99.8	99.7	99.6	100.0	100.0	100.0	99.5	100.0	100.0	99.7	99.9	99.8
Net All of the time/More than half the time (count)	1632	138	8	1484	1308	77	6	151	12	463	299	461	250	343	417	156	81	48	697	623	248
(%)	81.0	43.7	61.5	88.2 B	89.2	88.5	46.2	90.4 I	63.2	93.9 L	94.6 L	85.2 M	77.6	88.9 P	88.3 P	78.0 Q	59.6	52.2	91.6 U	81.4 U	59.0
	EFH													QR	QR	R					
(5) All of the time (count)	1331	91	7	1231	1082	67	3	132	9	417	259	362	185	294	345	119	57	33	593	492	191
(%)	66.1	28.8	53.8	73.2 B	73.8	77.0	23.1	79.0 I	47.4	84.6 M	82.0 M	66.9	57.5	76.2	73.1	59.5	41.9	35.9	77.9 U	64.3 U	45.5
	DEFH													QR	QR	R					
(4) More than half of the time (count)	301	47	1	253	226	10	3	19	3	46	40	99	65	49	72	37	24	15	104	131	57
(%)	14.9	14.9	7.7	15.0	15.4	11.5	23.1	11.4	15.8	9.3	12.7	18.3 K	20.2 K	12.7	15.3	18.5	17.6	16.3	13.7	17.1	13.6
(3) Half of the time (count)	219	71	5	143	121	8	2	11	4	22	13	61	50	33	40	22	26	14	48	84	86
(%)	10.9	22.5	38.5	8.5	8.2	9.2	15.4	6.6	21.1	4.5	4.1	11.3 K	15.5 K	8.5	8.5	11.0	19.1 O	15.2	6.3	11.0	20.5 ST
	EFH																				
(2) Less than half of the time (count)	68	34	-	34	26	1	3	3	1	14	3	12	3	5	8	15	6	10	25	31	
(%)	3.4	10.8	-	2.0	1.8	1.1	23.1	1.8	5.3	2.6	0.9	3.7 J	0.8	1.1	4.0	11.0 NO	6.5 N	1.3	3.3 S	7.4 ST	
	DEFH																				
Net Rarely/Never (count)	91	73	-	17	14	2	-	3	3	3	10	13	14	24	4	4	32	54			
(%)	4.5	23.1	-	1.0	1.0	1.1		0.6	10.5 EHO	0.6	3.1 JK	1.8	2.1	6.5 N	3.3 N	26.1 NOP	0.5	4.2 S	12.9 ST		
	DEFH																				
(1) Rarely (count)	54	42	-	11	7	1	1	1	1	3	5	4	8	10	14	4	4	19	30		
(%)	2.7	13.3	-	0.7	0.5	1.1	7.7	0.6	5.3 E	0.6	1.6	1.0	4.0 O	7.4 N	15.2 NOP	0.5	2.5 S	7.1 ST			
	DEFH														P						
(0) Never (count)	37	31	-	6	2	-	1	-	-	5	3	6	5	4	10	13	24				
(%)	1.8	9.8	-	0.4	0.1		7.7			1.6 JK	0.8	1.3	2.5	2.9	10.9 NOP	0.8	1.7 S	5.7 ST			
	DEFH						5.3 EH					L									

HISPANIC MARKET CONNECTIONS, INC. - HISPANIC DATABASE - SOUTHERN CALIFORNIA - MAY 1992

Table 8.4b

HISPANIC MARKET CONNECTIONS, INC. - HISPANIC DATABASE - SOUTHERN CALIFORNIA - MAY 1992

1. Do the people in this house speak Spanish?

		<- LANGUAGE USAGE->				TELEVISION MEDIA USAGE: SPANISH TV								TELEVISION MEDIA USAGE: ENGLISH TV							
								<- WEEKDAY -->			<- WEEKEND -->					<- WEEKDAY -->			<-- WEEKEND ->		
	TOT	SPAN DEP	SPAN PREF	NO PREF	ENGL PREF /DOM	TOT SOME SPAN	NON WTC-HERS	LHGT	MED	HVY	LGHT	MED	HVY	TOT SOME ENGL	NON WTC-HERS	LGHT	MED	HVY	LGHT	MED	HVY
TOTAL	2014	962	664	267	117	1827	187	628	643	492	340	415	842	1431	582	737	383	233	386	354	449
	100.0 %	100.0 %	100.0 %	100.0 %	100.0 %	100.0 %	100.0 %	100.0 %	100.0 %	100.0 %	100.0 %	100.0 %	100.0 %	100.0 %	100.0 %	100.0 %	100.0 %	100.0 %	100.0 %	100.0 %	100.0 %
		(B)	(C)	(D)	(E)	(F)	(G)	(H)	(I)	(J)	(K)	(L)	(M)	(N)	(O)	(P)	(Q)	(R)	(S)	(T)	(U)
No Answer	4	3	1	-	-	4	-	-	-	4	1	-	3	1	3	-	-	1	-	-	1
	0.2	0.3	0.2			0.2				0.8	0.3		0.4	0.1	0.5			0.4			0.2
Any Response	2010	959	663	267	117	1823	187	628	643	488	339	415	839	1430	579	737	383	232	386	354	448
	99.8	99.7	99.8	100.0	100.0	99.8	100.0	100.0	100.0	99.2	99.7	100.0	99.6	99.9	99.5	100.0	100.0	99.6	100.0	100.0	99.8
Net All of the time/More than half the time	1632	920	527	171	10	1559	73	482	578	462	244	350	780	1079	552	615	256	143	325	266	286
	81.0	95.6C DE	79.4D E	64.0E	8.5	85.3G	39.0	76.8	89.9H	93.9H I	71.8	84.3K	92.6K L	75.4	94.8N	83.4Q R	66.8	61.4	84.2T U	75.1U	63.7
(5) All of the time	1331	820	384	115	8	1276	55	364	479	406	180	283	676	828	502	483	191	109	255	202	215
	66.1	85.2C DE	57.8D E	43.1E	6.8	69.8G	29.4	58.0	74.5H	82.5H I	52.9	68.2K	80.3K L	57.9	86.3N	65.5Q R	49.9	46.8	66.1T U	57.1U	47.9
(4) More than half of the time	301	100	143	56	2	283	18	118	99	56	64	67	104	251	50	132	65	34	70	64	71
	14.9	10.4E	21.5B E	21.0BE	1.7	15.5G	9.6	18.8J	15.4	11.4	18.8M	16.1	12.4	17.5O	8.6	17.9	17.0	14.6	18.1	18.1	15.8
(3) Half of the time	219	31	111	53	24	178	41	93	52	18	52	49	46	199	20	79	63	49	38	55	76
	10.9	3.2	16.7B	19.9B	20.5B	9.7	21.9F	14.8IJ	8.1J	3.7	15.3M	11.8M	5.5	13.9O	3.4	10.7	16.4P	21.0P	9.8	15.5S	16.9S
(2) Less than half of the time	68	5	22	21	20	52	16	32	10	3	26	10	8	63	5	27	25	8	10	17	30
	3.4	0.5	3.3B	7.9B C	17.1BC D	2.8	8.6F	5.1IJ	1.6	0.6	7.6LM	2.4	1.0	4.4O	0.9	3.7	6.5	3.4	2.6	4.8	6.7S
Net Rarely/Never	91	3	3	22	63	34	57	21	3	5	17	6	5	89	2	16	39	32	13	16	56
	4.5	0.3	0.5	8.2B C	53.8BC D	1.9	30.5F	3.3IJ	0.5	1.0	5.0LM	1.4	0.6	6.2O	0.3	2.2	10.2P	13.7P	3.4	4.5	12.5ST
(1) Rarely	54	3	3	16	32	27	27	16	3	5	13	4	5	53	1	8	23	22	5	10	34
	2.7	0.3	0.5	6.0B C	27.4BC D	1.5	14.4F	2.5I	0.5	1.0	3.8LM	1.0	0.6	3.7O	0.2	1.1	6.0P	9.4P	1.3	2.8	7.6ST
(0) Never	37	-	-	6	31	7	30	5	-	-	4	2	-	36	1	8	16	10	8	6	22
	1.8			2.2B C	26.5BC D	0.4	16.0F	0.8IJ			1.2M	0.5		2.5O	0.2	1.1	4.2P	4.3P	2.1	1.7	4.9ST

HISPANIC MARKET CONNECTIONS, INC. - HISPANIC DATABASE - SOUTHERN CALIFORNIA - MAY 1992

Table 8.4c

HISPANIC MARKET CONNECTIONS, INC. - HISPANIC DATABASE - SOUTHERN CALIFORNIA - MAY 1992

6. Would you say you speak English...

	TOT	COUNTRY OF BIRTH								TIME RESIDED IN THE U.S.				ANNUAL INCOME (*$1000)					EDUCATION		
		U.S. (B)	PRTO RICO P.R.	OUTS. U.S./ P.R. (D)	MEX-ICO (E)	EL SALV ADOR (F)	CUBA	TOT CENT AMER (H)	TOT STH. AMER (I)	0-5 (J)	6-9 (K)	10-19 (L)	20+ (M)	LESS THAN 12.4 (N)	12.4 TO 23.9 (O)	24.0 TO 34.9 (P)	35.0 TO 49.9 (Q)	50+ (R)	GRDE SCHL (S)	HIGH SCHL (T)	HIG-HER EDUC (U)
TOTAL	2014 100.0%	316 100.0%	13 100.0%	1682 100.0%	1467 100.0%	87 100.0%	13 100.0%	167 100.0%	19 100.0%	493 100.0%	316 100.0%	541 100.0%	322 100.0%	386 100.0%	472 100.0%	200 100.0%	136 100.0%	92 100.0%	761 100.0%	765 100.0%	420 100.0%
No Answer	795 39.5%	13 4.1%	-	781 46.4%	699 47.6%	40 46.0%	5 38.5%	74 44.3%	2 10.5%	299 60.6%	169 53.5%	210 38.8%	90 28.0%	191 49.5%	191 40.5%	56 28.0%	19 14.0%	7 7.6%	430 56.5%	246 32.2%	72 17.1%
Any Response	1219 60.5%	303 95.9%	13 100.0%	901 53.6%	768 52.4%	47 54.0%	8 61.5%	93 55.7%	17 89.5%	194 39.4%	147 46.5%	331 61.2%	232 72.1%	195 50.5%	281 59.5%	144 72.0%	117 86.0%	85 92.4%	331 43.5%	519 67.8%	348 82.9%
Net Very well/Well	668 33.2% EFH	281 88.9D	10 76.9	376 22.4	310 21.1	19 21.8	6 46.2	36 21.6 FH	13 68.4E	54 11.0	46 14.6	140 25.9J	141 43.8J KL	79 20.5	128 27.1	76 38.0N O	81 59.6N OP	69 75.0N OP	92 12.1	306 40.0S	259 61.7ST
(4) Very well	383 19.0% EFHI	232 73.4D	3 23.1	147 8.7	118 8.0	7 8.0	5 38.5	16 9.6	4 21.1	15 3.0	15 4.7	53 9.8J K	63 19.6JK L	38 9.8	67 14.2	42 21.0N OP	51 37.5N OP	50 54.3N OP	43 5.7	171 22.4S	165 39.3ST
(3) Well	285 14.2% EFHI	49 15.5	7 53.8	229 13.6	192 13.1	12 13.8	1 7.7	20 12.0 FH	9 47.4BE	39 7.9	31 9.8	87 16.1J K	78 24.2J KL	41 10.6	61 12.9	34 17.0	30 22.1N	19 20.7	49 6.4	135 17.6S	94 22.4ST
Net A little/Very little	551 27.4%	22 7.0	3 23.1	525 31.2B	458 31.2B	28 32.2B	2 15.4	57 34.1B	4 21.1	140 28.4	101 32.0	191 35.3	91 28.3	116 30.1	153 32.4R	68 34.0R	36 26.5	16 17.4	239 31.4U	213 27.8U	89 21.2
(2) A little	380 18.9%	17 5.4	3 23.1	359 21.3B	309 21.1B	20 23.0B	1 7.7	43 25.7B	3 15.8	95 19.3	71 22.5	123 22.7	69 21.4	71 18.4	94 19.9	48 24.0	25 18.4	15 16.3	151 19.8	153 20.0	72 17.1
(1) Very little	171 8.5%	5 1.6	-	166 9.9B	149 10.2B	8 9.2B	1 7.7	14 8.4B	1 5.3	45 9.1	30 9.5	68 12.6M	22 6.8	45 11.7R	59 12.5R	20 10.0R	11 8.1	1 1.1	88 11.6T	60 7.8U	17 4.0
Mean	2.72	3.68D EFHI	3.00	2.40	2.36	2.38	3.25	2.41	2.94	2.12	2.21	2.38	2.78	2.37	2.48	2.68	3.03	3.39	2.14	2.80	3.17
Standard deviation	1.05	0.66	0.71	0.97	0.96	0.95	1.17	0.95	0.83	0.85	0.89	0.98	0.95	1.04	1.07	1.04	1.02	0.82	0.96	1.02	0.92
Standard error	0.03	0.04	0.20	0.03	0.03	0.14	0.41	0.10	0.20	0.06	0.07	0.05	0.06	0.07	0.06	0.09	0.09	0.05	0.05	0.05	0.05

columns tested (n_k) (sig=.05) BD, BEFHI, JKLM, NOPQR, STU

CHAPTER 9

- Tianguis Stores: The Right Idea at the Right Time

- Bank of America's Introduction of System-Wide Bilingual ATMs

- Western Union

- CIBA Vision's Illusions

- Inter-American Book Services: Selling Spanish-Language Books through Direct Marketing Vehicles

- California Avocado Commission: Hispanic Advertising Campaign

- Education Now And Babies Later (ENABL)

- Immigration and Naturalization Service Amnesty

Principles in Action:
Case Studies

Editor's Note: These case studies were reprinted with the cooperation of the organizations that were involved. Each was written by a different contributor.

■ Tianguis Stores:
The Right Idea at the Right Time

BACKGROUND

In 1985, the Vons Grocery Companies identified a unique opportunity in the Hispanic community. They determined that 4.5 million Hispanics had been under-served by the supermarket community in southern California, and that 80 percent of them were of Mexican origin with a strong nostalgia for their traditional foods.

With no Hispanic/Mexican supermarket, the only options for people in the community were the independent grocers. The other large supermarket chains were finding ways to reach the Hispanic market, but mainly with a cookie-cutter mentality; even with the best efforts, it wasn't enough to have just an ethnic aisle.

The Tianguis club card.

Hispanic products were frequently lost among a vast array of Asian products.

Vons was visionary and created Tianguis, the first supermarket specially designed with the Hispanic customer in mind. The name *Tianguis* is an Aztec word, from the Nahuatl language, meaning "marketplace." Vons felt this name provided high-awareness and differentiated it from the competition. Vons recognized the importance of fresh produce among Hispanics and made the produce section four times larger than the average supermarket.

The first Tianguis—covering 80,000 square feet—opened in Montebello, California, in January 1987. That same year Valdés Zacky Associates, Inc., a full-service advertising and promotional agency, was awarded the account and given the assignment of creating the grand opening campaign for the next two Tianguis to open in El Monte and Cudahy, California.

PHASE I
Objective

Develop an identity for a 100 percent Hispanic supermarket. The advertising objective was to establish *the* source for Hispanic, and particularly Mexican, grocery needs.

Creative Strategy

Target Group: Hispanic females 18–49.

Role of Advertising: To invite Hispanics to discover Tianguis.

Main Message: Tianguis satisfies all your Mexican grocery needs because it has "el sabor de lo nuestro"/"the taste of our heritage."

Reasons Why:

✧ Everything at Tianguis is fresh.

✧ Many items made on premises/"acabados de hacer."

✧ Wide variety to choose from.

✧ Low prices.

Support:

✧ In-store bakery and tortillería.

✦ Produce area 4x normal size.

✦ Weekly featured specials.

Slogan: "Venga a disfrutar del sabor de lo nuestro"/"Come enjoy the taste of our heritage."

The agency felt this slogan best described the personality of Tianguis, since the word "sabor" in Spanish encompasses a lot more than "taste." It pertains to all the senses, it's a feeling, it describes an experience. Therefore, under the slogan, "Venga a disfrutar del sabor de lo nuestro," the grand opening commercials were an invitation to discover and enjoy Tianguis as a festive grocery shopping experience, but also as a family outing. The commercials also feature an item/price donut for the co-op advertisers. The campaign's success was apparent both by its selection by advertising professionals as one of the top six Hispanic campaigns and in its results.

Results

Stores number two and number three registered the highest revenues generated for any store opening in the history of the Vons chain. Store number one's revenues increased $100,000 during each new store's first-week openings. As for the co-op advertisers, Carnation, Kimberly-Clark, and Plantation were able to project and achieve 25 percent sales increases during on-air periods. More Pepsi-Cola was sold in one week in three Tianguis locations than in Vons' 180 stores.

Due to the success of Tianguis and the acquisition of the Safeway stores by Vons, more Tianguis stores opened between 1989 and 1990. Given the stores' new needs, between 1987 and 1990 Valdés Zacky Associates created several campaigns, adapting the creative strategy to ensure future success. However, the advertising objective and the slogan remained untouched.

As a result of maintaining awareness of Tianguis among Hispanics as *the* source for Mexican grocery needs, sales between 1989 and 1990 increased 11 percent.

PHASE II
Objective

Establish link between Vons and Tianguis: By 1990, with nine Tianguis stores, Vons was successfully fulfilling the needs of the Hispanic community. Valdés Zacky Associates was hired to estab-

Audio: Ahora en Tianguis, Tianguis Club es la manera más fácil y moderna de ahorrar.

Now at Tianguis, Tianguis Club is the easiest and most up to date way to save.

Venga al puestito donde le echamos una mano,

Come to the booth where we give you a hand

llenando una simple y sencilla solicitud.

filling out a simple application.

ahorros en cientos de productos.

of products right in your hands.

En la caja sólo tendrá que

At the cash register you just

apretar el botón azul

press the blue button

Venga al puestito, hágase socio gratis y

Come to the booth, become a member,

comience a ahorrar.

and start to save.

Pronto recibirá su tarjeta personal
de Tianguis Club,

*You'll soon receive your personal
Tianguis Club card,*

poniendo en sus manos

putting savings on thousands

y deslizar su tarjeta.

and slide your card through.

En su recibo verá todo lo que ahorró.

*On your receipt you'll see
all you've saved.*

*One of the Tianguis TV
spots showing how to get the
Club card.*

lish a tie between both Vons and Tianguis stores for future opportunities by conveying Vons ownership. No one could better establish such a connection than Bill Davila, who not only is president of and spokesperson for Vons, but also the creator of Tianguis.

Creative Strategy   Valdés Zacky Associates decided to formulate a campaign that put a face on the Tianguis name. This transition spot, entitled "First Step," takes viewers back to 1985, where Bill Davila presents his innovative idea to the Vons management group. He tells the group, "It's time for Vons to take the first step and create a market of markets for the Hispanic . . . what I am talking about is a Tianguis!" As the spot returns to the present, Davila states, "Today Tianguis is a reality, and no matter how good we think we are, the day we think we are good, that will be the day we will take a step backwards."

Results   This successful sixty-second spot succeeded in connecting Vons and Tianguis in the consumer's mind. It not only helped in the perception of Tianguis' quality among Hispanics and reinforced Vons commitment to the Hispanic community, it provided the opportunity to introduce features that were going to be available in both stores, such as the "Club" and electronic couponing.

PHASE III
Objective   Introduction of the Club and electronic couponing: Vons brings electronic couponing to Hispanic consumers via VonsClub and TianguisClub. The objective is to increase the competitive edge with a unique product, and offer Hispanics an education in easy savings.

Message: Tianguis and Vons are the first to bring Hispanics the easiest, simplest, worry-free way to have automatic savings; they don't even need a bank account. Bill Davila is again used as the unifying spokesperson.

Slogan: "Ahorrar está en sus manos"/"Savings at your fingertips."

Creative Strategy   This campaign was supported with TV, radio, and outdoor advertising, including transit ads. It was necessary to develop the application forms and other collateral materials in the simplest way. Although the VonsClub card had been in existence, Vons supported it in Spanish for the first time. It was designed and introduced from scratch as the TianguisClub card.

The messages were simple: Vons explained what the card was, how to get it, and what the benefits were through customers who provided testimonials and were shown interacting with Davila.

A key in-store tactic was directing consumers to a newly created "Puestito" (kiosk) in Tianguis. Here Tianguis personnel would guide customers through the application process and explain the use of the Club card, alleviating any consumer confusion.

Results

✧ TianguisClub sign-ups per store averaged 3,500 a week, greater than Vons or its upscale market Pavilions during the general market campaign introduction.

✧ VonsClub Hispanic media support increased sign-ups 30 percent over normal sign-ups in Vons stores.

✧ The amount of average Club transactions are 150 percent higher than nonmember transactions.

✧ After one year, 50 percent of Tianguis regular customers are TianguisClub members.

CONTRIBUTOR'S PROFILE

Case Study Contributor: Dolores Valdés Zacky

Agency: Valdés Zacky Associates, Inc., Los Angeles, California

Client: The Vons Companies

Media: Television, radio, outdoor, and transit advertising

■ Bank of America's Introduction of System-Wide Bilingual ATMs

BACKGROUND

Bank of America is a major commercial U.S. bank, headquartered in San Francisco, California. The bank enjoyed a solid market share of over 30 percent of California's more than 8 million Hispanic consumers. In addition, the Hispanic consumer segment was the fastest-growing consumer segment in the bank's portfolio. A primary Hispanic attitude and usage research study conducted by the bank revealed that 95 percent of the respondents felt that it was very important to have Spanish-language services available to them.

In order to better service this dynamic portion of the bank's portfolio, a decision was made to convert the entire Automated Teller Machine (ATM) system from English-only screens to bilingual (English-Spanish) screens. Also, because a significant portion of the bank's Hispanic clientele had savings-account only relationships with the bank, providing bilingual ATM services would make it easier for this clientele to use the many checking account products the bank offers. Spanish-language ATMs would also strengthen the bank's position in the market by demonstrating to California's Hispanic population that Bank of America was sincerely interested in having them as clients. Spanish-language ATMs would further decrease branch operational costs by absorbing the frequent in-branch cash/check deposit and withdrawal transactions that made up a significant portion of the Hispanics account activity.

OBJECTIVES

✧ Increase VERSATEL Card usage among branches in high density Hispanic serving areas.

✧ Reduce the number of in-branch transactions and convert them to lower cost ATM transactions.

✧ Motivate Hispanics who currently do not bank with Bank of America to open deposit accounts.

✧ Motivate Hispanics to use ATMs more often.

✧ Demonstrate to all California Hispanics that Bank of America is sincerely interested in having them as clients and wants to make their banking as simple and convenient as possible.

CONSUMER TARGET

✧ Primary: First-generation Spanish-language dependent Hispanic VERSATEL cardholders who never or seldom use VERSATELLER ATMs due to language barrier.

✧ Secondary: Spanish-language dominant Hispanics who never or seldom use VERSATELLER ATMs due to language barrier. These individuals may or may not be current Bank of America clients.

FRAME OF REFERENCE

✧ Primary/Secondary: ATMs exist as a convenient alternative to going into the branch to obtain cash and take care of other routine banking transactions. Operation of ATMs is too complicated for the target market because the prompts on the screens aren't in Spanish.

✧ Identifier: All Bank of America VERSATELLER ATMs are now bilingual . . .

✧ and provide unprecedented banking convenience for Spanish-speaking individuals.

✧ Purchase Motivator: Primary and secondary target groups will utilize a bank that is perceived as being safe and trustworthy, provides easy access to savings, and is committed to providing services in a language the target audience understands. Bank of America's ATMs meet these needs because they are easy to use, reliable, and convenient.

Bank of America . . .

POINTS OF DIFFERENCE

✧ has more ATMs than any other bank in California and all will be bilingual;

✧ has more convenient locations;

✧ offers a Spanish-language toll-free (1-800) number for customer service;

✧ is committed to providing services to Hispanic consumers in Spanish to make banking easier;

✧ is the only major California bank to offer bilingual checks.

✧ VERSATELLER ATMs all over California are accessible and easy-to-use for Spanish-dominant Hispanics.

COMMUNICATION OBJECTIVES

✧ Educate Spanish-speaking ATMS non-users about the different banking transactions that can be accomplished at VERSATELLER ATMs.

✧ Motivate Hispanics to open savings or checking accounts because Bank of America provides more ATMs and is committed to providing more services in Spanish than the competition.

CREATIVE STRATEGY

Banking with Bank of America is now easier/better than any other California bank for Spanish-dominant Hispanics because Bank of America provides all its California VERSATELLER ATMs in their language of choice. VERSATELLER ATMs are easy to use and conveniently located throughout the state. As a result of having Spanish-language ATMs and other customer services in Spanish, Hispanics will see that the Bank of America is truly committed to this market.

TONE/ POSITIONING

Communication was planned to position the Spanish-language feature as an add-on to the bank's VERSATELLER ATM service that would make ATM convenience accessible to those who prefer to conduct their banking in Spanish. The tone was planned to be upbeat, emphasizing the VERSATELLER ATMs now "speak" Spanish, as well as English. The feature was also positioned as a matter of choice—it is entirely up to each customer to conduct their banking in English or Spanish. The objective was to introduce the service to Bank of America's Spanish-speaking clients while reassuring English-speaking clients that they will continue to see all-English prompts on the screens.

MEDIA AND PUBLICITY PLAN

Total statewide conversion was completed in March 1991. A statewide blitz consisting of alternating flights of Spanish-language television and radio was executed in April and May. This was supported by ongoing outdoor and in-branch signage and collateral. A publicity plan was also developed that included the placement of Spanish-speaking bank spokespersons in statewide Spanish-language television and radio interviews. Press packets explaining the bilingual ATM roll-out were also prepared for both English- and Spanish-language media.

RESULTS

The addition of bilingual capabilities to all of Bank of America's ATMs proved to be very successful on a number of fronts. First of all, it proved to be one of the most distinguishing facts that differentiated the bank from its California competition. As a result of this strategy, along with the bilingual check series and Spanish-language tele-servicing, Bank of America continues to be considered the premier bank for Hispanics in California and continues to maintain the dominant share of the market with a consistent increase of well over 5,000 Hispanic banking households per month.

Also, within three months of the addition of the bilingual prompts on the screens, the bank's ratio of VERSATEL cards issued to cards used set a new national record for the industry.

As more and more Hispanic clients have become used to the ATMs, the bank's cost of doing business has decreased while its ability to provide more services and greater convenience to Hispanic clients has increased.

The best evaluation of these marketing efforts came from one of the bank's clients. After the bilingual ATM roll-out, the bank received the following comments from a customer:

> Dear Bank of America,
>
> I am writing to thank you for incorporating the Spanish-language into your ATM system. This is a major event in my life and my husband's. I read about this service in yesterday's newspaper. Last night we went to our local bank and after many years of banking with Bank of America, my husband was able for the first time to use the machine rapidly and easily without my help, by choosing the Spanish-language mode.
>
> My husband has about 20 relatives/friends in the area, most of whom have been similarly limited by their lack of English. At the next family reunion I will make a point to let them know of your new service. [This will also, 1) make the women more independent, 2) get them used to using plastic cards—most do not have cards of any type but rely on cash.]
>
> Also . . . I believe your new service is opening a door of access which will not only increase your business but lead to increased financial well-being and self-esteem in the lives of many . . . individuals. I am thrilled . . . You have given [younger people who come here with nothing but their willingness to work] control of their money. Thank you . . .

Case Study Contributor: Ennio L. Quevedo-García

Company: Bank of America, San Francisco, California

Media: Spanish-language television and radio, outdoor and in-branch advertising, press releases

CONTRIBUTOR'S PROFILE

■ Western Union

BACKGROUND

In the early to mid-1980s Mexico was taking a beating. Inflation mocked the value of its currency, unemployment soared to record levels, and two major earthquakes destroyed its key telecommunications facilities. Foreign affairs compounded Mexico's problems when Arab oil over-production created lower demand for Mexico's petroleum. With Mexico unable to make timely payments on its debt, its credit-worthiness slipped, as did the flow of international dollars into its banks. In the midst of this economic severity, two rates of exchange for the peso emerged: a controlled rate set by banks and a free rate, which fluctuated according to street demand. This adverse backdrop set the scene for much of Western Union's success in building its consumer money transfer business to Mexico.

Bienvenidos a los Estados Unidos

Mexicans sought economic opportunity in the United States, which soon became the beneficiary of an unskilled to semi-skilled labor pool of Mexican immigrants. North American corporations had a new and increasingly viable population to which they could market their goods and services. Perhaps the most fortunate companies were those whose businesses were communications related. Mexicans had left their families in their homeland in search of employment and the American dream. No matter what the outcome of their journey north, those pioneers had to communicate with a distant family while supporting that dream.

Western Union had long been in the business of transferring money for consumers from one point to another. It had distinguished itself as number one in its field and had an agent network that rivaled the size of the McDonald's franchise. The business was, at the time, primarily domestic, but "tolerating" a sluggish business to Mexico. The business was weighted down by an out-of-date revenue sharing agreement struck with the Mexican government some 20 years earlier. The constraints of that agreement left Western Union little room to optimize the profit margins; it had to focus on ways to deliver volume instead.

Understanding the Customer

In the early 1980s, the critical mass of Hispanics in the United States was composed of Mexicans and it was growing in record numbers. This, coupled with the increased amount of Spanish-language media utilized by giants like AT&T and Procter & Gamble, seemed to justify some marketing attention by Western Union.

One of the major challenges in planning the marketing effort was attempting to understand the customer base. Trying to research it would prove difficult, given it was largely undocumented. The Simpson Rodino Act, which granted amnesty to thousands of undocumented Mexicans, had not yet been passed. Applying traditional research techniques using a questionnaire and clipboard would have sent customers right into the arms of the "casas de cambio"/"money exchange houses" whose tactics for converting money and sending it were sometimes questionable. Nonetheless, these exchange houses represented the primary competition at the time.

Discovering the Competition

With little understanding of what drove the Hispanic money transferral business and what created the extraordinary swings in its volume, Western Union marketing specialists hit the streets. Accompanied by two bicultural members of the Spanish-language ad agency account team, marketers set out to go "undercover" into the barrios of southern California, Texas, and Chicago.

Marketers visited small money exchange houses and learned how they used the wildly fluctuating free rate of exchange of the peso to manipulate business. This enabled Western Union to read the signals and stave off competitive incursions. (Eventually, this became unnecessary once Mexico stabilized its currency in accordance with its promise to the International Monetary Fund.)

Western Union sent money transfers using the competition and contrasted the results with Western Union on price, delivery time and method, and density of coverage in Mexico. They uncovered the "shell game" perpetrated on unsuspecting Mexicans by some unsavory businesses and created a campaign that built trust in Western Union. They expanded their core of Spanish-speaking agents to accommodate the anticipated increase in demand.

Defining & Meeting Customer Needs

Western Union customers could send messages with their money transfers. The messages contained the destination, point of origin, and a marketer's dream—the purpose or application of the transaction. A survey of these messages provided another discovery for Western Union.

Going back twelve months, Western Union ordered a random pick of approximately 35,000 of the messages that accompanied the money transfers. They read and catalogued each money transfer message by destination and purpose. During the analysis, they determined that more than one-half of them were going to a very specific group of states in Mexico, whose locations were plotted on a large map. Western Union learned that each message had very precise information as to how the money was to be distributed, what it was to be used for, how much of it was to be put in the bank, and what event, such as a birthday, it commemorated.

Armed with this information, Western Union's ad agency was able to clear the use of the appropriate Mexican state songs for the radio campaign and create copy that played back just the right message to appeal to the ever-increasing numbers of recent arrivals into Western Union's Spanish-speaking agent locations.

CONTRIBUTOR'S PROFILE

Case Study Contributor: Bonnie A. Morrow, AT&T, New Jersey (formerly of Western Union)

Agency: Conill, Inc., New York, New York

Client: Western Union Financial Services, Inc.

Medium: Radio

Creative Director: Christian Dobles

■ CIBA Vision's Illusions

BACKGROUND

More than 23 million Hispanics reside in the United States. In fact, this number makes the U.S. Hispanic population the largest "Hispanic nation" within any non-Hispanic country. CIBA Vision and marketing research company Dorland Sweeney Jones (DSJ) found this high-profile population to be one of the most promising marketing opportunities for its Illusions® colored soft contact lenses for dark eyes.

Primary and secondary research conducted by DSJ found some remarkable facts about Hispanics. First, Hispanic females are highly expressive in nature, using their fashionable style of dress and their eyes, in particular, to express themselves. Second, regarding the product Illusions, independent research discovered that "Hispanics are 65 percent more likely than non-Hispanics to say they are interested in buying colored contact lenses" (Telemundo Group, Product Usage Study, 1990). Third, Hispanics trust and respect sources of authority, especially their eye care professionals and other health-care professionals.

THE PRODUCT

Illusions are soft contact lenses that change dark eyes into shades of blue, green, amber, and grey in a way that feels comfortable and looks natural.

PROBLEM

The challenge involved how to implement a "push-pull" campaign targeting U.S. Hispanics, a communications effort designed to reach both the professional eye-care audience and a receptive consumer audience to generate awareness about the unique benefits of Illusions soft contact lenses for dark eyes.

STRATEGY

The first line of attack was to convince eye-care professionals that if they stocked Illusions, the increase in business from Hispanic women could help them expand their practice. The second line was to convince the target consumer audience of Hispanic women that Illusions soft contact lenses for dark eyes are a product of preference when they want to change their look and enhance their natural beauty. It was important to convey that their eye-care professional can help them with all their vision-care needs.

SOLUTION

DSJ and CIBA Vision implemented the Hispanic Opportunity, the first comprehensive Hispanic marketing campaign in the vision-care industry. The multifaceted program included an educational, practice-building workshop for eye-care professionals in key Hispanic markets, as well as an innovative Spanish-language consumer advertising and promotional campaign in print and broadcast media, targeting not only Hispanic women but eye-care professionals in key Hispanic markets.

Practice-building workshops for eye-care professionals were held in three cities: San Antonio, Houston, and Los Angeles. DSJ created the format, inviting regional eye-care professionals and their staff to attend a seminar conducted by Hispanic market research

CIBA vision print ad.

experts and leading Hispanic eye-care professionals. The workshops delivered valuable market-specific insights about meeting the vision-care concerns of Hispanic patients in their communities.

In conjunction with the practice-building workshops in the target markets, CIBA Vision sponsored a Hispanic-consumer radio promotion. A series of six one-minute *novelas,* or soap operas, entitled "Ilusiones," aired for three weeks in San Antonio, Houston, Miami, and on the number-one-rated station in Los Angeles. The series, produced in Spanish by DSJ, depicted one man's search for his "illusion"—a mysterious, beautiful woman who wears Illusions soft contact lenses.

The DJs at each of the regional stations invited listeners to call into their stations to audition for the dramatic lead in the final *novela* episode. Callers were then invited to a live radio remote contest, also held in each market, to compete for the part.

Concurrent with this broadcast promotion, DSJ developed professional and consumer patient materials, direct mail, and ad co-op slicks—all in Spanish. These were designed to assist in educating and promoting both the product benefits and the radio *novela* episodes and contest.

DSJ achieved its primary objective of increasing awareness about Illusions soft contact lenses among Hispanic consumers and educating eye-care professionals about the opportunities for growth in reaching this receptive audience.

RESULTS

In each of the cities, there was significant attendance from major optical chains and the private eye-care professional community at the practice-building workshops. The radio promotion was also successful; during the first week of the promotion alone, the participating radio stations received approximately 20 to 30 calls per hour. These calls were a direct result of the radio *novela,* and the respondents who called requested more information about Illusions soft contact lenses. At the mall remotes, conducted by the participating radio stations, over 300 people attended to watch the contestants try out for the *novela* talent search and to obtain more information about Illusions contact lenses.

To date, participating eye-care professionals polled in all of the participating markets stated that there is a dramatic increase in the number of people inquiring about Illusions.

Case Study Contributors: Michael J. Heinley and Robert J. Morrison

CONTRIBUTOR'S PROFILE

Agency: Dorland Sweeney Jones, Philadelphia, Pennsylvania

Client: CIBA Vision

Media: Radio, direct mail, public relations, promotional materials, educational workshops

Creative Director: Robert J. Morrison

Art Director: Ron Lewis

Copywriters: Robert J. Morrison and Jim Shaw

■ Inter-American Book Services: Selling Spanish-Language Books through Direct Marketing Vehicles

BACKGROUND
Selling Spanish-language books in the United States is no easy task. However, there is a clear need for this product for two major reasons. First, the use of Spanish within the Hispanic community is still predominant (although in some cases Hispanics have had very limited education in the Spanish language, they still have some need for Spanish-language books because they provide a link with Hispanic culture).

Second, there is the proximity of the United States to Spanish-speaking America. From Mexico to Patagonia, the United States has for the last 200 years had a continuous link with a market of 300 million Spanish speakers. The most important market is Mexico, which is not only the United States' closest neighbor but also its third most important trade partner after Canada and Japan. The proximity of Spanish-speaking America to the United States has always had important economic, political, and cultural implications for this country; and thus, there is a clear need for information, in all areas of knowledge, about the countries of Spanish-speaking America. U.S. academics, independent researchers, and citizens with a vested interest in Spanish-speaking America, as well as a small segment of college-educated people from these countries who reside in the United States, also have a need for Spanish-language books.

These two reasons define two distinct segments of the population in need of Spanish-language books that make up the market segments for these products.

Inter-American Book Services, Inc. (IBS) identified these needs and chose direct marketing as the most efficient manner of reaching its market. It recognized that the availability of Spanish-language books is very limited, although areas such as Miami, New York, and Los Angeles have developed a limited market through Spanish-language bookstores. The following case study examines the operation of this company during its first year, the marketing process that was followed, and the results obtained.

IBS defines its objectives as follows: To address the needs of all users of Spanish-language books in the United States by providing the same variety and availability of these books as one would expect from a good bookstore in any Spanish-speaking country.

OBJECTIVE

In order to fulfill this objective, IBS signed contracts with 15 different publishers, including the largest Spanish-language publishing groups in the world, and arranged to import all the books—originally published in Mexico, Spain, and Argentina—directly from Mexico into southern California.

In order to achieve distribution on a national scale, IBS decided to reach consumers through direct marketing vehicles, mainly direct response advertising on Spanish-language TV, and direct mail catalogs.

By distributing an extensive catalog with a wide array of topics, IBS was providing the same variety found in bookstores in Mexico City or Buenos Aires to U.S. residents, including those living in areas with a low Hispanic population.

Based on the analysis previously described, IBS defines its potential market as two distinct segments:

MARKET

✦ The U.S. Hispanic Segment: IBS defined the typical member of this segment as the mass Spanish-speaking Hispanic consumer in need of a variety of Spanish-language books. Because the consumer profile for this segment shows low educational levels in either Spanish or English and low readership levels of any type of printed materials, including periodicals, IBS made a preliminary decision to promote only a reduced number of topics. After IBS visited a number of neighborhood bookstores, the company decided to promote books that would fulfill a practical need, such as dictionaries and self-improvement titles, and books covering current topics that haven't reached the Spanish-language market. This second area was defined in much the same fashion as Time-Life Books and other companies that concentrate on mass market subjects such as mystery, the occult, and other related topics.

⬧ The Academic Segment: The academic segment was divided into two subsegments:

The cover of El Mundo del Libro *catalog.*

1) Native Spanish speakers, Spanish-language speakers, and Spanish-as-a-second-language speakers with high income and educational levels.

2) All academic and research institutions in need of Spanish-language books.

It was evident that the U.S. Hispanic market represented the majority of IBS's potential market. The Hispanic market represented a low-income segment estimated to represent 70 percent of all U.S. Hispanics, or about 4 million households, in 1990. In contrast, the academic segment represented no more than 50,000 names including academic institutions.

IBS divided its strategy into two areas: mainstream (U.S. Hispanic market) and specialty (academic market).

MARKETING STRATEGY

IBS released a direct-response TV promotion every six weeks aimed at the Hispanic consumer. Strategically, this was the main source of revenue for IBS, which required continuity in order to meet key strategic goals, namely:

Mainstream

✧ To achieve recognition of the brand name, El Mundo del Libro.

✧ To generate revenue and cash flow to support staff and normal operations.

✧ To generate income to be used to finance the development, production, and distribution of the book catalog.

IBS further divided its mainstream strategy into two types of TV promotions:

✧ Promotions for books with a permanent consumer need, such as dictionaries, books that address pregnancy, sex education, child education, and self-improvement, and the Bible. These promotions were expected to produce a steady demand with small fluctuations throughout the year.

✧ Promotions for books with a seasonal appeal or need, such as mystery, sports, prophecy, and religious titles. These promotions bank on seasonal needs or a specific opportunity that develops for a variety of reasons. One of the most successful TV promotions was a package of four books called *Prophecies*, which was released at the beginning of the Gulf War.

Specialty IBS decided to release a 24-page catalog, two times a year, distributing 30,000 copies each time. The catalog was promoted as a book club, providing membership numbers and a frequent buyer discount system. The catalog was divided into five sections resembling the way bookstores are normally organized. The five sections were:

- ✧ Discount price titles and special promotions

- ✧ Spanish and Ibero-American literature

- ✧ World literature translated into Spanish

- ✧ History, philosophy, essays, biographies, dictionaries, religion, mystery, and esoteric titles

- ✧ Self-improvement, sex education, cooking, pregnancy and child-care, gardening, and manual skills titles

IBS's "specialty" strategy also intended to meet a number of goals:

- ✧ Recognition of El Mundo del Libro brand name among academic institutions

- ✧ Recognition as the source of the largest variety of Spanish-language books anywhere in the United States, with new releases as current as those entering the Spanish-speaking American markets

- ✧ Enough revenue to make this segment profitable

MEDIA STRATEGY IBS negotiated per inquiry (P.I.) rates and TV schedules with
Mainstream Univisión and Galavisión with ROS (Rotate on Schedule) insertions or fixed positions depending on availability of time.

- ✧ As a rule of thumb, IBS would schedule three to four spots a day, including prime-time spots.

- ✧ The regular release schedule was for a minimum of two weeks which could be extended indefinitely based on sales levels.

IBS identified specific lists available that met the profile for this segment:

Specialty

✧ The subscribers to the Spanish-language edition of *Americas* magazine, published by the Organization of American States (OAS). List profile: Median age is 55, mean income is $44,000, about 40 percent are not native Spanish-speaking subscribers, many subscribers are academic institutions.

✧ The subscribers to *Medico Interamericano,* a Spanish-language magazine for physicians. List profile: 95 percent of subscribers are physicians educated in Spanish-speaking America; most are in a high-income bracket.

✧ IBS sent over 700 catalogs to colleges and universities specifically identified as having a department of modern languages that included Spanish or a department of Latin American studies.

During its first year of operation, IBS was able to produce revenues of roughly $1,050,000, which was considered very positive for its first year. Of total sales, 93 percent came from direct-response TV as expected. Gross promotional profits averaged 35 percent, and gross operating profit provided margins close to 10 percent. Thus, IBS had a profitable operation for many months.

RESULTS

While TV promotions provided several "big hits," the catalog response was only 1.7 percent, which produced a gross promotional margin of only 7 percent. Although it was enough to cover direct costs, it did not justify the substantial hours put in by the staff to produce it. However, the catalog fulfilled functions important to IBS executives: increasing awareness of Hispanic culture at its best and promoting the habit of reading. For these reasons, IBS decided to maintain the catalog as long as it produced enough to pay all direct costs involved in its operation.

The TV promotions experienced most of their success with book promotional packages that fulfilled permanent needs. The *Prophecies* promotion, including a volume on Nostradamus, was lucky to be released at the same time that the conflict between Iraq and Kuwait exploded and operation Desert Storm commenced. This promotion was the fastest-selling item for IBS and would have continued to sell steadily if inventory had not been exhausted.

Although IBS did a very good job of securing inventory imported from Mexico "just in time" for the promotion, it was impossible to maintain continuity for this promotion for an indefinite period of time. Although sales were gradually decreasing, they reached a plateau that could have been maintained if advertising time would have remained available.

The largest selling promotion over a long period of time (11 months) was the Spanish-language Larousse dictionary, *El Pequeño Larousse Ilustrado*, which, as predicted, fulfilled a permanent need. The next best-selling promotions were a Spanish-English dictionary and sexual education and pregnancy information packages. These, too, fulfilled permanent needs.

In summary, of total revenues produced by direct-response TV advertising during the first year, the following promotions made the largest contributions:

Prophecies promotion #23.3%

Larousse dictionary #22.7%

Follow-Me dictionary #7.9%

Sexuality books #5.4%

Pregnancy books #4.9%

STRATEGIC HURDLES IBS was able to produce a profitable operation from the very start and was able to maintain an efficient procurement of inventories imported from Mexico, which at the beginning of the business was considered a possible bottleneck. However, IBS found it increasingly difficult to be able to secure advertising time from all sources in order to maintain optimum sales levels. Three major factors contributed to this obstacle:

1) The main sources of time for IBS—Univisión and Univisa (Televisa's U.S. operation)—were also using the network to market videos, music, and other items through direct-response advertising, making it difficult to secure time for IBS.

2) Books generally produce lower responses than most products such as music videos and audio packages. Thus,

since one spot with IBS produced less per-spot revenue for the medium, the TV networks normally preferred to sell an item with higher demand.

3) The media had been experiencing a constant change of owners and Univisión was again being put on the selling block, which contributed to a level of uncertainty and cautiousness.

IBS was able to create a profitable operation. However, the consumer habits of its primary market and the uncertainty that persisted in the media made it very difficult for IBS to remain profitable.

RESULTS

Books are unfortunately a relatively low-demand item and today, in 1993, neither Univisión nor Telemundo accept P.I. (per inquiry) advertisers. With Univisión in new hands once again, prospects for direct-response advertising remain to be seen. Until now, inventories appear to be low in both the networks and key spot markets. Since rates normally go up when inventories are low, Spanish-language media should enjoy higher revenues after years of limited growth. This should eventually release time for direct-response advertisers. However, past experience and current trends show that only "hot ticket items" would provide enough revenue for the media and for direct-response advertisers in order to achieve profitable results in a promotion. Thus, for books, only a very hot item could make it to the top of the chart of Spanish-language direct-response TV advertising.

Case Study Contributor: Alvaro de Regil

Agency: Mercatec Direct Associates, Los Angeles, California

CONTRIBUTOR'S PROFILE

Client: Inter-American Book Services, Inc.

Media: Television, print, direct mail

Creative Director: Silvia Fernandez de Ortiz

Art Directors: Benito Martinez Creel and Maria Amparo Escandon

El aguacate va con todo. ¡Qué Sabor!

One of the avocado campaign's in-store posters promoting the avocado as a versatile fruit.

■ California Avocado Commission: Hispanic Advertising Campaign

BACKGROUND

In 1991 the California Avocado Commission (CAC) launched a six-week advertising campaign in Fresno, California, targeting the Hispanic consumer market. The challenge was to motivate this target market, which already over-indexed in avocado usage, to increase frequency and consumption. The Fresno campaign was so successful that marketing agency Sosa, Bromley, Aguilar & Associates proposed it be expanded into three additional markets in 1992.

✧ The U.S. Hispanic population is growing five times faster than the general population, and more than 50 percent of this population resides in California and Texas.

✧ Based on test market results, advertising increased avocado consumption among Hispanics.

✧ During a period of advertising support, the Fresno Hispanic consumer purchased 10.7 avocados per month versus the 9.4 purchased during a period of no advertising. In addition, fre-

An in-store poster showing another way to serve avocado.

quency of avocado purchase once a week or more increased from 41 percent to 56 percent.

✧ There was an opportunity in the top California and Texas avocado markets to maximize grower return via a Hispanic market campaign.

✧ Floridian and Chilean avocados were in the markets, however there was no advertising to support sales.

✧ Los Angeles, Fresno, San Antonio, Dallas, and Fort Worth were chosen as target markets due to the high incidence of avocado consumption and Spanish-dominant Hispanics in each market.

✧ Hispanic women 18 to 49 years old, Spanish dominant, and the primary grocery shopper, were chosen as the target audience.

OBJECTIVE The advertising campaign's objective was to increase Hispanic sales and usage of California avocados in the Hispanic market, a segment in which the product already experienced a high incidence of usage.

MARKETING STRATEGIES
✧ Expand Fresno campaign to four top Hispanic ADIs.

✧ Create awareness through advertising and media promotional packages.

✧ Increase frequency of usage by communicating new uses for avocados.

✧ Utilize radio, print, and outdoor media to communicate creative messages.

✧ Utilize in-store merchandising to support creative message and generate immediate sales.

✧ Measure effectiveness of campaign through quantitative research.

MESSAGE The creative message focused on increasing frequency of avocado use among Hispanics rather than attempting to increase the number of Hispanics using avocados. The executions introduced new uses for avocados. The campaign also reminded the consumer of more traditional avocado dishes, thus featuring the avocado as a versatile fruit.

    ✧ Expanded Fresno test to include Los Angeles, San Antonio, Dallas, Fort Worth, and Fresno.

Outline of 1992 California Avocado Commission Plan

    ✧ Campaign ran January to May and included a six-week launch and a maintenance schedule.

    ✧ Baseline media plan (radio, print, outdoor) was enhanced at selected periods through promotions. Promotional packages included radio remotes, live liners, and recipe contests.

In order to measure the objective of increasing Hispanic sales and usage of California avocados, quantitative research was conducted including:

RESEARCH

    ✧ Hispanic Awareness and Usage Tracking Study (San Antonio and Los Angeles)

    ✧ Sales Tracking Study (San Antonio)

The study was conducted in April/May 1992. In 1990, Sosa conducted an awareness and usage study in Los Angeles that was used as a benchmark before launching the campaign. The results for the 1992 study were compared, when applicable, to the data obtained in the study conducted in 1990.

Hispanic Tracking Study
BACKGROUND

    ✧ To determine the opportunities for expanding avocado consumption among Hispanics.

OBJECTIVES

    ✧ To track advertising awareness, attitudes, and usage of avocados among Hispanics in Los Angeles and San Antonio.

    ✧ To measure the impact of the CAC Hispanic advertising campaign.

A total of 300 interviews were completed in Los Angeles and San Antonio (150 in each market). In order to participate, respondents had to meet the following qualifications: Hispanic female; primary grocery shopper; Spanish dominant and bilingual; 18 to

METHODOLOGY

54 years of age; watch at least five hours of Spanish-language TV per week; past users, current users, or non-users of avocados.

OBJECTIVE   ✧ To track sales among Hispanics and non-Hispanics before and during the California Avocado Commission's Hispanic advertising campaign.

METHODOLOGY   The movement of avocado sales in San Antonio was tracked through H.E.B.'s Scanner Data Service, provided by KWEX-TV. The data represented the sales activity of five Hispanic stores and five non-Hispanic stores of comparable sales revenue and square footage.

RESULTS   Results from the awareness and usage tracking study show clear signs that the California Avocado Commission's Hispanic Advertising campaign reached the Hispanic market and managed to accomplish the following:

✧ From 1990 to 1992 advertising awareness increased among Hispanics in Los Angeles (from 30 percent to 35 percent). Almost one-half of the Hispanics in San Antonio (47 percent) were aware of Spanish advertising for avocados.

✧ Virtually all Hispanics (98 percent) were current avocado users (in Los Angeles and San Antonio). In Los Angeles, purchase of avocados increased significantly from 1990 to 1992 (from 81 percent to 97 percent).

✧ An average of 17 avocados were purchased in the past month among current users in Los Angeles and San Antonio. In Los Angeles, the number of avocados purchased in the prior month increased significantly (18, versus 10 in 1990).

The findings of the sales tracking study show that the campaign had a positive impact in the H.E.B. stores that were monitored accomplishing the following:

✧ When the campaign was launched in February, comparing 1991 sales to 1992, avocado units sold in Hispanic stores increased from 23,000 to 107,000, while those sold in non-Hispanic stores went from 19,000 to 42,000.

✧ Avocado sales increased in the month of April 1992 compared with 1991 sales, even through the average price per unit increased.

Case Study Contributors: Patricia Perea (Research) and Palmira Arellano (Public Relations)

Agency: Sosa, Bromley, Aguilaw and Associates, San Anotnio, Texas

Client: California Avocado Commision

Media: Radio, newspaper, in-store posters, outdoor, and bus shelters (transit)

Creative Director: Federico Traeger

Art Director: Ruben Cubillos

Account Management: Ernest Bromley

CONTRIBUTOR'S PROFILE

■ Education Now And Babies Later (ENABL)

Unintended teen pregnancy exacts an enormous toll both on the individuals involved and on society. The problem is particularly severe in California, which has a higher percentage of young people than most other states and the second highest rate of reported teen pregnancy in the country. In 1989, 11.4 percent of all live births in California were to teenage mothers, of which more than a third were to girls 17 years or younger. This was an increase of 25 percent over 1980 (California Health and Welfare Agency, 1991). Yet the teenage birthrate doesn't tell the whole story. Studies show that the birthrate for this group represents only half of the pregnancies among California adolescents.

Teenage mothers are far less likely to complete high school and will start their adult life economically handicapped. The consequences for society are enormous. California teen mothers represent $225 million expended annually in Aid to Families with Dependent Children (AFDC) grants and food stamps and com-

BACKGROUND

prise 11 percent of current AFDC applications. In 1985, California spent more than $3 billion on families that were begun when the mother was a teenager.

In addition to the startling statistics on unintended teen pregnancy, the increase in sexually transmitted diseases and, notably, the appearance and spread of AIDS have brought a renewed emphasis on sex education in communities and schools. Many sex education programs and mass media campaigns are typically knowledge based, implying an individual's understanding of the consequences of personal actions. But research has shown that until the age of 16, a young person's ability to recognize the potential impact of his or her choices is limited. Thus, there is a need to create educational programs specific to the needs of this young audience—programs that consider and address the pubertal changes and social and peer pressures that exert significant influence on this group.

The state of California Department of Health Services, Office of Family Planning, developed a program to address these needs. Called Education Now And Babies Later (ENABL), the program is the educational component of Governor Pete Wilson's comprehensive initiative to reduce the incidence of teen pregnancy in California. ENABL is a broad informational and educational program for young men and women to help them learn and practice the skills necessary to postpone sexual activity.

The primary audience is California boys and girls ages 12 to 14. This age group was selected because the ENABL program is designed to reach kids before they have become sexually active, helping them to modify current attitudes regarding sexual activity and to ultimately change behavior. The Hispanic community, having the largest incidence of teen pregnancy in California, is a primary ethnic target. The program also targets the African-American, Asian, and non-Hispanic white communities. The secondary audience is parents of 12- to 14-year-olds, with a special emphasis on Hispanic parents.

OBJECTIVES   ✧ To create awareness among the target audience that they do not have to feel pressured to engage in sexual activity before they are ready.

✧ To attain an advertising recall score of 50 percent.

✧ To change attitudes about early sexual behavior by introducing carefully researched messages sensitive to the physical, cultural, demographic, psychosocial, and behavior characteristics of California youth.

✧ To create awareness and inform parents of 12- to 14-year-olds about the program so that parents can talk with their teens about the pressures they face with regard to engaging in sexual activity.

Advertising, Marketing, and Other Programs

In addition to the advertising campaign produced by San Francisco ad agency Gardner, Geary, Coll & Young, the California Office of Family Planning has funded 28 ENABL direct education projects which will bring the ENABL curriculum to more than 200,000 teens throughout 30 California counties, as well as to parents and the general community. Edelman Worldwide headed up a statewide public relations program, including promotional activities, that began in May 1992 and will continue through 1994. The ethnic public relations firms were Lagrant (African-American), Imada Wong (Asian-American), and VME (Hispanic-American).

CREATIVE STRATEGY

The creative strategy was to convince the primary target audience that they can say and hear "no" to sex while maintaining their self-esteem and that of the other person. Today's teens are experiencing enormous pressure to become sexually active. They are pressured by their friends and by society. They see and hear messages to engage in sexual activity on TV, on the radio, and in the magazines they read. Gardner found, through extensive formative research, that teens do not respond to or absorb authoritative or parental messages. "Just say no" makes teens tune out and turn off. Instead, teens speaking to their peers in their own language about the realities of the pressures they face is more effective. "If you're not ready, you're not alone" is the central theme in all communications to the teen target. It is very important to the teens that they don't feel that they are struggling with the issue alone. It is supportive of the teen's own self-esteem because it does not make the teen feel wrong for wanting sex, or for waiting. It gives them the choice to say no. Importantly, it is validated by all ethnic groups.

Gardner's findings with regard to the attitudes and values of the Hispanic community were instrumental to the final creative product and media plan. From their research they learned that there is a marked difference in attitudes about sexual issues between the Hispanic community and other ethnic communities in California. In the Hispanic culture, discussion of sexual issues is taboo. Young girls—"good girls"—do not engage in sexual activity prior to marriage—no discussion. The advertising had to send a message to Hispanic parents that the pressure to engage in sexual activity is a reality to their kids and show them that by talking to their children, they can help them resist these pressures.

MEDIA STRATEGY Television and radio were chosen because of their unparalleled ability to effectively reach and impact teens. One hundred percent of the teen advertising dollars was placed in these two media vehicles in order to achieve maximum impact and awareness from the advertising effort. Both television and radio have the ability to carry an emotional message and deliver it with impact to the young teen target. Prime-time programs chosen on Fox were "Beverly Hills 90210," "In Living Color," "The Simpsons," and "Married with Children." Fox leads in teen audiences with 8 out of the top 10 most-watched programs by teens, including Hispanic, African American, and non-Hispanic white teens alike. "Fresh Prince of Bel Air" and "Blossom" were chosen on NBC because they are the #2- and #3-rated shows. The ad agency wanted to capture the after-school viewing by teens, so early fringe/prime access programs were chosen, such as "Who's the Boss," "Charles in Charge," and "The Cosby Show." These shows average between a 4.0 and 11.0 teen rating, depending on the market. MTV Internacional was chosen to target the Hispanic audience because the network enjoys the same high recognition among teens as does basic MTV. Both Fox and MTV allowed advertisers to reach teens in an environment they consider "cool," making the ads more likely to impact behavior.

Radio complimented the television advertising by adding both reach and frequency. Album-oriented rock stations and contemporary hit radio were chosen, reaching over 90 percent of California's teens.

Television and print were also used to reach Hispanic parents of 12- to 14-year-olds. Ads were aired extensively on Telemundo and Univisión. Prime-time soaps (*novelas*) like "Velo Negro" and "Muchachitas" were integral to the media mix. Print ads were placed in major Spanish-language newspapers across California.

Hispanic Market Connections headed up the formative phase of the research, working closely with Gardner, Geary, Coll & Young in carrying out the research and interpreting the findings. IOX Assessment Associates was responsible for the media evaluation research.

RESEARCH

ENABL print ad: "Don't wait/talk to your children."

Formative Research   A total of 21 focus group discussions were conducted throughout the state of California to research the issue of sexual pressure as well as the ethnic communities being targeted. The groups took place with boys and girls, 12 to 14 years old, parents of 12- to 14-year-olds, and others who influence teens. Separate groups took place for each of the ethnic groups—Hispanic, African American, non-Hispanic white, and Asian. The moderators also represented the ethnic and gender diversity of the groups.

ENABL print ad: The Spanish headline warns parents that "More kids are getting involved in after-school activities."

ESTOS DIAS, MAS NIÑOS ESTAN PARTICIPANDO EN ACTIVIDADES DESPUES DE LA ESCUELA.

Si usted piensa que sus hijos solo están jugando, prepárese para una sorpresa.

Ahora, más y más niños están participando en actividades de manera diferente. Están teniendo relaciones sexuales. Y lo están teniendo cada vez más jóvenes. Desde los 12, 13 y 14 años.

Muchas veces participan por presión de sus amistades.

Y muchas veces, el resultado es mal afortunado. Veinte mil niñas en California dejan la escuela cada año por embarazo. Y las estadísticas muestran que las niñas hispanas son las que menos regresan a la escuela.

Hay una solución. Un programa nuevo, patrocinado por el estado, llamado "Educación Ahora, Hijos Después" (ENABL) es específicamente diseñado para enseñarle a los niños de 12 a 14 años en aprender lo que necesitan para controlar la presión de sus amistades y posponer relaciones sexuales.

Queremos ayudar. Pero no lo podemos hacer solos. Usted también tiene que hablar con sus hijos. Ellos necesitan saber que usted entiende sus problemas. Y que su familia está allí para apoyarlos.

No es fácil. Pero juntos podemos hacer la diferencia.

No espere. Hable con sus hijos hoy.

Comprométase. Antes de que lo hagan ellos.

ENABL

COMPROMETASE. ANTES DE QUE LO HAGAN ELLOS.

Two California school districts were chosen for the evaluation of ENABL advertising. The Sacramento Unified City School District functioned as the higher-intensity media site and the Santa Monica-Malibu Unified School District functioned as the lower-intensity media site. Prior to the campaign, questionnaires were distributed to more than 1,100 eighth-graders at three Sacramento schools and four Santa Monica schools. At the end of September 1992, approximately one month after the conclusion of the initial six-week ENABL advertising campaign, questionnaire data were gathered from almost 1,300 Sacramento and Santa Monica students. Post-campaign data were collected from over 1,100 students at the same sites about one month after the conclusion of the 1993 campaign.

Evaluative Research

✧ Total net awareness was nearly 80 percent at both sites, well exceeding the project goal of 50 percent awareness.

**RESULTS
Campaign
Awareness**

✧ From mid-campaign to post-campaign, the number of students who demonstrated unaided recall of the ENABL advertisements more than doubled in the higher intensity site.

✧ For radio advertisements, total net awareness was significantly greater in the higher-intensity site.

✧ Students surveyed at the higher-intensity site had better responses (which is to say responses more in line with the ENABL objectives) on all questionnaire items for which there were significant differences (e.g., "best age" for having sex, most guys/girls my age have had sex, more guys/girls are waiting to have sex, sex with people you don't know well is okay, sex is okay for two people who love each other).

**Normative
Perceptions**

Total scores from the higher-intensity site increased on all three items and were significantly different from scores of students at the lower-intensity site (e.g. stop dancing with guy/girl making moves at you, could refuse to go to guy's/girl's house, avoid sex despite pressure from guy-/girlfriend).

Confidence

Significantly smaller proportions of students had sex for the first time in the higher-intensity site than in the lower-density site.

**Sex-Related
Behavior**

Case Study Contributor: Gayle Geary

**CONTRIBUTOR'S
PROFILE**

Agency: Gardner, Geary, Coll & Young, San Francisco, California

Client: State of Claifornia Department of Health Services, Office of Family Planning

Media: Television, radio, and print

Creative Director: John Coll

Senior Copywriter: Marcie Judelson

■ Immigration and Naturalization Service Amnesty

BACKGROUND   The Immigration Reform and Control Act of 1986 mandated a public awareness program to communicate to illegal aliens the conditions and process under which they could legalize their status in the United States. An important objective of the Immigration and Naturalization Service (INS) was to encourage as high a number of eligible illegal aliens as possible to apply for legalization. La Agencia de Orcí & Asociados was selected to manage the entire advertising program.

STRATEGY   La Agencia designed a series of multimedia and multilingual campaigns throughout the United States and Puerto Rico. Initially, the basic thrust would be to communicate specific information regarding the major issues inhibiting the application process.

Issues such as family separation, deportation in case of ineligibility, and how to prove length of residence were discussed in depth in advertising placed in radio, newspapers, magazines, and public affairs programming. Television, radio, and out-of-home were used to generate immediate and sustained awareness, as well as to motivate those eligible to apply.

PROGRAM   A highly rated television analysis program was conceived. "La Nueva Ley: Analisis a Fondo" ("The New Law: A Thorough Analysis") was produced and aired on Los Angeles' Spanish television station, KMEX, and on other Univisión affiliates.

Although a majority of the target audience was Spanish-speaking, it was deemed essential to communicate the message in as

INS print ad: "Let me tell you what Immigration said about how to prove how long we've lived in the United States."

many languages as available, to assure the greatest possible coverage. To accomplish this, a radio campaign in 48 languages was developed and run.

Informative advertising ran in over 108 daily newspapers (in English, Spanish, Chinese, Japanese, Korean, Tagalog, Laotian, Vietnamese, and Cambodian). Magazine advertising ran in major publications such as *U.S. News & World Report.*

Public relations and community affairs efforts conducted by

Audio: Millones de inmigrantes   están por alcanzar su meta.   La meta

Millions of immigrants   *are about to reach their goal.*   *The goal*

por medio de su esfuerzo.   De asegurar un futuro brillante   para sus hijos.

through their efforts.   *Of providing a bright future*   *for their children.*

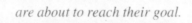

en este largo viaje.   Pero si no se toma   antes del 4 de mayo,

in their long journey.   *But if it's not taken*   *by May 4th,*

de vivir en este gran pais

of living legally

legalmente.

in this great country.

De superarse

Of succeeding

(Music and Train Effect)

Aplicar para la legalización

Applying for legalization

es el último paso

is the last step

la oportunidad

the opportunity

se perderá para siempre.

will be lost forever.

No se quede atrás. Aplique ya.

Don't get left behind. Apply now.

other organizations and agencies contributed to the outstanding success of the program.

RESULTS   ✧ Thorough research was a basic part of the program. Results were measured on a regular basis and adjustments to the program were made as needed.

✧ Survey research confirmed that nearly 95 percent of the target audience was aware of the law and its key provisions. Having achieved a high level of awareness, the agency was able to communicate the requirements for legalization and how to meet them. By the end of the campaign more than 90 percent of the people the INS wanted to reach knew what steps to take and how to take them.

✧ An interesting conclusion of the research concerned the image of the INS, the government agency empowered to implement the law. It was learned that the INS had a reputation for professionalism and fairness, and could be relied upon to tell the truth.

✧ The image of the INS, already positive, improved as the law was implemented and more applicants went through the process.

✧ The clearest demonstration of the success of the campaign was the number of those eligible who filled out an application and paid the application fee.

✧ Approximately 3.2 million applications went through the process, well beyond expectations.

CONTRIBUTOR'S   **Case Study Contributor:** Héctor Orcí
PROFILE
Agency: La Agencia de Orcí & Asociados, Los Angeles, California

Client: Immigration and Naturalization Service (INS)

Media: Television, radio, magazines, newspapers, and outdoor

Creative Director: Norma Orcí

Sourcebook:

Who to Call for What

■ *Consultants*

JUAREZ AND ASSOCIATES, INC.
12139 National Blvd.
Los Angeles, CA 90064
Phone: (310) 478–0826
Fax: (310) 479–1863

Type of Consultation: Offers research and management consulting services to government, institutional and private sector clients: general management; survey and socioeconomic research; program review and evaluation; general and Hispanic marketing; employment, training and development services. Complete bilingual capabilities in English and Spanish. Geographic areas served: U.S., Latin America, and Spain. Small minority-owned firm. **Founded:** 1971. **Principal Executive:** Nicandro F. Juarez, President. **Staff:** 25.

MARKET DEVELOPMENT, INC.
1643 6th Ave.
San Diego, CA 92101
Phone: (619) 232–5628
Fax: (619) 232–0373

Type of Consultation: MDI specializes in full-service qualitative and quantitative research for the U.S. Hispanic market and Mexico. Custom research services include Spanish-language focus groups (in-house staff of bilingual moderators), concept testing and consumer surveys. Standardized research services include: Consumer Linkage, a structured technique for generating advertising strategies; and Hispanic Copy Trac, a quantitative copy-testing system for Spanish-language commercials. Also offered is Hispanic Omnibus and Hispanic Teen Omnibus, national surveys of the Hispanic market, conducted quarterly. Consumer surveys and omnibus study are supported by an in-house, 35 station bilingual telephone interviewing facility. Firm's strength is strategic counsel in U.S. Hispanic and Latin American marketing/advertising, especially cross-cultural consumer behavior. MDI serves a wide range of industries, including, but not limited to: consumer durables, consumer non-durables, and services. Geographic areas served: U.S., Mexico and Latin America. Small, minority, woman-owned firm. **Founded:** 1978. **Principal Executives:** Loretta H. Adams, President; Henry Adams-Esquivel, Executive Vice President; Roger S. Sennott, Vice President. **Seminars and Workshops:** Transcultural Marketing/Advertising: Rationale, Methods and Strategy Development; Strategic Cross-Marketing in Specific Product Categories/Industries. **Staff:** 30.

TARGET MARKETING RESEARCH GROUP, INC.
PO Box 8653
Miami, FL 33255–8653
Phone: (305) 262–1606
Fax: (305) 262–0372

Special Note: Maintains office at 5805 Blue Lagoon Dr., Ste. 185, Miami, FL 33126–2019.

Types of Consultation: Specializes in conducting custom

primary marketing research among U.S. Hispanic and Puerto Rican consumers on a national level. Design, administer and analyze qualitative and quantitative projects. Industries served: marketing research industry, advertisers and advertising agencies, as well as government agencies. Geographic areas served: U.S. and Caribbean. Small, minority-owned firm. **Founded:** 1989. **Principal Executive:** Martin G. Cerda, President. **Staff:** 8.

MARTHA GARMA ZIPPER

5715 Silent Brook Ln.
Rolling Meadows, IL 60008
Phone: (708) 397–1513
Fax: (708) 397–9016

Type of Consultation: Hispanic qualitative research consultant specializes in the Hispanic market. Conducts Hispanic research in fluent Spanish. Covers all facets of a qualitative project (focus groups or individual depth interviews: design and translate screeners and discussion guides, coordinate fieldwork, moderate in English or Spanish, and provide simultaneous translator as well as analyze and summarize observations). Industries served: consumer products and services, education, food, health care, transportation, restaurants, hair care, financial industries, retail, advertising, packaging, promotions, and telecommunications. Geographic areas served: U.S. Small, minority owned firm. **Founded:** 1986. **Principal Executive:** Martha Garma Zipper. **Seminars and Workshops:** The Value of Research among Hispanics. **Staff:** 1.

■ *Directories*

BURRELLE'S HISPANIC MEDIA DIRECTORY
BURRELLE'S MEDIA DIRECTORIES

75 E. Northfield Rd.
Livingston, NJ 07039
Phone: (201) 992–6600
Fax: (201) 992–7675
Free: 800–631–1160

Newspapers, magazines, newsletters, radio and television programs, and other media serving the interests of the Hispanic population. Entries include publication or station name, address, phone, names and titles of key personnel, description of publication or program. **Frequency:** Irregular; previous edition 1989; latest edition August 1990.

HISPANIC AMERICANS INFORMATION DIRECTORY

Gale Research Inc.
835 Penobscot Bldg.
Detroit, MI 48226–4094
Phone: (313) 961–2242
Fax: (313) 961–6083
Free: 800–877–GALE

About 4,900 sources of information on a variety of aspects of Hispanic American life and culture, including national, state, and local organizations; publishers of newspapers, periodicals, newsletters, and other publications and videos; television and radio stations; library collections; museums and other cultural institutions; Hispanic studies programs and research centers; federal and state government agencies; and awards, honors, and prizes. Entries include name, address, phone, name and title of contact, description of services, activities, etc. **Frequency:** Biennial, odd years.

HISPANIC MEDIA & MARKETS DIRECTORY

Standard Rate & Data Service
3004 Glenview Rd.
Wilmette, IL 60091
Phone: (708) 256–6067
Fax: (708) 441–2264
Free: 800–323–4601

Over 1,000 Hispanic-targeted media, including radio and television stations, newspapers, consumer and business publications, outdoor advertising, and direct mail lists. Entries include company name, address, phone, telex, names and titles of contact and other key personnel, subsidiary and branch names and locations, description of projects and services, market information, and media rates. **Frequency:** Quarterly.

■ *Electronic Resources*

CHICANO DATABASE ON CD-ROM

University of California, Berkeley
Chicano Studies Library
3404 Dwinelle Hall
Berkeley, CA 94720
Phone: (415) 642–3859
Fax: (415) 642–6456

Contains more than 42,000 citations, with abstracts, to literature written by and about Chicanos (Mexican Americans) and other Latinos in the United States. Corresponds to *Arte Chicano: An Annotated Bibliography of Chicano Art* (from 1965 to 1981), *The Chicano Anthology Index*, *The Chicano Index* (from 1989 to date) and *The Chicano Periodical Index* (from 1967 to 1988). Also includes the Latinos and AIDS database, produced by the Chicano Research Center at the University of California, Los Angeles, which provides about 200 citations to journal articles, books, and reports on AIDS as it relates to Latin Americans. **Electronic mail address:** cslassistantlibrary.berkeley.edu. **Format:** CD-ROM. **Language used in database:** English. **Subject coverage:** All topics pertaining to the Chicano (Mexican-American) experience including information on other Latinos in the United States.

DEMOGRAPHIC LATINO PROFILES

Latino Institute
228 S. Wabash, 6th Fl.
Chicago, IL 60604

Phone: (312) 663–3603
Fax: (312) 663–4023

Contains population figures as well as data on the primary status, income, educational attainment, school enrollment, and labor force status of Latinos in the Chicago, Illinois area within the following geographic areas: the city of Chicago; 77 community areas within Chicago; 14 Chicago-area suburbs with significant Latino population; Cook, DuPage, Kane, Lake, McHenry, and Will counties; Metropolitan Chicago (six-county area); suburban metropolitan Chicago; the state of Illinois; and the Fourth U.S. District. **Format:** Batch access. **Language used in database:** English. **Subject coverage:** Latino demographic data pertaining to the Chicago, Illinois area.

HAPI ONLINE

University of California, Los Angeles
Latin America Center
405 Hilgard Ave.
Los Angeles, CA 90024
Phone: (310) 825–1057
Fax: (310) 206–2634

Contains more than 180,000 citations to periodical articles, documents, book reviews, original literary works, and other materials appearing in scholarly journals of interest to Latin Americanists. Also covers journals treating United States-Mexico border issues and Hispanic groups in the United States. Sources include more than 400 journals published in North and South America and in Europe. Corresponds to *Hispanic American Periodicals Index (HAPI)* and the HAPI Online database and in part to the Latin American Studies, Volume I: Multidisciplinary CD-ROM product. **Format:** Batch access. **Language used in database:** English. **Subject coverage:** Topics relating to Latin America in the areas of the humanities and social sciences, including business and industry; the United States and Mexico border region; Hispanic groups in the U.S.

MINORITY MARKETS ALERT

EPM Communications, Inc.
488 E. 18 St.
Brooklyn, NY 11226
Phone: (718) 469–9330
Fax: (718) 469–7124

Contains the complete text of *Minority Markets Alert,* a monthly newsletter covering current research on the buying patterns of minority consumers. Covers trends, lifestyles, priorities, attitudes, and consumer and demographic patterns of Hispanic, Black, and Asian American groups. Each summary contains complete contact and price information. Sources include reports and studies conducted by research companies, government agencies, and universities. **Format:** Online. **Language used in database:** English. **Subject coverage:** Trends within Hispanic, Black, and Asian American markets.

■ *Journals and Magazines*

HISPANIC BUSINESS

360 S. Hope Ave., Ste. C
Santa Barbara, CA 93105–4017
Phone: (805) 682–5843
Fax: (805) 687–4546

English-language business magazine catering to Hispanic professionals, executives, and entrepreneurs. **Established:** 1979. **Frequency:** Monthly. **Subscription:** $18.

HISPANIC REVIEW OF BUSINESS

Latin National Publishing Corp.
2 Penn Plaza, Ste. 1500
New York, NY 10121
Phone: (212) 564–4255

Magazine reporting on Hispanic business. **Established:** 1981. **Frequency:** 10x/yr. **Subscription:** $26.

HISPANIC TIMES MAGAZINE

PO Box 579
Winchester, CA 92596
Phone: (708) 790–9488

Magazine focusing on business and careers (English and Spanish). **Established:** 1978. **Frequency:** 5x/yr. **Subscription:** $30; $3.50 single issue.

MINORITIES AND WOMEN IN BUSINESS

Venture X, Inc.
PO Drawer 210
Burlington, NC 27216
Phone: (919) 229–1462
Fax: (919) 222–7455

Magazine networks with major corporations and small businesses owned and operated by minority and female entrepreneurs. **Established:** October 1984. **Frequency:** 6x/yr. **Subscription:** Free to qualified subscribers; $15; $36 three years.

MINORITY BUSINESS ENTREPRENEUR

924 N. Market St.
Inglewood, CA 90302
Phone: (310) 673–9398
Fax: (310) 673–0170

Business magazine for the ethnic minority business owner. **Established:** Fall 1984. **Frequency:** 6x/yr. **Subscription:** Free to qualified subscribers; $12.

■ *National Hispanic Organizations*

HISPANIC ORGANIZATION OF PROFESSIONALS AND EXECUTIVES
87 Catoctin Ct.
Silver Spring, MD 20906
Phone: (301) 598–2535
Stanley Valadez, Executive Director

Promotes Hispanic participation in free enterprise and political systems. Fosters development of Hispanic professionals and executives and seeks an increase in their number; acts as catalyst in formation of private enterprise endeavors and community programs. Works to establish links among national and international professional and executive sectors. Holds annual awards dinner. Serves as sponsoring organization for: Hispanic Cultural Institute; Hispanic First Federal Credit Union; Hispanic Heritage Foundation; HopeAmerica Investment Clubs. **Founded:** 1973. **Members:** 990. **Publications:** Newsletter, semiannual.

INTERRACIAL COUNCIL FOR BUSINESS OPPORTUNITY
51 Madison Ave., Ste. 2212
New York, NY 10010
Phone: 800–252–4226
Fax: (212) 779–4365
Lorraine Kelsey, Executive Officer

Assists minority businessmen and women in developing, owning, and managing business ventures with substantial employment and economic impact. Services include business feasiblity studies, financing, market development, and other technical assistance to start or expand minority-owned companies. Offers free management training courses. **Founded:** 1963. **Publications:** Annual report. Newsletter, monthly.

LULAC FOUNDATION
400 1st St. NW, Ste. 721
Washington, DC 20001
Phone: (202) 628–8516
Fax: (202) 628–8518
Elva Perez, Executive Director

Individuals committed to the improvement of economic, educational, health, and social conditions in America. Seeks to create an alliance between Hispanics and corporate America. Serves as a research, organization, training, and education resource on issues of importance to the U.S. Hispanic community. **Founded:** 1973. **Members:** 35. **Publications:** *The Future of Puerto Rico, Voices from the Americas, U.S. Immigration Reform, U.S. Foreign Policy in Latin America, If Not Contadora, Then What?,* and *The English Only Movement: An Agenda for Discrimination* (booklets).

THE MEDIA INSTITUTE
1000 Potomac St. NW, Ste. 204
Washington, DC 20007
Phone: (202) 298–7512
Patrick D. Maines, President

Encourages and promotes the development of knowledge and understanding of American media and communications. Conducts research into the legal, economic, and political aspects of the media and communications industry and its role in American society. Maintains a multidirectional program of research that focuses on media performance, the role of new technologies, and communications policy issues; operates the First Amendment Center, Hispanic Media Center, Center for Media Analysis, and Center for the Protection of Creative Rights. Sponsors luncheon discussion series and seminars. **Founded:** 1976. **Publications:** Books, research studies, monographs, and conference proceedings.

NATIONAL ASSOCIATION OF MINORITY WOMEN IN BUSINESS
906 Grand Ave., Ste. 200
Kansas City, MO 64106
Phone: (816) 421–3335
Fax: (816) 421–3336
Inez Kaiser, President

Minority women in business ownership and management positions; college students. Serves as a network for the exchange of ideas and information on business opportunities for minority women in the public and private sectors. Conducts research; sponsors workshops, conferences, seminars, and luncheons. Maintains speakers' bureau, hall of fame, and placement service; compiles statistics; bestows awards to women who have made significant contributions to the field. **Founded:** 1972. **Members:** 5000. **Publications:** *Today,* bimonthly. Newsletter.

NATIONAL COUNCIL OF LA RAZA
810 1st St. NE, 3rd Floor
Washington, DC 20002
Phone: (202) 289–1380
Fax: (202) 289–8173
Raul Yzaguirre, President

National umbrella organization working for civil rights and economic opportunities for Hispanics. Provides technical assistance to Hispanic community-based organizations in comprehensive community development, including economic development, housing, employment and training, business assistance, health, and other fields. Conducts research programs; compiles statistics; bestows awards; advocates on behalf of Hispanics. Offers private sector resource development training, proposal writing seminar, and board of directors training. Provides policy analysis. **Founded:** 1968. **Members:** 147. **Publications:** *Action Alerts,* periodic. *Agenda,* quarterly newsletter. *Backgrounders, Issue Briefs,* periodic. *Education Network News,* quarterly newsletter.

Elderly Network News, quarterly newsletter. *Policy Analysis Monographs,* periodic. *Poverty Network News,* quarterly newsletter. Also publishes handbooks and manuals, statistical analyses, and news releases.

NATIONAL HISPANIC CORPORATE COUNCIL

2323 N. 3rd. St., Ste. 101
Phoenix, AZ 85004
Phone: (602) 495–1988
Fax: (602) 495–9085
Joanne Samora, Director

Companies interested in exploring the business potential of the growing Hispanic market. Acts as clearinghouse of Hispanic marketing information, expertise, and counsel. Helps identify Hispanic executives among major U.S. companies and provides networking development opportunities for member organizations. **Founded:** 1985. **Members:** 70. **Publications:** Newsletter and annual report.

NATIONAL MINORITY BUSINESS COUNCIL

235 E. 42nd St.
New York, NY 10017
Phone: (212) 573–2385
Fax: (212) 573–4462
John F. Robinson, CEO and President

Minority businesses in all areas of industry and commerce. Seeks to increase profitability by developing marketing, sales, and management skills in minority businesses. Acts as an informational source for the national minority business community. Programs include: a legal services plan that provides free legal services to members in such areas as sales contracts, copyrights, estate planning, and investment agreement; a business referral assistance program that provides technical assistance in developing foreign markets; an executive banking program that teaches members how to package a business loan for bank approval; a procurement outreach program for minority and women business owners. Conducts continuing management education and provides assistance in teaching youth the free enterprise system. Bestows awards. **Founded:** 1972. **Members:** 400. **Publications:** *Corporate Minority Vendor Directory,* annual. *Corporate Purchasing Directory,* annual. *NMBC Business Report,* bimonthly. *NMBC Corporate Purchasing Directory,* periodic.

NATIONAL SOCIETY OF HISPANIC MBAS

PO Box 2903
Chicago, IL 60690–2903
Phone: (312) 782–5800
Fax: (312) 782–4339
Victor Artas, Jr., President

Hispanic individuals with Master of Business Administration degrees; MBA candidates; interested others. Promotes business education among Hispanics; works to increase Hispanic representation in business. Sponsors speaker series and educational programs; maintains job bank; awards scholarships. Bestows Brillante Award. **Founded:** 1988. **Members:** 900. **Publications:** *The Bottom Line,* quarterly. Newsletter.

■ *Newsletters*

MINORITY MARKETS ALERT

EPM Communications Inc.
488 E. 18th St.
Brooklyn, NY 11226
Phone: (718) 469–9330

Contains reports of research on minority consumers. Profiles the Black, Hispanic, and Asian American populations. Recurring features include news of research, book reviews, and notices of publications available. **First published:** 1989. **Frequency:** Monthly. **Price:** $189/yr., U.S. and Canada; $229 elsewhere. **Online through:** NewsNet Inc., 945 Haverford Rd., Bryn Mawr, PA 19010, (215) 527–8030; Predicasts, 11001 Cedar Ave., Cleveland, OH 44106, (216) 795–3000.

THE MINORITY TRENDSLETTER

Center for Third World Organizing
3861 Martin Luther King Way
Oakland, CA 94609
Phone: (415) 654–9601

Analyzes issues and trends of particular concern in the Black, Asian, Latino, and Native American communities by surveying "mainstream" media coverage and issuing a different perspective. **Frequency:** Quarterly. **Price:** $20/yr. for individuals, U.S.; $50 for institutions.

■ *Newspapers*

HISPANIC LINK WEEKLY REPORT

Hispanic Link News Service
1420 N St., N.W.
Washington, D.C. 20005
Phone: (202) 234–0280
Fax: (202) 234–4090

Consumer publication covering issues and trends of U.S. Hispanics. **First published:** 1983. **Frequency:** Weekly. **Price:** $113/yr for individuals; $128/yr for institutions.

HISPANIC REPORTER

3121 W. Temple St.
Los Angeles, CA 90026
Phone: (213) 487–5095
Fax: (213) 385–0269

For English-speaking Hispanics and those interested in the Hispanic marketplace. **First published:** 1992. **Frequency:** Weekly. **Subscription:** Free.

MUNDO HISPANICO

Mundo Hispanico, Inc.
Box 13808, Sta. K
Atlanta, GA 3024–0808

Phone: (404) 881–0441
Fax: (404) 881–6085

Reports Hispanic news; and publishes calendar of events (tabloid format). **First published:** 1979. **Frequency:** Fortnightly. **Subscription:** $30.

MUNDO—SPANISH NEWSPAPER

El Mundo, Inc.
845 No. Eastern Ave.
Las Vegas, NV 89101
Phone: (702) 649–8553
Fax: (702) 649–7429

Spanish-language newspaper covering general Hispanic news. **First published:** 1980. **Frequency:** Weekly. **Subscription:** $40.

■ *Representatives of Hispanic Media*

ADVERTISING BROADCASTING SYSTEM, INC.
Represented Media: Radio
El Paso, TX 79903
Gateway Central Plaza,
2211 E. Missouri, Ste. E–237
P.O. Box 79923–3425
Enriqueta Gomez, Armando De Leon, M. Elena Lazo
Phone: 915–542–2969
Fax: 915–542–2958

AMERICAN MINORITIES MEDIA
Represented Media: Newspaper
Santa Barbara, CA 93101
214 E. Gutierrez St.
Alanna Velasquez, Dawn Henson
Phone: 805–963–7676
Fax: 805–963–7677
New York, NY 10128
1556 Third Ave., Ste. 409
Kim Dolan, Lisa Bank
Phone: 212–360–1960
Fax: 212–360–6372

AMIGO INTERNATIONAL MEDIA
Brownsville, TX 78521
3505 Boca Chica Blvd., Ste. 220
Rick Shaw
Phone: 512–544–4553
Fax: 512–544–4556

ARTESA/MARKETING SERVICES
Represented Media: Newspaper, Free Standing Inserts, Consumer/Trade Magazines, TV, Radio.
Hollywood, CA 90028
6725 Sunset Blvd., Ste. 406
Holmes Stoner

Phone: 213–469–8204, 469–0280
Fax: 213–469–6193

BAJA TV/RADIO SALES
Represented Media: Radio, Television
San Diego, CA 92108
4420 Hotel Circle Court, Ste. 365
Greg Reddick
Phone: 619–298–3274
Fax: 619–298–3197

CABALLERO SPANISH MEDIA, INC.
Represented Media: Radio
New York, NY 10016
261 Madison Ave., 18th Fl.
David Haymore, Eduardo Caballero,
Manny Ballestero, Steven Kabatsky
Phone: 212–697–4120
Fax: 212–697–9151
Chicago, IL 60601
205 N. Michigan Ave., Ste. 2015
Maria Dwyer
Phone: 312–565–4888
Fax: 312–819–1970
Los Angeles (Santa Monica), CA 90405
2714 Pico Blvd., Ste. 208
Chris Nevil, Andrea Golden-Mohr, Leonov Garcia
Phone: 213–450–5656
Fax: 213–452–0584
Dallas, TX 75219
3500 Maple Ave., Ste. 1320
Charles Crawford, Rocky Crawford, Barbara Gasc
Phone: 214–522–1888
Fax: 214–522–7406
Atlanta (Marietta), GA 30067
1640 Powers Ferry Rd., Bldg. 5, Ste. 300
Charles Maisano, Carol Darnes
Phone: 404–953–1111
Fax: 404–953–0417
Detroit (Southfield), MI 48075
4000 Town Center, Ste. 290
Tom Perry, Jan Gore
Phone: 313–358–8500
Fax: 313–358–2468
San Francisco, CA 94111–1525
750 Battery St., Ste. 340
Liz Dasher
Phone: 415–772–2740
Fax: 415–772–2758
Houston, TX 77057
MCO Plaza, 5718 Westheimer, Ste. 1705
Cary Minor, Marlea Zwiebel
Phone: 713–785–2345
Fax: 713–266–6925
Minneapolis, MN 55404
1111 Third Ave., South, Ste. 450
Craige Iwaszko, Monique Lichttenegger
Phone: 612–339–2626

Fax: 612–341–9832
Philadelphia, PA 19102
   The Bellevue
   Broad & Walnut Streets, 9th Fl.
   Beryl Naturman, Kathleen O'Connor
   Phone: 215–732–3380
   Fax: 215–735–5216
Portland, OR 97201
   4700 S.W. Macadam Ave., Ste. 303
   Georgia Hess, Laura Goldstein
   Phone: 503–223–1700
   Fax: 503–223–4580
Seattle, WA 98121
   2505 Second Ave., Ste. 515
   Kelly Chandler, Bonnie Grosby
   Phone: 206–728–4117
   Fax: 206–443–1872
St. Louis, MO 63102
   10 S. Broadway, Ste. 500
   Phone: 314–231–0000
   Fax: 314–241–0049
Boston, MA 02116
   31 St. James Ave., Ste. 809
   Greg Martin, Kelly Ryan
   Phone: 617–426–3374
   Fax: 617–482–9560
Charlotte, NC 28210
   6135 Park South Drive, Ste. 103
   Jim Peacock, Karen (Ragan) Wood
   Phone: 704–552–7761
   Fax: 704–556–0022
Denver, CO 80231
   10200 East Girard Ave., Ste. 247, Bldg. C
   Jeff D. Edgley, Denise Hoffman
   Phone 303–368–0334
   Fax: 303–368–0355
Kansas City, MO 64114
   1156 W. 103rd St., Ste. 215
   Eugene Gray
   Phone: 816–471–3502
Irvine, CA 92715
   18662 MacArthur Blvd., Ste. 475
   Chris Nevil
   Phone: 714–261–5757

CBS HISPANIC MARKETING
Represented Media: Broadcast
New York, NY 10019
   51 West 52nd St., 18th Fl.
   Gerardo Villacres, Adriana Grillet,
   Gustavo Szulansky, Rafaela Travesier
   Phone: 212–975–3005
   Fax: 212–975–5384
Los Angeles, CA 90028
   6121 Sunset Blvd., Ste. 516
   Deanna Levy
   Phone: 213–460–3716
   Fax: 213–460–3298

CHARNEY/PALACIOS & CO.
Represented Media: Newspapers, Consumer/Trade Magazines
Miami, FL 33156
   9200 S. Dadeland Blvd.
   Charles J. Charney, Grace Palacios
   Phone: 305–670–9450
   Fax: 305–670–9455

R. B. COLLINS & ASSOC.
Represented Media: Consumer/Trade Magazines
New York, NY 10016
   88 Lexington Ave.
   Bob Collins
   Phone: 212–889–9017

CRESMER, WOODWARD, O'MARA & ORMSBEE, INC.
Represented Media: Newspaper
New York, NY 10022
   866 Third Ave.
   States D. Tompkins, John Morrison, Pamela Bender
   Phone: 212–750–4040
   Fax: 212–935–9514
Atlanta, GA 30328
   6205 Barfield Rd., N.E., Ste. 270
   Gail Johnson
   Phone: 404–256–7893
   Fax: 404–252–7756
Dedham, MA 02026
   990 Washington St., Ste. 316, South
   David Harken
   Phone: 617–326–8871
   Fax: 617–326–8429
Chicago, IL 60601
   One E. Wacker Dr.
   Richard A. Mitchell
   Phone: 312–321–6360
   Fax: 312–321–6364
Dallas, TX 75240
   13601 Preston Rd., Ste. 917E
   Bob L. Walker
   Phone: 214–960–7085
   Fax: 214–960–8986
Troy, MI 48084
   2855 Coolidge Highway, Ste. 218
   Rick Knight
   Phone: 313–649–4030
   Fax: 313–649–3843
Los Angeles, CA 90010
   4929 Wilshire Blvd., Ste. 415
   Harlan Evans
   Phone: 213–936–2800
   Fax: 213–936–2828
North Miami Beach (Miami), FL 33179
   1550 N.E. Miami Gardens Dr., Ste. 302
   R. Peter Evans
   Phone: 305–945–2266

Fax: 305–947–2299
Minneapolis, MN 55402
    821 Marquette Ave., Ste. 910
    John C. Berg
    Phone: 612–339–6879
    Fax: 612–337–5799
Philadelphia, PA 19102
    1411 Walnut St., Ste. 400
    Robert Kramer
    Phone: 215–568–1880
    Fax: 215–568–6226
San Francisco, CA 94104
    Russ Building, 235 Montgomery St., Ste. 1020
    Robert C. LaFontaine, Lee Allder
    Phone: 415–981–2882
    Fax: 415–981–2730
Aurora (Denver), CO 80014
    3025 S. Parker Rd., Ste. 109
    Greg Appel
    Phone: 303–337–5968
    Fax: 303–337–0257

DOHERTY & COMPANY
Represented Media: Consumer Magazines
Chicago, IL 60601
    307 N. Michigan Ave.
    Pat Doherty, Dick Meenahan
    Phone: 312–726–6025

EASTMAN RADIO, INC.
Represented Media: Radio
New York, NY 10019
    125 W. 55th St.
    Carl Butrum, Steven Moskowitz,
    Lindsay Berry, Charlie Sislen
    Phone: 212–424–6400
    Fax: 212–424–6415/6407
Chicago, IL 60611–3964
    444 N. Michigan Ave., Ste. 3270
    Diane Nader
    Phone: 312–836–0850
    Fax: 312–836–0424
Detroit (Troy), MI 48084–2870
    3310 W. Big Beaver Rd., Ste. 545
    Tom O'Brien
    Phone: 313–643–7555
    Fax: 313–643–6339
San Francisco, CA 94105–1575
    100 Spear St., Ste. 1950
    Brian Robinson
    Phone: 415–512–9320
    Fax: 415–512–9013
Seattle, WA 98121
    2200 Sixth Ave., Ste. 707
    Sandy Runnion
    Phone: 206–441–6773
    Fax: 206–441–6819
Los Angeles, CA 90048

    6500 Wilshire Blvd., Ste. 330
    Andrew Rosen
    Phone: 213–966–5108
    Fax: 213–852–0961
Dallas, TX 75201–1817
    300 Crescent Court, Ste. 410
    Gary Andon
    Phone: 214–999–2127
    Fax: 214–855–1473
Houston, TX 77027–5150
    2900 Weslayan, Ste. 625
    Steve Johnson
    Phone: 713–960–1252
    Fax: 713–960–8861
St. Louis, MO 63102–1795
    10 Broadway, Ste. 570
    Brett Cervantes
    Phone: 314–241–7040
    Fax: 314–241–9031
Philadelphia, PA 19103
    8 Penn Center, Ste. 1320
    Karen Crane
    Phone: 215–557–6610
    Fax: 215–557–7313
Boston, MA 02116–4396
    Statler Office Bldg., Ste. 225
    Peter Kadetsky
    Phone: 617–357–1666
    Fax: 617–357–1665
Atlanta, GA 30305–1579
    6 Piedmont Center, Ste. 720
    Marlene Kunis, Rich Farquhar
    Phone: 404–365–3090
    Fax: 404–816–5703
Minneapolis, MN 55402–3385
    Piper Jaffrey Tower, Ste. 2860
    Rob Myers
    Phone: 312–836–0856
Denver, CO 80206
    222 Milwaukee St., Ste. 209
    Gerriann Sullivan-Ward
    Phone: 303–393–6552
    Fax: 303–321–1087
Salt Lake City, UT 84107–2972
    575 E. 4500 South, Ste. B200
    Kathy Bingham
    Phone: 801–266–1480
    Fax: 801–266–2365
Portland, OR 97201
    1500 S.W. 1st St., Ste. 320
    David Lichtman
    Phone: 503–222–2122
    Fax: 503–222–1474

J. L. FARMAKIS, INC.
New Canaan, CT 06840
    Box 1004
    Jack Farmakis, Jan Anderson, Debbie Erichs

Phone: 203–966–1746
Cedar Rapids, IA 52407
　　Box 4446
　　Russ Parker
　　Phone: 319–895–6723

GALAVISIÓN
Represented Media: Television
Los Angeles, CA 90067–5010
　　2121 Avenue of the Stars, Ste. 2300
　　Daniel Crowe, Tom Donahue
　　Phone: 310–286–0122
New York, NY 10153–0001
　　767 Fifth Ave., 12th Fl.
　　John Pero
　　Phone: 212–826–5400

GANNETT NATIONAL NEWSPAPER SALES
Represented Media: Newspaper
New York, NY 10022
　　535 Madison Ave.
　　Sheldon Lyons, Bette Ann Yarus
　　Phone: 212–715–5300
Chicago, IL 60611
　　444 N. Michigan Ave., Ste. 200
　　Jim Moore
　　Phone: 312–527–0550
Detroit (Troy), MI 48075
　　340 E. Big Beaver Rd., Ste. 150
　　Tom Howell
　　Phone: 313–357–7910
Los Angeles, CA 90025
　　11111 Santa Monica Blvd., Ste. 2100
　　Charles Williams
　　Phone: 213–444–2100
Dallas, TX 75244
　　5001 LBJ Freeway
　　Heritage Sq. Tower II, 7th Fl.
　　Tammi Tharp
　　Phone: 214–387–5265
Melbourne, FL 32940
　　1237 Mira Vista Lane
　　Dan O'Connell
　　Phone: 407–259–8964

J. C. GATES & COMPANY
Represented Media: Radio
Las Vegas, NV 89109–4302
　　3700 Las Vegas Blvd. South
　　James C. Gates, Juanita Haddy Landon
　　Phone: 702–795–7600

GILLIS BROADCASTING REPRESENTATIVES
Represented Media: Radio
Los Angeles (Toluca Lake), CA 91602
　　10153 1/2 Riverside Dr., No. 181
　　Jim Gillis

Phone: 818–505–1097
New York, NY 10001
　　11 Penn Plaza, Ste. 2219
　　Joseph Savalli
　　Phone: 212–239–3288
Dallas, TX 75234
　　14330 Midway Rd., Ste. 207
　　Jack Riley
　　Phone: 214–788–1630
Atlanta (Decatur), GA 30033
　　Drawer 33100
　　Daniel Haight
　　Phone: 404–633–9080
Chicago (Highland Park), IL 60035
　　3059 Priscilla Ave., Ste. 208
　　Robert A. Lazar
　　Phone: 312–433–6032

EUGENE F. GRAY
Represented Media: Radio
Kansas City, MO 64114
　　1156 W. 103rd St., Ste. 215
　　Eugene F. Gray
　　Phone: 816–471–5502

GREYSTAR ONE
San Diego, CA 92108–3845
　　2878 Camino del Rio South, Ste. 260
　　Arthur Williams
　　Phone: 619–497–2230

HERBERT E. GROSKIN & CO.
Represented Media: Radio
New York, NY 10016
　　280 Madison Ave., Ste. 1011
　　Herbert Groskin, Dianna Sabia Groskin, Vicki Paige
　　Phone: 212–689–5850
　　Fax: 212–689–5885

HISPANIC TELECOMMUNICATIONS GROUP, INC.
Represented Media: Television, Radio National Network, Outdoor, Magazines
Los Angeles, CA 90036
　　5455 Wilshire Blvd., Ste. 1405
　　Manny Montana
　　Phone 213–936–7117
　　Fax: 213–936–7153

KATZ & POWELL RADIO
Represented Media: Radio
New York, NY 10016
　　470 Park Avenue S., Ste. 1400
　　Shelly Katz, George Gollub, Melissa Halmos, Mitch Katz
　　Phone: 212–545–0600
Los Angeles, CA 90211
　　200 N. Robertson, Ste. 342

Susan Laronge, Blaise Tracy
Phone: 310–274–8885
Chicago, IL 60611
Tribune Tower, Ste. 2602
435 N. Michigan Ave.
Douglas Levy, Shawna Ryan
Phone: 312–467–0200
Detroit, MI 48080
22971 Nine Mile Rd.
Ken Patt, Mike Martin
Phone: 313–773–7700
Boston, MA 02116
100 Boylston St.
George C. Bingham
Phone: 617–482–4370
Atlanta, GA 30305
3423 Piedmont Rd. NE, Ste. 540
Staci Solomon
Phone: 404–264–4553
San Francisco, CA 94123
1870 Jefferson St., Ste. 203
Richard Ferrante
Phone: 415–986–1147
Dallas, TX 75234–3001
3003 LBJ Freeway, Ste. 127
Sherry Terry
Phone: 214–243–8770
St. Louis, MO 63105
Box 50269
Bruce Schneider
Phone: 314–991–4261
Portland, OR 97201
1512 S.W. 18th St.
Richard Gohlman, Sanna Hern
Phone: 503–226–2911
Seattle, WA 98109
701 Dexter N., Ste. 216
Mick Tacher, Kelly Chandler
Phone: 206–285–1913

KATZ HISPANIC MEDIA
Represented Media: Radio
New York, NY 10019
125 W. 55th St.
Elena Soto, Jeff Hodge
Phone: 212–424–6497
Fax: 212–424–6208
Atlanta, GA 30305–1579
6 Piedmont Center, Ste. 712
Glen Woosley
Phone: 404–365–3061
Fax: 404–816–5708
Boston, MA 02116–4396
Statler Office Bldg., Ste. 216
Jane Rodophele
Phone: 617–357–1670
Fax: 617–357–1658
Chicago, IL 60611–3964

444 N. Michigan Ave., Ste. 2970
Phone: 312–836–0860
Fax: 312–245–9262
Dallas, TX 75201–1817
300 Crescent Court, Ste. 400
Leslie Falmar
Phone: 214–999–2091
Fax: 214–855–7854
Detroit (Troy), MI 48084–2870
3310 W. Big Beaver Rd., Ste. 545
Tom O'Brien
Phone: 313–643–6495
Fax: 313–643–6339
Houston, TX 77027–5150
2900 Weslayan, Ste. 610
Glenda Beasley
Phone: 713–961–5094
Fax: 713–629–0303
Los Angeles, CA 90048–4922
6500 Wilshire Blvd., Ste. 200
Eduard D'Abate
Phone: 213–966–5095
Fax: 213–852–1206
Minneapolis, MN 55402–3385
Piper Jaffray Tower, Ste. 2990
Dennis Sternitzky
Phone: 612–339–9904
Fax: 612–339–2005
Philadelphia, PA 19103–2113
8 Penn Center, Ste. 1350
Vince Gambino
Phone: 215–564–2533
Fax: 215–567–5850
Portland, OR 97201
1500 S.W. First Ave., Ste. 320
David Lichtman
Phone: 503–222–2122
Fax: 503–222–1474
St. Louis, MO 63102–1795
10 S. Broadway, Ste. 570
Brett Cervantes
Phone: 314–241–7040
Fax: 314–241–9031
San Francisco, CA 94105–1575
100 Spear St., Ste. 1900
Doreen Cappelli-Sofia
Phone: 415–777–3788
Fax: 415–974–1663
Seattle, WA 98121
3131 Elliot Ave., Ste. 620
Larry Lustig
Phone: 206–284–4383
Fax: 206–284–4928
Represented Media: Television
New York, NY 10019
125 W. 55th St.
Elena Soto, Jeff Hodge
Phone: 212–424–6497

Fax: 212–424–6208
Atlanta, GA 30305–1579
    Six Piedmont Center, Ste. 710
    Sant Perez
    Phone 404–365–3100
    Fax: 404–816–5548
Boston, MA 02116–4396
    Statler Office Building, Ste. 220
    David Henderson
    Phone: 617–542–5458
    Fax: 617–357–1677
Charlotte, NC 28209–3649
    5821 Fairview Rd., Ste. 407
    Bob Schellenberg
    Phone: 704–553–0220
    Fax: 704–553–1547
Chicago, IL 60611–3964
    444 N. Michigan Ave., Ste. 3200
    Doug Cook
    Phone: 312–836–0500
    Fax: 312–836–5489
Cleveland, OH 44115–2107
    Keith Building
    1621 Euclid Ave., Ste. 1718
    Ray Mendelsohn
    Phone: 216–621–7924
    Fax: 216–623–8363
Dallas, TX 75201–1817
    300 Crescent Court, Ste. 400
    Cheryl Pollitt
    Phone: 214–978–4900
    Fax: 214–978–4992
Denver (Englewood), CO 80111–2702
    One DTC, 5251 DTC Parkway PH5
    Scott Gudzak
    Phone: 303–740–8765
    Fax: 303–796–2930
Detroit (Troy), MI 48084–2870
    3310 W. Big Beaver Rd., Ste. 501
    David Blaszkowski
    Phone: 313–649–6381
    Fax: 313–649–2086
Houston, TX 77027–5150
    2900 Weslayan, Ste. 625
    Ron Speck
    Phone: 713–961–5195
    Fax: 713–961–5814
Jacksonville, FL 32202–5015
    1 Independent Square, Ste. 2201
    Greg MacGregor
    Phone: 904–358–2914
    Fax: 904–632–2347
Kansas City, MO 64105–2112
    1100 Main Street, Ste. 1890
    Denise Winslow
    Phone: 816–842–2606
    Fax: 816–221–7731
Los Angeles, CA 90048–4922

6500 Wilshire Blvd., Ste. 200
    Kim Lipit
    Phone: 213–966–5000
    Fax: 213–658–6443
Miami (Hollywood), FL 33021–6927
    3440 Hollywood Blvd., Ste. 480
    Jay Doro
    Phone: 305–961–3881
    Fax: 305–964–4518
Minneapolis, MN 55402–3385
    Piper Jaffary Tower, Ste. 2885
    Anne Lane
    Phone: 612–339–7711
    Fax: 612–339–1335
Philadelphia, PA 19103–2113
    8 Penn Center, Ste. 1350
    David Handler
    Phone: 215–567–7950
    Fax: 215–567–6338
Portland, OR 97201
    1500 S.W. First Ave., Ste. 320
    Jodi Rogaway
    Phone 503–226–3973
    Fax: 503–228–4967
St. Louis, MO 63102–1795
    10 S. Broadway, Ste. 550
    Ed Adams
    Phone 314–231–1868
    Fax: 314–231–3620
San Francisco, CA 94105–1575
    100 Spear St., Ste. 1900
    Diedre Bailey
    Phone: 415–777–3377
    Fax: 415–978–9657
Seattle, WA 98121
    3131 Elliot Ave., Ste. 620
    Nancy Davis
    Phone: 206–284–3088
    Fax: 206–284–5733
Tampa, FL 33607–1462
    7650 West Courtney Campbell Causeway, Ste. 450
    Tom Barrett
    Phone: 813–287–8686
    Fax: 813–287–0953
Washington, DC 20036–2304
    1233 20th St. N.W., Ste. 203
    Cliff McKinney
    Phone: 202–872–5880
    Fax: 202–872–0263

LOTUS HISPANIC REPS
Represented Media: Radio
New York, NY 10017
    50 E. 42nd St.
    Rick Kraushaar, Robert Albright, Yvonne Luna
    Phone: 212–697–7601
    Fax: 212–697–8215
Los Angeles, CA 90028

6777 Hollywood Blvd.
Peggy Martin, Vicki Kramer, Mary Maher Hawley
Phone: 213–464–1311
Fax: 213–464–0549
Chicago, IL 60601
203 N. Wabash
Julie Sayre
Phone: 312–346–8442
Fax: 312–346–6580
San Francisco, CA 94111
447 Battery St., Ste. 300
Dave Specland
Phone: 415–773–8244
Fax: 415–563–5334
Dallas, TX 75251
7616 LBJ Freeway
Mark Munoz
Phone: 214–960–1707
Fax: 214–960–1721
St. Claire Shores (Detroit), MI 48080
22971 Nine Mile Rd.
Ken Patt, Mike Martin
Phone: 313–773–7700
Fax: 313–774–4889
Coral Gables (Miami), FL 33134
2655 LeJeune Rd., Ste. 510
Joe Cabrera
Phone: 305–446–3069
Fax: 305–445–0148

M. P. & M. MARKETING
Ecuador—Jose de Antepara
921 y 9 de Octubre, Piso 2
P.O. Box 09–01–752
Guayaquil
Ing. Xavier Marquez
Phone: 287794–288881–288970
Fax: 593–4–289690

MAJOR MARKET RADIO SALES
Represented Media: Radio
New York, NY 10017
100 Park Ave.
Warner Rush, Dave Kaufman, Jeff Wakefield, Amy Levy
Phone: 212–818–8900
Chicago, IL 60601
233 N. Michigan, Ste. 2021
Michael B. Disney
Phone: 312–938–0999
Los Angeles, CA 90024
10880 Wilshire Blvd., Ste. 1212
Phone: 213–474–5311
Philadelphia, PA 19103
1703 Spruce St.
Mary Mullen
Phone: 215–985–1330
Detroit (Southfield), MI 48075
4000 Town Center, Ste. 290

Jim Hagar
Phone: 313–358–2060
Boston, MA 02114
4 Longfellow Place, Ste. 1710
Linda Madonna
Phone: 617–523–0357
San Francisco, CA 94111
750 Battery St.
Austin Walsh, Howard Silver
Phone: 415–922–9600
Dallas (Irving), TX 75038
1350 Walnut Hill Lane, Ste. 100
Elaine Jenkins
Phone: 214–580–1595
Atlanta (Marietta), GA 30067
1640 Powers Ferry Rd., Bldg. #5, Ste. 360,
Mark Stang
Phone: 404–859–0075
St. Louis, MO 63102
10 Broadway, Ste. 500
Karin Dutcher
Phone: 314–231–9005
Seattle, WA 98121
2505 2nd Ave., #515
Doug Frame
Phone: 206–728–8016
Portland, OR 97201
4700 S.W. Macadam, #303
Phone: 503–222–4892
Pittsburgh, PA
Phone: Zenith 6670
Indianapolis, IN
Phone: 800–621–7010
Milwaukee, WI
Phone: 800–621–7010
Minneapolis, MN 55404
1111 Third Ave. S., Ste. 454
Mary Rooney
Phone: 612–341–3089

MCGAVREN GUILD RADIO
Represented Media: Radio
New York, NY 10017
100 Park Ave.
Peter Doyle, George Pine, Michael Rich
Phone: 212–916–0500
Chicago, IL 60601
205 N. Michigan Ave., Ste. 2015
Greg Noack, Richard Topper
Phone: 312–565–4888
Detroit (Southfield), MI 48075
4000 Town Center, Ste. 290
Cathy Moran
Phone: 313–358–8500
Philadelphia, PA 19102
The Bellevue
Broad & Walnut Sts.
Charles Reilly

Phone: 215–732–3380
Dallas, TX 75038
    1350 Walnut Hill Lane, Ste. 100
    Don Hall
    Phone: 214–518–9600
Atlanta (Marietta), GA 30067
    1640 Powers Ferry Rd., Bldg. 5, Ste. 300
    Anthony Maisano, Kay Olin
    Phone 404–953–1111
St. Louis, MO 63102
    10 S. Broadway, Ste. 500
    Mark Riordan
    Phone: 314–231–0000
Los Angeles, CA 90024
    10880 Wilshire Blvd., Ste. 1215
    Jeff Dashev, Eden Lucas
    Phone: 310–470–3383
Boston, MA 02116
    31 St. James St., Ste. 809
    Tom Poulos
    Phone: 617–423–0606
Houston, TX 77057
    5718 Westheimer, #1705
    Jill Galarneau
    Phone: 713–266–7667
Seattle, WA 98101
    1411 Fourth Ave. Bldg., Ste. 1106
    Michelle Robinson
    Phone: 206–223–1183
Minneapolis, MN 55404
    1111 Third Ave. S., Ste. 450
    Kate Miller
    Phone: 612–333–8717
Portland, OR 97201
    4700 S.W. Macadam Ave., Ste. 303
    Georgia Hess
    Phone: 503–223–1700
San Francisco, CA 94111
    750 Battery St., Ste. 340
    Todd Lawley
    Phone: 415–772–2700
Charlotte, NC 28210
    Two South Executive Park, Ste. 103
    6135 Park Rd.
    Jim Peacock
    Phone: 704–552–7761
Denver, CO 80231
    8547 E. Arapahoe Rd., Ste. J313
    Greenwood Village
    Susan Sorenson
    Phone: 303–766–2448

METRO 8-SHEET NETWORK, INC.
Represented Media: Outdoor
New York, NY 10017
    51 E. 42nd St., Ste. 820
    Robert Dragotta
    Phone: 212–867–7557

Fax: 212–867–7571
Chicago, IL 60602
    6 N. Michigan Ave., Ste. 1514
    Phone: 1–800–438–7328
Los Angeles, CA 90212
    400 S. Beverly Dr., Ste. 214
    Phone: 213–205–2182

ART MOORE, INC.
Represented Media: Radio
Seattle, WA 98121
    2200 6th Ave., Ste. 707
    Greg Smith, Sandy Runnion, Patti Berube,
    Ruth Hallett, Linda Oberst
    Phone: 206–443–9991
    Fax: 206–443–9998
Portland, OR 97201
    4800 S.W. Macadam Ave., Ste. 200
    Teddi Jones, Barbara Barry
    Phone: 503–228–0016
    Fax: 503–228–0556
Denver, CO 80206–5010
    222 Milwaukee St., Ste. 209
    Gerriann Ward, Adriana Vernon
    Phone: 303–321–2354
    Fax: 303–321–1087
Salt Lake City, UT 84107–2972
    575 East 4500 South, Ste. B–200
    Kathy Bingham
    Phone: 801–266–3576
    Fax: 801–266–2365

NAHP
Represented Media: Newspaper, Consumer/Trade Magazines
    Zeke Montes
    Phone: 708–656–6666
    Fax: 708–656–6679

THE PAPERT COMPANIES
Represented Media: Newspaper
Chicago, IL 60611
    400 N. Michigan Ave.
    Nancy Fredsall
    Phone: 708–822–9116
Dallas, TX 75201
    400 N. St. Paul, Ste. 800
    S. W. Papert, Jr.
    Richard Jones
    Phone: 214–969–0000
Detroit (Southfield), MI 48075
    21711 W. Ten Mile Rd., Ste. 238
    Ed Chevalier
    Phone: 313–357–3933
Kansas City, MO (Prairie Village, KS) 66208
    2200 W. 75th St., Ste. 202
    Bob Linton

Phone: 913–432–6600
Los Angeles, CA 91401
    5430 Van Nuys Blvd., Ste. 312
    Elizabeth Avery
    Phone: 818–990–3475
Memphis, TN 38157
    5050 Poplar Ave., Ste. #1702
    Joe Sullivan
    Phone: 901–767–6572
Minneapolis, MN 55402
    Chamber of Commerce Bldg.
    15 S. Fifth St., Ste. 1104
    Mark Kinderwater
    Phone: 612–338–1958
New York, NY 10165
    60 E. 42nd St.
    3802 Lincoln Bldg.
    Gary Tozzi
    Phone: 212–687–4750
San Francisco, CA 94107
    185 Berry St., Ste. 6103
    Jon Edwards
    Phone: 415–957–9490
Seattle (Federal Way), WA 98003
    31919 1st Ave., South, Ste. 124
    Phone 206–946–5191
Atlanta, GA 30319–1457
    4170 Ashford Dunwoody Rd., #G–3
    Brian Karp
    Phone: 404–255–8858
Woburn (Boston), MA 01801
    10 Tower Office Park, #313
    Frank Standley
    Phone: 617–932–0909
    Fax: 617–938–9304
Denver, CO 80230
    303 E. 17th Ave., #700
    Sandra Burtis
    Phone: 303–832–1520

PTS MEXICAN MEDIA ADVERTISING, INC.
Represented Media: Radio
Chula Vista, CA 91910
    590 G. St., Ste. 8
    Gabriel Ruiz
    Phone: 619–691–5378

RADIO TIME SALES/INTERNATIONAL
Represented Media: Radio
San Francisco, CA 94133
    559 Pacific Ave.
    Sam Posner
    Phone: 415–391–1984
    Fax: 415–788–3844
New York, NY 10016
    347 Fifth Ave., Ste. 1007
    Elaine Herzstein
    Phone: 212–679–3910

Chicago, IL 60601
    333 N. Michigan, Rm. 2032
    John Murphy
    Phone: 312–346–3334
Detroit, MI 48226
    1553 Woodward Ave., Ste. 925
    Eleanore Krupp, Mary George
    Phone: 313–961–3353
Los Angeles (Glendale), CA 91208
    1383 Opechee Way
    Jack Kabateck
    Phone: 818–500–7201
Dallas, TX 75236
    3003 LBJ Freeway
    Tamela Bembebek
    Phone: 214–243–8764
Seattle, WA 98109
    701 Dexter N., Ste. 216
    Mike Sheppard, Kelly Chandler
    Phone: 206–285–1913
Portland, OR 97201
    1512 S.W. 18th Ave.
    JoAnna Ebert
    Phone: 503–226–2911
Atlanta (Decatur), GA 30033
    Drawer 33100
    Dan Haight
    Phone: 404–633–9080
St. Louis, MO 63105—Box 50269
    Bruce Schneider
    Phone: 314–991–4261

REGIONAL REPS CORP.
Cleveland, OH 44115
    1100 Chester Ave., Ste. 100
    Stuart J. Sharpe, Robert A. Stern
    Phone: 216–781–0035
Cincinnati, OH 45203
    Holiday Park Tower
    644 Linn St.
    Joseph C. Hearn
    Phone: 513–651–1511
Atlanta, GA 30338
    4480 North Shallowford Rd., Ste. 115
    Michael E. Povlo, Jack M. DeHaven
    Phone: 404–394–7377

RILEY REPRESENTATIVES
Represented Media: Radio
Dallas, TX 75244
    14330 Midway Rd., Ste. 216
    Jack Riley
    Phone: 214–788–1630
    Fax: 214–490–6438
    Houston phone: 713–759–0549
Chicago, IL 60606
    20 N. Wacker Dr., Ste. 540
    Howard Weiss

Phone: 312–263–3340
Fax: 312–263–8494
Detroit (St. Claire Shores), MI 48080
   22971 Nine Mile Rd.
   Ken Patt, Mike Martin
   Phone: 313–773–7700
   Fax: 313–774–7700
San Francisco, CA 94133
   559 Pacific Ave.
   Sam Posner
   Phone: 415–391–1984
   Fax: 415–788–3844
Atlanta (Decatur), GA 30033
   Drawer 33100
   Daniel A. Haight, Arlette G. Haight
   Phone: 404–373–2662
   Fax: 404–373–4658
Los Angeles (Toluca Lake), CA 91602
   10153-1/2 Riverside Dr., No. 181
   Jim Gillis
   Phone: 818–505–1097
   Fax: 818–505–1099
Pittsburgh, PA 15217
   6326 Forward Ave.
   Roger Rafson
   Phone: 412–421–2600
   Fax: 412–421–6001
New York, NY 10001
   Eleven Penn Plaza
   Joe Hoffman
   Phone: 212–239–3288
   Fax: 212–563–1301

ROSLIN RADIO SALES, INC.
Represented Media: Radio
New York, NY 10022
   515 Madison Ave., Ste. 1104
   Marvin Roslin, Alan Korowitz, Zim Barstein,
   Frank Truglid, George Patitis, Steve Heimer
   Phone: 212–486–0720
Boston, MA 02116
   229 Berkeley St., Ste. 31
   Jeff Finkel
   Phone: 617–262–3400
Chicago, IL 60601
   54 W. Hubbard St., Ste. 100
   Chris Brandli
   Phone: 312–644–0269
Philadelphia, PA 19102
   260 S. Broad St., Ste. 200
   Jeff Finkel
   Phone: 215–735–3947
Los Angeles (Beverly Hills), CA 90210
   200 N. Robertson
   Barry Poles
   Phone: 310–278–8098
Dallas, TX 75204
   4144 N. Central Expressway #660

Shannon Clark
Phone: 214–823–7092
Atlanta, GA 30326
   3355 Lenox Rd., N.E., Ste. 750
   Lisa Hanrahan
   Phone: 404–266–0614

SAVALLI BROADCAST SALES NAB
Represented Media: Radio & Television
New York, NY 10001
   Eleven Penn Plaza, Ste. 962
   Joseph Savalli, Gladys Swanson
   Phone: 212–239–3288
   Fax: 212–563–1301
Chicago, IL 60606
   20 N. Wacker Dr., Rm. 540
   Howard C. Weiss
   Phone: 312–263–3340
Atlanta (Decatur), GA 30033
   Box 33100
   Dan Haight, Arlette Haight
   Phone: 404–633–9080
Dallas, TX 75244
   14330 Midway Rd., Ste. 209
   Jack Riley, Liz Tunnell
   Phone: 214–788–1630
Los Angeles (N. Hollywood), CA 91602
   11332 Camarillo St.
   Hugh Wallace
   Phone: 818–980–3212
   Fax: 818–980–8464
San Francisco (Napa), CA 94558
   666 Wall Rd.
   Ward Glen
   Phone: 707–944–9115
Philadelphia, PA 19118
   15 W. Highland Ave.
   Robert Dome
   Phone: 215–242–3660
Boston, MA 02116
   100 Boylston St.
   George C. Bingham
   Phone: 617–482–4370
Kansas City, MO 64114
   1156 W. 103rd St., Ste. 215
   Gene Gray
   Phone: 816–471–5502
Detroit (St. Clair Shores), MI 48081
   21714 Lakeland St.
   Ken Patt
   Phone: 313–445–0491

SBS NETWORK
Represented Media: Radio
New York, NY 10019
   26 W. 56th St.
   Mickie Reyes, Barbara Rosenthal, Isabel Martin,
   George L. Ortiz

Phone: 212–541–6700
Fax: 212–541–8535
Los Angeles, CA 90028
5700 Sunset Blvd.
Rick Taylor
Phone: 213–962–3712
Fax: 213–466–8259
Miami, FL 33145
1411 Coral Way
Joe Rey
Phone: 305–854–1830
Fax: 305–856–8812

THE TACHER COMPANY. INC.
Represented Media: Radio
Seattle, WA 98109–5005
211 6th Ave., Ste. 200
Mick Tacher, Denise Norman, Kari Burns, Greg Tacher
Phone: 206–727–2222
Fax: 206–441–2738
Portland, OR 97201
1512 S.W. 18th
Richard Gohlman, Lori Ware
Phone: 503–226–2911
Fax: 503–226–6596

TELEMUNDO GROUP, INC.
Represented Media: Television
New York, NY 10019
1740 Broadway, 18th Fl.
Sual P. Steinberg, W. Gary McBride, Donald M. Travis,
Peter J. Housman II, M. Alexander Berger, Gustavo G. Godoy,
Peter D. Roslow, T. Morrison, Adrea D'Amico,
Michael Gillespie
Phone: 212–492–5500
Fax: 212–459–9498
Los Angeles, CA 90048
6300 Wilshire Blvd., Ste. 1220
Silvia Mendoza, Mario Mendoza
Phone: 213–658–6868
Fax: 213–653–2367
Chicago, IL 60611
435 N. Michigan Ave., Ste. 1310
Maura Donohue
Phone: 312–321–1911
Fax: 312–321–1916
San Francisco, CA 94104
250 Montgomery St., Ste. 510
Suzanne Avila-Armstrong
Phone: 415–421–4848
Fax: 415–421–6602
Hialeah, FL 33010
2340 West 8th Ave.
Olga Luis
Phone: 305–883–0987
Fax: 305–888–9270
Dallas, TX 75240

1140 One Lincoln Center
5400 LBJ Freeway
Roger Ashley
Phone: 214–661–2560
Fax: 214–661–2605

UNIVERSAL BROADCASTING CORPORATION
Represented Media: Radio
Mineola, NY 11501
40 Roselle St.
Howard Warshaw, Jeffrey D. Warshaw
Phone: 516–741–1200

UNIVISIÓN
Represented Media: Television
New York, NY 10158–0180
605 Third Ave., 12th Fl.
Raul Torano, Peter Von Gal
Phone: 212–455–5200
Fax: 212–867–6710
Secaucus, NJ 07094–2998
24 Meadowland Pkwy., 3rd Fl.
George Blank, Mike Durney
Phone 201–348–2841
Fax: 201–617–7255
Miami, FL 33178
9405 N.W. 41st St.
Evelyn Castillo
Phone: 305–471–4021
Fax: 305–471–4027
Los Angeles, CA 90045
6701 Center Drive West, 15th Fl.
Patricia Testa
Phone: 310–338–0700
Fax: 310–348–3619
San Francisco, CA 94124
2200 Palou Ave.
Rudy Balderrama
Phone: 415–824–4384
Fax: 415–824–1906
Chicago, IL 60611
401 E. Illinois St., Ste. 325
Brian Pussilano
Phone: 312–321–8200
Fax: 312–321–8223
Irvine (Orange County), CA 92714
2030 Main St., Ste. 235
Steve Mandela
Phone: 714–474–8585
Fax: 714–474–8385
Irving (Dallas), TX 75039
600 E. Las Colinas Blvd., Ste. 566
Jack Hobbs
Phone: 214–869–0202
Fax: 214–869–2636
Bingham Farms (Detroit), MI 48025
30700 Telegraph Rd., Ste. 3640
Mark Brown

Phone: 313–540–5705
Fax: 313–540–2419

HUGH WALLACE, INC.

North Hollywood (Los Angeles), CA 91602
11332 Camarillo St.
Hugh Wallace, Bill Mendell, Beverly Allen, Mary Williams
Phone: 818–980–3212
New York, NY 10001
11 Penn Center
Joe Hoffman, Tom Pazlar
Phone: 202–239–3288
Fax: 212–562–1301
Chicago, IL 60606
20 N. Wacker Dr.
Howard Weiss, Jeff Brunstein
Phone: 312–263–3340
Fax: 312–263–8494
San Francisco, CA 94608
2000 Powell St., Ste. 700
Jim Potts
Phone: 415–420–0828

■ *Research Centers*

BROOKLYN COLLEGE OF CITY UNIVERSITY OF NEW YORK
CENTER FOR LATINO STUDIES

1205 Boylan Hall
Bedford Ave. & Ave. H
Brooklyn, NY 11210
Phone: (718) 780–5561

Contact: Prof. Hector Carrasquillo, Codirector

Research Interests: Promotes research and develops projects concerning the sociology, economics, and politics of Latinos, especially Puerto Ricans living in New York and on the island. Collaborates with College and community groups on research and programs of mutual interest and disseminates information within the College and in the community.

COLUMBUS MINORITY BUSINESS DEVELOPMENT CENTER

233 12th St., Ste. 621
PO Box 1696
Columbus, GA 31902–1696
Phone: (706) 324–4253
Fax: (706) 324–0335

Contact: Edward G. Dawson, Project Director

Founded: 1982. **Research Interests:** Marketing research on economic and general business conditions of minority businesses, especially in the area of construction. **Meetings/Educational Activities:** Sponsors seminars and workshops in management training, taxes, procurement, finance, and bonding.

MICHIGAN STATE UNIVERSITY
JULIAN SAMORA RESEARCH INSTITUTE

216 Erickson Hall
East Lansing, MI 48824–1034
Phone: (517) 336–1317
Fax: (517) 336–2221

Contact: Dr. Richard A. Navarro, Director

Research Interests: Social, economic, educational, and political condition of Latino communities, especially in the Midwest. Studies concern multicultural education, literacy, telecommunications, demographics, economic development, community development, family, and youth. **Publications:** Julian Samora Working Papers Series; Julian Samora Research Institute Occasional Papers Series; Institute Research Report Series. **Meetings/Educational Activities:** Sponsors a speakers series and periodic conferences.

MINORITY BUSINESS
INFORMATION INSTITUTE

130 5th Ave., 10th Floor
New York, NY 10011
Phone: (212) 242–8000
Fax: (212) 989–8410

Contact: Earl G. Graves, Executive Director

Founded: 1970. **Library Holdings:** Maintains 2200 volume library of books, periodicals, and reports focusing on minority businesses. **Publications:** *Index to Black Enterprise,* periodic. Magazine.

NATIONAL COUNCIL OF LA RAZA, POLICY ANALYSIS CENTER

810 1st St. NE, Ste. 300
Washington, DC 20002
Phone: (202) 289–1380
Fax: (202) 289–8173

Contact: Charles Kamasaki, Vice President for Research

Founded: 1968. **Research Interests:** Research and policy analysis from a Hispanic perspective, including studies on education, employment and training, immigration, civil rights enforcement, housing and community development, Hispanic poverty, the elderly, business and economic development, energy, language issues, substance abuse, and AIDS. Prepares demographic analysis of Hispanic Americans. Provides technical assistance to Hispanic community-based organizations, answers inquiries, and makes referrals. **Publications:** Research reports; policy analyses; *Agenda* (quarterly newsletter); *Education Network Newsletter* (quarterly); *Poverty Project Newsletter* (quarterly); *Ancianos Network Newsletter* (quarterly). **Meetings/Educational Activities:** Offers internships and fellowships in policy analysis studies. Sponsors seminars, workshops, and an annual conference in July, open to all. **Library:** Maintains a reference collection on Hispanic issues; Diane Cabrales, information specialist.

NATIONAL HISPANIC RESEARCH CENTER

2727 W. 6th St., Ste. 270
Los Angeles, CA 90057
Phone: (213) 487–1922
Fax: (213) 385–3014

Contact: Carmela G. Lacayo, President

Founded: 1975. **Research Interests:** Conducts bilingual social science research on the Hispanic community, particularly elderly persons. **Publications:** *Legislative Bulletin* (quarterly). **Library:** 2,500 volumes on Hispanics and aging.

NATIONAL HISPANIC UNIVERSITY
NATIONAL HISPANIC CENTER FOR ADVANCED STUDIES AND POLICY ANALYSIS

135 E. Gish Rd., Ste. 201
San Jose, CA 95112
Phone: (415) 451–0511
Fax: (415) 451–4648

Contact: Dr. B. Roberto Cruz, President

Founded: 1981. **Research Interests:** Hispanic policy issues, including studies of education, immigration, housing, census data, employment, media, philanthropy, international relations, Hispanic women, recreation and leisure, civil rights of minority language students, special education, minority business enterprises, community economic development, special markets, youth development, and Latin American relations. Emphasizes dropout prevention and Hispanic consumer markets. **Publications:** *State of Hispanic America* (annually); *NHU Update*. **Meetings/Educational Activities:** Sponsors periodic seminars and conferences. **Library:** 20,000 volumes on bilingual education; Maira Elena Riddle, director student services.

NORTHERN ILLINOIS UNIVERSITY
CENTER FOR LATINO AND LATIN AMERICAN STUDIES

140 Carroll Ave., B–3
De Kalb, IL 60115
Phone: (815) 753–1531
Fax: (815) 753–0198

Contact: Michael J. Gonzales Ph.D., Director

Founded: 1985. **Research Interests:** Latin America and the Latino experience in the U.S.

STANFORD UNIVERSITY
STANFORD CENTER FOR CHICANO RESEARCH

Cypress Hall, E Wing
Stanford, CA 94305
Phone: (415) 723–3914
Fax: (415) 725–0353

Contact: Fernando Mendoza, Director

Founded: 1980. **Research Interests:** Issues of Latino children and women, and Latino empowerment issues in education, business, government, law, and the media.

UNIVERSITY OF CALIFORNIA, LOS ANGELES
CHICANO STUDIES RESEARCH CENTER

180 Haines Hall
Los Angeles, CA 90024–1544
Phone: (213) 825–2363
Fax: (213) 206–1784

Contact: Antonio Serratta, Assistant Director

Founded: 1970. **Research Interests:** Stimulates, coordinates, and assists faculty research on public policy issues, changing demographics, history, and culture of the Chicano/Latino community. **Publications:** *AZTLAN; International Journal of Chicano Studies Research;* Monograph Series; Anthology Series; Occasional Paper Series. **Meetings/Educational Activities:** Holds Chicano Lecture Series (fall, winter, and spring quarters). **Library:** 12,000 monographs and theses/dissertations on Chicano/Mexican studies; Richard Chabran, associate librarian.

■ *Top 25 Hispanic-owned Businesses*

GOYA FOODS, INC.

100 Seaview Dr.
Secaucus, NJ 07094
Phone: (201) 348–4900
Joseph Unanue, CEO

Number of Employees: 1,600. **Founded:** 1936. **Rank in 1993:** 1. **1992 Sales:** $453.00 million. **Type of Business:** Hispanic food manufacturing and marketing.

BURT ON BROADWAY AUTOMOTIVE GROUP

5200 S. Broadway
Englewood, CO 80110
Phone: (303) 761–0333
Lloyd G. Chavez, CEO

Number of Employees: 600. **Founded:** 1939. **Rank in 1993:** 2. **1992 Sales:** $422.76 million. **Type of Business:** Automotive sales and service.

SEDANO'S SUPERMARKETS

5252 W. Flager St.
Miami, FL 33134
Phone: (305) 444–7824
Manuel A. Herran, CEO

Number of Employees: 1,500. **Founded:** 1962. **Rank in 1993:** 3. **1992 Sales:** $224.56 million. **Type of Business:** Supermarket chain.

GALEANA VAN DYKE DODGE

28400 Van Dyke
Warren, MI 48093
Phone: (810) 573–4000
Frank Galeana, CEO

Number of Employees: 334. **Founded:** 1969. **Rank in 1993:** 4. **1992 Sales:** $186.3 million. **Type of Business:** Automotive sales and services.

CAL-STATE LUMBER SALES, INC.

2704 Transportation Ave.
San Diego, CA 92050
Phone: (619) 336-1186
Benjamin Acevedo, CEO

Number of Employees: 98. **Founded:** 1984. **Rank in 1993:** 5. **1992 Sales:** $169.64 million. **Type of Business:** Wood product sales.

ANCIRA ENTERPRISES, INC.

6111 Bandera Rd.
PO Box 29719
San Antonio, TX 78238
Phone: (512) 681-4900
Ernesto Ancira, Jr., CEO

Number of Employees: 300. **Founded:** 1983. **Rank in 1993:** 6. **1992 Sales:** $168.00 million. **Type of Business:** Automotive sales and services.

INTERNATIONAL BANK OF COMMERCE

PO Drawer 1359
Laredo, TX 78040
Phone: (210) 722-7611
Dennis E. Nixon, CEO

Number of Employees: 650. **Founded:** 1966. **Rank in 1993:** 7. **1992 Sales:** $160.70 million. **Type of Business:** Financial services institution.

HANDY ANDY SUPERMARKETS

2001 S. Laredo St.
San Antonio, TX 78207
Phone: (512) 227-8755
A. Jimmy Jimenez, CEO

Number of Employees: 1,705. **Founded:** 1983. **Rank in 1993:** 8. **1992 Sales:** $148.00 million. **Type of Business:** Supermarket chain.

FRANK PARRA AUTOPLEX

1000 E. Airport Fwy.
Irving, TX 75062
Phone: (214) 721-4300
Tim Parra, CEO
Mike Parra, CEO

Number of Employees: 284. **Founded:** 1971. **Rank in 1993:** 9. **1992 Sales:** $146.62 million. **Type of Business:** Automotive sales and services.

NORMAC FOODS INC.

9500 NW 4th St.
Oklahoma City, OK 73127
Phone: (405) 789-7500
John C. Lopez, CEO

Number of Employees: 255. **Founded:** 1970. **Rank in 1993:** 10. **1992 Sales:** $142.77 million. **Type of Business:** Meat products manufacturer.

LLOYD A. WISE, INC.

10440 E. 14th St.
Oakland, CA 94603
Phone: (510) 638-4800
Steve Rodman, CEO

Number of Employees: 291. **Founded:** 1914. **Rank in 1993:** 11. **1992 Sales:** $137.21 million. **Type of Business:** Automotive sales and services.

INFOTEC DEVELOPMENT, INC.

3611 S. Harbor Blvd., Ste. 260
Santa Ana, CA 92704
Phone: (714) 549-0460
J. Fernando Niebla, CEO

Number of Employees: 600. **Founded:** 1978. **Rank in 1993:** 12. **1992 Sales:** $126.03 million. **Type of Business:** High-tech engineering.

CTA INC.

6116 Executive Blvd., Ste. 800
Rockville, MD 20852
Phone: (301) 816-1200
C. E. (Tom) Velez, CEO

Number of Employees: 1,280. **Founded:** 1979. **Rank in 1993:** 13. **1992 Sales:** $115.94 million. **Type of Business:** Aerospace/defense systems.

CAPITAL BANCORP

1221 Brickell Ave.
Miami, FL 33131
Phone: (305) 536-1500
Abel Holtz, CEO

Number of Employees: 632. **Founded:** 1982. **Rank in 1993:** 14. **1992 Sales:** $114.17 million. **Type of Business:** Financial services institution.

COLSA CORP.

PO Box 1068
Huntsville, AL 35807
Phone: (205) 922-1512
Francisco J. Collazo, CEO

Number of Employees: 700. **Founded:** 1980. **Rank in 1993:** 15. **1992 Sales:** $112.00 million. **Type of Business:** Engineering services.

TROY FORD
777 John R.
Troy, MI 48083
Phone: (810) 585–4000
Irma B. Elder, CEO

Number of Employees: 115. **Founded:** 1968. **Rank in 1993:** 16. **1992 Sales:** $111.09 million. **Type of Business:** Automotive sales and services.

CAREFLORIDA INC.
7950 53rd St., NW
Miami, FL 33166
Phone: (305) 591–3311
Paul L. Cejas, CEO

Number of Employees: 194. **Founded:** 1973. **Rank in 1993:** 17. **1992 Sales:** $110.60 million. **Type of Business:** Health insurance.

GASETERIA OIL CORP.
144–31 Farmer's Blvd.
Springfield Gardens, NY 11434
Phone: (718) 525–9076
Oscar Porcelli

Number of Employees: 450. **Founded:** 1973. **Rank in 1993:** 18. **1992 Sales:** $108.00 million. **Type of Business:** Gasoline stations.

EAGLE BRANDS, INC.
3201 Milam Dairy Rd., NW
Miami, FL 33122
Phone: (305) 599–2337
Carlos M. de La Cruz, CEO

Number of Employees: 200. **Founded:** 1984. **Rank in 1993:** 19. **1992 Sales:** $97.95 million. **Type of Business:** Wholesale beer distributor.

PRECISION TRADING CORP.
1401 88th Ave., NW
Miami, FL 33172
Phone: (305) 592–4500
Israel Lapciuc, CEO

Number of Employees: 35. **Founded:** 1979. **Rank in 1993:** 20. **1992 Sales:** $96.00 million. **Type of Business:** Consumer electronics.

CONDAL DISTRIBUTORS, INC.
2300 Randall Ave.
Bronx, NY 10473
Phone: (212) 824–9000
Nelson Fernandez, CEO

Number of Employees: 250. **Founded:** 1968. **Rank in 1993:** 21. **1992 Sales:** $95.00 million. **Type of Business:** Wholesale food distributor.

TELACU
5400 E. Olympic Blvd., Ste. 300
Los Angeles, CA 90022
Phone: (213) 721–1655
David C. Lizarraga, CEO

Number of Employees: 600. **Founded:** 1968. **Rank in 1993:** 22. **1992 Sales:** $93.00 million. **Type of Business:** Economic development corporation.

ROSENDIN ELECTRIC, INC.
880 N. Maybury Rd.
San Jose, CA 95133
Phone: (408) 286–2800
Raymond J. Rosendin, CEO

Number of Employees: 650. **Founded:** 1919. **Rank in 1993:** 23. **1992 Sales:** $91.00 million. **Type of Business:** Electrical contracting.

MEXICAN INDUSTRIES IN MICHIGAN, INC.
1616 Howard
Detroit, MI 48216
Phone: (313) 963–6114
Henry J. Aguirre, Founder

Number of Employees: 800. **Founded:** 1979. **Rank in 1993:** 24. **1992 Sales:** $87.50 million. **Type of Business:** Automotive trim manufacturing.

THE VINCAM GROUP
9040 Sunset Dr.
Miami, FL 33143
Phone: (305) 271–9920
Carlos A. Saladrigas, CEO

Number of Employees: 6,500. **Founded:** 1985. **Rank in 1993:** 25. **1992 Sales:** $85.30 million. **Type of Business:** Employee leasing.

Index

a

Acculturated Hispanics
    advertising to 228, 229
    media habits of 228
Acculturation 11, 164, 165, 188, 266, 384
    business and 188
    external factors in 165
    Hispanics and 257
    indicators of 374
    individual traits and 166
    internal factors in 165
    managing 180
    process 164
    rate of 176
    segmentation and effects on marketing 326
Adults, Hispanic See Hispanic adults
Advertisers 280
Advertising 315
    to bilingual Hispanics 227
    bilingual or Spanish-language 124

    budgets 349
    campaigns 254, 345
    Catholic church and 347
    emotionally-driven 124
    expenditures 280
    exposure parameters 264
    language and 217, 218, 220, 227
    public transportation and 271
    in radio 264, 278, 345
    recall and 217
    in television 257, 345
Advertising agencies
    selecting a Hispanic agency 349
Advertising Broadcasting System, Inc. 460
Affluent families by Hispanic subgroup
    number of (1990) 132
    percentage of (1990) 133
Affluent Hispanic households 118
    Arizona (1990) 153
    California (1990) 149
    Colorado (1990) 154
    Florida (1990) 152
    Illinois (1990) 153

in states with largest Hispanic population 148
  New Jersey (1990) 150
  New Mexico (1990) 154
  New York (1990) 150
  Texas (1990) 151
Affluent Mexican households 118
Age composition
  of the Hispanic population 85
  of the Hispanic population: in percentages 86
Age distribution
  of mainland Puerto Rican population (1992) 103
  of U.S. Central and South American population (1990) 110
  of U.S. Cuban population (1992) 106
  of U.S. Mexican population (1992) 99
  of U.S. White and Hispanic populations (1988) 79
Age of discovery 13
American LIVES®, Inc. 390
American Minorities Media 460
Amigo International Media 460
Ancira Enterprises, Inc. 473
Apparel 125
  annual average expenditures by Hispanic households 143
Arbitron 267
Areas of Dominant Influence (ADI)
  Hispanic ADIs 311
  and Hispanic print media (1993) 307
Arizona
  affluent Hispanic households (1990) 153
  Hispanic affluence in 119
  metropolitan areas with large Hispanic concentrations 75
Artesa/Marketing Services 460
Automated teller machines (ATMs) 420
Automobile use among Hispanics 324

b

Babalaos 201
Baja TV/Radio Sales 460
Balceros 199
Bank of America 419

Bilingual and monolingual Spanish-speakers
  age 5 and older in the U.S. (1990) 241
  measurement of 225
Bilingual Hispanics in the U.S. 224
  and actual vs self-perceived language ability 224
  and emotional vs rational language usage 227
  English proficiency among 225
  levels of 226
  marketing to 224
Bilingual households
  English vs Spanish usage in 226
Bilingual switching 226
Bracero Program 191
Brand name recognition 317, 318
Brazil
  and definition of Hispanic 11
Broadcast media 278 *See also* Media
Brooklyn College of City University of New York
  Center for Latino Studies 471
Burrelle's Hispanic Media Directory 456
Burt on Broadway Automotive Group 472

c

Caballero Radio Network 268
Caballero Spanish Media, Inc. 460
Cable television, Hispanic 260
Cadena Radio Centro 268
California
  affluent Hispanic households (1990) 149
  affluent Hispanics in 118
  demographic profile of language segments in Southern California (1992) 242
  English and Spanish-Language Proficiency segments in Southern California (1992) 244
  immigrant population and 51
  media usage profile by language segments in Southern California (1992) 248
  metropolitan areas with large Hispanic concentrations 70
  radio listening habits of adults (1993) 303
  retail store information and language segmentation in Northern California (1991) 306

retail information sources by language segments in
Southern California (1992) 247
Spanish and English Proficiency of Hispanic Men and
Women in Southern California 357
television viewing habits of adults 304
value orientation differences between language segments
in Southern California (1992) 246
California Avocado Commission 438
Cal-State Lumber Sales, Inc. 473
Capital Bancorp 473
Careflorida Inc. 474
CBS Hispanic Marketing 461
CBS Hispanic Radio Network 268
Central Americans
consumerism and 61
demographics (1990) 67
fashion sense of women 333
households 112
marital status and (1990) 111
Charney/Palacios & Co. 461
Chicago
demographic profile of language segments (1994) 243
English and Spanish-language proficiency segments
(1994) 245, 249
Chicano Art Movement 194
Chicano Database on CD-ROM 456
Chicano murals 194
Children See Hispanic children
CIBA Vision 426
Clothing See Apparel
CNN Radio Noticias 268
Collins, R. B. & Assoc. 461
Colorado
affluent Hispanic households (1990) 154
Hispanic affluence in 119
metropolitan areas with large Hispanic concentrations
74
Colsa Corp. 473
Columbus Minority Business Development Center 471
Commercials See Advertising
Communication
cultural 12, 171, 210
key to effectiveness of 171
Communicative media strategy 275
Computer-aided telephone interviewing (CATI) 382
Conceptual marketing framework 316

Conceptualization
issues 377
process 372, 386
Condal Distributors, Inc. 474
Conjunto 195
Consumer
miscellaneous expenditures (1990–1991) 157
food expenditures (1990–1991) 156
housing expenditures (1990–1991) 155
life-styles and formal education 54
life-styles and income 54
life-styles and occupation 54
market understanding 11
profiles 361
targeting through radio 266
Contact lenses 426
Continental Hispanic population 163
Cost per interview (CPI) 382
Countries with large Spanish-speaking populations (1990) 26
Coupons
Hispanic consumer use of 339
usage by language segments 360
Cresmer, Woodward, O'Mara & Ormsbee, Inc. 461
Crosstabs 388
CTA Inc. 473
Cuban Americans
affluence and 118
age distribution and (1992) 106
characteristics of 198
consumerism and 59
dominant cultural influences of 199
food and 202
health and 201
households (1992) 107
income of households and families 108
language and 199
legal status of 199
literature and 202
marital status and (1992) 107
migration and 199
music and 201
political issues of 201
presence in the United States 199
religion and 201
self-identification of 200
size and location of population 198

socioeconomic characteristics of 200

sports and 202

states with large populations of (1990) 106

theater and 202

values of 200

women's fashion sense 333

Culture 13, 164

adaptation and sensitization process and 385

advertising aspects of 219

affinity with 166

Anglo-American 188

attunement to 161

building a base 177

communication and 12

context of products and services 323

differences between Hispanics and American middle class 208

diversity among U.S. Hispanics 189

dominant themes within 166

food and 122

values in 373

Curanderos 201

Customs 16

∂

data analysis process 372

data bias 317

introduced by sampling methods 318

data gathering methodology 317

data extrapolation process 372

Demographic Latino Profiles 456

Demographic profile

of language segments: Chicago (1994) 243

of language segments: Southern California (1992) 242

of U.S. Hispanic women (1990) 365

Demographics

advertisers and 39

businesses and 39

Hispanic households and 46

marketers and 39

El Diario de Las Américas 270

El Diario-La Prensa and Noticias del Mundo 270

Disposable income among Hispanics 117

Doherty & Company 462

Door-to-door

interviews 392–394

vs telephone studies 392

e

Eagle Brands, Inc. 474

Eastman Radio, Inc. 462

Economic integration of Hispanics 257

Ecosystemic model 182, 184, 185, 206, 343

Education

attainment by Hispanics 102

women and 365

Education Now and Babies Later (ENABL) 443

Effective frequency for marketing 290

Effective reach in marketing 290

Emotional appeal 340

Emotional positioning 341

English- and Spanish-language proficiency segments

Chicago (1994) 245, 249

Southern California (1992) 244

English dominant Hispanics 228

English preferred Hispanics 228

English proficiency

of Hispanic Men and Women in Southern California 357

English- and Spanish-language Radio

listening habits by language preference: weekdays 292

listening habits by language preference: weekends 292

English- and Spanish-language TV

viewing habits by language preference: weekdays 291

viewing habits by language preference: weekends 291

English-language networks

average ratings 286

Ethnic identification 374, 384

Ethnicity

Hispanic 10, 373

U.S. population and 78

Exosystem 185

Expenditures by Hispanics, Non-Hispanics, and African-Americans

comparative annual average (1990–1991) 144

Exploratory assessment study 321

Exposure parameters 264

Familismo 167

Family

    households, definition of 47

    dynamics and effects on marketing 336

    in Hispanic culture 167

    interdependency in Hispanic culture 187

Family life

    cultural variations between Mexican-Americans and

        Anglo-Americans 206

Farmakis, J. L., Inc. 462

Feria Mundial Hispaña 7

Festivals, Hispanic 7, 32

Financial products 117

Florida

    affluent Hispanic households (1990) 152

    Hispanic affluence in 119

    immigrant population 51

    metropolitan areas with large Hispanic concentrations
        73

Food 121

    expenditures (1990–1991) 156

    preferences 122, 138

    size of Hispanic households and purchases of 122

Footwear 125

Foreign-born Hispanics 9

    as consumers 42

    banks and financial institutions and 42

    from Spanish-speaking Latin America (1990) 83

    lifestyles and 42

    marketing to 326

    studies of 379

    values by language preference 353–356

Fox television network 446

Galan, Neby 258

Galavisión 258, 284, 463

Galeana Van Dyke Dodge 472

Gannett National Newspaper Sales 463

Gaseteria Oil Corp. 474

Gates, J. C., & Company 463

Geographic distribution 10

    and Hispanic markets 40

Gillis Broadcasting Representatives 463

Goya Foods, Inc. 472

Gray, Eugene F. 463

Greystar One 463

Groskin, Herbert E., & Co. 463

Grupos cumbieros 195

h

Handy Andy Supermarkets 473

HAPI Online 457

HBO en Español 259

Hispanic adults

    coupon usage by language segments 360

    radio preferences in Los Angeles area 294

Hispanic affluence 117

Hispanic Americans Information Directory 456

Hispanic businesses 6

    growth of 27

    ranked by city 28

Hispanic Business 259, 377, 457

Hispanic children

    in bilingual families 337

    general market and 366

    marketing to 335

    role in Hispanic culture 168

Hispanic consumers 3, 128, 256

    availability of demographic information on 317

    habits of 115

    language preference and 373

    mind-set of 320

Hispanic culture
    characteristics of 168
    values and 188
Hispanic Database©, Media Questions (1990) 401
Hispanic demographic growth
    and effect on sampling models 318
Hispanic family households
    definition of 47
Hispanic heritage 5
Hispanic Heritage Festival 7
Hispanic homeowners 123
Hispanic households
    affluence of 148
    and bilingual switching 226
    clothing expenditures in 143
    definition of 46
    demographic changes and 331
    expenditures of 136
    income gains (1983–1990) 131, 132
    income (1982–1990) 20
    income (1983–1992) 147
    incomes above $50,000 130
    incomes of 130
    projections 1990–2000 88
    projected gains 1990–2000 89
    in U.S. (1970–1992) 87
Hispanic income 115, 116, 174
    by country (1990) 145
    in Midwest 116
    per capita (1990) 27, 211
    sources of 119
Hispanic labor force 81
Hispanic language segmentation 15
Hispanic Link Weekly Report 459
Hispanic LIVES© (Lifestyles, Interest, Values, Expectations)
    390
Hispanic market 3, 129
    consumer data issues and 371
    data on 317, 318
    by generation 352
    language segmentation and 239
    language usage and 215
    net advertising expenditures (1993) 311
    opportunities in 121
Hispanic Market Connections 15, 274, 390
    and English proficiency study 225

and language segments study 230
and language-based segmentation 230
Hispanic marketing
    evaluating environment 316
    marketing teams and 348
Hispanic media 253
    organizations 253, 295
    preferences 278
Hispanic Media & Markets Directory 456
Hispanic Media and Market Source 377
Hispanic men
    marriage within same origin subgroup 358
Hispanic Organization of Professionals and Executives 458
Hispanic population
    age composition and 85
    age composition (in percentages) and 86
    age distribution (1988) of 79
    by country of origin 82, 109
    by generation 87
    continental 163
    distribution by national origin 33
    growth of 66
    loss in southern states 92
    1960–1990 19
    1980–2000 19
    1992–2050 77
    of selected states (1990) 25
    as percentage of U.S. population (1960–1990) 20
    sex composition of the U.S. (March 1992) and 98
    states with the largest (1980, 1990) 91
    trends in U.S. 4
    by type of origin (1990) 23
Hispanic print media 269
    and areas of dominant influence (ADI) (1993) 307
Hispanic Radio Network 268
Hispanic readership 270, 303, 305
Hispanic Reporter 459
Hispanic research indicators
    area of residence 372
    behavioral and psychological 373
    ethnicity and 373
    legal status 372
    marketing directions and 373
    self-identification 372
    Spanish surname and paternal ancestry 372
    strength of ethnic identification 373

Hispanic Review of Business 457

Hispanic self-identification 22

Hispanic spending 115, 120

Hispanic subgroups 8, 51

    and marriage of same origin 358

    those linguistically isolated in the U.S. and four states
        (1990) 237

Hispanic teenagers

    general market and 366

    marketing to 335

    television viewing habits and 338

Hispanic Telecommunications Group, Inc. 463

Hispanic Times Magazine 457

Hispanic U.S. elected officials (1993) 30

Hispanic women

    birthrate of 331

    body language and 334

    characteristics of 332

    cultural values and 333

    diversities among 330

    education and 365

    literacy rates among 331

    marketing to 330

    marriage within same origin subgroup 358

    by occupation 359

    participation in labor force 332

    religious values and 333

    U.S. demographic profile (1990) 365

    in the work force (1980–1990) 366

Hispanic World Fair 7

Hispanic youth

    acculturated 337

    growth of market 335, 367

    as market 44, 53

    marketing to 334

    media usage and 338

    unacculturated 337

Hispanic yuppies (*Huppies*) 229

Hispanics

    affluent households among 148

    chronology of presence in U.S. 34

    defined 7, 66, 373

    educational attainment of 102

    English dominant 228

    English preferred 228

    involvement in American society 175

linguistically isolated 236

Home entertainment, Hispanic 122

Home ownership

    in California and Chicago 158

    among Hispanic subgroups 123, 140

    rate of 122

Home purchases, Hispanic 123

Household expenses

    additional expenses 137

    comparative annual average (1990–1991) 134

    comparative major expenses (1990–1991) 135

Household income of Hispanics, Non-Hispanics, and African
    Americans 147

Household projections (1990–2000) 26

    for Hispanics 88

Household purchasing decisions

    and teenager influence 222

Households 88–89, 366

    without families 48

    family statistics and 45

    multicultural 13

    1990–2000 88–89, 366

    size 47

    South American 112

    with telephones (1993) 351

    in transition 90

    U.S. Hispanic (1970–92) 87

Housekeeping expenditures

    comparative annual average (1990–1991) 142

Housekeeping supplies/equipment 125

Housing 122

    comparative annual average expenditures (1990–1991)
        139

    expenditures by market segment (1990–1991) 155

Houston Metropolitan Area

    Weighted Sampling Plan by Hispanic Population Density
        398

Hughes Communications 259

Hugh Wallace, Inc. 471

Huppies 229

i

Illinois
    affluent Hispanic households, 1990 153
    Hispanic affluence in 119
    metropolitan areas with large Hispanic concentration 73
Immigrants
    California and 51
    communication strategies for 276
    and metropolitan areas 50
    reasons for coming to U.S. 24
Immigration 5, 41
    housing costs and 122
    U.S. net 1992–2050 80
Immigration and Naturalization Service Amnesty 450
Immigration Reform and Control Act of 1986 450
Income
    gains in Hispanic households (1983–1990) 131
    Hispanic national median 116
    Hispanics above the U.S. median 146
Indicators of Hispanic culture and business 31
Infomercials 276
Information overload and advertising effectiveness 217
Infotec Development, Inc. 473
Insurance 121
Inter-American Book Services 430
International Bank of Commerce 473
Interracial Council for Business Opportunity 458

j, k

Juarez and Associates, Inc. 455
Katz & Powell Radio 463
Katz Hispanic Media 269, 464

l

Labor force
    participation 81
    participation among Mainland Puerto Ricans (March
        1992) 105
    participation among U.S. Cubans (March 1992) 108
    participation among U.S. Mexicans (March 1992) 101
Language 14
    advertising and 218, 384
    comfort with 385
    differences between English and Spanish 181
    emotional responses to advertising and 219
    Hispanic market and 215
    marketing and 384
    preference for Spanish 14
    proficiency in 385
    translations and 220
    usage 385
    usage of Spanish 13
Language preference
    Miami ADI and 240
    and time spent listening to English- and Spanish-language
        radio 292
    and time spent watching English- and Spanish-language
        TV: weekdays 291
    and time spent watching English- and Spanish-language
        TV: weekends 291
Language segmentation 230, 337
    by key Hispanic markets 239
    media preference in California and 277
    retail store information in Northern California (1991) 306
Language segments
    Chicago, demographic profile of (1994) 243
    media usage and 232
    psychographic profiles of 232
    sociodemographic profiles of 231
    Southern California: demographic profile of (1992) 242;
        for media usage (1992) 248; for retail information
        sources (1992) 247
Latin America
    influence of indigenous cultures 14
    Spanish-speaking foreign-born persons from (1990) 83
Latino, defined 8

Latino Voices (survey) 8

Life cycle model 182, 183

    Linguistically isolated households 223

    defined 14

    in the U.S. 222

    Mexicans and 223

Literacy rates

    among Hispanic women 331

Long-term investments 117

Los Angeles

    adult Hispanics and coupon usage in 360

    Hispanic radio listening habits in 304

    radio program preferences of adult Hispanics in
        294

Lotus Hispanic Radio Network 268

Lotus Hispanic Reps 465

Lulac Foundation 458

m

Machismo 168

Macrosystem 185

Major Market Radio Sales 466

Marielitos 199

Marital status

    of mainland Puerto Rican population (March 1992)
        104

    of U.S. Central and South American population (1990)
        111

    of U.S. Cuban population (March 1992) 107

    of U.S. Mexican population (1992) 100

Market

    U.S. Hispanic 129

Market advertisers

    20 leading Hispanic (1991–1993) 310

    50 leading Hispanic (1993) 308

Market competition 387

Market Development, Inc. 455

Market diversity management 387

Market expectations 44

Market growth

    Hispanic subgroups and 52

    management of 387

Market segmentation 387, 388, 392

    geographical 392

    language-based 392

Market subgroups 40

Market trends 43

Marketing

    to affluent Hispanics 118

    to bilingual Hispanics 224

    framework for 182

    language segmentation and 230

    research services 376

    to U.S. Hispanics 316

    to U.S.-born Hispanic segment 327

    unsuccessful campaigns 344

Marketing research

    Hispanics and 371

    services for 376

Marriage

    within same origin subgroup 358

Maryland

    metropolitan areas with large Hispanic concentration 75

McGavren Guild Radio 466

Media 7

    Hispanic consumers and 256

    Spanish and English preference and 385

    strategies for mass media/multiple media 272, 277

    U.S. Hispanic 253, 256

The Media Institute 458

Media strategy 275

Media usage 15

    advertising and 384

    broadcast 278

    dynamics of 255

    Hispanic dynamics 255, 272

    language segments and 232

    marketing and 384

    profile by language segments: Southern California (1992)
        248

Mesosystem 185

Mesosystem model of market analysis 343

Metro 8-Sheet Network, Inc. 467

Metropolitan areas

    Hispanic gains (1980–1990) and 94

    with large Hispanic concentration 76

    with 100,000 or more Hispanics (1980 and 1990) 96

    with 100,000 or more Hispanics (1990) 92

Mexican-American art 194

Mexican Americans
    affluent households among 118
    art and 193
    characteristics of 190
    consumerism and 54
    cultural influences of 191
    fashion sense of women 333
    food and 196
    health and 193
    income of households and families (1991) 101
    immigration-related events 190
    language and 191
    marital status (1992) and 100
    political issues and 192
    presence in the United States 190
    religion and 193
    self-identification of 191
    socioeconomic characteristics of 192
    sports and 196
    values of 192

Mexican demographics (1990) 67

Mexican households
    affluence among 118
    makeup of (March 1992) 100
    and income (1991) 101

Mexican Industries in Michigan, Inc. 474

Mexican literature 195

Mexican music 194

Mexican-origin population of 100,000 or more (1990) 98

Mexican population
    age distribution (March 1992) and 99
    size and location of 190

Mexican theater 195

Mexican women
    fashion sense of 333

Miami ADI and language preference 240

Michigan State University
    Julian Samora Research Institute 471

Microsystem 185, 187

Midwest
    Hispanic income in 116

Migration 5
    reasons for 10
    settlement patterns 10

Minorities and Women in Business 457

Minority Business Entrepreneur 457

Minority Business Information Institute 471

Minority Markets Alert 459

The Minority Trendsletter 459

El Misisipi 269

Money transfer business 424

Moore, Art, Inc. 467

M. P. & M. Marketing 466

MTV 258

MTV Internacional 446

Multimedia audiences (1991) 285

Mundo Hispanico 459

Mundo—Spanish Newspaper 460

Music Television (MTV) 258

Música Norteña 195

n

NAFTA *See* North American Free Trade Agreement

NAHP 467

National Association of Minority Women in Business 458

National Council of La Raza 458
    Policy Analysis Center 471

National Hispanic Corporate Council 459

National Hispanic Research Center 472

National Hispanic University
    Center for Advanced Studies and Policy Analysis 472

National Minority Business Council 459

National organizations 7

National Society of Hispanic MBAs 459

National Television Index (NTI) 261

New Jersey
    affluent Hispanic households (1990) 150
    Hispanic affluence in 118
    metropolitan areas with large Hispanic concentration 74

New Mexico
    affluent Hispanic households (1990) 154
    Hispanic affluence in 119

New York
    affluent Hispanic households (1990) 150
    immigrant population and 51
    Hispanic affluence in 118

metropolitan areas with large Hispanic concentrations
(1980–1990) 72
Nielsen Hispanic household panel 319
Nielsen Hispanic Television Index (NHTI) 233, 260
Nielsen Media Research 260
Noncash benefits 116
Nondynamic (still) media 272
Normac Foods Inc. 473
North American Free Trade Agreement (NAFTA) 326, 387
Northeast
Hispanic income in 116
Northern Illinois University
Center for Latino and Latin American Studies 472
Novelas 258
El Nuevo Herald 270

o

Operation Bootstrap 196
La Opinión 270, 279
Orquesta tejana 195
Outdoor Advertising 271

p

The Papert Companies 467
Parra Autoplex, Frank 473
People Meter 261
Platt Amendment 199
Politics 7
Portugal
and definition of Hispanic 11
Precision Trading Corp. 474
Primary Hispanic Radio 268
Print media 269, 279 *See also* Hispanic print media
Product integration 276
Product or service life cycle
status check of 320
Product recognition 273, 275

PTS Mexican Media Advertising, Inc. 468
Public transportation
advertising and 271
Puerto Ricans
age distribution: mainland (1992) 103
characteristics of 190
demographics (1990) 69
dominant cultural influences of 196
food and 198
health and 198
households (1992) 104
households and families and income: mainland (1991)
105
language and 196
labor force: mainland (1992) 105
legal status of 196
literature and 198
marital status: mainland (1992) 104
migration and 196
music and 198
political issues of 198
population and consumerism: island 58
population and consumerism: mainland 56
religion and 198
self-identification of 197
size and location of 196
socioeconomic characteristics of 197
sports and 198
states with 100,000 or more (1990) 103
theater and 198
values of 197
women's fashion sense 333

Quinceañera 16
Radio 264, 278
advertising in 345
Hispanic listening habits and 266
language preference and 278, 292
program preferences of adult Hispanics in Los Angeles
area 294
Spanish-language listening habits 293

switching language format 266
 targeting Hispanic consumers and 266
Radio Time Sales/International 468
Readership levels
 socioeconomic conditions of Hispanics and 270
Regional Reps Corp. 468
Religious art 194
Renting 122
Research
 defining 372
 implementation process 372
 managing/avoiding abuses in 374
 methodology 385
 qualitative 376
Retail
 information sources by language segments: Southern
  California (1992) 247
 store information and language segmentation: Northern
  California (1991) 306
Retroacculturation 170, 221, 229
Riley Representatives 468
Rosendin Electric, Inc. 474
Roslin Radio Sales, Inc. 469

♪

"Sabado Gigante" 276
Sales growth 388
Salsa 201
Sample plan development process 374
Sampling
 issues 377
 plan development 380
 weighted by Hispanic population density: Houston 398
Santeria 201
Santeros 201
Savalli Broadcast Sales NAB 469
SBS Network 469
Sedano's Supermarkets 472
Segmentation of Hispanic market 386
Sentiments 16
Sex composition of U.S. Hispanic population by origin (1992)
 98

Short acculturation scale 399
Simpson Rodino Act 425
Social attributes 16
Social networks 5
Sociodemographic differences
 marketing strategies and 324
South Americans
 consumerism and 61
 households 112
 population and marital status (1990) 111
Southern California Language Usage Statistics 408
Southwest
 income in (Hispanic) 116
 population in (Hispanic) 116
"Spanglish" 221
Spanish and English proficiency
 Hispanic Men and Women: Southern California 357
Spanish-dominant households
 television watching and 285
 viewership of top-rated general market programs: adults
  299
Spanish-English Bilingual Study 378
Spanish Information Service 269
Spanish International Communication Corporation (SICC)
 257
Spanish International Network (SIN) 257
Spanish language
 books 430
 diaries 267
 media 257
 newspapers 269
 popularity and usage in the U.S. 221, 249
 proficiency segments: Chicago (1994) 245, 249
 radio and 264
 radio listening habits and 293
 Southern California and (1992) 244
 testing and 378
Spanish monolingual and bilingual population 5 years and over
 238
Spanish network coverage by market 296
Spanish-only study 377
Spanish-speakers
 in households in the U.S. (1990) 222
 increase in 221
 population (1990) 235
Stanford University Center for Chicano Research 472

States

with Central and South American populations of 100,000 or more (1990) 110

with highest percentage of Hispanics (1990) 21

with Hispanic household incomes above the U.S. median 146

with large Cuban populations (1990) 106

with largest Hispanic population (1980, 1990) 91

with Mexican-origin population of 100,000 or more (1990) 98

with Puerto Rican population of 100,000 or more (1990) 103

Statistical manipulation of data 318

Stereotypes 173

Supermarkets

Hispanic customers and 414

Survey

issues 377

techniques and research practices 382

"Switching language" radio format 266

t

The Tacher Company, Inc. 470

Target Marketing Research Group, Inc. 455

El Teatro Campesino 196

Teenagers See also Hispanic teenagers

Fox network and audience 446

Telacu 474

Telemundo Group, Inc. 258, 276, 470

Telemundo Network Profile 283

Telephone

interviews 392, 394

penetration 141

services 124, 125

spending, Hispanic and 124

studies 395

Televisa 259

Television 257

advertising 345

audience shares among men 18 and over 287

audience shares among women 18 and over 288, 289

average ratings for English-language networks 286

National Television Index 261

National Hispanic Television Index 233, 260

top-rated programs of Hispanic adults 298

top-rated programs of men 301

top-rated programs of Spanish-dominant adult Hispanics 299

top-rated programs of Spanish-dominated and general audience among women (1993) 302

top-rated programs of total adults and Hispanic adults (18–49) 298

top-rated programs of women 300

viewing patterns 263, 282, 285

watching by Hispanic adults in California 304

Texas

affluent Hispanic households (1990) 151

Hispanic affluence in 119

immigrant population and 50

metropolitan areas with large Hispanic concentrations (1980–1990) 71

Tianguis Stores 413

Tichenor Spanish Radio Group 269

Traffic Audit Bureau 272

Translation

dangers of 172

English into Spanish 220

Tropicales modernos 195

Troy Ford 474

u

U.S. Census

language questions and (1990) 241

U.S.-born Hispanics 9

marketing to 327

studies 379

values by language preference 353–356

U.S. population

ethnic distribution of 78

percentage of Hispanics (1960–1990) 20

alternative projections of by race/ethnicity (1980–2040) 84

racial or ethnic distribution 78

Spanish speaking 221

Universal Broadcasting Corporation 470

University of California, Los Angeles
    Chicano Studies Research Center 472
Univisión Group 257, 276, 470
Univisión Network Profile 282
Upscales 379

Values 15
    American culture and 188
    language segment differences: Southern California and
        (1992) 246
    middle-class Hispanic and American differences 207
    U.S.-born vs. foreign-born by language preference
        353–356
The Vincam Group 474
Virginia
    metropolitan areas with large Hispanic concentrations 75
Volumetric data, Hispanic 319
Vons Grocery Companies 413

Washington, D.C.
    metropolitan areas with large Hispanic concentrations 75
Western Union 424

White population
    age distribution and (1988) 79
Winner-type donors profile 391
Wise, Lloyd A., Inc. 473
Women *See also* Hispanic women
    demographic profile of U.S. Hispanic 365
    education and non-Hispanic 365
    fashion sense of Cuban 333
    fashion sense of Puerto Rican 333
    fashion sense of U.S. Mexican 333
    financial earning power 49
    households and 48
    labor force and 49
    Spanish-dominant, top-rated television programs of 302
Work force
    Hispanic women and (1980–1990) 366

Youth *See* Hispanic youth
Yuppies 229
Zip codes
    Hispanic population density and 380
    targeting Hispanic neighborhoods and 378
Zipper, Martha Garma 456